MR FIVE PER CENT

THE MANY LIVES OF CALOUSTE GULBENKIAN

THE WORLD'S RICHEST MAN

JONATHAN CONLIN

P

PROFILE BOOKS

This paperback edition published in Great Britain in 2020 by
Profile Books Ltd
29 Cloth Fair
London EC1A 7JQ
www.profilebooks.com

First published in Great Britain in 2019 by
Profile Books Ltd

3 5 7 9 10 8 6 4

A CIP catalogue record for this book is available from the British Library.

ISBN 978 1 78816 043 8
eISBN 978 1 78283 444 1

Text design by Sue Lamble
Typeset in Garamond by MacGuru Ltd
Printed and bound in Great Britain by CPI Group (UK) Ltd, Croydon CR0 4YY

For Richard Roberts (1952–2017)

CONTENTS

ILLUSTRATIONS

Black-and-white plates

Calouste Gulbenkian in 1892, in his early twenties. (© private collection)
Gulbenkian's parents Dirouhi and Sarkis. (© private collection)
Gulbenkian as a child, with cousins in local costume. (© private collection)
Gulbenkian with his tutor Setrak Devgantz. (© private collection)
An oil well in Baku: Gulbenkian visited in 1888.
Gulbenkian and his wife Nevarte on their wedding day, 1892.
Nevarte in Paris ten years later. (© private collection)
Gulbenkian's son Nubar in 1901, aged five. (© private collection)
Nubar with his younger sister Rita. (© private collection)
The only portrait of himself that Gulbenkian commissioned, painted by
     Charles Joseph Watelet in 1912.
Gulbenkian's British passport photograph.
Gulbenkian and Nubar with the Iranian prime minister Timurtash in
     London, 1931. (BP Archive)
Henri Deterding, managing director of Royal Dutch-Shell, and for a
     time Gulbenkian's closest friend. (Courtesy Royal Dutch-Shell)
Exterior of Gulbenkian's palace at 51 Avenue d'Iéna in Paris.
Gulbenkian's imposing ground-floor office at Avenue d'Iéna.
Views of the roof terrace and beyond at Avenue d'Iéna.
Gulbenkian's fine bedroom – never used, as he slept at the Ritz every night.
The ornate dining room, complete with wall tapestries of cherubs
     cavorting in trees.
The main foyer at Avenue d'Iéna, with a Rodin bronze and Houdon's *Apollo*.
The grand staircase, seldom used by visitors.
Houdon's life-size marble of Diana, bought from the Hermitage by
     Gulbenkian in 1930.
Gulbenkian on holiday in Fez in 1932.
The Hotel Aviz in Lisbon, Gulbenkian's home during the Second World
     War. (Courtesy Câmara Municipal de Lisboa)

The flamboyant Nubar cutting a dash among English country tweeds. (Courtesy Mark Samuelson)

The Gulbenkians' sixtieth wedding anniversary in 1952.

Gulbenkian at ease in wartime Lisbon with one of his beloved white cats.

The 84-year-old recluse with his faithful secretary Isabelle Theis in 1953. (© AP/TopFoto)

Three key figures in Gulbenkian's legacy: his son Nubar, confidant Cyril Radcliffe, and José de Azeredo Perdigão, who shepherded the Foundation to Portugal.

Colour plates

Ghirlandaio's *Young Woman* (*c.* 1490), acquired by Gulbenkian in 1929.

Two items from Gulbenkian's collection of jewellery by René Lalique.

The Artist in his Studio (*c.* 1878) by Edgar Degas, bought by Gulbenkian in 1919.

Rembrandt's *Pallas Athene* (*c.* 1657), bought from the Hermitage by Gulbenkian in 1930.

Thomas Gainsborough's *Mrs Lowndes-Stone* (*c.* 1775): Gulbenkian expected this type of portrait to 'flirt' with him.

Two of Gulbenkian's 'decorative' pictures: Hubert Robert's *Le Tapis Vert* (*c.* 1776) and Stanislas Lépine's *L'Estacade* (*c.* 1882).

Portrait of Gulbenkian's daughter Rita and a self-portrait (both 1942) by her husband Kevork Essayan. (© private collection)

Carved stone head of an official, one of the Egyptian antiquities acquired for Gulbenkian by the archaeologist Howard Carter.

All photographs not otherwise credited above are copyright © Calouste Gulbenkian Foundation, Lisbon

MAPS

AUTHOR'S NOTE

On Names

Although Gulbenkian referred to his home city as Constantinople rather than Istanbul, both names were used in the nineteenth century. For convenience's sake I have used Istanbul throughout. I use modern spellings when referring to other places within today's Republic of Turkey. In keeping with the practice of the *British Journal of Middle Eastern Studies* and other journals, I do not transliterate Arabic, Armenian or Persian personal or place names where a Europeanised version exists (hence Mosul, not Mawsul).

On Values

To provide a sense of scale, some of the historical values cited in the text are immediately followed by sterling or dollar equivalents in parentheses (or square brackets, where a value appears in a quotation). These are estimates of the 2015 RPI equivalent of the historical value in question, made using Lawrence Officer and Samuel H. Williamson's Purchasing Power Calculator, accessible online at www.measuringworth.com.

The Ottoman Empire around 1880

Ottoman Empire

Nominally part of the Ottoman Empire

400 kilometres

300 miles

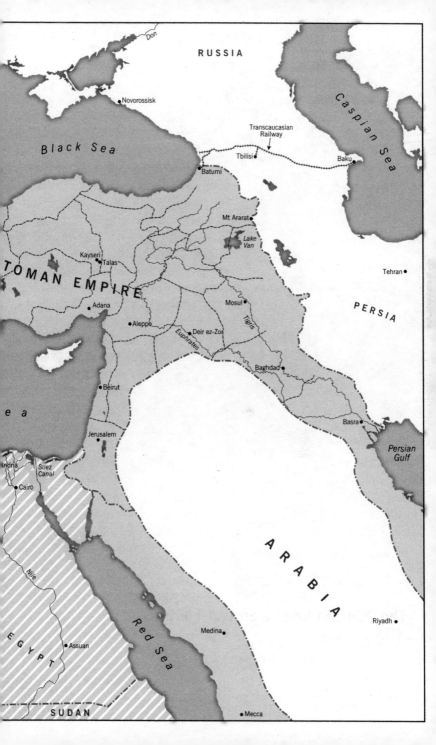

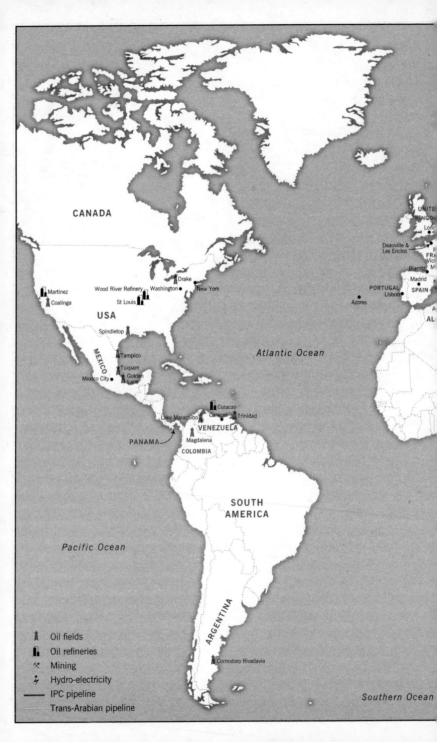

Gulbenkian's world

The Red Line Agreement of 1928

INTRODUCTION: DRAWING THE LINE

Every map has its legend. The map attached to the Red Line Agreement of 31 July 1928 is no exception. This agreement saw the companies we know as BP, ExxonMobil, Total and Royal Dutch-Shell join forces in the Middle East. Instead of fighting each other for control of the region's oil, they would collaborate in a joint venture: the Turkish Petroleum Company. TPC was Calouste Gulbenkian's baby, or rather his 'house', established in 1912. In 1914 the British Foreign Office had given its blessing: rival powers were to cooperate not only in the oil-rich Ottoman provinces of Mosul and Baghdad, but in the entire 'Ottoman Empire in Asia'.

In 1928, however, the 'Ottoman Empire in Asia' was a distant memory. In the First World War the empire had collapsed, triggering a wave of genocidal violence which killed a million of Gulbenkian's fellow Armenians. A patchwork of French and British mandates and protectorates was developing into new nation-states we know today as Iraq, Jordan and Saudi Arabia. Unsurprisingly, therefore, when it came to defining the 'Ottoman Empire in Asia' as it had been in 1914, the oilmen who found themselves in Ostend that day in 1928 were in something of a fix.

All was confusion until Calouste Gulbenkian intervened:

> When the conference looked like foundering, he again produced one
> of his brainwaves. He called for a large map of the Middle East, took
> a thick red pencil and slowly drew a red line round the central area.

'That was the Ottoman Empire which I knew in 1914,' he said. 'And I ought to know. I was born in it, lived in it and served it. If anybody knows better, carry on ...'

Gulbenkian's TPC partners inspected the map, and it was good. This account, taken from Ralph Hewins's 1957 biography, continues: 'Gulbenkian had built a framework for Middle East oil development which lasted until 1948: another fantastic one-man feat, unsurpassed in international big business.'[1]

The 1916 Sykes–Picot Agreement had seen woefully ill-informed imperial proconsuls carve out Syria, Iraq and Jordan using a series of straight lines, lines which paid scant regard to physical or human geography. Perhaps the most notorious example is 'Churchill's Sneeze', the triangular indent in Jordan's southern border that supposedly resulted from the statesman's momentary distraction in 1921. In Hewins's account Gulbenkian's gesture is more sprezzatura than sneeze, and is accompanied by claims to an expertise the others around the table lacked, expertise born of personal and professional experience. The tone and the narrator's portentousness, however, lend Gulbenkian the statesman's authority to determine the fate of millions with the stroke of a pen.

In his lifetime Gulbenkian studiously avoided the press, to the extent that today those who recognise the name often confuse the secretive Calouste with his publicity-seeking son Nubar; Londoners in particular fondly recall Nubar's chauffeur-driven taxicab. Calouste's secretiveness has previously made it difficult to establish even basic facts about his family, education and career. Many contemporaries and some historians have equated such secretiveness with duplicity, rather than modesty. It is common to find Gulbenkian referred to as 'a shadowy Armenian manipulator', a 'detested' figure whose influence, like his 5 per cent, derived 'from the liberal dispensation of bribes'.[2]

Other oil histories have been kinder. In his Pulitzer-winning history of the oil industry, *The Prize*, Daniel Yergin places Gulbenkian on a par with the great Rockefeller, Getty and Mattei as 'one of the great buccaneer-creators of oil'.[3] If Calouste Gulbenkian is known today it is as the man who drew the red line, a milestone in the history of the oil industry and the Middle East. The 1928 Red Line Agreement embodied Gulbenkian's personal claim to 5 per cent of TPC's oil, a claim which he later vested in a company, Partex, which continues to this day.

Yet on closer inspection the legend falls apart. Although the map was certainly left until the final phase of the negotiations that culminated at Ostend, Gulbenkian showed little interest in it. The map does not feature in the memoirs Gulbenkian dictated for private circulation in 1945. He was not even at Ostend that fateful day. The anecdote is one of several myths invented by Gulbenkian's son, which tell us more about Nubar's feelings for his father (pride, resentment, sometimes affection) than they do about the man himself.

Disposing of the red line legend might seem foolhardy in a biographer. Yet it is important to recognise that the others round this table were powerful empires and multinational companies, staffed by hundreds of employees, backed by armies of soldiers and sailors, as well as taxpayers and shareholders. They were hardly going to let Gulbenkian, an individual with no company or state behind him, scrawl red lines over their maps. Gulbenkian had fought hard to get his quarrelsome British, French and American partners to agree to cohabit in his 'house', and successfully defeated repeated attempts to defenestrate him. But he was not particularly bothered about the course of the red line itself. Nor was it his style to make pretty speeches. He worked as a back-room fixer, an intermediary between the worlds of business, diplomacy and high finance, a figure very different and more interesting than the Gulbenkian of legend.

The spider at the centre of an emerging international oil and banking industry, Gulbenkian held empires and multinationals to ransom for more than fifty years. He would not have come to wield such power, however, had he not been an exceptionally skilled negotiator and financial architect. Oilmen from California to the Caucasus sought him out for his skill in raising capital on the stock markets of New York, London and Paris. He played an important if previously unacknowledged role helping both Royal Dutch-Shell and Total establish themselves as oil majors.

Gulbenkian's deals introduced American oil companies to the Middle East, and brought Royal Dutch-Shell to America – as well as to Mexico, Venezuela and Russia. The embryonic oil industry Gulbenkian found at the start of his career in 1900 was one dominated by a single oil producer and a single company: the United States and Standard Oil. At his death in 1955 the world oil industry was no longer an American monopoly, but an international cartel. This cartel's members, the so-called 'Seven Sisters', each produced oil from several countries. Several new 'sisters' have appeared since. But the oil industry's structure of multinational production, integration and partnerships remains the same: the web woven by Gulbenkian is with us still.

Born in Istanbul in 1869, Gulbenkian came of age in the Ottoman Empire, only to see this familiar world tear itself apart in genocide and war. He was not the only Ottoman Armenian to find refuge in the West. But he was the only one to make it big in this unfamiliar world. Far from holding him back, the destruction of his homeland and a loner personality became keys to his success: as a secretive man without loyalties to any one empire, state or company, Gulbenkian could present himself as the ulti-mate honest broker. For 'westerners' he was a trusted source of intelligence on the Middle East. For 'easterners' he was someone to turn to in order to find out what the Great Powers and their mighty oil companies were up to. This was as true of Sultan Abdülhamid II in 1900 as it was of the Shah of Iran and Ibn Saud of Saudi Arabia four decades later. Gulbenkian was a diplomat in the service of both the Ottoman and Persian empires. Even Stalin sought Gulbenkian's advice, rewarding him with Rembrandts from the famous Hermitage Museum. No other business figure in the history of the oil industry wielded such influence, over such a scale, for so long.

Gulbenkian's story is timely. Whether we look back to the First World War and Sykes–Picot a century ago, or whether we consider the ongoing war for control of Iraq or current debates about capitalism, politics and identity, Gulbenkian is hiding in plain sight, challenging us to pin down the source of his fabulous wealth and influence. How did a man who knew nothing of geology and who never visited Iraq, Saudi Arabia or any of the Gulf states lay claim to 5 per cent of Middle East oil production? Once he secured this stake, how did he manage to hold on to it, and so become the richest man on earth? How did a shy recluse bridge divides of East and West which seem insurmountable today?

Gulbenkian built a fabulous palace in Paris which he filled with trea-sures, not only paintings from the Hermitage, but Greek coins, Egyptian antiquities, Persian carpets, Iznik faience and Japanese netsuke. Today his collections are housed in Lisbon, next to the headquarters of the foun-dation which bears his name and which remains one of the wealthiest foundations in the world. Yet the great collector himself never slept in his palace. He lived in hotels. He held four different passports and intended his foundation to be equally international in ambition. This freewheeling, cosmopolitan spirit reflected the pre-1914 world of unrestricted inter-national exchange of capital, technology and people. This globalisation subsequently went into retreat, until the 1980s. Now the tide is going out again: free enterprise and free movement are under assault from Right and Left. Trade disputes are trumped up. Sinister 'citizens of nowhere' are made up. And the cheers and the votes roll in. Surely Gulbenkian, the ultimate 'citizen of nowhere', has something important to tell us at this moment in history.

As Al Jazeera recently put it, Gulbenkian was 'the world's first oil fixer, broker and deal-maker'.[4] However, alongside the negotiator, financier, collector and diplomat, he was also a family man. Revealed here for the first time, Gulbenkian's vast personal archive allows us to count the cost of his ceaseless activity on those he loved. His solicitousness as husband, father and grandfather led him to subject his family to relentless surveillance and control. At different times his wife, son and daughter attempted to break free. His son even took Gulbenkian to court. All failed to escape that other web, of money, power and affection which Gulbenkian spun around them. There are many Gulbenkians, therefore, to discover beyond that of the Red Line Agreement.

In the 1920s the line which most exercised Gulbenkian was that separating Turkey from the new state of Iraq. Despite being 'Turkish', TPC's relations with the Turks were poor. The British-mandatory regime in Iraq was more likely to confirm the company's rights to Mosul's oil. For TPC, therefore, it was crucial that Mosul's oilfields end up on the Iraqi side of any Turkish–Iraqi border.

After the Lausanne Conference of 1923 failed to reach agreement the border question was referred to the League of Nations. The League appointed a former prime minister of Hungary, Count Pál Teleki, to lead a commission of inquiry. In June 1925 Gulbenkian proposed to get Teleki's maps drawn so that the Mosul oilfields were on the 'right' (Iraqi) side of the border. Teleki's cartographer, he explained to his TPC partners, was the old Ottoman cartographer, an Armenian named Zatik Khanzadian. Khanzadian knew of Gulbenkian's role in TPC and had approached Gulbenkian through a mutual schoolfriend, Aram Djevhirdjian:

> Khanzadian knows all the crooks [*sic*] and corners of the place, and as the other members [of the commission] are not cartographers, it remains for him to make up the map according to certain instructions regarding topographical positions; I am given to understand that he can turn this as he likes, and so Khanzadian desires to get into personal

and confidential touch with me, relying on my position and name to keep the whole thing [secret]. He is desirous of knowing which are the points that our company would like to remain on the side of Iraq.[5]

Why bother with conventions, protocols and treaties when international borders could be fixed your way, for just £2,000 (£100,000)? Others might go to the starting line. Gulbenkian went straight to the finish.

PART I

APPRENTICE, 1869–1914

'Even if all Constantinople were to work itself up into a rage against me my reputation would not suffer, for it is not in Turkey that I strive to shine.'
C. S. Gulbenkian

ONE

ISTANBUL, 1869

Calouste Gulbenkian's life story is many things, but a rags-to-riches story it is not. The eldest of three brothers, Calouste was born in 1869 into a wealthy Ottoman Armenian family in Istanbul, capital city of the vast Ottoman Empire. For little Calouste, travelling between Europe and Asia would have been routine, as the family straddled the Bosphorus. The family home and Calouste's first school, Aramyan-Uncuyan, were on the Asian side of the city, in Kadıköy.[1] The family's offices and warehouses were on the European side. Holidays were spent on the Princes' Islands, in the nearby Sea of Marmara.

One of the earliest images we have of Calouste shows him standing somewhat stiffly in European clothes alongside two others in the customary dress of Mesopotamia, which the Ottoman sultans had conquered in the early sixteenth century. The pair on the right are probably relatives, perhaps members of the Kouyoumdjian family of Baghdad. The Gulbenkians were merchants and money changers, in regular communication with partners in major Ottoman cities, such as Izmir, Beirut and Baghdad, as well as further afield, in lands which had formerly been Ottoman, such as Bulgaria and Egypt, and also Marseille and Manchester. They exported the empire's raw cotton, wool, mohair and opium, importing cloth from Manchester, glassware from France and kerosene from Baku. The Gulbenkian offices occupied several rooms inside Büyük Valide Han, a vast seventeenth-century complex of workshops, warehouses and offices that

still looms halfway between the Grand Bazaar and Sirkeci Station, the terminus of the Orient Express.

Though there were several hundred thousand Ottoman Armenians
living in Istanbul (representing 15 per cent of the total population), the
Armenian community's merchant elite (the *amiras*) consisted of a mere 165
families.[2] Unsurprisingly, members of this remarkably mobile caste inter-
married constantly. Calouste's mother, Dirouhi, was already a Gulbenkian
before she married Sarkis Gulbenkian.[3] Calouste's youngest brother would
later marry a Kouyoumdjian. Whatever the nature of the relationship
between Calouste and the man in the keffiyeh, therefore, it is clear that
such visitors would hardly have seemed exotic to young Calouste, growing
up in the large house at 1bis Lorando Street.

Alongside these Armenians the Kadıköy household also included
Turks, Greeks and maybe even one or two French. It was their job to do
the laundry, cook the meals, make Sarkis's coffee (he had only to clap his
hands for a fresh cup to appear) and carry Calouste to and from school on
their shoulders. Though these servants were not members of the Armenian
Church, it was common in the Ottoman period for members of different
faiths to observe each other's holidays.

With the important exception of the parish church, school was the
only truly segregated environment Calouste would have known in this
multi-ethnic imperial city. Lessons and services were delivered in Armenian. The Gulbenkians may have written to each other in Turkish, but they
used the Armenian alphabet when doing so (the combination brought
added security to their communications). On an official level, however, the
Armenian community or *millet* was identified as second-class: exempted
from some civil duties, such as military service, but subject to certain taxes
and restrictions not imposed on the Sultan's non-Armenian subjects. Many
of the city's *amiras* elected to take foreign citizenship in order to escape
these restrictions and enjoy the special protections and tax exemptions
extended to foreign nationals under bilateral conventions, the so-called
'capitulations'.[4]

Sons of the Rose Lord

Armenians had been living in Istanbul since the eleventh century, several
centuries before the Ottomans arrived. The Gulbenkians, however, were

relative newcomers. The brothers Sarkis and Serovpe had arrived around 1850 from a much smaller town in central Anatolia: Talas. Though there is no evidence that Calouste ever visited, there would have been no doubt in his family's mind that Talas was 'home'. The Gulbenkians were the wealthiest residents of Talas, which numbered around 800 Armenian, 900 Greek and 500 Turkish households. They owned the biggest house (fifteen rooms). They were the biggest exporters of *jehri* (a plant harvested for dye) and owned the smartest shops in 'Little Alexandria', Talas's shopping street.[5] They built the town's two Armenian schools and gymnasium, and paid to rebuild the Armenian church in stone. Wherever he settled, in New York or Nice, a Gulbenkian was expected to continue paying his share of the running costs of these family institutions, to continue sending funds 'home' for distribution among the needy.

Perched on a ridge of purplish-grey limestone beneath Mount Erciyes, Talas looks out over the much larger city of Kayseri, simmering on the hot plain below. When the great British explorer Gertrude Bell passed through Talas in 1909, her companions warned her to keep her wits about her. Her guide Fattûh and the *zaptieh* (constable) assigned to protect her swapped cautionary tales:

'Upon a day [said the *zaptieh*] the devil came to Kaisarîyeh. "Khush geldi," said the people, "a fair welcome," and they showed him the streets and the bazaars of the city, the mosques and the khâns, all of them. When he was hungry they set food before him till he was well satisfied, but when he rose to depart, he looked for his cloak and belt and they were gone. The devil is not safe from the thieves of Kaisarîyeh.'

'God made them rogues,' said Fattûh.

'What can we do?' observed the *zaptieh* philosophically ... 'the world is all one.'

'Great travelling they make,' continued Fattûh. 'In every city you meet them.'[6]

More than a century later, another traveller to Kayseri (the author) paused to admire the Armenian church. A passer-by stopped. 'If you like it,' he said, pointing up at the church, 'we can sell it to you.'

If the Kayserians were renowned wheeler-dealers, then Kayserian Armenians were particularly adept at spotting new opportunities. They were also notorious for their disputatiousness, thanks to the long-running feud between the Melkonians and the Frenkians, Armenian Kayseri's answer to the Montagues and the Capulets, which obliged all the Armenians in the region to pick a side. Wealthy Armenians with carriages regularly commuted back and forth, eager to swap the baking summer heat in Kayseri for the cool orchards and meadows up in Talas.

Above the entrance to Vart Badrikian, the boys' school in Talas, stood a dedication stone with an inscription recording how:

> Noble offspring of Gulbenk of Vart Badrik's line, four sons following the good path with love, the eldest Avedik, the younger Gullabi, Kalousd, Kerovpe, with their sisters Marina and Serpouhi and for the soul of their brother Hovhannes, dedicate this school to the nation this October 1847.

Born in Talas in 1800, Gullabi Gulbenkian was Calouste Gulbenkian's grandfather. Vart Badrik was the warlord from whom all Gulbenkians claim descent: 'Gül benk' is the Turkified version of Vart Badrik, or 'Rose Lord'.

Vart Badrik had ruled the south shore of Lake Van in the eleventh century, when that region formed part of the Armenian principality of Vaspourakan. When Vaspourakan was folded into the Byzantine Empire in 1021, its leading Armenian families and retainers were moved west, to Cappadocia. Though Vart Badrik's reputation was fearsome, this probably did not give the rather shy and retiring Calouste much by way of schoolyard credibility. 'Benk' is close to the Persian word *benek*, meaning birthmark – uncomfortably close for Calouste, who was duly called 'spotty-face' at school.

In 1847 the 'nation' to which the Gulbenkians dedicated their school was not a nation-state or even a political cause. The last of the Armenian kingdoms had been conquered by the Mamluks in 1375, and thereafter Armenians in Anatolia had made lives (sometimes very successful ones) as subjects of the Ottoman Empire, just as fellow ethnic Armenians had as subjects of the Byzantine, Persian and Mughal empires – occasionally rising to high imperial office. In this context 'nation' referred to a set of institutions by which Ottoman Armenians governed their community, as one of the *millets* or ethnic groups into which the Sultan's subjects were divided.

The Armenians were among the first peoples to convert to

Christianity, and loyalty to the Armenian Church and Armenian rite alongside the Armenian language held the community together in unpropitious circumstances. Unsurprisingly for an Ottoman Armenian *amira*, Calouste was comfortable with this noumenal 'nation' and never expressed a desire to revive a national 'homeland'. Loyalty to the Sultan was another tie Ottoman Armenians shared. Loyalty was exchanged for protection within the Sultan's realm, for the right to practise one's religion and for certain other privileges.

If this was the arrangement, it was one the Sultan would fail to keep after 1895, subjecting his Armenian subjects to coordinated waves of violence. As one former Talas resident recalled, 'In the years 1915–1916 the Armenians were exterminated. They massacred some, exiled others. The Turks appropriated their fields, their houses. This way, they became the lords of the place.'[7] The churches and school were desecrated, quarried for their stone. Even the dedication stone from the boys' school would have vanished, had it not been acquired by the sole remaining Armenian resident, in exchange for 100 sheep. To the west, Istanbul's Armenian population collapsed, from 25 per cent in 1914 to 8.5 per cent in 1920.[8] Yet Gulbenkian's world view hardly changed. As late as 1923 he was still describing his family's position within this system in unreconstructed terms – to a former Young Turk minister, no less. 'We, who have at all times been very loyal subjects and friends of the country,' Gulbenkian wrote, deserved better than to be persecuted, which in his case involved confiscation of the family's properties in Istanbul. 'I resent this most deeply,' he continued, 'on account of my relations and my position. You can hardly overlook the fact that I have at all times and always sought the revival of our country, and I believe that I have given many proofs of that in the past.'[9]

The 'revival of our country' was the aim of the so-called Tanzimat reforms introduced by Sultan Abdülmecid in 1839. This wide-ranging and highly ambitious programme sought to modernise the empire's tax system, economy, armed forces and administration, and even to replace the patchwork of self-governing ethnic communities with a unitary Ottoman society and identity. The reforms continued under Abdülmecid's successor, Abdülaziz, but came to stop in 1876, with the accession of a conservative hardliner, Abdülhamid II. A child of the Tanzimat, Gulbenkian continued to hope that this 'revival' might come about, longer than most of his fellow Ottoman Armenians did.

Gladstone's Sweet Song

Unlike the Armenian and Greek *millets*, Ottoman Turks and Arabs had done little to avail themselves of the opportunities presented by the Tanzimat reforms. Muslim families were unwilling to expose their children to the broader curriculum and new ideas advanced by the regime, or by American missionaries who operated free schools across the Empire (including in Talas).[10] They preferred to send their sons to madrasas, where they gained few skills other than the ability to repeat sections of the Koran from memory. Hopes that educational reforms would foster the emergence of a Muslim bourgeoisie were disappointed. Ottoman Turks and Arabs were slower to adopt the *alla franga* habits that the Gulbenkians had assumed in the mid-nineteenth century: wearing western-style clothes, eating off individual plates at a table (rather than from a communal dish on the floor), serving women first (rather than the men) and so on.[11]

Armenians and Greeks continued to dominate international as well as domestic trade and manufacturing of all kinds. Even in a system as venal as the Ottoman Empire, after all, you had to have some nous to hold a copper, kerosene or ferry concession. You had to understand the basic technology and finance, read accounts and have a sense of international markets and how they worked. Even if you didn't know the chemistry behind refining crude oil into kerosene or how a steamship worked, you had to have the languages and diplomacy to hire and manage those who did, be they Russian, Scottish or French. Turks and Arabs did not see these skills as important. To the vast majority of the Sultan's subjects, including Armenian farmers and shepherds on the plain of Adana or around Lake Van, they probably were not very useful. There was enough work to fill the daylight hours without worrying about steamships, cotton gins or even better breeds of angora sheep.

Well travelled, well educated, polyglot and bred to trade, the Gulbenkians and their fellow *amiras* of Istanbul were perfectly positioned to channel western European investment and technology and set it to work across the Ottoman Empire. Whether they were interested in a true Ottoman cosmopolitanism, a new culture that might supplant their Armenian one, is far less evident. After 1875 the emergence of a revolutionary Armenian politics aroused long-dormant dreams of an 'Armenian National Homeland'. These developments challenged the claim of the *amiras* and the Armenian Apostolic Church to lead the Armenian community. Different members of the Gulbenkian clan were pulled in different directions. While those of Sarkis's generation struggled to make sense of it all, for Calouste's generation thoughts of derring-do on behalf of the *patrie* could be rather exciting.

A number of factors, therefore, led some Ottoman Armenians to begin casting about for a protector to replace the Sultan in the years after 1875. In the east of Anatolia, one obvious push factor was the Sultan's indifference to the oppression of Armenians. A matching pull was the Russian advance into the neighbouring Caucasus. For decades the Russians had posed as guardians of the Orthodox Churches. There was a large Armenian community in Tbilisi who did very well out of this Russian move southwards. The same tunnels, roads and railways which served to project Russian power into the Caucasus could be used by Armenian traders like the Mantashevs to export carpets, kerosene and other products to Russian markets. The Russians also brought peace and stability, which was always good for business. Russian Cossacks transplanted or simply liquidated the petty mountain and hill khanates who had been robbing Armenian caravans for centuries. Many eastern Armenians saw Russia as a hegemon they could trust.[12] If they could afford it, they sent their boys to be educated in Tartu (now Estonia, then part of the Russian Empire) and St Petersburg.

But eastern Anatolia was a long way from Istanbul; western and eastern Armenians spoke different dialects. Western Armenians looked to Britain, Russia's great rival. In particular they looked to one man, William Ewart Gladstone, founder and conscience of the Liberal Party, who served as prime minister four times between 1868 and 1894. Gladstone's charisma and rhetorical skill won him a cult-like following in the 1870s. Gladstone encouraged his hearers (enfranchised or not) to make politics something into which they could invest all their Christian convictions and moral values, something powerful enough to bend events to its almost divine will.

Like many thoughtful High Anglicans with Tractarian leanings, Gladstone had taken a strong interest in the Orthodox Churches' theology and liturgy. In the 1840s he even hoped to reunite Christian Churches of East and West. Instead of having been cursed by the Reformation to be nothing more than a theological halfway house, the Anglican Church might become the centre of a truly catholic (as in universal) Church. Hopes of restoring Church unity were dashed in 1870, when the Roman Catholic Church, led by Pope Pius IX, headed down a conservative,

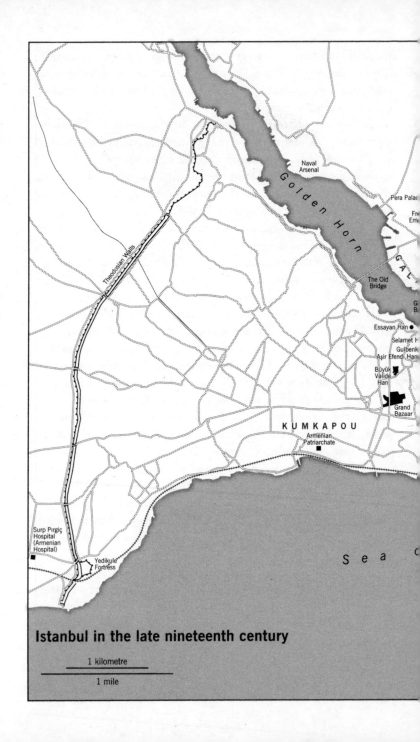

Naval
Arsenal

G o l d e n   H o r n

Pera Pala

Fr
Em

GA

The Old
Bridge

G
B

Essayan Han ●

Selamet H
Gulbenk
Aşir Efendi Han

Büyük
Valide
Han

Grand
Bazaar

K U M K A P O U

Armenian
Patriarchate

Theodosian Walls

Surp Pırgiç
Hospital
(Armenian
Hospital)

Yedikule
Fortress

S e a   o

Istanbul in the late nineteenth century

1 kilometre

1 mile

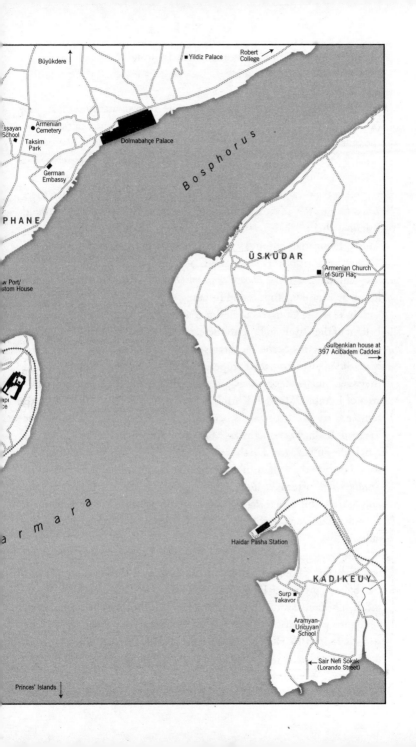

Büyükdere

Yildiz Palace

Robert College

Essayan School

Armenian Cemetery

Taksim Park

Dolmabahçe Palace

German Embassy

Bosphorus

ÜSKÜDAR

Armenian Church of Surp Haç

PHANE

w Port/ stom House

Gulbenkian house at 397 Acibadem Caddesi

api ce

armara

Haidar Pasha Station

KADIKEUY

Surp Takavor

Aramyan-Uncuyan School

Sair Nefi Sokak (Lorando Street)

Princes' Islands

ultramontane path. But Gladstone retained a strong affinity for the Armenian and other eastern Churches. The Armenians were, before anything else, fellow Christians.

In October 1875 news reached Britain that an attempted uprising of Orthodox Christians in Herzegovina was being violently put down by the Sultan. By June of the following year accounts of Ottoman atrocities had whipped up a public campaign. Britain had long seen herself as the champion of upstart nations escaping imperial yokes, championing the Greeks in their war of independence from the Sultan. It helped when there was a face to put to such campaigns, someone who could be led round Britain gathering cheers, as Garibaldi and Kossuth (both rebels against the Austro-Hungarian Empire) were in the 1860s. In the case of the so-called 'Bulgarian Horrors', that leader was Gladstone himself. In September 1876 his pamphlet *Bulgarian Horrors and the Question of the East* appeared, followed by a speaking tour round Britain.

In 1878 the Congress of Berlin convened to redraw the Balkan map, in light of the Ottoman Empire's defeat in the Russo–Turkish War. Unlike the Montenegrins, Serbs, Bulgarians and other Balkan peoples, the Armenians did not hail from the European part of the Ottoman Empire, nor did they seek independence; they just wanted security. The Armenian patriarch of Istanbul, Mkrtich Khrimian, travelled to Berlin in 1878, but was refused entry to the formal deliberations of the Congress. Article 61 of the Treaty of Berlin was nonetheless hailed as an Armenian victory. Under this article the Sultan agreed to the appointment of two British monitors who would oversee the welfare of the Armenian communities in the provinces or *vilayets* of eastern Anatolia. Unfortunately, neither the British nor the Sultan took this article very seriously, and it remained unimplemented. Once back in Downing Street in 1880, Gladstone did little to lean on the Sultan.

There was, admittedly, a lot on his plate. In 1886, while Gulbenkian was attending school in London, Gladstone floated 'the Hawarden Kite', a trial balloon proposing Home Rule for Ireland. The 'Kite' sent shockwaves through Britain, destroying the Liberal Party. By the time Gladstone began denouncing Ottoman treatment of the Armenian community in 1890, he and his Liberal Party were a spent force. Nearly blind and not long for this world, as late as 1894 Gladstone could still move the faithful to righteous fury.[13] When invited by campaigners such as the indefatigable James Bryce, an impressive roster of bishops, lords and MPs were willing to sit on committees of Armenian philanthropic organisations such as the Anglo-Armenian Association (established 1893). But it was no longer very clear what this sound and fury actually signified. Listening to the old familiar song and clucking over lurid accounts of atrocities threatened to become nothing more than a genteel exercise in getting oneself worked up.

Unfortunately, the Armenian community in Britain and the western Armenian community generally failed to notice that, from Gladstone in 1876 through to Edward Grey in 1896, politicians saved their most promising rhetoric for periods when they were out of office. An exercise in Gladstonian piety, good manners and speechifying was received as a commitment on the part of Her Majesty's Government to intervene. When the railway engineer Henry Barkley arrived in Kayseri in 1890 on his journey through Anatolia, every Armenian he met assumed him to be the advance party of the British Army, come to deliver on all the rhetoric. 'You are notoriously the richest people in the world,' one Talas Armenian pointed out to him, 'therefore, if you do not come to govern us as you ought, you are at least bound to assist us Christians by spending, say twenty or thirty millions in making roads, railways, bridges, and other useful works.'[14]

Prudent Patriots

Other Ottoman Armenians were not going to wait on the Russians, the British, the Americans, or anybody else. They would emancipate themselves through revolutionary socialism, fomented by well-organised Armenian parties with their own international networks. The radical socialist Hnchakian Revolutionary Party was established in 1887, followed three years later by the Armenian Revolutionary Federation, or Dashnak Party. For *amiras* like the Gulbenkians, these were shocking and unsettling developments. Alongside a nostalgia for an Armenian *yerkir* or homeland, these parties were prepared to advocate violence to advance their aims. In the words of one 1891 proclamation, they would lead an awakening of the slumbering Armenian people 'gun in hand'. The Dashnaks' breathtaking occupation of the Imperial Ottoman Bank in Istanbul in 1896 demonstrated how serious such proclamations were. Feuding between Dashnaks and Hnchaks could be equally violent.

All such parties appealed to the large body of Armenian peasant farmers stuck in the middle, who had little time or inclination for ideology and who knew the real *yerkir*, which was something quite different from the romantic pastoral peddled by those who had never tilled the soil. Without the means of articulating or disseminating its own political stance, this central community remained something of a mirror, reflecting the beliefs of those who appealed to it. From the mid-1890s onwards, these isolated communities bore the brunt of Ottoman violence. In some cases, as in Zeytoun, they fought back, to the cheers of Dashnaks and Hnchaks, who were rarely in a position to offer anything more by way of support.

What were all these thundering speeches, party manifestos and daring acts of violence to the Gulbenkians? What did they mean to Calouste, a child of Tanzimat-era Istanbul and, later, a student in London during Gladstone's third administration? To *amiras* they represented so many threats to business as usual, and not much more. Such indifference has led twentieth- and twenty-first-century Armenian historians to describe the *amiras* as token Armenians, lacking in patriotic 'substance'. *Amira* generosity to their community can even be perceived as guilt money. Gulbenkian's brother-in-law claimed that Gulbenkian's contribution to Armenian causes had been 'trifling' and that he had not been 'a good Armenian'.[15]

Some *amiras* even found themselves tarred as collaborators. Perceptions of Harutyun Paşa Dadian (1830–1911) are revealing in this regard. Educated in Paris, Dadian came from an impeccable Armenian family (linked to the Gulbenkians by marriage) and worked in the Ottoman Foreign Ministry from 1848, rising to become a vizier in 1887. Challenged on his record in later life, Dadian replied that 'however dangerous the position in which a population as weak as ours finds itself, it is our duty to work faithfully for the State, to avoid insurrection and thereby prevent terrible retribution. Is not prudent patriotism still patriotism?' To an Armenian writing in 2002, it was a 'craven excuse'. Both the Gulbenkians' and the Dadians' philanthropy were cases of 'token Armenians' salving guilty consciences.[16]

The Gulbenkians did not see Armenian and Ottoman as conflicting identities. The labels were interdependent: how could the Armenians understand themselves as the 'loyal *millet*' without the Sultan to be loyal to? Perhaps this identity was flimsy. The loyalty consisted largely in what one did not do (rebel, bear arms, try to convert others), rather than what one did. The fashion for western European clothing and manners added a further cosmopolitan aspect. At times this, too, seems to sit a bit oddly. In the photograph with his Baghdad cousins, little Calouste's British-style clothes are a bit baggy here and there. A childhood spent in this cosmopolitan world, in a household with British and French servants, with relatives regularly passing through on their travels between the family's far-flung trading branches, must have shaped Gulbenkian's mind-set. It may not have trained him to be a 'good Armenian', but it certainly prepared him for the role he would fill in the world of international business.

TWO

MARSEILLE, LONDON AND BAKU, 1883–8

The Gulbenkians described their family as 'oriental', which they took to mean patriarchal. Children were brought up by nurses, tutors and governesses, with limited access to their parents. Fathers were distant, revered figures whose word was law. They arranged for their sons to learn the business by working for relatives abroad or elsewhere within the empire. They also arranged marriages: sons were supposed to marry fellow Armenians of a similar rank, rather than an *oddar*, or non-Armenian; daughters were married off between the ages of thirteen and sixteen. Cousins and extended relatives were always welcome in each other's houses, whether for a visit or for a much longer stay.

Calouste kept one of his father's copybooks of outgoing correspondence, which gives a sense of how such a family functioned. In these letters, written in the usual mixture of Turkish vocabulary and Armenian alphabet, the distinction between servants and relatives blurs. Both are addressed using pet names, some French ('Monsieur Jacques'), some Turkish ('Haci Hanim' or 'Lady Pilgrim', a title commonly given to anyone who had made the pilgrimage or *hajj* to Jerusalem). A tutor or other family retainer might serve several generations of the same family. When they became too old to do so, they were not dismissed but provided for, and often came to act as unofficial courts of appeal in family disputes. This was certainly true of 'Baron' Setrak Devgantz, who served as Calouste's tutor, and later as tutor to his only son, Nubar. In some cases these servants were in fact distant relatives who had fallen on hard times.

In October 1883 Sarkis sent his eldest son west, to live with Sarkis's brother-in-law, Hagop Selian, in Marseille. Having finished his studies at the Armenian school in Kadıköy, Aramyan-Uncuyan, it would have been normal for Calouste to have gone on to attend either St Joseph's or Robert College, Istanbul's leading French- and American-administered colleges. The decision to aim for an English school and university suggests that Sarkis's business was going very well, allowing him to imitate the example set by the very richest *amiras*, who had begun to send their sons to Eton and Harrow.

Sarkis's letter to Selian in Marseille, however, suggests another reason:

> We don't want to send him to boarding school, as Calouste always has nightmares. He slept in his mother's room right up to his departure for Marseille ... He cannot express himself. His mother always coddles him, and so he is nervous and shy. He hardly says a word. In Turkey he wouldn't say 'hello' to a girl; I think he thinks it's immoral. We sent him to Europe hoping to change his character.[1]

Calouste was accompanied by 'Baron' Devgantz. The pair had their photograph taken shortly after arriving. Having Devgantz with him doubtless helped Calouste make the difficult transition from a warm, Turkish-speaking family environment to something less familiar. Devgantz was also there to report to Sarkis on Calouste's progress and to give reassurance that Calouste was keeping away from both alcohol and the Joliette, Marseille's entertainment quarter.[2]

One of the most important ports on the Mediterranean, Marseille was the natural entry point for those travelling to France from Istanbul – at least until the Orient Express railway opened in 1888. Its importance as a trading centre ensured that it already had a sizeable Armenian community in 1884, including the Selian family, who also hailed from Talas. Alongside his formal studies at the École de Commerce and his lessons with Devgantz, Calouste presumably helped out a bit in the offices of Selian and Gulbenk, giving him his first real taste of his father's line of business.

In Marseille Calouste learned basic business skills such as accounting at the École de Commerce. Given the importance of French as a means of polite communication, Calouste probably had a smattering of it when he arrived in Marseille. He now perfected it, and spent his evenings starting to learn English. He took his lunch in a hotel. Rather than seeing this as a waste of money, Sarkis approved: it saved time. The individualist in Calouste came to appreciate the efficiency and anonymity of hotel living at a young age (he was only fourteen), along with the freedom from repetitive chitchat, temperamental cooks and the other tribulations of eating in one's own house. In 1884, however, Calouste probably welcomed being able to talk Turkish with his relatives in the evenings. Such conversation would be harder to come by in London.

School Days

In the summer of 1884 Calouste travelled to London, this time without Devgantz. Acting on the advice of associates from the London firm of W. H. Cole & Co., Sarkis had decided to enrol his son at King's College School.[3] Henry Cole, his son Alfred Clayton Cole (a future Governor of the Bank of England) and a certain Mr Baxter (also of W. H. Cole & Co.) clearly knew Sarkis well and took a close interest in his son's welfare. 'Caloost' was duly admitted into Mr Greare's fifth-form class, and accommodation was found in the Ealing home of the chaplain, the Reverend Henry Belcher.[4]

King's College School was squeezed into the basement floor of King's College, the university established in 1829. The two shared a headmaster and several other masters, as well as a building, and students at the school regularly 'went upstairs' – that is, transferred into the college. The main entrance gave on to the Strand, which had long been one of London's busiest thoroughfares. The main block ran south to Victoria Embankment, overlooking the Thames. As a relatively new foundation, the school lacked the cachet of other London public schools, such as Westminster and St Paul's. Yet its fees were not cheap by the standards of the day.

All students had to study Divinity, Mathematics, English Language, Literature and History. Otherwise the Upper School was divided into a 'Classical' side, which gave an Oxbridge-style education in Classics, and a 'Modern' side, intended to prepare boys for the Department of Applied Sciences in King's College, as well as for the civil service exams and 'Mercantile Pursuits'. Calouste was admitted to the 'Classical' side, even though his father stated that he simply wanted him to 'improve your

English and French, finish college and come back to start work as a businessman'.[5]

The basement of King's was cramped. The school's sports ground was some distance away and otherwise there was only a narrow courtyard in which to let off steam. This was a serious drawback in this era of 'muscular Christianity', when public school sports gained an almost cult-like following, revered for the manly character traits they supposedly instilled. It was hard to imagine the plots of novels like Thomas Hughes's *Tom Brown's School Days* (1857), itself based on Rugby School, being translated to a basement in the Strand.

The more unpleasant aspects of public school life were clearly in evidence at King's. In one letter home Calouste reported that a boy had been 'murdered' by fellow pupils on the corridor which ran down the centre of the college building.[6] Twelve-year-old Charles Fisher Bourdas had died a few days before, nine days after receiving 'quite a dozen blows ... with the fist' from other boys at the school.[7] These boys regularly formed a gauntlet at the bottom end of the corridor, where they could catch lower school boys returning to class from the dining room, punching them as they tried to get past. Even as he lay on his deathbed, paralysed in both legs, Bourdas refused to 'split' (tell tales) on those who had hit him. It went against the honour code of the school.[8] In the scandal triggered by his death, this code was dubbed 'a system of terrorism' by the Home Secretary, Sir William Harcourt.[9]

Although the school registers of the time do include some other non-European names, as a boarder Calouste was probably more exposed to such roughhousing than day boys like Bourdas were. One old boy, Edward Wakefield, later recalled observing 'a most painstaking effort to roast a boy in half an hour', as well as having 'thrashed a big hulking fellow whom I caught tormenting a puny-looking youngster of Jewish appearance, who turned out to be a son of Baron Rothschild'. Thrashing a bully rather than 'splitting' on him was *Tom Brown* manliness at its best. Truth and fiction overlapped completely: Wakefield explained that the attempt to cook a boy was due 'not to cruelty, but the careful reading of School novels'.[10]

At 63 Warwick Road, the Reverend Belcher's Ealing villa, there were only four boarders. Calouste took the place vacated by Joseph Kamauoha, one of a cohort of well-born Hawaiians sent by King Kalakaua to be educated in Britain.[11] Although not quite so strange a bird of passage as Kamauoha, Calouste faced the same high expectations and risks. His job was to keep his head down and assimilate as quickly as possible. Each day he dined at Gatti's on the Strand at 6.30 p.m., then walked home across the parks, retiring to bed at 8 p.m. The other boarders waited until Belcher retired before sneaking out to the music hall. They returned wearily in the small hours, just as Calouste awoke to put in six hours' reading before attending college.[12] Homesick, Calouste took to spending Saturdays with the Balians, an Armenian family famous for providing the architects who designed many of the Sultan Abdülhamid II's palaces. While Sarkis was grateful to Khosrov Balian for his hospitality, he did not want his son to be a burden and eventually ordered Calouste to stop pestering them.[13]

His mother, Dirouhi, did not write to Calouste herself, and so her views and instructions had to be relayed via her husband's letters. There being no underground railway in Istanbul, apart from a short underground funicular linking Galata and Pera, Dirouhi was worried at the thought of her sixteen-year-old son going to school every day on the District Line. He should not jump off a moving train.[14] 'Your mother says you should not work so hard,' Sarkis added in October 1884, 'but I think you should work even harder.'[15] In November Calouste asked for his father's permission to travel to Marseille to spend Christmas with the Selians. This was refused. He begged. 'You shall not go to Marseille for Christmas. Never! Never! Never! You must stay at Belcher's house and study,' thundered Sarkis.[16]

It seems that Calouste was being bullied by fellow boarders. He wired his father that he was 'broken-hearted' at the thought of spending Christmas alone in London. Sarkis backed down and ten days later Calouste arrived in Marseille.[17] Over the holidays reports of the abuse Calouste had been subjected to at Belcher's got back to Istanbul via the Selians, and Sarkis agreed that Hagop Selian should accompany Calouste on his return to London and investigate. Having initially refused to believe Calouste's reports, accusing him of slandering Belcher, Sarkis agreed that Calouste should move out of Warwick Road. He could live with the Balians until Easter.[18]

Applied Sciences

In January 1885 Calouste 'went upstairs' to King's College's Department of Applied Sciences, despite having spent only a term at the school.[19] Sarkis continued to waver over the direction his son's studies should take. Was

Calouste in London to acquire fluency in English and other skills of value
to the family's import-export business? Or was he there to acquire knowledge of new sciences whose utility was less immediately obvious? When
Calouste first expressed an interest in studying geology and mechanical
engineering, in October 1884 his father replied, truthfully enough, that
such subjects were 'unknown in Turkey'. Sarkis thought that these dis-
ciplines might be useful in the future, however, and was happy for his son
to proceed.

One month later Sarkis changed his mind: Calouste should drop any
thought of engineering and geology, and only study English, French and
Maths at King's. In the evenings he could do English Literature, English
History and commercial law. There would be no demand for anything
else. Calouste got his father to agree to allow geology two weeks later, but
mechanical engineering was too 'dirty'. A Gulbenkian did not get himself
oily working on machines.[20] Clearly this debate was as much about prestige as it was about 'useful' knowledge.

In July 1885 Trinity term ended and Calouste left London to spend
the holidays at home, travelling via Vienna, a journey which took five days.
His parents had not seen him in a year and a half. His brothers, Karnig
and Vahan, were now fifteen and seven years old respectively. He wrote to
Cole, apparently the first letter he ever wrote in English:

> As I had promised to write you a short time after my arrival in Con-
> stantinople and to inform you on my pastime & how I got alone [*sic*]
> on my voyage. I now take this opportunity of fulfilling my promise.
>
> You know that I am not an Englishman and having only spent
> 10 months in mastering what little I have been able to acquire; I know
> you will look over any little mistakes I may make here & specially when
> I tell you that this is my first attempt to write to you all being of my
> own style & composition & this is the result of 10 months hard study
> in England.
>
> After having said 'Adieu and au Revoir' to England on Saturday
> morning (the 27th ult[imo]). After a few hours sailing on the same
> morning the shores of the 'La Belle France' were seen. We then crossed
> victorious Germany, Great Austria, newly civilized Austria & poor
> Bulgaria.
>
> After a few days the 'Danae' is sailing with a fresh breeze 'en route'
> for Byzance. In the morning I got up very early to view the spectacle

presented to us by the beauty of the Bosphorus. I am unable to describe to you its supernatural beauty which is not I am aware unknown to you.

So I arrived safe & sound on Thursday morning. In another letter I will write to you how I pass my time & on Armenia (all I can tell you about). My father & mother present to you their best compliments.

I remain yours very truly

Calouste S. Gulbenkian

P.S. I wrote this letter on the 25th inst. but was forgotten at the office.[21]

The letter is a charming jumble of phrases Gulbenkian is proud at having picked up in conversation ('safe & sound'), borrowings from his English language textbook ('style & composition') and bons mots doubtless intended to give an air of the seasoned and polite traveller. While his English became fluent, even as an adult he made the odd mistake, usually when trying to quote an English colloquialism or idiom that had caught his fancy. 'Nooks and corners' became 'crooks and corners', for example.

In later life Calouste was also guilty of inflating the qualifications he earned at King's. He claimed to have gained a 'First Class Degree in Engineering'. Such a degree did not exist at that time. Compared with France and particularly the German states, Britain had been slow to create university faculties of science and engineering. Oxford only opened a Department of Engineering Science in 1908. The aim of the Department of Applied Sciences at King's was not to confer specialised degrees but to provide 'a system of general education of a practical character for young men who are to be engaged in professional employments, such as Civil Engineering, Telegraphy, Surveying, Architecture, and the higher branches of Manufacturing Art'.[22]

What Calouste in fact earned was an associateship of the Department of Applied Sciences, awarded at the end of Michaelmas term 1887, thanks to having won the 2nd Year Physics prize (jointly) and the 3rd Year prizes in both Physics and Practical Physics. Although two prizes were enough to earn the associateship, he also earned Certificates of Merit in 2nd Year Mechanics and Arts of Construction, as well as a Certificate of Distinction in 3rd Year Physics.[23] Alongside these he also studied practical chemistry, geology, geometrical and mechanical drawing, surveying and an activity known simply as 'Workshop'. There were more than 150 lectures a term to attend, with exams at the end of the year. In July 1887 he also sat an external, state examination in magnetism and electricity, gaining an advanced certificate (first class), a stand-alone qualification.[24]

In later life Gulbenkian also claimed to have studied under Ernest Rutherford, the New Zealand-born pioneer of nuclear physics, as well as the great William Thomson, Lord Kelvin, who helped formulate the second law of thermodynamics.[25] Thomson was showered with honours and even gave his name to a unit of measurement (the kelvin, used to measure absolute temperature). But Rutherford did not move to Britain until 1907 and Thomson never taught in London. While Rutherford was plain fabrication, in Kelvin's case Gulbenkian was confusing William Thomson (physicist) with his former teacher John M. Thomson (chemist). The latter was much less distinguished.[26]

If Gulbenkian had a mentor at King's, it was the physicist Herbert Tomlinson (1845–1931), whose name could again be confused with Thomson's. In this golden age leading scientists such as T. H. Huxley were also charismatic public speakers, adept at capturing and holding the attention of non-specialists with their rhetoric, as well as carefully prepared illustrations. Tomlinson, too, was known for Huxleyesque displays of bravura: 'It was a tradition that in his final lecture on sound, which he gave at the end of the course on Physics, he finished by playing *God Save the Queen* by dropping tuned blocks of wood in proper succession on the lecturer's table.'[27] Tomlinson's research was attuned to the needs of industry, rather than 'pure' physics.[28] If Gulbenkian thought of pursuing further studies in Paris (as he later claimed), it was presumably in research similar to Tomlinson's, and using Tomlinson's contacts.

The petroleum industry and related sciences were both in their infancy in this period. Though Gulbenkian studied Geology and Practical Physics at King's, these courses were more interested in coal and steam than in petroleum and electricity. Studying these subjects alongside several others, Gulbenkian did not go into much depth. This by no means rendered him unqualified to be an 'oilman'. Of his contemporaries in the oil industry, only Sir John Cadman (chairman of Anglo-Persian) had a degree in Geology, gained at the University of Durham in 1899. King's gave Gulbenkian sufficient knowledge of mathematics, engineering, geology and physics to be able to talk intelligently about petroleum, and even to explain the underlying principles that made, say, a steam turbine or generator work. More than that was unnecessary. It was the finance that came to fascinate him, not the science.

The process of discovering, extracting and refining oil was an art, not a science. So long as kerosene remained the predominant product there was little motivation for companies to invest in their own laboratories and in university training. Progress was made not in the laboratory but in the field, by trial and error, and a good deal of luck. Considering how expensive the errors were, in lives, money and environmental damage, it is remarkable that it took so long to comprehend the underlying principles. This short-term perspective reflected the limited financial means available to oilmen. Gulbenkian's later work would permit the industry to adopt a longer-term perspective, by giving oilmen access to capital markets and by building stable international collaborations.

Pangloss in Baku

Having completed his education in London, Gulbenkian presumably spent Christmas 1887 in Istanbul, remaining there until late September 1888, when he set off for Baku. The journey to Batumi took three days by steamship. Gulbenkian then caught the Transcaucasian Railway east to Kutaisi and Tbilisi, where he stayed for a fortnight before proceeding to Baku, on the Caspian side. After ten days exploring the city and surrounding oilfields and refineries he caught the train back to Batumi.[29]

This month-long voyage formed the basis of Gulbenkian's travelogue *La Transcaucasie et la Péninsule d'Apchéron: Souvenirs de voyage* (1891). The narrator's perspective is that of a learned French tourist travelling to satisfy his own curiosity. It reveals little of what this young Ottoman Armenian experienced, and a lot about his pretensions. 'We all know the passage in Xenophon relating to Kerassunde,' writes Gulbenkian at one point, with all the breezy confidence of a nineteen-year-old who never mastered classical Greek. For all his insistence that he is 'communicating to the reader my impressions as a tourist rather than my conclusions as an explorer', the author of *La Transcaucasie* does not wear his learning lightly.

Gulbenkian's ship has scarcely cleared Istanbul harbour before 'we' find ourselves surveying the available literature on the archaeology, anthropology, geology, history and natural history of the Caucasus. Gulbenkian regularly cites works published in French, English, German and Russian (the last two of which were as alien to him as classical Greek).[30] Intended to create the impression that he was in fact (contrary to his own modest self-appraisal) a fellow 'explorer', these references suggests that much of *La Transcaucasie* was mugged up after the fact, in a library in Paris.

In between these learned passages we get a good deal about landscape and mythology. With their eye for the picturesque and attention to colour, Gulbenkian's landscape descriptions are closely modelled on those found in travelogues by Théophile Gautier and Alexandre Dumas.[31] These descriptions, as well as the long discussions of bird life, were given short shrift by the archaeologist Georges Perrot of the École Normale Supérieure in Paris. Gulbenkian had shown Perrot around during the latter's passage through Istanbul, and asked him for advice on editing and publishing his manuscript. Perrot was ruthless in his criticism of the draft, which needed 'rewriting from the first line to the last'. He arranged matters with a leading French publisher, Hachette, and found a doctoral student, Samuel Chabert, to do the rewriting.[32]

Readers would, one suspects, have been surprised to discover that the author was not in fact arriving in Istanbul for the first time. Did Calouste even hear 'the sonorous tones of the muezzin calling the faithful to evening prayer' after a childhood spent in the city? Did 'oriental customs' and the 'picturesque and so pretty' dress of the natives really strike him any more? We will never know. Perhaps Gulbenkian believed, with Gautier, that 'To travel through a country, one has to be a foreigner.'[33]

Even in a four-week trip which rarely strayed from the hotels strung along the new railway, Gulbenkian surely experienced much that did not make it into his book. He may have been sent on business by Sarkis. S. & S. Gulbenkian traded in Caucasian kerosene, among many other things. There may have been fellow Gulbenkians that Calouste could call on en route. In Georgia as elsewhere the Armenians had long established themselves as advisers, translators and bankers to local princelings and other notables. By 1890 they controlled Tbilisi's duma or parliament, and they had built the city's largest cigarette factories, leather works and silk mills.[34] In cultural terms Tbilisi remained one of the most important centres of the Armenian community, with its own Armenian theatre and literary tradition.

One of the pillars of the Armenian community in Tbilisi was Alexander Mantashyantz, better known as Alexander Mantashev. Son of a Tbilisi textile merchant, Alexander had been sent in 1866 to Manchester, where

Ottoman cotton was woven into fabric for re-export (including back to the empire). Starting in the 1830s, various wealthy Armenian clans had established footholds there, often sending sons over at sixteen. By the time Mantashev arrived, a wealthy if small community had built up in what was now the Victorian shock city of steam-powered mills and relentless, profit-seeking hustle.

In 1872 Mantashev returned to Tbilisi, opened a textile warehouse and followed his father into the duma. With Russian colonisation had come the city's first modern banks, and Mantashev lost no time in joining the board of the Tbilisi Russian State Bank and the Commercial Bank, rising to become chairman of the latter, as well as its largest shareholder. Like the great Andrew Mellon of Pittsburgh, Mantashev of Tbilisi got into oil via one of his creditors, Mikael Aramyants, who had borrowed heavily to invest in railway tank cars to transport his oil to market. By a similar process of acquiring shares in return for non-performing loans, Mantashev acquired a stake in another Armenian oil company, A. Zatouroff. In 1899 he renamed the company A. I. Mantashev & Co.[35] In later life Mantashev became one of the wealthiest Armenian oil magnates.

Arriving in Baku in November 1888, Gulbenkian found few sights. He thought the old Persian centre sadly decayed and the new 'White Town' dull, 'no theatre, no music, no greenery, no water, not even any earth where plants can grow'.[36] After two days he set off to explore the oilfields of the Absheron peninsula, as well as the refining centre of Tchernagorod, the 'Black Town'. He was lent a carriage by an Armenian oilman, Hovhannes Zovianoff. Once refined into kerosene, Zovianoff's oil would have been transported by railway tank car to Batumi for transfer into tins. Packed into a wooden box, two of these four (imperial) gallon tins made up a 'case'. Along with the Russian *pood*, the case was the main unit of measurement employed in the oil industry. Finding supplies of tin and especially wood to make these cases was a constant headache, literally a bottleneck in production.

The largest producers in Baku were the Nobels. An émigré family from Sweden, the Nobels of St Petersburg built an engineering, armament and munitions company whose Izhevsk factory supplied the Russian armed forces. In 1873 Robert Nobel visited Baku to buy wood for rifle stocks, only to be distracted by the potential of oil. The Nobels set up their oil firm, Branobel, in 1879. An initial share capital of 3 million roubles was quintupled in just twelve years.[37] Deep pockets, excellent organisation and

investment in research by Dmitri Mendeleyev (who formulated the peri-
odic table of elements) and others gave Branobel a significant advantage
over the hundreds of smaller Armenian, Russian and 'Tatar' (Azeri) operators who struggled with poor equipment and hand-to-mouth financing.

Branobel's focus was on the domestic market, which it served via
a massive network of tank farms and sales offices across the Russian
Empire. Nobel's products, which included vaseline and lubricants as well
as kerosene and mazut (heavy oil, for firing train and ship engines), were
transported across the Caspian to Novorossisk, and then carried up the
Don on barges. In 1877 Branobel launched the first oil tanker, *Zoroaster*.
By 1888 Branobel had 25,000 employees and owned half of the tank cars
running the Baku–Batumi line. A model employer by the standards of the
time, Branobel provided far better housing than any equivalent firm, as
well as operating a savings and profit-sharing scheme for their workers.
Its facilities were wonders of technology and tours were given for foreign
visitors. It seems highly likely that Gulbenkian took up this opportunity.
Needless to say, Branobel was deeply feared and resented by all other Baku
producers and refiners.[38]

Nobel faced a foreign challenger in Rothschild Frères, the Paris branch
of the renowned banking dynasty. In 1886, two years before Gulbenkian's
trip, it bought out two Russians, Bunge and Palashkovsky, who had established the Batoum Oil and Trade Society, known by its Russian acronym,
Bnito.[39] Rothschilds relaunched this as the Société Commerciale et Industrielle de Naphte Caspienne et de la Mer Noire, with modest capital of
1 million roubles. As a bank, Rothschilds lacked technical knowledge.
Although the Société Caspienne had its own fields and refinery around
Baku, as well as a Black Sea tanker fleet, the Rothschilds did not seek to
acquire more. Instead they extended large credit lines at moderate rates to
all comers. The loans were repaid in kerosene, and those who borrowed
were banned from selling through anyone else. While Branobel focused on
Russia, the Société Caspienne served the export markets: western Europe,
India and the Far East. Thanks to the lack of rival sources of capital needed
to invest in new plant, tank cars and tankers, many took Rothschilds up
on the offer.[40]

In an industry divided among what we now call 'upstream' (finding
and lifting the oil), 'midstream' (transporting it) and 'downstream' (refining, selling and marketing it) activities, a company has to control only one
phase to control them all. This had been amply demonstrated by John

D. Rockefeller's Standard Oil, founded in 1870 to exploit the oilfields of northwestern Pennsylvania. Rockefeller had leveraged his control of refineries and railways to control price swings and pressure well owners to hand over their operations to Standard in exchange for shares in the company. Those who complied were promised an end to volatility and uncertainty, to 'that cut-throat policy of making no profits'. Those who refused the modest proposals of Rockefeller's lieutenants were pushed to the wall. The tactics employed relied on secrecy and ruthlessness: a refiner who resisted might find himself facing a 'barrel famine', a mysterious interruption in the supply of the barrels he needed to ship his products.

'Our plan,' Rockefeller promised, would 'make the oil business safe and profitable'. By keeping out of the drilling part of the industry Standard avoided the associated risks (dry holes), while making healthy profits on refining, transport and marketing. By the mid-1880s Standard controlled roughly 90 per cent of US refining capacity and 80 per cent of the US market for sales of refined products. Unsurprisingly, Standard was already facing rivals' accusations of anti-competitive behaviour, such as the discounts and rebates it secured from railways.[41] Strictly speaking, however, the Standard Oil Company did not own the network of companies under its sway; it was then illegal for one corporation to own shares in another. Instead, the shares were held by the company 'in trust' for its shareholders, under the 1882 Standard Oil Trust Agreement. Within a few decades, 'trust' became a byword for untrustworthiness, popularly associated with shady business practices that supposedly left consumers at the mercy of oligarchs with politicians in their pockets.

Thanks to discoveries on the Absheron peninsula, Russian production in the previous ten years had increased tenfold, reaching 23 million barrels in 1888.[42] A pipeline linking Baku and Batumi was under construction. Nobel had driven Standard out of the Russian market and was beginning to look for other outlets in western Europe. Standard's initial response was to drop prices. Instead of pulling back, however, in 1888 Nobel and Rothschilds each set up marketing companies in Britain. Standard was obliged to follow suit, establishing Anglo-American. All three began joint ventures with distributors in other European countries, a further step towards becoming international companies. Gulbenkian's trip to Baku thus coincided with a key turning point in the world oil industry: the beginning of a shift from an industry dominated by Standard and American (Pennsylvanian, for the most part) production to today's industry, dominated by a handful of companies with production scattered across the world. Baku's gushers were the impetus for this shift.

Compared with the tank farms and refineries of today, of course, those Gulbenkian would have seen in 1888 were rudimentary. The Absheron peninsula was an ugly, smelly and dangerous patchwork of rival claims, webbed with three-inch pipelines. 'Tanks' consisted of walls of earth shovelled out of the ground, in which lakes of crude sat, slowly evaporating, reflecting the sky like an obsidian mirror. The first generation of 'refineries' were bench stills, glorified stewpots in which crude had to be cooked in batches, rather than continuously flowing through and being separated into its various fractions.

Thanks to the waxy nature of Baku crude, copious amounts of sulphuric acid were required to 'wash' it. Although Nobel's Mendeleyev and other Russian chemists made key advances towards continuous refining and pressure cracking in the 1880s, the process required new equipment and specialist knowledge – and hence was not widely used.[43] Once the kerosene had separated out and been drawn off, the heavy residues had to be scraped out before the still could be used again. To save time this was often done while the interior of the still remained fiercely hot, by lowering in heavily wrapped men on ropes to chisel away at the crust. Although it was already clear by 1880 that crude also contained useful lubricants and heavy fuel oil (mazut), many operators flared off or simply dumped all but one product: kerosene, used for lighting. Given the average kerosene yield for Baku crude was a mere 30 per cent, the waste was colossal.[44]

In 1878 six drillers brought in from Pennsylvania sank the first drilled wells on the peninsula, drawing a line under the age-old method of digging pits with shovels and waiting for crude to seep into them.[45] 'Drilling' involved raising and dropping a heavy steel bit at the end of a long cable, pausing occasionally to bale out the crushed rock using a tubular bucket. In a sense the sheer volume of crude on the Absheron peninsula at shallow depths (compared with Pennsylvania) discouraged innovation. Thanks to layers of gas, this crude was often under considerable pressure and hence did not require pumping. But this pressure could be a curse as well as a blessing. Small-scale operators often struggled to bring gushers under control, allowing them to run unchecked for weeks on end. Thanks to the methane which often erupted with the crude, accidental explosions and fires were woefully common. The workforce who bore the brunt were Tatars. Little notice was taken of them by the Russians or Armenians except when brooding resentment flared into unrest. The Caucasian oil industry was a spectacle of waste and disorder. When Gulbenkian visited the fields he took an armed guard.

For a tourist, the highlight of a visit to the peninsula was the Zoroastrian fire temple on the Surakhani plain, to which Parsee pilgrims had come for centuries to worship the 'eternal fire', a natural gas vent. The last priest had departed in 1880 and one suspects that the structure Gulbenkian admired was a latter-day confection run up for the visit of Tsar Alexander III.[46] Although Gulbenkian is romantic enough to regret the departure of the Parsees, otherwise his account of the peninsula's industry is enthusiastic. Even when he is 'soaked from head to toe by a shower of oil', Gulbenkian's spirits are undampened. Indeed, his conclusions are so upbeat as to sound Panglossian. 'Everything therefore is for the best. The past is encouraging, the present superb and the future dazzling.'[47]

THREE

YOUNG MAN IN A HURRY, 1889–96

In the summer of 1889 Gulbenkian fell in love, in Bursa, while playing dominoes with Nevarte, the daughter of Ohannes and Virginie Essayan. Calouste was twenty, Nevarte was fourteen. All such meetings were, of course, heavily chaperoned by governesses and tutors like Devgantz. Parents, aunts and uncles were rarely out of earshot, and younger siblings could not be trusted to keep secrets. While boys like Calouste could snatch some moments of freedom, daughters rarely had any time alone until they married. A servant slept in Nevarte's room, and in order to write letters unobserved Nevarte had to somehow work out how to make herself wake up in the middle of the night, without waking the maid up as well.

Writing letters was easy compared with working out how to get them to the right person. Such was the fear of their falling into the hands of parents, servants or others that billets-doux were sent without salutation or signature, in French, *vouvoyant* (using the formal *vous* rather than *tu*), giving false dates, avoiding intemperate expressions ('ma chère') and sometimes using disguised handwriting. Gulbenkian's earliest surviving love letter observes these rules, somewhat cack-handedly: it is written in French on a piece of 'Sarkis and Serovpe Gulbenkian' headed notepaper:

> Excuse me, my friend, that I did not come to the garden today. Yesterday evening papa was looking at me so oddly that I fear he suspects something. He has forbade me walking out with that young girl, saying

that she is too young to accompany me. So don't expect to see me in the garden anymore. We will see each other at B[üyük]D[ere] – if you go there. I think we will see each other in a month's time at the latest. Oh, my friend, I know that it is pointless to remind you of your promise but for God's sake do not forget your vow not to reveal to anyone anything of what has passed between us ... Au revoir, your faithful friend.

If I appear cold towards you if and when you come to B[üyük] D[ere] please do not take any notice, it will be to allay any suspicions. Excuse me this scrawl and love me.

If you have something to tell me you could write it on a piece of paper and give it to this girl, she does not know French. Destroy this paper. Best wishes.[1]

Sarkis had evidently twigged that Calouste was no longer afraid of talking to girls and was prepared to say a good deal more than 'hello' to them. The creases indicate that this paper was folded up very small, so as to fit into the hands of a young servant and be passed without being seen. Nevarte did not destroy it.

Asked about the Essayan firm in 1893, the Istanbul branch of Crédit Lyonnais reported that they were 'A very good house, with an estimated capital of at least 3m francs. Affairs prudently and well managed ... They and the Gulbenkians are the two leading Armenian firms in our area.'[2] The families were well known to each other: they mingled in Pera, where the Essayans lived in winter, and in Büyükdere, where the Essayans had a large *yalı* (summer house) right on the Bosphorus. In 1878 Serovpe Gulbenkian and Ohannes Essayan were both appointed trustees of Surp Pırgiç, Istanbul's Armenian hospital, where the Gulbenkians later built a family burial ground.[3] The families shared servants, too: after serving as Calouste's tutor Devgantz returned to Istanbul, where he gave Nevarte lessons in Armenian.

There would have been nothing shocking about a girl marrying at fourteen. Nevarte's mother, Virginie, was married at fourteen, to a man sixteen years older. Such matches were arranged between the parents, and provided plenty of gossip for the entire community. Although affection was less important than ethnicity and status, daughters did have the power to veto an otherwise approved candidate. It seemed unlikely that Nevarte would object to Calouste, however. Her English governess, 'Miss Louisa', even had to admonish her charge to mask her feelings for Calouste. 'I do wish you would not blush every time we see that boy,' she remonstrated, 'he will notice and be so conceited about it.'[4]

A proposal was made on 5 June 1889.[5] Unfortunately, Nevarte's father, Ohannes Essayan, agreed with Sarkis Gulbenkian: Nevarte was still a child, too young to marry. Ohannes wanted to wait until she was eighteen. This prospect seemed to depress Calouste rather more than it did Nevarte. 'What a sentimental letter you wrote me yesterday!' she told him in one letter. 'I certainly hope you are sincere in what you write, but I beg you, moderate your language. We saw each other two days ago and already you want to meet again. What are you going to do when you go to London? We won't see each other for two years. It is time we got used to it, my friend.' After signing off (without using her name), Nevarte added, 'I beg you not to sign yourself "your slave". I am not looking for a slave, but a friend. Remember: no name, no date.'[6] As it happens, the Essayans left for Geneva, Paris and London several months before Gulbenkian left Istanbul.

The Essayans

Like the Gulbenkians, the Essayans were Cappadocians, from Kayseri, but had moved westwards to Istanbul slightly earlier. They were also several decades ahead when it came to opening branches of the family merchant house in Britain. Essai Essayan probably arrived in the United Kingdom in 1866.[7] 'Essai Essayan & Co.' appears in Slater's Manchester and Salford directory for 1867.[8] Such directories suggest a community of Ottoman merchants with offices in the same building, Globe House at 25 Sackville Street. They included Armenians such as the Mantashevs and Mosditchians, Ottoman Greeks such as Theologos N. Pervanoglou and Ottoman Turks such as C. Karayoussoufoglu. By 1876 Globe House also housed George Essayan, who may have been Nevarte's grandfather.[9] The Mosditchians were related to the Essayans by marriage.[10] As ever, family and business went hand in hand.

George (Kevork in Armenian) and the other Essayans were major contributors towards the construction of the first purpose-built Armenian church in Manchester, erected in Chorlton-on-Medlock in 1870. In 1874 they were on the committee that established the Union of Manchester Armenians. The Essayans were, in short, pillars of the growing Armenian community in Manchester.[11] A listing in a directory did not mean that these families were full-time Mancunians, however. As usual, family members would have moved regularly between Manchester, Istanbul and other trading centres.

Even with fellow Armenians around, Victorian Britain could be a challenging posting. Long considered useful for commercial reasons, British citizenship became even more valuable as coordinated violence against the Ottoman Armenian community escalated. To apply for naturalisation papers one had to be able to prove five years' residence in the United Kingdom. Meguerditch, Nevarte's uncle, went out to Liverpool in 1871 and remained in the country until taking citizenship in 1876.[12] Her father, Ohannes, followed in 1873. Lonely and depressed by the 'awful weather', Ohannes wrote to his wife back in Istanbul of how his sense of isolation was increased by his lack of English and French.[13] Nevarte herself was born in London, in 1875.

In 1879 the brothers Ohannes and Meguerditch set up their own firm, 'O. & M. Essayan', in the City of London. They remained at 34 Old Broad Street for several years, and retained offices in the neighbourhood until the firm was wound up in 1912. Listed initially as 'merchants', it seems that the brothers moved into banking during the 1880s. The constant vigilance demanded of a merchant gave way to the more relaxed life of a rentier. Neither Meguerditch nor Ohannes seems to have been very entrepreneurial, nor did they make much of an effort to train their sons up to the business. Presumably when their father died (in the 1880s?) the large inheritance they received left them uninterested in continuing the daily grind.

With his low, murmuring voice, carefully trimmed moustache and tendency to chew his words, Ohannes Essayan was a forbidding presence at mealtimes, one of the few occasions during the day when little Nevarte and her four younger siblings would have had any contact with him. It was forbidden to laugh at table, at pain of risking one of Ohannes's rare but violent outbursts of temper. After Ohannes's death in 1901 Nevarte's mother, Virginie, enjoyed a long and happy widowhood as the centre of the Armenian community in Nice, blossoming into something of a socialite. As a young wife and mother in Istanbul, however, Virginie was a marginal figure, anxious and browbeaten by her mother-in-law, Anna.[14] Not that this discouraged sixteen-year-old Nevarte from dreaming of engagement. Like a blushing bride practising her future signature over and over, she repeatedly inscribed an early photograph 'To my fiancé' (in French) on the back.[15]

Ohannes's own education had been neglected, as his poor command of languages demonstrates. This made him all the more anxious to give his children an excellent education. Although Nevarte never went to school (university would have been unimaginable for a young lady), she did receive instruction in some sciences, such as astronomy, in addition to more socially acceptable subjects, such as Armenian and French. Much of Nevarte's childhood was therefore spent not with her parents, but with a bevy of French- and English-speaking governesses and tutors. Eager to praise her progress in order to continue in employment, they may have fostered a certain vanity in Nevarte, a tendency to be overly light-hearted and flirtatious: in a word (an Armenian one), *tetevsolik*.

An Electrician of the Highest Order

Travel to Baku and back in late 1888 does not seem to have lessened Calouste's sense of impatience and frustration at being in his home town once more. His father, Sarkis, was now running S. & S. Gulbenkian on his own, Serovpe having died in 1886. Calouste courted the patronage of foreigners passing through Istanbul. For the French archaeologist Georges Perrot, he was happy to talk about the city's antiquities. For a certain Mr Sweeney, who worked at the US Consulate, he was happy to talk wool, and provide information later published in the State Department's 'Asiatic Sheep and Wool Report'.[16]

Gulbenkian was pulling every lever he could reach to get his name in print. In May 1889 the *Levant Herald* of Istanbul published an article by him entitled 'Travels in the Land of Oriental Carpets'.[17] This described the kind of carpet looms and the traditional carpet patterns used in the Caucasus. He was also writing to geologists endeavouring to find out more about the oil-bearing structures of the Caucasus.[18] He spoke to Perrot about his plans for a longer travelogue that addressed petroleum as well as carpets, and Perrot came up trumps. Alongside the book itself (published in August 1891) Perrot got the chapters from *La Transcaucasie* that dealt with carpets and oil published separately in the *Revue d'archéologie* and the prestigious *Revue des deux mondes*, in January and May respectively.

In later life Gulbenkian claimed that *La Transcaucasie* established his reputation as an 'oil expert'. This was pure fabrication. Faced with earlier, livelier accounts by travellers who had spent more time in the Caucasus, *La Transcaucasie* sank without trace.[19] The book did, however, help Calouste and Nevarte to present the former as a serious prospect to Nevarte's reluctant parents. This was probably Calouste's principal justification for seeing the book into print, rather than simply giving it up as a bad job. He was certainly eager to make the most of his King's College qualifications. These, he claimed, were equivalent to those held by graduates of the École Normale Supérieure, who carried the title *docteur*. Nevarte challenged this, correctly pointing out that Calouste's qualifications were more similar to the less distinguished *bachelier ès sciences*. Calouste's amour propre did not take this well:

> I am a civil engineer and an electrician of the very highest order: I was the youngest and by far the youngest among my fellow students who received their diplomas with me, some of whom entered the [Royal Engineers], thanks to their diplomas which are prized everywhere. Had I wanted to continue my studies at the École Normale it would have been to deepen my knowledge of astronomy, mathematics and to undertake other studies of an advanced kind.[20]

Here Gulbenkian breezily claims that the decision not to proceed to further study in Paris had been his own, rather than his father's.

Given that Virginie Essayan had forbidden her daughter to write to Calouste, he could hardly send the Essayans a copy of *La Transcaucasie*, although he had had special gift copies printed on fine Japanese paper. Nevarte had to ask to borrow a copy from Calouste's cousin. Her hackles rose sympathetically when an Armenian newspaper in Istanbul, *Arevelk*, published a hostile review. 'The impudence of *Arevelk* is revolting! Of course you didn't have to send money in order to get your articles translated by someone else! What an idea! What ever will they think of next?!'[21] She reassured Calouste that a rival known only as 'Z.' lacked his education and intelligence. Z. could never get published in the *Revue des deux mondes*. But 'articles in reviews don't make any impression on men of business,' she noted, 'and least of all on father'.[22]

A born socialite who sparkled in company, Nevarte claimed to find her own charisma startling. 'I find admirers wherever I go,' she informed Calouste from Évian. 'I don't know what they see in me; I am far from being beautiful or pretty, I don't dress in any special way and I do not wear jewellery, and yet wherever I go people are transfixed.' She went on to describe her daily routine and her favourite activities: morning walks with her brother Yervant (who attended Harrow), writing letters, keeping a journal, dreaming by a window overlooking the lake, dancing in the evening. Calouste was making her more serious, leading her to spend some of each evening examining her conscience. But at the end of the day Nevarte's priorities were clear. 'I like to chat, laugh, have fun and get some compliments now and then.'[23]

Unfortunately for Calouste, alongside 'my beloved C' there was also the aforementioned Z., an S. and, worst of all, an M. There was also a V., that is Vahan Essayan, Nevarte's cousin, and G., Gullabi Gulbenkian, Calouste's cousin. M.'s family was poorer than the Essayans and the Gulbenkians. He nonetheless drew strong support from the grandes dames of the Armenian community in Paris. Though he could not make Nevarte rich, M. was, they reasoned, well brought up. Ohannes had enough money for both of them. This M. and Nevarte had corresponded. Although Nevarte stated that she had only addressed him in her letters as 'Monsieur', given false dates and written nothing compromising, she nonetheless feared that M. would use these letters to blackmail her. In Paris itself M. stalked Nevarte.[24]

Things reached a crisis point in August 1891, during a Channel crossing. Nevarte's parents invited S. to call on them in their cabin. Trying to avoid him, Nevarte feigned seasickness and went on deck by herself, only to be followed by S., who seized the opportunity to grab her hand and kiss it. Having apparently considered herself and Calouste to be engaged in spirit, if not in letter, Nevarte knew that Calouste would be shocked. 'I let S. kiss my hand in secret, yes, I encouraged him ... I fell from Charybdis to Scylla trying to make myself forget this whole story with M., I was frivolous, I craved distraction and not having any other means of passing the time ... Oh, that is enough, I cannot write more.'

Nevarte resolved to remain single until she came of age. She would then train as a teacher and continue her 'life of expiation' by working as the headmistress of a school for poor Armenians that she would endow herself. 'I am fed up with life and have no desire to ruin the life of whomever would take me in marriage.' Though histrionic, there is no denying the tear stains which mark the page, or the strength of the emotions Nevarte was experiencing. A postscript explains that her servant, hearing the scratching of Nevarte's pen stop suddenly, had entered the room to find her unconscious. Seeing the letter, the servant knew better than to call for help and thereby expose her mistress. 'What presence of mind!'[25]

The double standards of the time, as well as Nevarte's lack of anyone other than Calouste himself in whom to confide, placed her in a difficult position. There was little she could do to counter the rumours spread by the likes of M. and S. without further damaging her reputation. Calouste insisted that he was her adviser and confidant as well as her beloved. 'I'm your fiancé and your moral teacher, isn't that right,' he writes in one letter. 'I feel beholden to take charge of your education, for instruction without education is worthless.'[26]

Despite the obvious conflict between these roles, Nevarte was happy to agree to this arrangement. She began interrogating her own conscience and reporting to Calouste. Calouste's own behaviour was not up for discussion. While he expected Nevarte to give him chapter and verse about all her previous encounters with men, he would neither confirm nor deny the rumours of his own activities as a student in London.

Sometimes in these letters one senses that both parties are rehearsing lines they have heard elsewhere. Calouste did not seriously plan to die of grief (as he claimed in one letter), nor was Nevarte serious about spending the rest of her life as a spinster schoolteacher. The closing remark of Nevarte's letter praising her servant's good sense is a salutary reminder that these letters were being exchanged between young adults of a certain class who had no other outlets to express themselves. Nevarte may have 'forgot herself' out of sympathy when other young men paid her the compliment of appearing lovesick, but she must have had feelings of a different order to go along with Calouste's self-assigned role as 'moral teacher'. Though he was bullying in one sense, there are signs that Nevarte was aware of what was happening and happy enough to go through the motions of being the pretty penitent. The incident with S. and other 'crises' were, by dint of their emotional nature, experiences which may have tightened the bond of affection.

There were few other shared experiences available to them during their courtship, given the constant surveillance of Nevarte's parents. When Ohannes Essayan rented Cumberland House, by London's Marble Arch, Nevarte was at first at a loss as to how to keep lines of communication open. Eventually she worked out a system whereby Calouste wrote to a 'Mrs C. James', putting his letters in the post so that they would arrive between eleven and noon (there were then several deliveries a day). 'James' sounding like a common misspelling of their landlord's name, Dawes, her parents would assume any letters they intercepted were intended for her. 'James' was sufficiently different from 'Dawes', however, for Nevarte to be able to get the letter off whichever servant was charged with redirecting it.

Calouste's first letter written as 'H. Leonardi' to 'Mrs C. James' was full of code names: 'Uncle Thomas will sail next week for Sydney with Mrs Curzons.' Nevarte had to confess herself at a loss. Who was 'Uncle Thomas'? Who was 'Mrs Curzons'? She could, alas, understand Leonardi's final sentence: 'M. is more and more blackening your reputation. He is getting hideous, he seems to belong to the very lowest class of human beings.'[27] By exaggerating M.'s calumnies, Calouste posed as Nevarte's chivalrous champion.

A Wedding at the Métropole

In September 1891 the Essayans formally re-established relations with Gulbenkian. More than two years had passed since the first, unsuccessful proposal of marriage. Over the following months Gulbenkian paid visits to them at the Grand Hotel in Paris and the Langham in London, while Ohannes came round to inspect the Gulbenkians' new offices in the City. On 18 November 1891 Gulbenkian repeated his request for Nevarte's hand. This time he received a positive response. Quite what brought Ohannes and Virginie round is unclear. Though there had been other candidates, Nevarte's parents had not pushed any of them very hard and seem to have seen the Gulbenkians as a perfectly suitable family for their daughter to marry into. If Nevarte and Calouste still felt the same way about each other two years on, then the Essayans were not going to stand in their way.

Ohannes's mood can be gauged from a conversation he and Nevarte had on the train back to London from Harrow, where they had been visiting Yervant. She gave an account of it in a letter to Calouste. At the start of the journey, she noted, her father had as usual kept silent, until he began:

> [Armenian] 'I must speak with you, but not now, maybe in a few days.'
> [French] I said nothing. After a few seconds he went on, speaking very slowly, dwelling on each syllable.
> [Arm.] 'You have [Fr.] <u>sympathy</u> [Arm.] for him?'

[Arm.] 'Yes, father, pretty much.'

[Arm] 'What do you mean?'

[Arm.] 'Of all the boys I know, he's the highest in my estimation. He is [Fr.] serious [Arm.] and well educated.'

[Fr.] I can't recall everything I said, but I praised you a lot, he replied that he wanted to know my opinion of you; he had or rather was beginning to have a good opinion of you, and if he hesitated two years ago it was because I was then too young to judge properly whereas now even though I was still a child I was more [capable] of forming a judgement – he said lots of other things that I have unfortunately forgotten.

Although Ohannes 'did not mention the word "marriage" once', the message was clear to Nevarte: 'All is well, my darling!'

Ohannes also revealed that he and Virginie were worried about Calouste's health. It is unclear what exactly they were concerned about; apart from a bout of anaemia when he was thirteen, there is no record of Calouste being unwell before 1891. Although the Essayans could hardly ask him to visit a doctor, Calouste heard about this and secured a certificate of health from a doctor in Paris. Of course he could not show this to Ohannes and Virginie directly, as he did not officially know that this was a concern of theirs. Calouste told his cousin Gullabi, who told Nevarte, who told Ohannes that a certificate existed. In the same exchange in the railway carriage, Ohannes asked his daughter if she had seen it, presenting her with a perfect catch-22: either she had not seen it, in which case it might have been invented, or she had, in which case it was evidence that she and Calouste had been writing to each other, in defiance of her parents.[28] A report about the state of Calouste's body was not appropriate reading for a young lady. Indeed, Nevarte apologised for writing the word 'corset' in one letter to Calouste: it was extremely indelicate to do so, but she was trying to describe how she had tried and failed to use that item of apparel as a hiding place for his letters.[29]

The announcement of the formal engagement put the Armenian rumour mill into overdrive. When the wedding was delayed owing to Dirouhi catching typhoid it was claimed that Nevarte was having doubts, that she loved M., that Sarkis disapproved. Calouste was indifferent.[30] 'Even if all Constantinople were to work itself up into a rage against me my reputation would not suffer,' he wrote to Nevarte. 'For it is not in Turkey that I strive to shine, nor do I care how I measure up to Turkish standards.'[31] He had turned his back on Istanbul and all its Armenian *chan-chan* (Turkish: worthless chatter).

With the Essayans in Nice, Gulbenkian spent the spring of 1892 in London, with only Nevarte's photograph for comfort; she had presented it to him in a velvet wallet that she had embroidered herself. He was kissing it so often, he wrote, he was afraid he might spoil the photograph. Every spare moment was spent house-hunting, sometimes with Nevarte's sister Anna and Miss Louisa. A house near A. C. Cole's was the first to be considered, 10 Maresfield Gardens in Hampstead. Calouste considered this 'a very aristocratic street'. Then there was a house in Kensington, ruled out because it was too near the Royal Marsden Hospital. 'It's terrible, that, it gives me a very bad feeling,' he confessed. Finally he considered renting one of the new-fangled 'flats' in Buckingham Palace Mansions. Imagine, in a flat one could get by with just two servants![32]

The wedding took place on 12 June 1892 in the Whitehall Rooms at the Hotel Métropole, Calouste's home in London since 1891. An Armenian priest officiated.[33] Sarkis was there and Dirouhi too.[34] It is unclear if Calouste's brothers Karnig (now nineteen) and Vahan (fourteen) were present. They may have missed the seven-course reception dinner, which began with a *bisque d'écrevisses* and ended with a champagne mousse and *bombe Francillon*. The Bijou Orchestra under J. Pougher played highlights from operas by Rossini, Offenbach and Bizet. The festivities were, in short, *comme il faut*. The wedding portrait is somewhat stiff, even by the standards of the time. There was no honeymoon – Calouste was back at work the very next day.[35]

The Escape from Istanbul

Few records survive for the five-year period between Gulbenkian's marriage in June 1892 and his return to London in October 1897. In the intervening years he set up the London branch of the Gulbenkian merchant business, his father died and his only son, Nubar, was born. Founded with his uncle Garabed, 'C. & G. Gulbenkian' first appears in the London post office directory for 1892, listed as 'gen[eral] merchants' at St George's House, Eastcheap, in the City of London. This was a small office on the second floor, surrounded by the offices of soap manufacturers, shipbrokers and accountants.[36] Like S. & S. Gulbenkian, C. & G. did not specialise, importing a wide range of commodities from the Ottoman Empire: opium, rugs, cotton, wool and so on.

Fifty-six years old, Sarkis Gulbenkian's health was declining rapidly in 1892. He was unable to work without having Karnig or Vahan by his side. In 1888 Karnig had been sent to Marseille, following the same path blazed by Calouste. Unlike Calouste, however, he then returned to Istanbul rather than attending a British school.[37] Sarkis insisted that Calouste remain in London.[38] Calouste clearly returned at some point in the following year, as April 1893 found him sailing from Istanbul to Adana on the *Guadalquivir*. In Adana, in south-eastern Anatolia, Calouste arranged for a British engineer to come out and install new cotton-ginning equipment in the family's cotton works.[39] By the end of the year his father was dead, and as the eldest son he had to take charge.

Sarkis left an estate worth just shy of £T (Turkish lira) 75,000 (£8.6 million), £T 8,000 of which went to his widow, while the rest was divided equally among his three sons. The estate included houses, shops and *hans* across Istanbul. This was just Sarkis's personal fortune; most of his wealth would have been invested in S. & S. Gulbenkian and its allied family firms. Establishing how much he was worth is therefore difficult; it is indicative, however, that in 1895 more than £T 7,000 (£800,000) was withdrawn from the bank account of the successor firm to S. & S. Gulbenkian, Sarkis Gulbenkian Fils.[40]

There is almost no archival evidence available to indicate where Calouste was in 1894–5, or what he was doing. Clearly something happened to cause a rift between Sarkis's three sons. Letters exchanged a decade later suggest that Calouste cajoled his younger brothers into letting him speculate with their inheritances, by investing in South African mining shares. The Gulbenkians may have been among the many Ottoman Armenian merchants and *sarrafs* (money changers) to suffer heavy losses in such speculation. They certainly held shares in one investment trust caught up in the crash.[41] So did the Essayans.[42] Speculative losses may explain the aforementioned large withdrawals from the Imperial Ottoman Bank (IOB) account of Sarkis Gulbenkian Fils. It is also suggestive that the firm's manager in Baghdad, Istepan Turabian, was dismissed for speculating in mining shares, with the connivance of IOB's manager in that city.[43]

Record gold production in the Rand in late 1894 had brought about a boom in the so-called 'Kaffir Market' centred on London's stock exchange. Encouraged by Edgar Vincent, the mercurial new governor of IOB, mining shares also became a popular speculation on the Istanbul stock exchange, which had opened in 1866. IOB lent many investors large sums with which to speculate, while Vincent created the Eastern Investment Company as a vehicle through which to siphon off the profits he himself made speculating with the bank's money. The losses he kept on the bank's books.[44]

Unsurprisingly, given their dominance of Ottoman banking and finance, events on the Istanbul exchange were closely linked to a broader crisis of confidence among the Ottoman Armenian community, one itself linked to events far to the east, in the *vilayet* of Bitlis. Armenians there organised a tax revolt in 1894, angered by being asked to pay taxes to the Sultan on top of the established taxes to local Kurdish notables. The Ottoman authorities looked on as Kurdish irregulars 'pacified' their Armenian neighbours by means of wholesale slaughter. Fuelled by a fresh outburst of international outrage, Sultan Abdülhamid II repeated the same empty promises he had issued on previous occasions.

On 30 September 1895 members of one of the Armenian socialist parties, the Hnchaks, organised a demonstration in Istanbul. This ended in more anti-Armenian violence, with many of the city's Armenian population seeking refuge inside their churches. Istanbul's stock market (located in Galata) fell. Investors seeking to support their positions in South African shares suddenly found the banks reluctant to extend credit. A moratorium was declared on 1 November, which led to a run on IOB. On the 4th Vincent persuaded the Sultan that the run was an Armenian plot. The Sultan permitted Vincent to suspend payments for a month.[45] Though the situation improved thereafter, many small-time Galata brokers, as well as others tempted into the speculative boom, were ruined.

The Istanbul crash led to falls in Paris, Vienna and London. Desperate to grab the attention of the European powers, on 26 August 1896 a group of twenty-eight heavily armed Dashnaks, Armenian revolutionary socialists, invaded IOB's headquarters in Galata. Nine died in exchanges of fire with the Bank's guards. While Vincent made his escape over the roof, the Dashnaks laid explosives, determined to become martyrs by blowing up the bank unless their demands for international arbitration of the Armenian Question were met. Instead Vincent secured their safe passage to Marseille, ending a fourteen-hour siege.[46]

The attack served as catalyst for a massacre in which between 3,000 and 4,000 Armenians were killed by Muslim *softas* (students) and Albanian *başıbozuks* (irregular soldiers). The timing of the attacks and the standard-issue weapons subsequently recovered point to a coordinated slaughter in which these groups were invited to go on a forty-eight-hour looting and killing spree. Although the mob was largely kept to the old town, failing to cross the Galata Bridge, the violence menaced all Armenians in the city. This apparently included the Essayans and Gulbenkians.

According to family tradition, the Essayans made good their escape by taking one of the steamers operated by their ferry company, Essayan & Uncuyan.[47] They travelled to Alexandria. The story runs that the family's departure was a scramble to get on board before it was too late. 'We can't leave,' Virginie supposedly blurted out just as the steamer was preparing to leave, 'the laundry hasn't come home yet!' Ohannes's passport for the voyage, issued in Istanbul on 9 September – almost two weeks after the massacre began – suggests a more orderly departure.[48]

In the Essayans' large villa on the Asian side, the violence occurring over on the western shore may have seemed remote. The terror did not spread to Kadıköy, thanks, perhaps, to the intervention of Abdülhamid's ADC, Marshal Fuad Paşa.[49] The trigger for the family's departure was not the violence itself, but its aftermath. Under heavy diplomatic pressure to punish the perpetrators, the Sultan set up an Extraordinary Commission. The Commission pinned the blame for the violence on the Armenian victims themselves, and specifically charged the *amiras* with being the ringleaders.[50]

The Essayans faced prosecution by this Commission. They were also facing death threats from fellow Armenians, in particular from the Dashnaks. Badrig Gulbenkian and other leading *amiras* had made themselves unpopular with many Armenians by helping the Sultan replace Patriarch Ismirlian with a more pliable figure.[51] In a final irony, letters from Armenian revolutionaries to *amiras* demanding money with menaces were seized by the Ottoman security services – and taken as evidence that the *amiras* were in league with the Dashnaks.[52] The Sultan and Armenian revolutionaries were each accusing the Essayans of collaborating with the other. If the kangaroo court didn't get the *amiras*, a Dashnak bullet would. It was time to go.

Among the passengers on the Essayans' steamship was (supposedly) the Tbilisi-based Armenian oil magnate Alexander Mantashev.[53] Spotting a potentially useful patron, Gulbenkian is supposed to have latched on to the man, even ejecting his wife and infant son from the best cabin so that it could be offered to Mantashev. The picture of a young Calouste greasing up to a wealthy stranger on the Essayans' boat is hardly flattering, which may be why Calouste's son, Nubar, was so fond of rehearsing the story.[54] In reality the Essayans already knew Mantashev from Manchester. Nor is there much evidence that Calouste sought Mantashev's attention before 1899.[55] Calouste was probably miles away in London when this escape took place.

In the ten years after the completion of his studies at King's College, Calouste had come of age. He had repaid his father's investment in his education by giving the Gulbenkians a beachhead in the United Kingdom, a key step in the westward course followed by many Ottoman *amiras* in this period. Such a beachhead could also serve as an escape route, even if the escape was far less dramatic than was later recalled. Although Calouste had yet to specialise in the oil business, *La Transcaucasie* and especially his apparent enthusiasm for South African mining shares suggest that, like the Essayans, he was keen to move beyond the kind of merchant business practised by his father.

Calouste's pursuit of Nevarte had been sentimental and sermonising by turns. It takes a particular sort of 'friend' to include criticism of his beloved's moral upbringing and his future in-laws' parenting skills in his billets-doux. Perhaps we can see here an early example of Gulbenkian's insistence on 'moral values' in both professional and private life. He rarely defined these values, but the letters to Nevarte suggest a certain regimen: avoidance of gambling and equally irresponsible badinage; a modicum of amusement; rigorous self-examination and self-improvement. A man of his time and place, Gulbenkian also expected obedience to be shown to him, as both an educated man and the head of the household.

The marriage would be tested in the years to come. For all her youth and inexperience, the love letters suggest that seventeen-year-old Nevarte entered the relationship with her eyes open. At one point during their courtship she happened to be browsing in a Parisian jewellery shop with her mother when Mantashev came in with his latest mistress on his arm, 'a very pretty woman' whom he repeatedly addressed as 'my darling'. When they left Nevarte teased her mother, who was embarrassed at having encountered an Armenian gentleman she knew socially in such a compromising position.

> But I kept working it over in my head: how can a man buy jewellery for a woman who isn't his, and call her 'my darling'? Will you do the same? You will make me jealous if you do, not on account of the jewels

but because I don't want you calling other women 'my darling'. I can be fierce, can't I? I'm kidding, because I reckon this sort of thing happens all the time, and if this is the way things are then it is best that I start getting used to it.[56]

'You can be very arbitrary,' Nevarte recognised, 'as can I, perhaps more so than you. I won't give way, you won't give way.' 'These kind of thoughts aren't very encouraging,' she conceded. 'We are, both of us, fooling ourselves, but if we love each other sincerely and if we each close our eyes to the other's faults then everything will go well and we will be very happy.'[57]

FOUR

NOTHING MORE THAN A SPORT, 1897–1901

In October 1897 Gulbenkian returned to London, this time to stay. The years since his wedding in the Hotel Métropole back in 1892 had seen him knuckle down to work in the family's firm, at least until his father's death in 1894. The death of Sarkis Gulbenkian left Calouste as head of his branch of the family, including its three businesses, based in Istanbul, Marseille and London. Within a few years it became clear that Calouste was not willing to fill this role, preferring to strike out on his own into an entirely new field: the financing and promotion of London-based mining syndicates.

Despite his own heavy losses in the 1895 collapse, Gulbenkian was now drawn to the very heart of that same 'Kaffir Market', the racy corner of the London Stock Exchange which traded in volatile, small-capital South African mining companies. Within weeks of his return to London in 1897 he was in cahoots with Horatio Bottomley and Whitaker Wright, two of the most notorious figures in this market.

Gulbenkian seems an odd fit for this coterie, whose shenanigans epitomise 'naughty nineties' excess. The bookish swot who had stayed in his room to read while his schoolmates snuck out to the music hall had blossomed into 'Carloust', an investor in theatrical syndicates who gave dinners and stock market tips to 'Gaiety Girls'. Meanwhile a nervous as well as jealous Nevarte looked on from a distance, wondering if her husband would get out before the next crash.

Kangaroo Capitalists

The crisis in South African mining shares unleashed by the Jameson Raid should, one might have thought, have discouraged further speculation. Over New Year 1895/6 a group of armed conspirators crossed from British-controlled Cape Colony into the Boers' independent Republic of South Africa. The aim was to spark a revolt sufficiently impressive to give the British authorities an excuse to take control of the region and its recently discovered goldfields. Its failure caused Cecil Rhodes, Alfred Beit, Barney Barnato and the other mining magnates behind the conspiracy acute embarrassment. In June 1897 Barnato's body was fished out of the Atlantic somewhere south of Madeira and buried in Willesden Green in north London. He had been steaming back from South Africa when he fell overboard in highly suspicious circumstances.

Ten years younger than Barnato, Horatio Bottomley had promoted twenty or so mining firms in the heady years of the 'Kaffir' boom, eventually bundling them into two finance corporations. Pocketing subscribers' cash rather than investing it in mining operations, Bottomley's firms struggled to produce dividends, and the two mining investment trusts were merged in February 1897 as the Hansard Union, which went under shortly afterwards. A hearty character with the gift of the gab, Bottomley somehow convinced the public that he would see small investors right.

The failure of the Jameson Raid encouraged Bottomley and others to shift their focus from South African mines to western Australian ones, from the 'Kaffir' to the 'Kangaroo' market. Bottomley set up a new finance corporation, the West Australian Market Trust, whose shares were known as 'Westralians'. By Christmas 1897 he was back on form, regaling his fellow investors at a Christmas dinner. 'Ladies and gentlemen,' he began, 'I have said that the whole of the City of London is nothing more than a sport, and I am sure the simile does not apply to anything more than the history of the West Australian market.'[1]

Bottomley touted a lifestyle as much as he did mines: champagne, racehorses, theatre syndicates and lavish house parties at The Dicker, a rambling, much-extended exercise in what would later become known as stockbroker Tudor, albeit with the odd bit of castellation amidst the exposed beams and ornate bargeboards. It was never clear where the funds came from, but it wasn't very sporting to ask questions, especially when

Bottomley made it clear that you were his friend, one of a special group of insiders who were 'in on the ground floor'.

There was little honour among company promoters, and Bottomley often found himself defending his trusts against bear attacks from another promoter, James Whitaker Wright. A former Methodist preacher, Wright made his first fortune promoting silver mines in Leadville, Colorado, before joining the 'Kaffir circus' and setting up his own finance company, London and Globe. He, too, had his country house, Lea Park near Godalming in Surrey, which featured an underwater billiard room – that is, a room with an aquarium built over it – as well as a velodrome, theatre and observatory.

As we shall see, such larger-than-life figures (Wright weighed 220 pounds) did have a tendency to come to sticky ends, which only heightened their appeal to novelists eager to expose the decay of High Victorian society, with the mysterious speculator as Pied Piper luring aristocrats, churchmen and other innocents, poor as well as rich, to their doom. Augustus Melmotte in Anthony Trollope's *The Way We Live Now* (1875) was an early example of this genre. Company promoters were not all crooks, however, and it is important to note that activities which would now be considered insider trading were legal in the 1890s. Promoters provided a useful service in helping those who actually operated the mines to secure much-needed capital to buy plant and deepen shafts. They allowed small operators to amalgamate, consolidating operations.

Promoters thrived in this period because the 'accepting houses' (merchant banks) had little experience of or interest in organising new companies or introducing their shares to the market. Promoters in turn drew on more established firms of lawyers, accountants, brokers and advertising agencies. Setting up a private company could cost as little as £700 (£10,000); even less, if these firms agreed to take shares in lieu of cash payment.[2] Starting from 1895, companies began to be formed around patents as well as mines, helping develop the embryonic electrical and telecommunications industries, among others.

Investors struggled to find reliable information. The Companies Acts of 1856 and 1862 laid down the legal basis for public limited liability companies. They suggested that copies of balance sheets should be circulated to shareholders in advance of shareholder meetings, but this only became a requirement in 1929. Only in 1948 were such companies obliged to send a profit-and-loss account to shareholders. Many of these companies were private rather than public bodies and were not required to release any information at all.[3] For small-time investors, 'tips' from insiders or self-proclaimed insiders were all the guidance there was on how a company was doing.

In August 1897 Calouste wrote from Paris asking for a prospectus of the Joint Stock Institute, another of Bottomley's finance companies. Once in London he approached Bottomley, proposing to bring new investors into the Institute.[4] By January 1898 he had got a group of investors to put in a total of £30,000 (£3 million). In addition to his own money, which probably came from Nevarte's dowry, Gulbenkian persuaded his father-in-law, Ohannes, to invest on behalf of O. & M. Essayan. He also brought in several members of the Regnart family, who ran Maples department store. 'Do remember our policy,' Bottomley wrote to Gulbenkian from The Dicker. 'Buy Wholesale – sell retail [underlined three times].'[5] As their relations grew closer Gulbenkian began advancing ever larger sums to Bottomley, loans secured against shares in 'Joints' (Joint Stock Institute), 'Westralians' (West Australia Loan and General Finance Co.) and a bevy of other, more exotically named mining shares: Anacondas, Jumpers, Golden Horseshoes.

These shares could be very profitable. Gulbenkian bought 925 Golden Horseshoes at £9.25 in July 1898, selling in June 1900 at £16. He traded heavily in Sons of Gwalia, which rose from 2s to 6s in a similar space of time. He charged Bottomley a hefty 10 per cent interest on the loans. In many cases, however, Gulbenkian simply sold the shares (the collateral for the loan) on the rise, discharging the loan. He secured a bonus for every share sold to 'his' group of investors. A balance sheet he drew up in April 1898 showed a profit of £43,000 (£4.3 million) from the sale of 'Joints' and 'Market Trusts' alone. Making such a sum in six months left his family's merchant business seeming very small beer. This profit also overshadowed the £3,700 Gulbenkian made from his embryonic oil interests in the same period. Some of these profits were invested in much safer American and British railway shares and sovereign bonds.

Gulbenkian's relationship with Bottomley seems to have soured in 1899, when he suspected Bottomley of not being entirely open with him. Gulbenkian switched horses, from Bottomley to his rival, Wright. Between October and December 1900 Gulbenkian advanced eye-watering sums to Whitaker Wright, totalling £230,000 (£22.4 million). As usual these loans were at 10 per cent, and were secured against 'Globes' – that is, shares in Wright's London and Globe Finance Corporation – as well as in Le Roi

Mining, Victoria Gold, Standard Exploration, Nickel Corporation, Lake View Consols and Rossland Great Western Mines. These companies' gold mines included the spectacularly productive Ivanhoe mine near Kalgoorlie, also in western Australia.

Unfortunately, these companies were often heavily 'watered' – that is, massively overcapitalised – flooding the London market with shares. The original firm operating Ivanhoe had just £50,000 worth of share capital, but £1 million worth of shares were floated in London after Wright acquired and reorganised it. How much of the funds raised actually went into expanding mining operations (rather than into promoters' pockets) is unclear. On 28 December 1900 London and Globe announced its insolvency, Wright having failed in his attempts to prop up the price of Lake View Consols, presumably with funds borrowed from Gulbenkian. This failure seems to have caught Gulbenkian by surprise; he had advanced £75,000 (£7.3 million) to Wright just a week before, and that very day he drafted a letter to Wright outlining the terms of yet another loan.[6]

Though Gulbenkian had been selling them quickly, he was still left holding shares when the music stopped. Of course, the shares were security for loans; but could these loans be repaid? Wright went on the run. He wrote to Gulbenkian on 23 January 1901, asking him to transfer any unsold shares in Gulbenkian's position to one H. A. Malcolm, who worked for him – perhaps to squirrel them away before he (Wright) could be run down, as he eventually was, and put on trial for fraud. Gulbenkian duly did so. When Malcolm asked for Gulbenkian's help selling shares the next month, Gulbenkian replied that he was about to go on holiday and did not want to open a new account. On the reverse of his copy of this reply Gulbenkian scribbled a phrase in Armenian: 'What I say on the other side about going on holiday is a lie.'[7]

From Quality Street to Queer Street

Happily, it seems that Gulbenkian managed to sell many of the shares securing his loans to Bottomley and Wright before the loans became due, realising a healthy profit before it all came tumbling down. It was a very risky line of business to be in, however, with implications for Gulbenkian's marriage, family and private life. At first Gulbenkian seems to have tried to keep Bottomley at a distance, insisting on a certain formality. One letter from Bottomley of February 1898 is teasingly addressed to 'My dear "Mr Gulbenkian"', suggesting that Bottomley had previously attempted to address his partner as 'Gulbenkian', only to be rebuffed.[8] Gulbenkian took steps to ensure that his shares were held by nominees (stockbrokers' clerks living in Croydon and Catford), keeping his involvement secret. When he invited his father's old associates at W. H. Cole & Co. to participate they refused. The firm's partners had been in loco parentis during Calouste's days at King's. They were 'upset' to find him dealing with Bottomley, a man 'carefully shunned by the majority of the Stock Exchange'.[9]

Given his fondness for London chorus girls, Bottomley had taken the wise precaution of installing his wife in a villa near Monte Carlo. Nevarte spent most of 1897 and 1898 in a hotel in nearby Nice, along with her servants and a teething two year-old Nubar, who was royally spoiled by hotel staff, even as he continued to have regular tantrums. Nevarte was under firm instructions not to dance or flirt with other men. Nor was she to ride a bicycle (this was the height of the cycling craze). Nevarte suspected that this had little to do with a husbandly concern for her safety: 'Just admit that you are jealous of seeing me wear short skirts – it's the truth, isn't it!'[10]

When Horatio and his daughter Florrie joined Eliza Bottomley at Monte Carlo, however, Nevarte found herself under instructions from Gulbenkian to socialise with them. Eliza was far from a conversationalist, and Nevarte may have resented being seen keeping company with a former shop girl whose father had been a Battersea debt collector. Nevarte resented Calouste's attempts to use her sociable nature to further his own business interests. As she noted, there was something contradictory about Calouste's attitude, which alternated between instructions to court this or that individual from among the Hotel Excelsior's exclusive clientele and injunctions not to interact with strangers.

When Calouste's attempts to use her as 'an <u>instrument</u> for your business' extended to having her socialise with actor-managers and actresses, however, Nevarte drew the line. Calouste probably secured his entrée into this world through Bottomley, investing in a series of syndicates which took leases on the Royal Avenue Theatre and other London stages. In early 1898 Calouste asked Nevarte to move hotels in Paris so that she could give hospitality to actor-manager Seymour Hicks.[11] July found Hicks hailing Gulbenkian as 'my dear old friend', and passing him the lease of the Avenue Theatre as security for a loan to the American producer Charles Frohman, presumably to cover the costs of a season's run.[12] Equally at home on Broadway as in the West End, Hicks and Frohman collaborated on a number of productions, including J. M. Barrie's *Peter Pan* and *Quality Street*.

Gulbenkian also came to the assistance of hotel impresarios Richard D'Oyly Carte and César Ritz. Though small beer compared with his other ventures, investments in the entertainment and hospitality industries had their privileges. Gulbenkian's friendship with Ritz ensured his family special treatment in the latter's Paris and London hotels, while his friendship with Auguste Escoffier ensured a steady supply of well-trained chefs. Hilda Moody, star of *The Geisha* and *A Gaiety Girl* (both 1899), was the first of a series of noted actresses Gulbenkian squired around town. Nevarte was not pleased, and made her views known. Gulbenkian wrote to her mother, Virginie Essayan, in Istanbul, asking her to come to London and help him resolve the situation. Their daily arguments were 'making my life hell'. 'You know yourself how aggressive [Nevarte] gets and what a foul mouth she can have. She claims I am being immoral.'[13]

New Year's Day 1900 found Gulbenkian surprisingly bullish about Westralians, even if he no longer wanted to deal with the likes of Bottomley or Wright directly. Just because 'the whole Australian market is looked upon by the public with very great contempt as being the nest of unscrupulous gamblers, niggers, adventurers and etc' did not mean that there weren't 'really good and lasting mines in Western Australia'.[14] Gulbenkian was involved in reorganising Pride of Gwalia in 1901 and remained a director of the Westralian Mines and Finance Agency until it was wound up in 1904.[15]

Wright was eventually arrested in New York and extradited to Britain, where his trial for fraud at the Royal Courts of Justice began in January 1904. Immediately after hearing the court find him guilty of all charges, Wright retired to a side room, where he handed his watch to his solicitor with the words, 'I will not need this where I am going.' Wright then took cyanide and died within minutes. By this point Bottomley had returned to his earlier career as a journalist and politician, being elected MP for Hackney South. Parliamentary privilege did not extend to protecting him from charges of fraud, however, and he would serve a five-year sentence in Maidstone prison in the 1920s. Irrepressible and optimistic, there would be no cyanide pills or falls off steamships for this company promoter.

In September 1903 Bottomley ran into Gulbenkian in Paris and wrote to him later the same day:

> My dear 'Calouste,' seeing you this morning has set me thinking of the old days, and of the very unfortunate estrangement which has arisen between us. Don't you think we might bury the past? Will you and your wife dine with wife and me and Florrie and her fiancé somewhere tonight? Say 'yes' – and let us be friends once more, for, despite all our differences, I have a very warm corner in my heart for you.

Though he does not seem to have accepted this invitation, Gulbenkian did reply, albeit somewhat sententiously. He had no qualms about looking back. 'It has been one of the enjoyments of my life as you are aware, to have this moral satisfaction with everybody I have ever had any thing to do.'[16] Even when Whitaker's case came to trial Gulbenkian was relaxed. While he asked his broker to scan newspaper reports to see if either of them was named, he was confident that such a mention was 'not at all likely in view of our most clear legal distinct transactions'.[17]

Shady Lane

The Gulbenkians had been exporting kerosene from Batumi for some time and Sarkis Gulbenkian Fils continued doing so. The company also began buying and distributing Romanian oil products through its Varna (Bulgaria) branch, albeit without making any move to shift from shipping kerosene in cases to shipping it in bulk, in specially designed ships. None of the Gulbenkian partnerships were involved in 'upstream' activities – that is, in digging oil wells or in refining. Calouste's involvement in the financial restructuring of Russian oil companies was a new departure, one which he kept distinct from his work for the family firms. It began in early 1898, when he and Frederick Lane floated the Russian Industrial and Mining Company.

Born in 1851 to a family of immigrants from Malta, Frederick Lane was a partner in the London shipping agency Lane and Macandrew.[18] In 1884 the firm chartered the Nobel tanker *Petroleum*, shipping kerosene in bulk from Batumi to London for the first time. Nobel was more interested in the domestic Russian market, however, and so Lane turned his attentions to Nobel's biggest rivals, the Paris Rothschilds and their Société Caspienne. Starting in 1886, with a shipment to Calcutta, Lane's firm provided chartering services for Rothschild Frères, helping them transport kerosene

from Batumi to ports in the Far East.[19] In 1891 he brought together Rothschilds' production and refining capacity with the shipping capacity of
Marcus Samuel and Co.

Marcus and his brother Samuel Samuel ran a London-based general
merchant business inherited from their father, a self-made trader in seashells from east London. Lane and Marcus Samuel travelled to Baku
together in 1890. The Samuels began building a fleet of bespoke oil tankers
designed to transport oil in bulk. Now all they needed was the oil to fill
them. In 1891 Lane brokered a nine-year agreement giving the Samuels
exclusive rights to sell Rothschilds' Russian kerosene in the Far East. One
year later *Murex*, the Samuels' first bespoke oil tanker, arrived in Singapore.
Other tankers also named after types of seashells soon followed. In 1897
the Samuels established a new firm named Shell Transport and Trading.

As we shall see, 'Shady' Lane (the nickname was not used pejora-
tively) later brokered major deals involving the Rothschilds, Mantashev
and Royal Dutch-Shell. 'Considering the dominant position he eventually
assumed [Lane] was astonishingly uneducated,' noted a German oilman
who got to know him around this time. 'Like all Londoners of humble
background, in speaking he constantly struggled with that fatal letter
"h".'[20] Writing in his 1945 memoirs, Gulbenkian remembered Lane as 'a
very eminent commercial genius and organiser', 'the father of the British
oil industry'.[21]

Though its focus was the Russian rather than the British Empire,
otherwise the Russian Industrial and Mining Company was not that different from the flashier 'Institutes' and 'Trusts' operated by Bottomley
and Wright.[22] The ostensible purpose was the same: to acquire small yet
promising mining companies that had been founded abroad and inject
new capital for development. Over the next two years the company
acquired, reorganised and relaunched a series of Russian firms, creating
new London-based companies or forming syndicates, presumably with
a view to floating a company later on, should the enterprise in question
prosper. These companies mined gold in eastern Siberia, copper in Artany
(near Tbilisi) and both copper and gold in the Urals. Lane and Gulbenkian
were less successful as founders of entirely new ventures, and their Sakhalin
Syndicate searched in vain for oil on Sakhalin island in the North Pacific.[23]

Lane and Gulbenkian were on surer ground handling Caucasian oil
companies. After debating the issue at a Special Congress in May 1898, the
Russian authorities removed many of the restrictions on foreign investment

in the Caucasus oil industry that had been imposed in 1893. Russian Industrial and Mining was part of a resulting wave of inward British investment,
totalling £4.1 million (£400 million) by 1901, by which time annual Baku
production had risen from 516,000 (in 1897) to 11.6 million tons, the
highest recorded before the Soviet era.[24]

Russian Industrial and Mining's first coup was to secure control of
a firm formed by S. M. Schibaieff, a Moscow chemicals magnate who
had first visited Baku in the 1870s. Starting in 1880 with a small sulphuric acid plant, Schibaieff had gone on to acquire a number of fields on
the Absheron peninsula, using his chemical expertise to achieve yields of
kerosene, lubricants and other products that were matched only in Nobel's
refineries.[25] Schibaieff sold a controlling stake in his firm to a Dutch bank,
Labouchere Oyens, in late 1897. In February 1898 Lane and Gulbenkian
bought this stake and set up a new London-registered firm, the Schibaieff
Oil Company, with capital of £750,000 (£75 million) and an aristocrat
(Lord Wenlock) on the letterhead, as chairman. Gulbenkian served as
underwriter for the shares.[26]

In December 1898 the Company approached Georg Spies, a German-
born oilman who had developed several profitable fields to the north-east
of Grozny, along the Terek River, operating through a Russian company,
Spies Stücken.[27] In October 1900 Lane and Gulbenkian agreed with Spies
to form a parallel, London-based company, Spies Petroleum, and issue
£650,000 (£35 million) worth of shares.[28] By this point Russian Industrial
and Mining had also invested in oil wells in Texas and Indiana, sending
the great oil geologist Boverton Redwood to report on them.[29] It bought
several parcels of oil land from Mantashev, around which it floated yet
another new company.[30] Russian Industrial and Mining was growing short
of capital.[31] Unfazed, Gulbenkian proceeded to invest directly in these
new firms, and probably underwrote share offerings on London and, in
the case of Spies Petroleum, Paris as well.[32] He was also involved in establishing Bibi-Eybat Petroleum, which acquired the shares and oil leases of a
Russian firm of the same name. Once again, Boverton Redwood was sent
out to its fields (near Baku) to report.[33]

What did Gulbenkian bring to this business? Lane himself had visited
Baku on the Rothschilds' behalf back in 1890. Nearly twenty years older
than Gulbenkian, he had much more expertise in the oil business. Any
technical knowledge Gulbenkian may have retained from his studies was
not needed, nor were his family connections, which Gulbenkian probably

didn't want to call on anyway. As with Bottomley and Wright, Gulbenkian's contribution was capital, both his own and that of his friends. But we can also detect the first signs of his growing skill at negotiation and his nose for promising deals.

Thirty years old, Gulbenkian was still learning.

The End of the Partnership

The massacres unleashed across the Ottoman Empire in the wake of the 1896 Imperial Ottoman Bank attack led the Gulbenkian brothers to wind down their activities in central and eastern Anatolia. They closed branches in those areas and transferred funds to existing branches in Marseille and Varna. They considered opening new branches in Alexandria, Tianjin (near Beijing) and Hong Kong.[34] In late 1897 Gulbenkian's cousin Harutyun Gulbenkian was sent out to central Anatolia to collect outstanding debts from clients in the region, a centre of mohair production. He found that many of their clients had fled, while those who were left were starving. 'They don't have money,' Harutyun reported, 'they don't even have bread.'[35]

The decision to reinvest funds withdrawn from Anatolia in Varna seems to have been a case of making the best of a bad job. When the Gulbenkians' Varna manager Boaz Papasian died in 1899, the plan had been to wind down this branch as well, as it had returned no profit since being set up five years before. Bulgarian restrictions on currency movements made this impossible, however. Papasian was therefore replaced with a certain Hovassapian, a relation of Calouste's mother-in-law, Virginie.[36] Hovassapian does not seem to have been a very effective manager and he struggled to maintain good relations with either Calouste or Calouste's brother Karnig. Within a few months the Gulbenkians were accusing Hovassapian of cheating them and demanding that the Essayans compensate them for their losses.[37]

Meanwhile the 1899 recession in America added to the Gulbenkians' problems selling Aleppo and Mosul wool there.[38] With this, the Varna crisis and Dirouhi's declining health, it was clear that Calouste was needed back in Istanbul. Yet he claimed to be unable to return. Back in 1896 the Sultan had declared that any of his subjects who left without registering their intention to emigrate permanently would be prohibited from returning. This decision had been taken in an attempt to staunch the flow of

Ottoman Armenians from Istanbul in the wake of the 1896 massacres, an exodus which brought the city's economy almost to a standstill. Although Ottoman officials had reassured diplomats that these rules did not apply to rich Ottoman Armenians, Calouste apparently took them seriously and refused to risk attempting a return to Istanbul. For his brother Karnig, however, this was an excuse: as he noted, plenty of their relatives and business associates were moving freely in and out of the empire.[39]

Stock market coups with Bottomley fuelled Calouste's feelings of superiority and hostility towards his brothers, feelings that Nevarte sought to restrain. 'You have had a windfall with Bottomley and that makes me happier than I can say,' she wrote, 'but that is no reason to forget everthing else, your brothers and so on. Tomorrow may come a crash and you may be left hopeless.' It was wrong, therefore, for Calouste to write that he wished Karnig was dead, especially when he did not really mean it.[40] Other relatives also urged Calouste to make peace with his brothers.[41]

One thing Karnig and Calouste did agree on was that their youngest brother, Vahan, was a disappointment. Vahan turned twenty-one in 1899, becoming a partner in Sarkis Gulbenkian Fils. Like Calouste and Karnig before him, Vahan had been sent to Marseille. Instead of learning the family business with the Selians, however, he continued to pursue an interest in photography. Even worse, he began gambling and dabbling in radical Armenian politics, both activities Karnig saw as morally reprehensible and bad for business.[42]

In February 1899 Calouste had his brothers pack up and ship his and Nevarte's belongings from Istanbul to London, including nine crates containing paintings and sculpture.[43] After years of living in hotels, Calouste had bought his first house, 38 Hyde Park Gardens in London. It was here that their second child, a daughter named Rita, was born on 2 July 1900. The four-storey Bayswater terraced house overlooked Hyde Park, but was discreetly set back from Bayswater Road, at the bottom of a private road which even today remains inaccessible to non-residents. Gulbenkian had the interiors heavily renovated. Both the neighbourhood and the architect (Charles Mewès) were popular with nouveau riche bankers.[44]

A balance sheet that Gulbenkian drew up in 1898 around this time calculates his assets at £119,661 (£12 million).[45] He was significantly better off than Ohannes Essayan, who died in 1900 with assets of £27,542 (£2.7 million).[46] Having failed to train his sons in the business, control of O. & M. Essayan now passed to Ohannes's elderly brother Meguerditch.

In May 1901 Gulbenkian took the momentous decision of withdrawing from Sarkis Gulbenkian Fils (Istanbul), Gulbenk and Selian (Marseille) and C. & G. Gulbenkian (London). At the same time other adjustments were made: Vahan became a partner in C. & G. (he was already a partner in Sarkis Gulbenkian Fils) and Garabed Gulbenkian (Calouste's uncle) joined Sarkis Gulbenkian Fils (having already been a partner in C. & G.). Announcements appeared in the *London Gazette* and were sent to all companies with which these firms had dealings, officially informing them that Calouste was no longer responsible for the firms' debts, and vice versa.[47]

The rest of the Gulbenkians obviously knew of the brothers' disagreements and recognised that Karnig was not entirely the innocent victim. One senses that disagreements among partners who were also brothers and cousins were an accepted part of running an Armenian merchant house and nothing remarkable in themselves. Calouste's decision to retire, however, took his relatives aback. The official reason given was ill-health, but few believed it.[48] When his cousin Hovhannes Gulbenkian of the Beirut branch replied expressing scepticism, Calouste gave the real reason: he was leaving the partnership in order to focus on his work as a director of several large London-based companies.[49]

The 1901 withdrawal did not represent a complete cutting of ties. Such a severance would have been unprecedented, totally inexplicable. Karnig, Vahan and Garabed still looked to Calouste for advice in the years that followed and expected him to provide help if needed. They were aware of Calouste's growing reputation in the oil industry; this was proudly reported in Armenian newspapers published in Istanbul, such as *Byzantion*.[50] If anything, this success made it even harder to understand Calouste's diffidence.

'The genuine City Man talks of money,' wrote George Russell in his 1906 *Social Silhouettes*. 'What is so and so worth? What did he start with? How much did he lose in Kaffirs? What did he give for that place in Kent?'[51] In the five years since taking up permanent residence in London Gulbenkian had served his apprenticeship as a City Man, riding the second boom in 'Kaffirs' from start to bitter end, working closely with some of its most dynamic and colourful characters and learning at first hand how to reorganise and recapitalise companies. Thanks to his five years' residency, he now qualified for naturalisation as a British citizen, something he applied for in November 1902. On 1 December he became a British subject.[52]

For decades Ottoman Armenians had sought British, French and American citizenship as a means of securing diplomatic protection, as well as for its tax benefits. In Gulbenkian's case, however, naturalisation was more than that. In a career of restless movement and long periods spent in France and Portugal, Gulbenkian retained his British citizenship, right up until his death. Combined with his purchase of 38 Hyde Park Gardens, his withdrawal from the Gulbenkian companies and the transfer of his belongings from Istanbul, it represented a clear shift in his situation and perspective, from East to West. In 1892 he had informed Nevarte that he was deaf to Istanbul *chan-chan* and did not care about his reputation among the Ottoman Armenian community there. Ten years on, it was clear that London, not Istanbul, was the city where he 'sought to shine'.

FIVE

ASIATIC AND EUROPEAN, 1902–8

In 1903 Gulbenkian was acting as intermediary between the Paris Rothschilds' Frederick Lane and the Armenian oil magnate Alexander Mantashev. Peevish after a tough round of negotiations, Mantashev brooded as Lane read out the terms of their sales agreement clause by clause. After each clause Lane paused, first to allow Gulbenkian to translate into Armenian and then for Mantashev to confirm his agreement, also in Armenian. Mantashev's reply on each occasion was *'mayrt kunem'*, Armenian for 'I'll fuck your mother.' Gulbenkian rendered this in English as polite assent, whereupon Lane would thank Mantashev and move on to the next clause.[1]

Nubar enjoyed imagining his father as a lickspittle toady to Mantashev, who was seventeen years older than Calouste. Yet Calouste owed his entrée to the international oil industry not to Mantashev but to Lane. In the years since Calouste's visit to Baku, Mantashev had built his Russian-registered company, A. I. Mantashev, into one of the largest independent producers in the Caucasus. Alongside fields on the Absheron peninsula, it also owned lubricants and case-making plants, pipelines, docks, tank farms and railway tank cars. It was beginning to set up sales companies in Europe, such as Home Light in the United Kingdom. As other, much smaller Armenian operators went to the wall in the face of competition from Nobel and the Rothschilds' Société Caspienne, Mantashev was building an integrated oil company.

Whether on his own initiative or at the suggestion of Lane, in 1902 Gulbenkian put himself forward as an intermediary between these large Armenian-controlled Russian companies and the world's other big players. Gulbenkian's task was to convince his fellow Armenians of the value of joining syndicates aimed at dividing up Asian and European markets for kerosene, lubricants and other oil products. From a mere 10 per cent in 1880, Russian production in 1900 represented almost half of world oil production and hence could not be overlooked.[2] The sales cartel for Asia was Lane's brainchild, the Asiatic Petroleum Company, formally established in London in May 1903. The sales cartel for Europe was built around the Europäische Petroleum-Union (EPU), formed in Bremen in 1906, which brought all major European and Russian producers into one tent. EPU handled European sales of Romanian as well as Russian oil, and was managed by Deutsche Bank.[3]

The Asiatic and EPU cartels included Royal Dutch and Shell alongside the Paris Rothschilds and the Armenians. Both were designed to keep the partners from undercutting each other in the markets of northern Europe, the Mediterranean and Asia for kerosene (lubricants had their own cartels, drawn up along similar lines). If these price wars could be stopped, Asiatic and EPU could become powerful enough to strike sales agreements with the mighty Standard Oil, who dominated all markets. Of course, the risk each partner faced was that one of the others would cheat on them and suddenly strike their own deal with Standard. During a 1901 trip to New York Marcus Samuel visited Standard's offices at 26 Broadway, but no deal emerged.[4]

Thanks to his relationship with Lane, Gulbenkian was already a familiar figure to all the leading members of Asiatic and EPU – all except the Dutchman Henri Deterding, who became General Managing Director of Royal Dutch in 1902, a position he held until 1936. Royal Dutch had been founded in 1890 to exploit the oilfields of the Dutch East Indies (today's Indonesia). By the time Deterding took the helm its sales had almost reached parity with Shell's, even though it had fewer assets. Deterding probably met Gulbenkian shortly after moving to London in 1902; he participated (as a private investor) in a number of syndicates organised by Lane and Gulbenkian in the following years.[5]

Though the three worked closely together, their personalities were very different. Lane and Gulbenkian were softly spoken deal-makers with an eye for detail whose success owed much to an ability to represent multiple interests at one and the same time. Lane may have earned his 'Shady' nickname because nobody knew precisely for whom he was acting.[6] Deterding, by contrast, was emotional and mercurial, fixated on building his firm into a rival to the mighty Standard, whose supposed slights he lovingly nursed.[7]

Each partner entered the Asiatic and EPU agreements with their own expectations. Although officially Lane was negotiating as a representative of the Paris Rothschilds' interests, he took a broader view of Asiatic's potential to develop into a truly collaborative enterprise. He hoped to make Asiatic more than a partnership vehicle. He hoped it would become an independent entity, and develop new concessions.[8] Within a few years it became clear that Asiatic had helped Deterding to acquire control of Shell, as well as the Paris Rothschilds' oil companies, for Royal Dutch. Having begun in 1901 with a joint marketing company, in 1907 Royal Dutch and Shell 'merged' on a 60:40 basis. Asiatic also helped Royal Dutch learn about the Caucasus, a region it would enter aggressively after 1910, with Gulbenkian's help. If the tangled process of negotiating these cartels taught Gulbenkian anything, it was that Deterding was the one to follow – not Mantashev, or even Lane.[9]

Asiatic Petroleum

Although initially unwilling, on 20 June 1902 Marcus Samuel agreed to the Société Caspienne – that is, Rothschilds – becoming a third partner of the Asiatic Petroleum alliance, with one-third of the initial £600,000 capital. Gulbenkian was a part of these negotiations and was promised a 5 per cent commission.[10] This was probably conditional on Gulbenkian getting Mantashev and Mantashev's allies the Goukasoffs (fellow Armenians) to come inside Asiatic before Shell or Royal Dutch left for a better offer. From the beginning, Gulbenkian struggled to persuade the suspicious Armenians of the value of long-term collaboration. 'Without this partnership you and Mantashev will encounter all kinds of difficulties,' he wrote Goukasoff. 'Past experience has made it clear that we just cannot reach our goal by competition.'[11]

The Armenians were still hoping for an all-Russian cartel, however, and little progress had been made when negotiations in St Petersburg broke down in May 1902. Goukasoff had to be persuaded not to go in

with Nobel.[12] Further talks among Lane, Gulbenkian, Goukasoff and
Mantashev were held in August. The Armenians were offered two-fifths
of case oil sales within Asiatic's sphere of operations, which appeared in
the draft Articles of Association as a red-shaded area, a trapezoid that took
in east Africa and all of India, Australia, New Zealand and Asia, including
Japan.[13] They were to get 12 per cent of Asiatic, which would effectively
be a four-way split between them and Shell, Royal Dutch and the Société
Caspienne.[14]

Unfortunately for Gulbenkian, the Armenians preferred to remain
free and build up an independent European sales network through subsidiaries such as Home Light.[15] While Goukasoff agreed with Gulbenkian
that 'we should collaborate with big players, the current state of our firms
is not strong enough for us to stand with Rothschild and Nobel'.[16] Mantashev and Goukasoff were also concerned at rising inter-ethnic violence
between Tatars and Armenians, as well as Bolshevik agitation in the Caucasus. A young former seminarian named Joseph Stalin was among those
behind a new Soviet of Oil Workers in the Caucasus, organising strikes
and sabotaging wells and pipelines.[17] Russian production, which had
reached 11 million tons in 1901, now went into decline. The 11-million-ton
mark would be surpassed in the Soviet era; but by then world demand had
grown. Whereas Russian output had represented half of world output in
1901, in 1927 it was just 6 per cent.[18]

Had Gulbenkian simply been Mantashev's or Goukasoff's representative he might not have found himself in such a challenging position.
The main reason he was involved was probably because he had a proven
record for bringing the same parties together in a sales cartel, albeit one for
lubricants, a much smaller business than kerosene. Gulbenkian sent cables
and letters in all directions, trying to interpret the actions and mind-set of
Royal Dutch and Shell to the Armenians, and vice versa. He received little
by way of thanks. As he wrote to Lane, to the Rothschilds he appeared
'plus royaliste que le roi' in defending Mantashev's interests, while Mantashev's representatives resented his involvement, seeking to slander him as
a '"masked friend"'.[19]

Lane's response was to forward Gulbenkian's letter 'in strict confidence' to Maurice Baer of Rothschilds, adding his own explanation as to
why Baer's 'royaliste' charge was unfair to Gulbenkian:

The long and the short of it is, all the difficulty arises with G[ulbenkian] from the fact that, though in order to acquire the confidence of Mantashev he had to take up the position of representing Mantashev and [Goukasoff] also, his one aim has been, if possible, to become actually associated with [Société Caspienne] and her friends; and as their associate, using his influence and ability to guide and control Mantashev and Goukassoff. If he were definitely associated with us, his position would be clear, but naturally as long as he is outside us he apparently occupies the position of the representative of Mantashev and Goukassoff; while all his influence and ability has been used to frustrate their scheme, and force them to an alliance with us. This irritates him very much, and he wants to put an end to the situation.[20]

Two years later Lane was again having to stand up for Gulbenkian to the Paris Rothschilds, noting how Gulbenkian's nationality made him especially valuable as an intermediary with Mantashev and Goukasoff. 'He has the possibility of discussing with them in their own language,' Lane wrote,

> which puts him in touch with their sentiments and feeling, and this is an enormous power in the handling of them, while, at the same time, he is one upon whom we can absolutely rely. The difficulty to decide is, how to employ him? We have need of him, not simply in connection with the Asiatic, but in connection with every negotiation that is undertaken with this group, therefore, it is not in connection with the Asiatic simply, but in connection with the whole business of these groups, that I would like to see him employed.

Lane went on to note that he had discussed this with Gulbenkian, who was happy to take on this role. 'He has quitted business, and does not want to associate with anything that will mean labour in detail, or that would tie him such as the conduct of a business would.'[21]

The Europäische Petroleum-Union

In his 1905 letter Lane noted that the Rothschilds needed Gulbenkian not only for their dealings with Armenians, but for their oil businesses in England, France and in particular Naftaport, 'which he has led up to a certain point, but is liable to rupture'. Based in Berlin, the Deutsch-Rüssische Nafta-Import Gesellschaft was known to insiders as Naftaport, after its telegraphic address. Founded in 1899 to sell Nobel and Rothschild oil in Germany, its supply originally came exclusively from those two firms.[22] As with Asiatic, the hope in 1902 was to rope the majority of the Caucasian oil producers into a cartel, albeit one built around the European market.

Gulbenkian began trying to negotiate terms for the Armenian pro-ducers' entry into EPU in December 1902. Mantashev arrived in Paris with a proposal for a Mediterranean cartel: 35 per cent Mantashev, 25 per cent Rothschilds, 25 per cent Siderides (an Ottoman Greek with a case-making plant at Batumi) and 15 per cent Nobel. Rothschilds told him their share was too low, but explained that they would negotiate with Siderides and Nobel for the latter to allow Rothschilds 1 per cent and 3 per cent of their shares. This was agreed, only for Mantashev to start again, now proposing not only to take the 4 per cent Rothschilds had secured from the other partners, but to reduce Rothschilds' share even further. As Rothschilds' Baer wrote to Gulbenkian, 'This is no way to do business, and if M. Man-tashev refuses to back down then too bad: it's war in the Mediterranean.'[23] It was just the sort of shenanigans which gave the Caucasian Armenian oilmen a bad name, and which made a Gulbenkian necessary.

In February 1903 the board of Naftaport met. Terms for Mantashev and Goukasoff's entry were again on the table. It was proposed that Man-tashev take a 20 per cent participation of EPU, or 35 per cent if he came in with Goukasoff. In the end they secured 22 per cent jointly.[24] Detailed negotiations followed for other markets, such as France. Gulbenkian would, all agreed, be compensated (by Naftaport) with a 2 per cent com-mission on Mantashev's and Goukasoff's deliveries to France. Gulbenkian also had commissions of 10 per cent and 20 per cent respectively on Man-tashev's and Goukasoff's profits in their dealings with Rothschilds.[25]

In addition, Gulbenkian was elected to the board of Naftaport.[26] This brought him into contact with Deutsche Bank director Arthur von Gwinner, who would be an important figure in the negotiations for the Mesopotamian concession. Deutsche Bank was faced with the unenviable task of financing the Berlin–Bosphorus–Baghdad Railway, or *Bagdad-bahn*, an ambitious scheme dreamed up between Sultan Abdülhamid II and Kaiser Wilhelm II during the latter's state visit to Istanbul in 1898. Over two centuries the 'old' powers of Britain, Russia and France had each carved out their own sphere of influence within the Ottoman Empire, and each had a long history of intervening diplomatically and militarily to protect their economic interests. The Ottoman Empire had no such history with Germany, who seemed to be offering help with no strings attached.

For all its symbolic importance for international relations in the Near East, commercially the *Bagdadbahn* was a white elephant. Construction would only be possible, Gwinner recognised, if the Ottoman regime provided subsidies and London provided capital. In April 1903 he had seemed close to getting Barings and Ernest Cassel to lead a British contingent into this international effort, but a Turkophobic outburst in the press had panicked Foreign Secretary Lansdowne at the last minute.[27] Meanwhile any Ottoman subsidies or loans needed the approval of western chancelleries, as the purse strings were entirely in the hands of the empire's western creditors.

Oil offered a chance of making the *Bagdadbahn* pay. Under their 1899 concessions, the German railway companies controlled by Deutsche Bank had the mining rights to a twenty-kilometre strip flanking their line. Even if the actual route of the line (the *tracé*) became decidedly fuzzy several hundred miles short of Baghdad, it was already clear to the Germans and everyone else that this line could be routed so as to run straight through the most promising oil lands around Mosul.[28] The fact that Mosul lay within the British sphere of influence added to the intrigue. In 1904 Deutsche Bank secured an additional oil concession for the *vilayets* of Mosul and Baghdad.

Development of Mesopotamia's oil reserves promised to realise vast sums for the Sultan himself, quite apart from the royalties the concessionnaire would pay to the Imperial Treasury. In the 1880s Abdülhamid II's Minister of Finance, the Ottoman Armenian Agop Paşa, had acquired promising oil lands in Mesopotamia and passed them to the Ministry of the Civil List. The Sultan foresaw massive profits for the Civil List – that is, for himself as opposed to the Empire as a whole – but only if he could replace primitive hand-dug wells with drilled wells and the knowledge necessary to refine crude.[29] When two experts sent out to survey the Mosul area by Gwinner returned with less than cheering reports in 1905, the result was acutely embarrassing for the Minister of the Civil List.[30] Deutsche Bank's concession lapsed.

If the Ottoman Empire seemed a distant and difficult prospect, finding oil in Romania seemed more straightforward. Steaua Romana (Romanian

Star) had been taken over by Deutsche Bank and Wiener Bankverein in 1903. Gwinner put Georg Spies in charge of running Steaua. Spies was at a loose end, having been pushed out of the Caucasus oil firm which bore his name by Gulbenkian and Lane. He lobbied Romanian ministers for the state lands concession, a process not without its own baksheeshes (that is, paying bribes).[31] Meanwhile Gwinner reorganised Deutsche Bank's other interests in oil refining, storage and transport under a new holding company, established in January 1904.[32]

Deutsche Bank controlled far more distributing, refining and storage capacity than was necessary to process and sell Steaua's output. Gwinner therefore sought to secure additional supplies from the Caucasus and to create a sales cartel for all European markets. Lacking much confidence in his own staff, he looked to Lane to build the aforementioned holding company into this cartel, the Europäische Petroleum-Union, which was established in June 1904. As Gwinner wrote to Spies, Lane might be 'a first-class testicle' ('ein Couillon ersten Ranges'), but he was sharp.[33]

Even though many of them shared Gwinner's view of Lane, it was indeed 'Shady' Lane who in December led negotiations in Paris with Gwinner, Baer, Aron (both Rothschilds), H. Olsen (Nobel) and Sam Samuel (Shell) to transform EPU into a distribution and sales cartel for all of Europe, except the Balkans, Greece and Turkey. This would absorb all the partners' existing sales and distribution companies. Lane again hoped that Gulbenkian would persuade Mantashev and Goukasoff to come inside. The overall aim was clear: each producer would receive the same price per unit regardless of where within this European market his products were sold.[34]

Whereas the structure of Asiatic was relatively straightforward, EPU developed into a network of thirty interlocking finance, distribution, production and sales companies: American, Austrian, Belgian, British, Danish, Dutch, French, German, Romanian, Russian and Swiss. In London EPU bundled its partners' existing marketing entities (including Home Light) into a new company named British Petroleum.[35] Following Gulbenkian through this jungle is fiendishly difficult. He sat on the board of EPU not as anyone's representative (not even his own), but by dint of his relationships with several of the Belgian, British, Dutch, French, German and Russian firms involved, most of which he also had significant investments in. Here as elsewhere, his loyalties were difficult for others at the table to work out. Here as elsewhere, he made this a strength rather than a liability: without a clear 'home', Gulbenkian could appear as an honest broker.

In May 1906 Spies pointed out to Gwinner the importance of defending Steaua's interests within EPU. Without such a defence 'we will slide under the table and get raped by Lane'.[36] In the end they were 'raped' by Deterding. Although EPU signed a deal dividing European markets with Standard in May 1907, it got the smaller side of this 80:20 split. Supplies of Russian oil never increased to the expected levels, owing to the aforementioned political problems. As with Asiatic, so Royal Dutch used EPU to learn more about Romanian production prior to staging a big move into the area. Royal Dutch-Shell bought EPU in 1910.

The End of Sarkis Gulbenkian Fils

Despite a loan of £20,000 from Calouste and Nevarte in 1901, Sarkis Gulbenkian Fils had continued to struggle. The firm's losses in London, Marseille and Alexandria had reached an estimated £30,000 (£3 million) by July 1904. As losses mounted, Karnig proposed selling the *hans* and other Istanbul properties that the brothers had inherited from their father.[37] As Calouste observed to Hovhannes Gulbenkian, who ran the Beirut branch, the merchant business was looking old-fashioned. It was better to invest in property and shares.[38]

The decline of Sarkis Gulbenkian Fils was a contrast to the fate of their cousins' businesses in London and New York, where Badrig and his brothers were beginning to move from being general merchants to carpet manufacturers. As the eldest son of the eldest son, Badrig was head of the Gulbenkian clan and clearly saw his cousins' problems as his own, displaying more concern for the family's reputation than Calouste did. He generously gave both advice and £25,000 to Karnig in the summer of 1904. Asking Calouste to contribute £6,000, Badrig warned him that he was 'playing with fire' in letting his brothers go under. But even Badrig agreed that it was time to close down Sarkis Gulbenkian Fils and leave Istanbul behind.[39]

The final act came in 1907. On 30 April Sarkis Gulbenkian Fils was declared bankrupt in Istanbul, with debts of £57,000 (£5.4 million).[40] C. & G. Gulbenkian followed suit in London in July, with £59,000 worth of liabilities and just £13,000 in assets.[41] While the collapse of C. & G.

Gulbenkian was hardly noticed in London, in Istanbul the bankruptcy of Sarkis Gulbenkian Fils was a sensation. The French- and Armenian-language newspapers gave it extensive coverage; like everyone else, they wondered why Calouste was not helping his brothers.[42] A French consular officer named Picu sent reports about it back to Paris. Picu saw the firm's collapse as indicative of a wider malaise in Istanbul's Armenian merchant houses: a collapse in the Egyptian market and a rise in London interest rates had triggered a flight from the paper notes that Armenian merchant houses had been issuing since at least the 1870s.

In an economy without a central bank and short of gold, these notes operated as currency for everyday transactions. Roughly the size of a business card and printed on green, purple or red paper, they were typically repayable three months from their date of issue. Armenian churches seem to have issued such notes as well.[43] Picu reported that Armenian merchants had issued enormous amounts of this 'phoney paper'. One house valued at 2.5 million French francs had issued 4 million worth of notes. Various European banks had also chosen this moment to set up offices in Istanbul and were extending easy credit to attract business.[44] 'Under these circumstances a crisis was bound to arise sooner or later.'

Starting in late 1906 'a certain malaise' began to be felt in Istanbul as a result of the increase in the Bank of England rate in London, which ended the easy credit that had fuelled the crisis.

> From that point on the merchants of Constantinople found themselves struggling. Last spring [1907] came the collapse of a large Armenian house, Serkiz [sic] Gulbenkian fils. This was a shot across the bows of the local banks as well as those in London. It became difficult to place paper credit notes. Those merchants affected tried to liquidate their investments and reduce their exposure to the notes.

Armenian paper which had been accepted by fellow Armenians, Jews and certain German banks now became worthless. This in turn brought about a striking development: 'that mutual support which the Armenian houses had given each other now became a real danger to them.' In November 1907 a severe crisis seemed on the cards. The Ottoman Armenian merchant community had asked for a moratorium, but Picu thought they were unlikely to get one from the Imperial Ottoman Bank.[45] Cracks started forming within the community, too.

The bankruptcy left Calouste's brothers with a choice between entering a new line of work and trying to live frugally on their remaining investments, including the rents from the properties they still possessed in Istanbul.[46] For the younger brother, Vahan, Calouste had always been (as Vahan himself claimed) 'more of a father than a brother'.[47] Calouste had been best man at Vahan's wedding in 1902 to an Armenian from Bulgaria, Agavni Kouyoumdjian, which was held at 38 Hyde Park Gardens. Calouste tried to help Vahan find work in Manchester. After an expensive divorce, Vahan married a Frenchwoman and moved to Algiers, where he spent the rest of his life living off a dole from Calouste.[48] Vahan does not seem to have borne Calouste any ill-will. The same cannot be said of Karnig. Calouste had stood by and done nothing, Karnig wrote, while 'our company, which you founded and which bears our father's name', went to the wall. 'I will remember that to the end of my life.'[49] Karnig moved to Geneva and kept his word, refusing to have any contact with his older brother.

Having fallen severely ill in the summer of 1907, Calouste's mother, Dirouhi, died in June 1908. Shockingly, Calouste did not return to Istanbul to attend her burial at the Gulbenkian plot at Surp Pırgiç Hospital. For an Armenian of his class, with ample means to travel, his absence was conspicuous. One can only speculate as to why Calouste, who had been so close to his mother as a child, chose not to attend. Perhaps he resented Dirouhi for having allowed his father, Sarkis, to pack him off to Europe in 1884, when Calouste was so young and immature. Almost as shocking and disappointing to Badrig and the other Gulbenkians was Calouste's unwillingness to ensure that the family's long-held charitable obligations to Talas were kept up.[50]

The Collector

Calouste's relatives were certainly correct when they noted that the sums involved were 'a drop in the ocean' for him.[51] For the first half of 1902 he and Nevarte rented a magnificent property, Villa Paulette on Cap St Martin; 'amongst pine trees and in a lovely perfumed atmosphere looking in [*sic*] the blue sea in the sun', as he described it to Lane. In May 1905 Calouste felt rich enough to splash out on his first car, a 40hp Delaunay Belleville (Tsar Nicholas of Russia got his the following year).[52] He had helped his brothers, of course, with money and advice. Calouste may well have felt that Karnig, having made his bed, ought to lie in it. Calouste wasn't going to let himself be persuaded into throwing good money after bad by Karnig's 'silly old Anatolian-style arguments'.[53] Nor would he pay any heed to Istanbul *chan-chan* or the Ottoman Armenian press, both of which criticised his treatment of this brothers. 'My reply is "Let the bastards [*sriga*] bark",' he noted. 'Badrig is trying to discredit me out of envy.'[54]

Calouste's rising expenditure on art had not gone unnoticed by his family, and probably served to rub salt into these wounds. In December 1903 Garabed Gulbenkian wrote to Calouste expressing his surprise that the latter had paid £T 6,500 (£630,000) for a single painting. Garabed had heard the news from Gullabi, who had been told by Karnig. It was all grist to the Gulbenkian *chan-chan* mill.[55] The implication presumably was that, while one might legitimately spend some money on paintings to furnish one's home, the sums Calouste was paying were not so much inflated as simply outlandish. Calouste's first steps as a collector had admittedly been faltering; he acquired several eighteenth-century paintings whose attributions were subsequently questioned. In 1902 he told Lane Fox of the London dealer Thomas Agnew & Co. that he was tired of buying what he called 'convalescent pictures'.[56]

Seeking to educate himself in art history, in late 1903 he began a series of one-on-one tutorials at the Louvre with the curator and collector Camille Benoît.[57] Gulbenkian secured a letter of introduction to Bernard Berenson, the great expert on the Italian Renaissance, who would later form a corrupt professional partnership with the dealer Joseph Duveen.[58] Benoît assigned Gulbenkian homework, making him plough his way through the Louvre's Italian catalogue. Gulbenkian's collecting became more ambitious, if conventional. Although he continued to acquire saccharine nymphs by eminently forgettable nineteenth-century painters such as Charles Joshua Chaplin, otherwise his taste followed an established 'English' canon, embracing landscapes from the Dutch seventeenth-century Golden Age, Grand Manner portraits (Anthony van Dyck, Joshua Reynolds, Thomas Gainsborough) and Grand Tour scenes of Venice by Francesco Guardi, softened somewhat by a more French taste for eighteenth-century bibelots, furniture and sentimental portrayals of children by Jean-Baptiste Greuze. Opened to the public in 1900, the Wallace Collection in London was a clear inspiration, influencing Gulbenkian's taste just as it did that of J. P. Morgan, Henry Frick and Nélie Jacquemart.[59]

It was not unusual for collectors to seek the advice of dealers and museum curators such as Benoît. It was certainly not unusual for them to follow the market, as Gulbenkian did in paying high prices for eighteenth-century English mezzotints. The effort Gulbenkian invested in keeping abreast of art historical literature and periodicals such as the *Burlington Magazine* was unusual, however. Gulbenkian's relationship with the jeweller René Lalique was also remarkable: from his first purchase in 1899, Gulbenkian served as a mentor as well as a prized client, frequently lending items to exhibitions.[60] There is no evidence that Nevarte was ever permitted to wear the many necklaces and chokers acquired by her husband. Indeed, Gulbenkian's treasures were rivals for his affection: when he returned one eighteenth-century English portrait to Agnew in 1918 he justified his decision in personal terms. Although the lady portrayed had 'flirted' with him at first, Gulbenkian noted, he had concluded that they were not destined to be 'great chums' and decided on 'divorce'.[61]

When it came to collecting carpets and Islamic art, of course, Gulbenkian was drawing on generations of family experience. His father probably traded Caucasian and Persian carpets, among the many other commodities handled by S. & S. Gulbenkian. After Sarkis Gulbenkian's death carpets, Iznik tiles and other antiquities were one part of the family business which genuinely interested Calouste, more than it did his brothers. Calouste traded them with the great Istanbul collector Hagop Kevorkian for their joint account, and later developed new sources of supply inside Persia.[62] Unsurprisingly, some of the faience, carpets, coins and illuminated manuscripts Calouste traded ended up in his collection, along with 800 tiles.[63]

For Armenian-language newspapers like *Byzantion*, the extinction of one of Istanbul's leading merchant houses had been almost unthinkable: 'Surely there must be some resolution and Karnig effendi must continue his business, otherwise the brilliant name of the House of Gulbenkian will be stained.'[64] By 1908 it was evident that this had in fact come to pass, and *Byzantion* was not alone in feeling that Calouste Gulbenkian was partly responsible. For Calouste the bankruptcy completed a process of separation from his family's businesses which had begun in 1901, if not earlier.

As if to underline the point, Gulbenkian applied for the telegraphic address 'Gulbenkian, London'. In 1892 he had acquired it for a family firm, for C. &. G. Gulbenkian. Now he had his own individual address to go with his own individual office, at 17 St Helen's Place in the City.[65] With hindsight, it can seem as if he planned this from the beginning, as the concomitant to a long-held desire to blaze his own trail in the oil business. But in 1908 it was still not clear that his career lay exclusively in oil, even if by then he was a familiar figure to industry leaders such as Lane and Deterding.

If asked how Gulbenkian had got to this position, one suspects that Lane and Deterding might have had difficulty identifying a coherent step-by-step narrative. Lane struggled to find a clear name for Gulbenkian's position. Whatever name we choose, it is clear that Gulbenkian could not have reached it at all had he identified himself as Mantashev's representative, or anybody else's for that matter. If anything Gulbenkian presented himself as the put-upon honest broker who 'couldn't be nicer', but who ended up misunderstood, and accused by each side of being overly faithful to the other. It was a pose he would strike at regular intervals throughout the Red Line and Group Agreement negotiations in 1924–8 and 1945–8.

He could also present himself, perhaps more legitimately, as an investor with the long-term aims of this or that company at heart. From Lane's perspective, Gulbenkian was a wealthy man whose fortune lifted him above narrow mercenary concerns. Negotiating international sale cartels was, it seems, a *divertissement* for a man who had 'quitted business'. Thanks to a revolution in Istanbul, this retirement was about to get a lot busier.

— SIX —

YOUNG TURKS,
1908–14

The liberal Ottoman constitution of 1876 and the parliament it created had been suppressed almost as soon as they were born, in an attempt by Sultan Abdülhamid II to draw a line under the Tanzimat reform era. Yet reforms of army education ensured that western European ideas of liberalism, nationalism and constitutionalism fermented in the minds of a new cadre of officers, civil servants and teachers. Secret and not-so-secret societies sprang up, notably the Committee of Union and Progress and the Ottoman Freedom Society. In 1907 these groups had begun to coalesce, particularly in Salonica (Thessaloniki), and a set of leaders emerged who would shape the Ottoman Empire's violent transition into a secular nation-state: Enver (an officer stationed in Salonica), Cavid (a secondary school headmaster in Salonica) and Talaat (a post office official).

Unable to beat them, the Sultan decided to try coopting them. On 23 July 1908 Abdülhamid II reinstated the constitution of 1876. This so-called 'Young Turk Revolution' inspired many inside and especially outside the Ottoman realms to hope that the empire could in fact be reinvigorated. The revolution changed Gulbenkian's perception of the empire and of his own position relative to it. After his father's death in 1894 he had turned away from the empire and towards international finance and Caucasian oil. After 1908 Gulbenkian changed tack: rather than trying to sell the family's properties within the empire, he began looking for new farms and factories to buy.[1] The empire, it seems, was open for business.

The following four years saw Gulbenkian work closely with the new regime, and in particular the Finance Minister, Cavid. Gulbenkian became an Ottoman diplomat. He founded the National Bank of Turkey (NBT) in 1909 and the Turkish Petroleum Company (TPC) in 1912. Both sought to break the diplomatic logjam resulting from the struggle among European diplomats, financiers and investors for Ottoman concessions, be they loans, railways or oilfields. In both cases Gulbenkian's big idea was collaboration. International cartels would free the Ottoman government from the restrictions imposed whenever one single European power secured an exclusive concession. He was, in a sense, working to restore economic sovereignty to the Ottoman Empire.

After 1912 the climate in Istanbul grew darker. The Balkan Wars and the Italo-Turkish War fostered militarism, anti-western sentiment and a more racially defined Turkish patriotism that gave Gulbenkian pause. But he had other irons in the fire throughout this period. He assisted Deterding and Royal Dutch-Shell as they moved aggressively into Venezuelan, American and especially Caucasian oil, buying up small companies, merging them into larger entities, improving their management processes and floating new companies on the New York, London, Paris and Amsterdam stock markets.[2] Thanks to his apprenticeship with Bottomley, Wright and Lane, Gulbenkian was expert at these activities.

The National Bank of Turkey

Gulbenkian issued the prospectus for a National Bank of Turkey in December 1908. As he noted, 'Hitherto the Turkish government has been entirely in the hands of a group headed by the Deutsche Bank and the Imperial Ottoman Bank,' with the result that, 'so long as the old regime lasted, these Banks had a certain control over the business of Turkey'. The new regime was opposed to those banks and had asked Gulbenkian to assemble 'such a group of bankers as will enable them to undertake business on behalf of the Turkish government'. This new bank would be built on international cooperation and so work in the interests of the empire, rather than those of France, Germany or any other western power.[3]

Founded in 1863 as an Anglo-French joint venture, over time the Imperial Ottoman Bank had become almost entirely French-controlled. The Paris market's appetite for Ottoman debt seemed insatiable. But in order to be quoted on this market any loan had to have the approval of the French state, the so-called *côte*, granted conjointly by the Finance and Foreign Ministries. As Gulbenkian noted, this condition gave the French state a powerful tool for imposing its own demands on the Ottomans.

It could insist, for example, that money borrowed from France had to be spent on orders from French firms such as Schneider rather than German ones such as Krupp. French loans thus carried hidden costs, which rose markedly after 1908. Not only did loans come with longer shopping lists, they fuelled rumours that the French state might intervene directly to protect 'its' creditors, perhaps by invading Syria, France's sphere of influence within the Ottoman realms.[4]

Gulbenkian faced an uphill struggle trying to find alternative sources of capital for the Ottoman Empire. In 1910 about a third of the world's securities were quoted on the London market.[5] But the City had been badly burned in the 1875 Ottoman default, and its appetite for Ottoman bonds had further declined as a result of Gladstone's 'Bulgarian Horrors' campaign of 1877. Though the Kaiser's Turcophilia had prodded German banks to move into Istanbul, the Berlin money market was small compared with Paris and London, and was already struggling to cope with the massive demands imposed on it by the famous Baghdad Railway.[6] The NBT (which was not, despite its name, a central bank) hoped to get round this by casting its net widely, creating a large international consortium, including Ottoman investors.

It was at this point that Gabriel Noradunkyan, a childhood friend of Gulbenkian and sometime Ottoman Minister of Public Works, proposed that Gulbenkian get in touch with the Anglo-German banker Sir Ernest Cassel. A German-born Jew, self-made, with excellent ties to King Edward VII, Cassel had established his international reputation in Egypt, financing the Aswan Dam and establishing the National Bank of Egypt in 1898.[7] Privately, Gulbenkian feared that, with Cassel behind it, NBT might end up following the course previously taken by Deutsche Bank: having entered the Ottoman market making 'all kinds of promises', Deutsche had joined with IOB rather than competing with it. In any case, Gulbenkian noted, 'We have no advantages or business on hand to offer to Cassel to ask him to amalgamate with us.'[8] Cassel concurred, seeing the bank's draft statutes as 'not serious' and the founding directors as lacking in heft.[9]

The statutes had probably been drafted by F. E. Whittall, of the Istanbul commercial agents Gilchrist, Walker and Co. Whittall chaired the first minuted meeting of the bank's founders, held in Istanbul on 29 January 1909. Cavid was present at this meeting, along with two *paşas* also linked to the Committee of Union and Progress.[10] Also present was Reşid Sadi, who edited the Young Turk newspaper *İkdam*, as well as Gulbenkian's uncle Meguerditch Essayan. This meeting deputed Reşid Sadi to meet with Cassel in London and discuss the changes the latter proposed to make in the statutes.

Cassel clearly persuaded them as well as Gulbenkian that he would not allow NBT to become IOB's accomplice.[11] As a result of these discussions the old statutes were abandoned and a fresh application put together.[12] Cassel travelled to Istanbul, cabling Gulbenkian from Pera on 9 March asking him to come out and assist him with negotiations with Cavid and the Anglophile Grand Vizier Kâmil Paşa.[13] Gulbenkian was surprised that Cassel sought his advice. For Sorgoudje, the London manager of O. & M. Essayan, it was to be expected that Cassel, for all his experience of London banking, valued an adviser able to 'navigate the maze of intrigue and oriental snares'.[14] The more bankers like Cassel vied with each other to furnish 'Turks' with capital, Sorgoudje argued, the better. 'Turkey's needs are many and varied,' he noted, 'we who hail from this country will be the first to benefit.'[15]

Ernest Cassel was something of a role model for Gulbenkian, carving out a position for himself in finance similar to that Gulbenkian would later establish in oil. Unlike Gulbenkian's other mentor, Frederick Lane, Cassel did not work for anyone else. Seventeen years older than Gulbenkian, Cassel was a one-man band, supported by a tiny staff based in London. He travelled constantly, ceaselessly networking among bankers and states-men, organising the underwriting of sovereign debt issues from Brazil to Japan and the financing of vast engineering projects like the London Underground. For the Permanent Secretary to the British Treasury in 1903, Cassel was one of 'my first counsellors', one of 'those to whom any new Chancellor of the Exchequer should be introduced in his first weeks', along with 'Natty' Rothschild and John Baring.[16]

NBT's foundation was formalised by means of an *irade* (Sultan's decree) of 11 April 1909. A million pounds' worth of £10 shares were issued, the vast majority held by Cassel, his ally Lord Revelstoke (John Baring) and railway financier Alexander Henderson. The remainder were divided among Cavid, Essayan, Gulbenkian and various *paşas*. The presidency went to an Englishman, Henry Babington Smith, who had formerly sat on the council of Ottoman bond-holders. Having established his bank, Cavid's priority now was to secure a loan. Once again he turned to Gulbenkian.

Serving the Sultan

Cavid captivated western European observers in a way no previous Ottoman finance minister had. The American Embassy reported that Istanbul was 'swarming with capitalists' thanks to Cavid, 'a man of no mean talent, whose financial capacities are for the moment undisputed ... anxious to interest foreigners in the industrial awakening of Turkey'.[17] 'It seems as if the deputy for Salonika will, simply by the force of his personality, end the financial disarray,' reported the Belgian ambassador, 'and that under his leadership, as if by magic, the Empire will enter a new era of wealth and prosperity.'[18]

Unlike the majority of Young Turk leaders, Cavid did not have a military background. The son of a merchant of Salonica, he had joined the Ottoman Freedom Society in 1906, shortly before it merged with the Committee of Union and Progress.[19] In his *Ulum-u İktisadiye ve İçtimaiyye* (*Journal of Economic and Social Sciences*) and in his speeches Cavid pushed a liberal, free-market economics.[20] 'All countries and all civilisations have evolved and developed by opening their doors widely,' he wrote. 'Living off your own output within your own borders is not development.'[21]

On 4 December 1909 Grand Vizier Tevfik Paşa wrote to Gulbenkian confirming his appointment as Financial and Commercial Counsellor to the Ottoman Legation in London, following it up with a request to report to Cavid on Britain's financial situation.[22] In July Gulbenkian was appointed to the same position (*conseiller financier*) at the Paris embassy.[23] As a director of NBT, as a diplomat and as a private investor, he was soon caught up in negotiations for another Ottoman loan. These culminated in November 1910, when Cavid signed a £T 11 million (£1 billion) loan (issued in 1911) with a German consortium led by Deutsche Bank. Given France's fiscal hegemony, this was a shock, leading many to see the loan as part of a broader trend for the Young Turks to look to Germany as an ally that could (unlike Britain, France or Russia) be trusted not to claim its own sphere of interest in the empire. The 1913 German military mission to the Ottomans led by General Liman von Sanders was another step in that direction.

In reality, however, the 1911 loan was an attempt by Cavid and his Ottoman, German and British allies to replace a French monopoly with an international consortium. Even if it had not tendered for the 1909 Ottoman loan, the mere presence of NBT helped to strengthen Cavid's bargaining position. Cavid rejected IOB's initial loan terms. The French Foreign Ministry (the Quai d'Orsay) was well aware that Cavid, his 'alter-ego' Hüseyin Cahit (editor of the influential pro-CUP newspaper *Tanin*) and other leading Young Turks sat on NBT's Consultative Committee.[24] In mid-October 1909 a humbler IOB reached agreement with the Ottoman government for a £T 7 million loan, of which they gave NBT a 28.5 per cent share, at Cavid's request.[25]

Such was the parlous state of the empire's finances that Cavid and the new Anglophile grand vizier, Hakkı Paşa, were back the following summer, once again touring Europe's capitals in search of a lender. In London in July Cassel threw them a dinner, with Gulbenkian, David Lloyd George and Winston Churchill in attendance. French being the only language in common, Lloyd George was somewhat at a loss, but Churchill got on 'swimmingly' with Cavid.[26] Gulbenkian showed Cavid round the London stock exchange.[27] Despite the warm reception, Cavid came away with nothing but a vague promise that NBT 'would not leave him [Cavid] in the lurch' if negotiations in Paris failed.[28] Cavid duly moved on to Paris, where he signed an agreement with a syndicate led by Crédit Mobilier on 8 August, for a 4 per cent £T 11 million loan at 88.5 (that is, the Ottoman Treasury would receive 88.5 pence for every pound they had to repay, independent of interest charges), secured against the customs revenue of the *vilayet* of Istanbul.

But Crédit Mobilier represented only 15 per cent of this syndicate: alongside the other French investment banks with equal 15 per cent shares was Gulbenkian.[29] In *Tanin* Cahit hailed the loan as proof that the Ottoman Treasury was not dependent on IOB and congratulated Cavid on successfully separating the question of loans from that of concessions for river navigation, railways and petroleum. The Ottomans could now offer concessions to the highest bidder, rather than being obliged to award them to those who had lent them money.[30] The French ambassador, Bompard, fumed that the loan was 'a challenge to the French government'.[31] Asked in an interview if he had sidelined IOB, Cavid's reply was suave: 'No. IOB sidelined itself.'[32]

Unfortunately, the French government refused to accept this

treatment. They planned to make any French loan conditional on the Ottomans passing reforms to accounting procedures and on their placing orders with French firms. The reforms were French in inspiration, in so far as they were developed by Charles Laurent, First President of the Cour des Comptes.[33] After mistakenly reporting that NBT had secured a loan, *Le Temps* published a series of articles viciously attacking Cassel, seeking to dissuade any rogue French bank from collaborating with NBT.[34] Although Cassel was in Paris with propositions for a much larger loan, faced with such pressure he advised Gulbenkian that NBT would have to withdraw: the negotiations had lurched 'into the region of politics'. It was a case of 'force majeure'.[35]

Cassel told Grand Vizier Hakkı Paşa in London that their only hope was to ask the Foreign Office to mediate between them and the French.[36] Gulbenkian volunteered himself.[37] Gulbenkian and the Ottoman ambassador to Paris were duly invited to a meeting with the French Finance Minister, Georges Cochéry, on 5 October. At this meeting Cochéry stated that he would negotiate with Gulbenkian himself.

Gulbenkian began these negotiations by observing that IOB's high-handed behaviour did not reflect 'the profound transformation which had occurred in the political situation in Turkey'. He proposed a compromise.[38] On 6 October Cochéry told Gulbenkian and Naoum Paşa that he would be away from Paris for several days and that they should consult Foreign Minister Pichon in his absence. Pichon had told members of the Crédit Mobilier syndicate to 'stick by their loan contract right to the end'.[39] When Gulbenkian and Naoum called at the Quai d'Orsay the next day, Pichon handed them a memo laying out a scheme under which the *côte*, or permission to issue the loan in France, would be granted in exchange for the appointment of two French experts to a new Ottoman Cour des Comptes and a Direction Générale des Mouvements des Fonds.

Gulbenkian presented this memo to Cochéry as the Quai d'Orsay's suggestion, although it was actually a proposal which Crédit Mobilier had attached to their abortive August loan offer. Negotiations continued with Pichon, and a settlement had apparently been reached by 10 October 1910 for a £T 11 million loan, except that neither Cochéry nor Cavid had seen it. The French Foreign Ministry seemed happy enough to keep the French Finance Ministry in the dark.[40] Meanwhile, at Harrow, fourteen-year-old Nubar proudly read of his father's doings in the papers. 'I hope the loan comes off soon, for two reasons,' he wrote to Calouste. '1. For your glory and honour 2. because you can't come see me and give me a hug until it does.'[41]

Unfortunately, both Cavid and Cochéry refused to accept these terms.[42] Unfazed, Pichon instructed the Syndic des Agents de Change, Maurice de Verneuil, to meet with Gulbenkian behind Cochéry's back to discuss the 'Pichon' plan further. It was agreed that Verneuil would try again to secure Cochéry's approval if Gulbenkian tried to get Cavid's.[43] Far from Istanbul or Paris conspiring against each other, the French Foreign Ministry was conspiring against the French Finance Ministry, and Gulbenkian and Verneuil were conspiring to secure the *côte* – not for IOB or NBT, but for Crédit Mobilier.[44]

The French later concluded that the Ottomans had had a German offer in their back pocket all along. According to this theory, Gulbenkian was a 'straw man' who had been put forward by Cavid in order to 'make us show our cards', Gulbenkian being an intermediary the Turks could easily disavow.[45] This was not true. Berlin's offer to help the Ottoman government was intended merely 'to put some starch into the Turks', as Deutsche Bank's Karl von Helfferich put it, and to get Paris to be more accommodating.[46] Far from being in cahoots with Cavid, Gulbenkian shared the Quai d'Orsay's confusion at Cavid's rejection of the 'Pichon' plan.

As Gulbenkian noted, the idea of appointing the two officials was based on a reform proposal Cavid himself had put before the Ottoman Chamber of Deputies back in the spring. Why had a proposal which seemed acceptable a few months before now become an insult?[47] Cavid's cables to Gulbenkian are candid enough to suggest the answer: Cavid's room for manoeuvre within the Turkish cabinet had been reduced by the growing influence of the Minister for War, Mahmut Şevket Paşa, who consistently blocked Cavid's attempts to curb military spending.[48] The Belgian ambassador heard of 'violent scenes' between the two.[49]

Since 1909 the French government had been pushing for IOB and NBT to merge, and these negotiations ran in parallel with those for the loan.[50] While the French just wanted to absorb a troublesome rival, the Foreign Office sought to bring about a true merger, in the spirit of the 1904 Entente Cordiale.[51] Hugo Baring (brother of John) and Babington Smith were both in Paris in October 1910, and met regularly with Gulbenkian to discuss progress. They sought a 50:50 merger between the tiny NBT and the much larger IOB. Gulbenkian's negotiations with Cochéry had formed part of a strategy for achieving this. If the loan went to Crédit

Mobilier, so the thinking ran, a chastened IOB would be more willing to merge with NBT on a 50:50 basis.[52]

Although the loan ended up being issued by Deutsche Bank, the episode nonetheless demonstrates the extraordinary complexity of Gulbenkian's activities. In the case of the loan, which 'side' was he working for? Was he simply a 'straw man' for Cavid? Was he betraying NBT in working with Crédit Mobilier? One could see this exercise as some sort of shell game, seeking to find where Gulbenkian really stood amid this array of banks, ministries and empires. But that was not the game Gulbenkian had been playing: far from yoking himself exclusively to one, in 1910 Gulbenkian had been negotiating for the Ottoman government, the Quai d'Orsay, NBT, Crédit Mobilier and himself, all at the same time. This talent for evading attribution to this or that side would underpin much of his later success as a deal-maker in the world of oil.

Meanwhile struggles between Turkey and Greece over various Aegean islands led to a naval arms race. On paper the Ottoman navy had been the third-largest in the world in 1875, but Sultan Abdülhamid II's fear of a naval coup meant the fleet had been kept bottled up on the Golden Horn. Now Basil Zaharoff of the British firm Vickers stoked Ottoman fears by harping on about the risks posed by Greek dreadnoughts. Fearing that it might otherwise appear 'a broken reed', in 1911 NBT further encouraged this rearmament race by issuing Ottoman Treasury bills which financed the construction of a new Vickers-built dreadnought for the Ottoman navy, the *Reşadiye*.[53] In 1913 a second was ordered, the *Sultân Osmân-ı-Evvel*, the largest ever constructed. NBT took the ship itself as security while the Ottomans paid for it in monthly instalments.[54]

It did so in full agreement that the second ship was 'idiotic', given the state of Ottoman finances and the risk of escalation.[55] By July 1913, however, NBT and the Ottoman cabinet were boxed in by questions of prestige. A Navy Society had been formed shortly after the 1908 revolution, to collect funds for naval rearmament through voluntary subscriptions. Although Gulbenkian urged Grand Vizier Hakkı Paşa to sell the first ship, Hakkı and Cavid knew that no Ottoman cabinet could do so and expect to remain in power, such was the strength of patriotic feeling at stake.[56] For Gulbenkian the situation had become untenable. He wrote to Cavid in December 1912 asking to resign his post as *conseiller financier*: 'one has to sacrifice all [one's] self-esteem to be able to serve the country under these circumstances.'[57]

Turkish Petroleum

Under the pre-revolutionary regime the chief rivals for the Mesopotamian oil concession, Deutsche Bank and D'Arcy Exploration (which became Anglo-Persian), had secured competing concessions in 1904 and 1906 respectively. The Sultan's privy purse (the Ministry of the Civil List) had been acquiring oil lands in the *vilayets* of Mosul and Baghdad since 1877.[58] Yet the baksheesh that helped secure such concessions could also be employed to block rivals, while the semi-autonomous status of the Ministry of the Civil List further complicated matters. Hence the logjam which prevented any one concession from being developed: whenever one would-be concessionaire managed a step forward, its many rivals intervened to push it back.

Though frustratingly slow-moving and corrupt, the *ancien régime* had the virtue of familiarity. Deutsche Bank had built up good relations with Izzet Paşa, the Sultan's most notorious influence-peddler, as well as the powerful Melhamé family, who controlled the tobacco monopoly and other plum concessions. After the 1908 revolution these connections were worse than useless.[59] D'Arcy's lead concession-hunter in Istanbul, Henry Nichols, was delighted to see the tables turned. But the storm had also swept away the 'friends and assets' he had built up over four years. 'Halliss Bey, our pet official wirepuller and scoundrel', had also been discharged.[60] Meanwhile, as another German observer wrote to Helfferich, 'The extremists of both sides are at daggers drawn: the Utopians of the new regime and the Reactionaries of the old – the mediating middle class, which might otherwise bring about some sort of balance, is entirely absent.' Far from being over, 'the Revolution is ongoing'.[61]

In terms of oil concessions, the 1908 revolution seemed to leave everyone back at square one, unsure whom to bribe, or, indeed, whether bribes worked in this brave new world. Many of the Ministry of the Civil List's properties around Mosul were transferred to the Finance Ministry.[62] The revolution attracted strange new creatures to Istanbul, notably Americans, who now made their first tentative push into Middle East affairs. Two American challengers, Bruce Glasgow and Rear-Admiral Colby Chester, arrived in late 1909, offering the Turks the same alluring prospect the Germans had offered a few years before: plentiful capital for inward investment, without the political agenda. But what capital (if any) did such concession-hunters have? Did they even represent the companies they said they did?[63]

In July 1909 Gulbenkian, Lane and Deterding submitted a plan for a seventy-five-year oil import and distribution monopoly within the Ottoman realms, sharing the profits 60:40 with the Ottoman government. This 'Régie co-intéressée du pétrole de l'empire ottoman' would have been similar to the Régie des tabacs, the tobacco monopoly. Income from an import duty on oil products would have been used as security for a £T 1.5 million loan.[64] This oil monopoly was, however, also to include exclusive rights to exploit oil found within the Ottoman Empire, including the lands previously controlled by the Civil List. Unfortunately, Cassel was unenthusiastic.[65] The Foreign Office and State Department were also opposed, owing to prior commitments to rival would-be concessionaires.[66]

Gulbenkian continued to propose petroleum projects on behalf of Asiatic Petroleum, whose international character would, he held, appeal to Ottoman ministers. His uncle Meguerditch Essayan served as his man on the spot, tasked with ministerial liaison, 'backsheeshes' and above all with creating 'more and more difficulties', 'by hook or by crook', for rival concessionaires.[67] Rather than trying to secure the Tigris navigation concession for Gulbenkian and his friends in London, however, Meguerditch went to their rival, Lynch Bros., and tried to cut his own deal. Gulbenkian was furious. 'Are you the agent of myself and my friends; are you acting for your own account, on behalf of other Ottoman subjects, or what?' Rather than greasing the petroleum monopoly concession by giving free shares to influential individuals, Meguerditch tried to keep them for himself.[68]

Perhaps he was more naive than unreliable. Asked to ferret out Standard Oil's plans for the Ottoman Empire, he proposed to ask them direct. 'Now I ask you as a business man do you think for a moment that the Standard Oil people who are going to be our opponents, are likely to tell us what their intentions are?' Gulbenkian seethed.[69] In August 1910 relations broke down entirely. Essayan sued Gulbenkian before the Court of King's Bench in London for the £6,000 supposedly owed to him for his services in making trouble for their rivals, specifically 'in obtaining the rejection of Messrs Lynch Bros. as Concessionaires' for the Tigris navigation. The case went against Essayan in February 1911.[70]

Gulbenkian decided to try again to involve NBT. This time he met with a more favourable response from Cassel, and NBT sent an engineer, Robert Money, to tour the *vilayets* of Mosul and Baghdad.[71] This in itself was nothing remarkable: the Ottoman authorities, the British, the

Germans and even the French were all sitting on reports compiled from similar surveys dating as far back as 1889. The sheer number of such survey reports is one reason why it is hard to credit Gulbenkian's claim that it was his report to the Sultan which drew the latter's attention to the potential of Mesopotamian oil.[72] Regardless of when he submitted it, his report was hardly as significant as he made out.

NBT would not have set up an oil subsidiary had Deutsche Bank not been keen. Though Gwinner had passed on the offer to come in with Gulbenkian in his Turkish oil monopoly scheme in early 1910, he had been impressed by Gulbenkian's role in the loan negotiations later that year.[73] Gwinner explained to the German Foreign Office the advantages of having Gulbenkian on board: his presence demonstrated that the NBT group was 'petroleum-savvy'; Gulbenkian was 'a trusted counselor of the Young Turk regime in financial matters, and a link to the leaders of the Deterding group'.[74] In May 1911 Gwinner offered to take a share of NBT's proposed oil venture, in exchange for transferring the petroleum rights Deutsche Bank claimed through the Baghdad and Anatolian Railways.[75]

It was eventually agreed that shares in the new oil venture would be allocated as follows: 25 per cent each to Anglo-Saxon Petroleum (a Royal Dutch-Shell subsidiary) and Deutsche Bank, and 50 per cent to NBT (including Gulbenkian's 15 per cent holding).[76] The inclusion of Royal Dutch-Shell was down to Gulbenkian.[77] Though on paper Deterding had been in on the abortive Ottoman oil monopoly scheme, there is no evidence that he took much of an interest in Mesopotamia.

In October 1911 Gulbenkian drafted the articles of a new oil company and the Turkish Petroleum Company formally came into existence the following year.[78] The name Ottoman Oil Company had been proposed, but was already taken. Turkish Petroleum sounded more 'Young Turk'.[79] The TPC partners agreed not to involve themselves in the production of oil within the Ottoman Empire except through TPC.[80] This self-denial clause was an important part of Gulbenkian's vision for the joint venture: if Deutsche Bank or Royal Dutch-Shell wanted to do anything involving oil anywhere within the Ottoman Empire (that is, all of the Middle East bar Iran and Kuwait), they would have to do so as tenants of TPC, Gulbenkian's 'house'.

When Babington Smith informed the Foreign Office about TPC in August 1912, however, he was told that British backing had already been pledged to D'Arcy's Anglo-Persian. The Foreign Office proposed that

Anglo-Persian join TPC, but Anglo-Persian's managing director, Charles Greenway, refused. September marked the beginning of what would be an eighteen-month process by which the Foreign Office as well as the Board of Trade and the Admiralty endeavoured to broker an alliance.[81]

Back-room lobbying ensured that Gulbenkian's 15 per cent shareholding in TPC was not forgotten at the Foreign Office. Over lunch on 28 November 1913 Babington Smith informed Alwyn Parker of the Eastern Department that Gulbenkian had 'been the first mover in all this petroleum business'.[82] Grand Vizier Hakkı Paşa also warned Parker that the British government could not reallocate NBT's shares in TPC. Some belonged to Gulbenkian and he might sue them. Gulbenkian was 'a British subject of some substance ... prepared to put £150,000 [£13.3 million] himself into the Turkish Petroleum Company'.[83]

In these discussions it was noted that Gulbenkian was willing to reduce his 15 per cent to a smaller, non-voting participation of 5 per cent, to be carried by one or more of his TPC partners.[84] The fact that NBT had kept Gulbenkian's shareholding a secret nonetheless made a 'painful impression' on the Foreign Office. Foreign Secretary Grey was 'somewhat concerned that such important information should not have been communicated to us at an earlier date'. He asked for more information on the nature of Gulbenkian's holding, as 'a most important fact in the situation, and one which must inevitably influence [the British government] in determining their attitude in respect of their recognition of the title of the Turkish Petroleum Company'.[85] From the background information provided by Deutsche Bank it became 'fairly clear that Mr Gulbenkian actually engineered the formation of the Turkish Petroleum Company'.[86]

By March 1914, however, all of Gulbenkian's TPC partners were fed up playing pass the parcel with his 5 per cent. None of them were willing to carry it for him. Deutsche Bank and Anglo-Persian preferred to liquidate TPC and start again without him or Royal Dutch-Shell. 'It would certainly be a peculiar situation, not to say more,' noted Gwinner, 'that Mr Gulbenkian without any legal basis should be able to frustrate the intention of three European powers.'[87] The British and German governments agreed; Gulbenkian and Royal Dutch-Shell did not fit their vision of a 50:50 Anglo-German entity.[88]

For all his appreciation of Gulbenkian's expertise, Gwinner distrusted him.[89] He suggested that Gulbenkian's stubborn refusal to sell was inspired by Deterding: in other words that Gulbenkian's hidden participation had been intended to hand control of TPC to Royal Dutch-Shell. This was a fair charge to make. Conveniently, at the eleventh hour Deterding agreed that Royal Dutch-Shell would carry 2.5 per cent (that is, hold 2.5 per cent's worth of TPC shares on Gulbenkian's behalf) if Anglo-Persian did the same (thus making 5 per cent).[90] Anglo-Persian agreed. These arrangements were formally incorporated in the Foreign Office Agreement, signed on 19 March 1914: under this agreement Deutsche and Royal Dutch-Shell held 25 per cent each, and Anglo-Persian 50 per cent. Mr Five Per Cent had been born, though it would be many years before anyone referred to Gulbenkian as such.

From Deterding's perspective, the idea of Anglo-Persian having a 50 per cent share of such a large concession was an affront. Anglo-Persian had only been registered in 1909. Although it enjoyed exclusive oil rights to the southern half of Persia, since acquiring that concession in 1901 it had been burning its way through money. Its founder, William Knox D'Arcy, had tried hawking his rights to Cassel, Deterding, Alphonse Rothschild and British Foreign Secretary Lord Lansdowne. Nobody was interested in such a risky venture.[91] At the end of his financial tether, in 1905 D'Arcy reached a syndicate agreement with a Scottish oil company named Burmah, which agreed to stump up the capital needed to continue survey work.

Oil was struck at Masjid-i-Sulaiman in May 1908. Challenging working conditions and poor management nonetheless dogged Anglo-Persian's wells and its refinery on Abadan, an island in the Shatt al-Arab. When the first tanker arrived in December 1912 to load the very first shipment of Anglo-Persian kerosene, it emerged that there was insufficient stock to fill it. Having bailed the firm out once, Burmah was opposed to Anglo-Persian getting involved in Mesopotamia. In its view, Abadan was 'a scrap heap'. Anglo-Persian would have gone under had it not persuaded the Admiralty of its potential value as a reassuringly 'British' supplier to the Royal Navy.[92]

Within four days of the Foreign Office Agreement the British and German ambassadors made a joint demand to the Ottoman cabinet for the Mesopotamian oil concession. They viewed this as a quid pro quo for agreeing to an increase in Ottoman customs duties. On 28 June their efforts were rewarded with the so-called *Lettre Vizirielle*, which promised them the concession for the two *vilayets* of Mosul and Baghdad. There is little in Ottoman archives to suggest that Ottoman ministers saw this as anything more than a way of buying time.[93] Nothing in the *Lettre* itself or in the intentions of its authors justified its becoming the foundation stone of TPC's post-war success, let alone a determining factor in the economic development of the Middle East over the next fifty years. Yet it did.

An Unsolved Problem

Nor was it clear in 1914 that this was a concession worth having. Gulbenkian's decision to retain a share of TPC was a speculative one. It went against the advice of Cassel (who had sold all his TPC shares) and Lane, men whose skills and counsel Gulbenkian admired deeply. As early as 1909 it was clear, however, that Gulbenkian's vision differed from theirs. While Lane and Deterding saw the Turkish oil import monopoly as a financial end in itself, Gulbenkian saw it as a means to an end: an oil concession covering the entire Ottoman Empire. As Lane put it, Gulbenkian wished 'to obtain the concession and then act independently with it'. Lane insisted that this was not a sensible plan for a man like Gulbenkian:

> I grant you that the exclusive right to search for petroleum in Turkey is a very comprehensive one, and may be a very valuable one, but its value has got to be proved by expenditure of money, and when you consider the various experiences in the development of no matter what petroleum territories, unless in one or two exceptional cases, you will find that more money has been put into the ground than ever has been taken from it.

Frustrated at his friend's obstinacy, Lane could not avoid a dig as he outlined the two ways of tackling the Ottoman Empire's oil: to pump-and-dump shares in a company, or hold on to the shares, in the hope of some very distant prospect of pumping oil:

> To sell an unsolved problem to the ignorant at an immense profit (which no doubt with your knowledge of how to handle these Stock Exchange problems could readily be accomplished, even though there was not a drop of oil in the whole of Turkey), or, on the contrary, to take the risk of whether the thing is a payable or non-payable proposition. If I risk my own money, what is the prospect of making something of it? All depends upon what the production amounts to: no one can

tell what this will be. If it be a small production, there is very little in
it; if it be a large production, it will mean the expenditure of a vast
amount of money, and the success or non-success of the enterprise will
depend upon the amount of money, brains and experience put into it,
and the number of years that you will devote to it. It is a labour which
you could never undertake – it is against your nature.

Lane was prepared to pursue the import monopoly project, which offered
good rewards 'for the few months of labour we might devote to this business'. He was not ready to enter a business in which 'you could not expect
to see any reasonable result under 10 years'.

In spite of their 'real friendship', Gulbenkian would have to proceed
alone.[94] Lane and Gulbenkian would continue collaborating on a number
of mining, oil and industrial finance projects for several more years yet.
Lane's letter nonetheless demonstrates that Gulbenkian already had a
vision of what would later become the Turkish Petroleum Company. As
Lane predicted, TPC would require Gulbenkian to invest a vast amount
of his own money. Contrary to Lane's prediction, though, it would take
twenty-two years, not ten, to realise any return.

A Family on the Brink of War

Meanwhile tempers were flaring in the Gulbenkian household, reaching
crisis point in June 1914. When Nevarte began socialising with Serkiz
Duz, a member of an influential Ottoman Armenian family, Gulbenkian
exploded, shouting at his wife. 'He is making a spectacle of me,' Nevarte
complained to Devgantz, 'and my honour is questioned.' Although Calouste exchanged little other than badinage and stock tips with the actress
Mary Moore, Nevarte had her own suspicions.[95] To Calouste's surprise, she
not only continued meeting and dancing with 'that bastard', but 'Nubar
meets him, too.' This last struck Gulbenkian as particularly shocking. 'We
must be a model pair for our children,' he wrote to Nevarte. His only wish
was 'to be happy together'.[96]

As the example of Calouste's brother Vahan and his wife, Agavni,
demonstrated, there was a way out. 'Divorce would be the best solution
for you and Nevarte,' Devgantz wrote Gulbenkian, 'if Rita and Nubar were
adults. But in the current situation it would be catastrophic for Nubar as

well as for your career.' The crisis deepened with a dispute between the couple over who controlled certain investments which Gulbenkian had put in his wife's name, but which Nevarte believed had formed part of her inheritance. 'I am the master – It is I who has the money – I will flatten everything in my path,' Gulbenkian told his wife.[97] Nevarte seems to have followed her mother's advice to back down, and went to Germany, to visit Nubar and Devgantz and to take the waters at Bad Homburg.[98]

Having attended Harrow for just two years, in October 1912 Nubar enrolled at Bonn University, where he lived with Devgantz in leafy Pöppels-dörfer Allee. At Harrow Nubar's housemaster had reluctantly honoured Calouste's demands that Nubar be allowed home at the slightest sign of ill-health, and be spared what the housemaster described as 'the disciplinary and moral effect of football'.[99] Persuading a university to take Nubar on at sixteen must have been just as difficult. As a certain Professor Wilhelm pointed out, 'he is the youngest university student not only in Bonn, but in all of Germany.'[100] A punishing schedule of lectures and tutorials left him no time to socialise with other students. His father nonetheless pressured him to network. 'You must recognize,' Nubar complained, 'that I cannot run after a student shouting "You are noble, and hold a high position in society – come with me and I'll give you dinner at the Royal Hotel."'[101]

As a three-year-old, Devgantz now recalled, little Nubar 'would run down anyone who tried to stand in his way'. His determination to overcome any obstacle had not waned. 'That's a good thing,' Devgantz noted. 'But it is not good that he, a boy not yet of age, already glorifies the power of money … It does not bode well for his future.' Harrow had done little to tame a disposition to be '"uppish"', as his housemaster put it. Thanks to an indulgent father, Nubar was exceptionally well travelled for his age. His thirteen-year-old sister, Rita, at boarding school near Ascot, was envious. 'He will be getting so "blasé" in a few years when he has done everything there is to be done,' she noted. But when her brother *did* get bored of all the 'lovely places', she added, 'he can start all over again with me'.[102]

By the time the famously hot summer of 1914 came round it was clear to Gulbenkian that the Young Turks' experiment with a return to constitutionalism had failed. The Ottoman Empire had not, it seemed, been capable of using its new freedoms and new opportunities wisely. Gulben-kian seems to have seen the crisis in his own household in similar terms. 'The constitutional rights I have allowed in my household have proved an absolute failure,' he noted in June 1914, 'for, by reason of their education not being of a sufficiently ripe character, [family members] have been unable to enjoy such constitutional rights.'[103] A firmer hand was needed. Gulbenkian would be master in his own household.

PART II

ARCHITECT, 1914–42

*'If you have faith you get a deep conviction and self confidence...
then through something which you cannot explain you radiate all
round you this faith and then it goes on rolling and rolling.'*
C. S. Gulbenkian

'I have three friends: work, sun and sleep.'
C. S. Gulbenkian

SEVEN

PUT OUT MORE FLAGS, 1914–18

There was definitely something wrong with the canaries. In October 1914 they started falling ill. Gulbenkian had several cages of them in his Paris apartment, on the fourth floor of 27 Quai d'Orsay. Gulbenkian's Paris housekeeper, Madame Soulas, had taken the precaution of isolating the first canary that fell sick. It was getting hard to find birdseed. Back in August Germany had declared war on France, and Britain had declared war on Germany. Russia, Serbia, Montenegro and Japan were also at war. Paris was emptying, Soulas reported to Gulbenkian in London. The maid charged with looking after the canaries, Francine, was distraught. Vets being as scarce as birdseed, a doctor was called, but was unable to help.[1]

Although Gulbenkian had resigned as *conseiller financier* in early 1913, Cavid reappointed him in July 1914, needing his assistance with yet another loan.[2] Soulas went to the Ottoman embassy and secured a written declaration that the Gulbenkian apartment belonged to a member of the imperial delegation. She also bought an Ottoman flag. 'It is superb,' she informed Gulbenkian, 'and cost an almost imperial sum.' She put it for the time being in the hall with the other flags, ready to be used as required. There were now three available: Ottoman, British and French. On 5 November, unfortunately, the last two declared war on the first.

Gulbenkian's status as a naturalised Briton, an Ottoman diplomat and a French resident might have puzzled a less resourceful retainer. Soulas was not troubled. She would be sure to fly the right flag at the right time.

While she normally flew the Ottoman flag, to assert diplomatic status, she would replace it with the British and French flags, either 'when the news is bad' or 'if there is unrest in Paris'.

Meanwhile, in London, Gulbenkian agreed that economies should be made in his Paris household. The canaries' Évian water was to be replaced with tap water. The former had been 'a foolish luxury', he conceded. Three days later the sick canary died and Russia declared war on the Ottoman Empire.[3]

And the Devil Take the Last

The crisis found Nevarte in the Hotel Augusta, Bad Homburg, where she had gone to cool off after the problems in her marriage noted in the previous chapter. Nubar was still in Bonn with his tutor, Devgantz. On 31 July Nevarte cabled Gulbenkian reporting that she would travel to Folkestone if the international situation got any worse, picking up Nubar on the way. A few days later Nevarte, Nubar, Rita and Devgantz were in Nancy, however, trying to get to Paris in the entourage of the Ottoman ambassador. Owing to lack of petrol, they had to leave their landaulette car behind. By late August all were safely installed in the Grand Hotel, Eastbourne, where Nubar got down to reading the books on petroleum that Calouste sent him.[4]

Unbeknown to Nevarte, her brother-in-law Karnig also happened to find himself in Paris in August 1914, along with his wife, two children and two Armenian servants. Seriously short of money, Karnig asked his elder brother to lend him 50,000–100,000 francs, pledging seventy-five Imperial Ottoman Bank shares as security. The pair had not seen, spoken or written to each other in seven years. Karnig felt humiliated making such an appeal, 'wiping the slate clean of all your past egotisms'. Calouste's cabled reply was terse: 'everyone is overcome with troubles regret impossible to do anything.' Karnig moved his family to St Malo, then Neuilly, where his baby son, Sarkis, fell sick in December, dying in May 1917. Calouste did send funds to help with medical expenses. Meanwhile his youngest brother, Vahan, was safe in Algeria, living off a monthly stipend paid to him by Calouste.[5] Calouste's siblings had not recovered from the shipwreck of 1907. Now they never would.

Three thousand miles away in Mesopotamia, the Ottoman governor mobilised his troops on 4 August. The regime's pro-German sentiments had become increasingly obvious. Writing from Baghdad the previous March, Gertrude Bell claimed that the situation had deteriorated markedly over the previous three years: 'The tribes are all out of hand, everyone carries arms.'[6] Ottoman troops were not paid or provided with food or equipment, and so they simply requisitioned what they needed, favouring the 'Christian' merchants with their custom. In Baghdad ninety mules on their way to Anglo-Persian's wells were requisitioned. The British Acting Political Resident got them back, only to have the police take five while they were being watered, 'and no receipt given'.[7]

One month later the Resident was wondering if he shouldn't embark on what might well be the last Lynch steamship down the Euphrates, lest he himself be taken in an equally undocumented fashion. On visiting the city governor, or *vali*, however, he met with a surprisingly warm reception. The *vali* explained that he would ignore the Unionist agenda of inciting violence against British interests. 'He assured me [the] Moslem population of Mesopotamia would never rise against [the] English whose just character was known to all. He deprecated attaching undue importance to manifestoes by Unionists as they could not really appeal to Moslems.' The head of the Sunni community gave similar guarantees.[8] British fears that the Middle East might catch fire when the Ottomans declared *jihad* proved unfounded.

In Istanbul, of course, the Unionists ruled the roost. August found TPC representatives negotiating a concession agreement with Cavid. It was clear that the German ones were being treated differently from the English. 'If there is a declaration of war then we should have to skip,' noted one of the latter, 'and the devil take the last.'[9] A few days before, the imam Oubeid Ullah had preached at the Hagia Sofia: 'I bring you good news! Be glad!' he exulted. 'Twenty millions of *giaviour* [non-Muslims] are killing each other with most devilish instruments. May God make it more!'[10] On the 16th Louis Mallet arrived to take up his post as British ambassador, in less than propitious circumstances. Thanks to Churchill's requisitioning of the two National Bank of Turkey-financed ships, the *Reşadiye* and *Sultân Osmân-ı-Evvel*, anti-British sentiment had reached fever pitch.

It was common (and legal) in time of war for ship-building nations to requisition warships that had yet to be completed or delivered, in order to incorporate them into their own navies. Far from Britain's actions being aimed at the Ottomans, several other nations also had vessels requisitioned.

But inside the Ottoman Empire these nuances were lost. The Germans provided two replacement battleships, SMS *Breslau* and SMS *Goeben*, further nudging the Turks into an alliance with Berlin.

Within two months the *Midilli* and *Yavûz Sultân Selîm*, as they had now become, would be shelling Russian ports on the Black Sea. Their targets included the oil installations at Novorossisk. Caucasian-based production companies which Gulbenkian acquired for Royal Dutch-Shell found a major distribution channel blocked.[11] Otherwise, production in the Caucasus continued as normal; or rather, as near normal as anyone had any right to expect in a part of the world stalked by inter-ethnic violence, Bolshevik agitators, bandits, typhoid and vodka.[12]

Even after the Turks shelled the Russian ports in October Mallet seemed surprisingly sanguine. On 29 October 1914 the Turks entered an alliance with Germany. On 1 November Mallet left for Athens. Over the next five days Britain recognised Kuwaiti sovereignty and annexed Cyprus. The time for diplomatic fudges intended to spare Ottoman blushes was over. Britain also landed Indian troops at Fao, the mouth of the Shatt al-Arab, close to Anglo-Persian's refinery at Abadan. This would be the beachhead for the invasion of Mesopotamia, the British capture of Mosul and the creation of the British mandate of Iraq.

Shopping for Shell

Addressing the board of Royal Dutch-Shell in November 1914, Henri Deterding wrote bullishly of its prospects. Investments in production facilities in California, Mexico, Venezuela, Egypt and Borneo were creating positive network effects, as the company's rapidly expanding tanker fleet was now able to circumnavigate the world while minimising wasted journeys. 'We now go from London to the Gulf [of Mexico], load Kerosene there, and then we go through the Panama Canal to Shanghai, whence we go to Singapore or Borneo, load Benzine or Liquid Fuel for Europe, – and then start the same way over again,' Deterding noted. 'I do not think that anything proves so fully our enormously strong position.' Standard's tankers, by contrast, were condemned to travel back empty after runs from the Gulf of Mexico to Europe.[13]

Deterding had grounds to feel upbeat. Royal Dutch-Shell was now the world's largest (in net assets), most profitable and most international oil company.[14] Oil was now more than just grease and lighting, lubricants and kerosene: in 1911 Standard's sales of gasoline exceeded its kerosene sales for the first time; in 1912 the Royal Navy decided to switch from coal to fuel oil.[15] Standard was not, admittedly, the behemoth it had once been. In May 1911 the United States Supreme Court found the company guilty of conspiring to restrain trade, under the terms of the 1890 Sherman Antitrust Act.

Standard dissolved itself. The original holding company became Standard Oil of New Jersey (Jersey Standard). Thirty-three other firms were disaffiliated. Inheriting almost half of the original firm's assets (including much of its refining capacity and several European subsidiaries), Jersey Standard was five times the size of its next-largest 'sister', Socony (Standard Oil of New York), and bigger than all other American companies except US Steel.[16] Relations with its 'sisters' were friendly enough for Jersey Standard to retain much of Standard's formidable reputation. For Gulbenkian and other oilmen, the name on the letterhead may have changed, but they still referred to Jersey Standard as 'Standard Oil'.

The blistering pace of Royal Dutch-Shell's growth came at a cost. Management was shared between offices in The Hague and London. British rivals blackmailed His Majesty's Government into subsidising them, claiming that they would otherwise be absorbed into this supposedly 'foreign' trust. The so-called 'Shell menace' was born. In May 1914 Parliament voted to subscribe £2.2 million to Anglo-Persian in return for a 50 per cent shareholding and two seats on the board. The most powerful nation in the world had apparently determined that oil was a strategic commodity which could not be left to private enterprise. As it turned out, the government's directors had little to say on policy, and the relationship ended up being something of an embarrassment to both sides.[17] The capital and the diplomatic support, however, saved Anglo-Persian from the hole it had dug for itself in southern Persia. This coup was a striking example of the rewards of courting governments, of diplomacy.

Diplomacy was not Henri Deterding's strong suit. He and his colleagues were already pushed to find the capital, equipment and staff needed to work all their concessions. Many of these concessions were joint ventures, where the original concessionaires had handed over their leases in return for shares in a recapitalised company controlled by Royal Dutch-Shell. These minority shareholders were very much alive to the risk that the company would 'sit' on their concession (deliberately neglecting to exploit it, for fear of glutting the market). They needed careful managing. This was particularly important in Mexico and Venezuela, where minority share-holders' ties to dictators and other power brokers held the key to political risk. Gulbenkian helped Royal Dutch-Shell to overcome all these difficul-ties: he handled government liaison, reassured anxious concessionaires, managed share issues and kept Deterding under control. Without him, the pantechnicon would have soon come off the road. Thanks to him, the company had a very good war indeed. Even after paying dividends of 40 per cent, the combine was left with embarrassingly large amounts of retained earnings, which it did its best to 'lose' through creative accounting.[18]

In February 1907 General Antonio Aranguren had acquired a fifty-year concession for the districts of Maracaibo and Bolívar, in the Venezuelan state of Zulia. Aranguren came to London and joined forces with a New Zealander, Duncan Elliott Alves, subsequently forming an oil-focused syndicate with other, English investors in 1913. Meanwhile a well-connected lawyer, Max Rafael Valladares, was acquiring similar rights in the east of the country, which were transferred in 1912 to a New Jersey-based company, Caribbean Petroleum.[19] In 1915 and 1917 Shell took controlling stakes in Aranguren's Venezuelan Oil Concessions (VOC) and Caribbean respectively, paying Aranguren largely in shares. It also began constructing a large refinery on the nearby Dutch island of Curaçao.

The entity which acquired the VOC shares was a London-based investment trust named Burlington, established in 1913 with Venezuelan oil business in mind. In 1914–17 Burlington also made a series of advances to Caribbean, being paid in shares. Ownership of Burlington was divided up between Royal Dutch-Shell, Rothschilds (both the Paris and London branches), and an American company, General Asphalt.[20] Identifying Gulbenkian's interest in this business is fiendishly difficult, which was probably the intention.

A web of contracts linked Aranguren, Alves, Burlington, VOC, Car-ibbean, Royal Dutch-Shell and Gulbenkian.[21] It is clear that Gulbenkian was interested in these contracts on a number of levels: as a shareholder in Royal Dutch and in Shell, of course, but also through Burlington indi-rectly and through Caribbean and VOC directly. He seems to have made his own loans to VOC and Caribbean, being repaid in shares held for him by Burlington. Gulbenkian also had an option on 35 per cent of any further VOC share issues, which would prove very profitable.

Gulbenkian met with VOC's R. Hamilton Edwards and Aranguren

during their visit to London in the spring of 1915. Edwards's proposal was to issue £1 million worth of shares on the London market, with Edwards receiving £140,000 worth of shares for free as well as £35,000 in cash.[22] This was admittedly an ambitious proposal, given the instability of the country. General Juan Vicente Gómez had seized control of Venezuela in 1908, while President Cipriano Castro was off receiving medical treatment in Europe. Castro's followers conspired constantly thereafter. Indeed, in April 1915 Arévalo Cedeño invaded the country via Arauca (Colombia), for the second time. Though this invasion was put down and plans for other invasions kept getting deferred, Gómez's challengers redoubled their efforts to secure arms and funds from the United States government or private companies, in exchange for promises of oil and other concessions. Gómez's decision to remain neutral in the war riled the United States, which refused to recognise his regime.

Gulbenkian found Edwards, Aranguren and the other Venezuelans 'most difficult people to deal with'. Within a month, however, he managed to reach an agreement for a more digestible issue of 350,000 £1 VOC shares, some of which were given to the concessionaires in exchange for the titles to their concessions. Under a separate agreement between Gulbenkian and Deterding, the latter promised to form a £3 million holding company (VOC Holding) after the war, which would buy the concession from VOC for £500,000 in preference and £1.5 million ordinary shares. Deterding was to have the right to buy 460,000 preference shares at par and be given 350,000 ordinary shares, with Gulbenkian managing this share pool for fifteen years.[23] Such an arrangement left Gulbenkian in charge of managing the share price, and of trying to stop Aranguren and other concessionaires from dumping their shares on the market.[24]

Meanwhile Gulbenkian also tried to work out ways to minimise the risks to Royal Dutch-Shell of being too closely tied to Aranguren.[25] Reputedly the wealthiest citizen in Venezuela, Aranguren had ties to the anti-Gómez rebels and later contributed funds for an abortive revolution and invasion planned for 22 April 1919. This was deferred owing to lack of materiel and the plot being revealed by a *Gomecista* spy.[26] In June 1916 Aranguren sponsored an outbreak of violent unrest at Maracaibo, after he was replaced as acting president of the state of Zulia by a *Gomecista*. Troops loyal to the regime opened fire on a crowd endeavouring to prevent the new president from disembarking, killing twenty.

Thanks to such activities, VOC's concession was repeatedly

challenged in the courts, a cycle which tied the company up until a settlement was reached in May 1921.[27]

Gulbenkian also negotiated acquisitions of American companies such as Californian Oilfields and Roxana, which had wells in Oklahoma. Shell California was formed with a capital of $30 million and was soon constructing the Valley Pipeline to link its Coalinga field to a new refinery at Martinez. Gulbenkian managed an issue of additional Roxana shares in 1917, bringing its capital to $5 million and funding construction of new pipelines and a refinery at St Louis.[28] President Woodrow Wilson's attempt to eliminate holding companies proved less of an obstacle than might have been feared, largely thanks to the light-touch regulation offered by the state of Delaware.[29]

Soon Royal Dutch-Shell was lifting more oil inside the United States than Jersey Standard.[30] The natural corollary of this was the introduction of Royal Dutch to the New York stock exchange. Although he never travelled to the United States, Gulbenkian had been building ties with the New York investment bank Kuhn Loeb since at least 1907, often working through their Paris representative, Lionel Hauser. This relationship grew so tight over the following decade that Kuhn Loeb set up a dedicated telegraphic address for Gulbenkian: any telegram Gulbenkian wired to 'GULBLOB, New York' was certain of receiving special treatment from Mortimer Schiff, Otto Kahn or other leading figures at Kuhn Loeb.[31]

The illness of his first wife, as well as the strain of business, took its toll on Deterding in the summer of 1916, a situation which clearly concerned Gulbenkian.[32] This concern and the copious correspondence between the two indicate a deep friendship. For Deterding, Gulbenkian was someone in whom he could confide his deepest thoughts about himself, his wife and his colleagues at Royal Dutch-Shell:

> My dear friend. I think everything goes as well as can be expected on this earth taking in consideration my temperament. I have tried hard to change to more mortal views but if I do I become very insipid and/ or uninteresting. I feel I must either be all there or my whole [soul] and being is absent and I would not be H.D. Your words are of a very good and wise friend, in fact the only one who knows me thoroughly and likes me all the same. I want to have such a long talk with you when you are back. As regards America I think they ought to pay 4% as a commission but we can see what The Hague says.[33]

Gulbenkian appreciated the trust placed in him. 'I have penetrated so much in your private life, as your friend, you have allowed me to do so,' he noted, 'that I feel myself all the comradeship and the responsibility.' Though Gulbenkian wrote of how much he liked to hear about Deterding's 'inner life', Gulbenkian did not share his own 'inner life' with Deterding.[34]

In November 1915 the Foreign Office wrote to Anglo-Persian informing them that the 1914 Foreign Office Agreement 'has in the circumstances no longer any legal validity, and that they will decline to take this agreement into account when the moment comes to arrange for the future of the oil areas in these districts'. The way seemed open for Anglo-Persian's Charles Greenway to grab Deutsche Bank's 25 per cent of TPC.[35] The Germans had already reached a similar conclusion. They proposed cancelling the *Lettre Vizirielle*, so that Deutsche Bank could work the concession alone, defenestrating Anglo-Persian and everyone else.[36] In December 1917 the German Brennstoffkommando Arabien (militarised fuel survey) drilled test wells south-east of Mosul. They struck oil (albeit not the main field) and began planning pipelines. A year later the war had been lost.[37]

Building an Entente

Gulbenkian served Deterding and himself by acting as liaison between Royal Dutch-Shell and the French government, which began experiencing acute oil shortages in March and April 1917. While the French army had just 316 trucks, cars, tractors and planes at the start of the war, by the end they had 97,279.[38] The British had been the first to see the need for a special department with staff able to gain an overview of petroleum supply in wartime, formulating policy and coordinating between various civil, military and naval departments. Royal Dutch-Shell's Robert Waley Cohen was appointed honorary petroleum adviser to the British War Office in April 1917. A Petroleum Committee and Petroleum Executive followed in June and November, both under a minister, Walter Long. President Wilson established a Fuel Administration in August. France formed a Comité Générale du Pétrole.

While the British and Americans were able to call on the professional expertise of Jersey Standard, Anglo-Persian and Royal Dutch-Shell, in France there were fewer experts. This created an opening in Paris for Gulbenkian. In collaboration with Georges Bénard of the Paris banking house Bénard & Jarislowsky, Gulbenkian began lobbying officials in the French ministries of supply and commerce. With the British and American governments pushing their national champions, Gulbenkian confided to one French official, Royal Dutch-Shell was 'feeling a bit isolated'. This powerful oil combine was ready to relocate to France, provided 'it could find in France the political power base it lacked'.[39]

When it came to oil politics, it seemed, Royal Dutch-Shell was lonely; France was lonely. Gulbenkian proposed that they should feel lonely together. The gambit worked. When the aforementioned Comité Générale was formed the following year, Bénard was appointed its secretary. The Comité was chaired by a senator, Henri Bérenger, fondly recalled today as the 'father' of France's oil policy.[40] The policy was in fact furnished by Gulbenkian and his self-styled 'pupil', Bénard. Months before formal peace negotiations got started, they coached Bérenger on what to ask from the British government: full cooperation in Romania, the Caucasus, Persia and Mesopotamia, and the sale of Deutsche Bank's quarter-share in TPC to Royal Dutch-Shell.[41] Gulbenkian began managing Bérenger's private investment portfolio and even (according to Gulbenkian's secretary) provided a furnished apartment at 88 Boulevard de Grenelle.[42]

As Gulbenkian wrote to Edmond de Rothschild, the idea was 'to profit from the current situation, from the lack of oil in France, in order to put ourselves in the French government's good books and win their sympathy'. They should encourage the French to call an Anglo-French oil summit, he went on. This would be 'a master-stroke, putting Standard Oil right up against the wall and at the same time making us look good to the French government'.[43] The summit took place in November 1917. Gulbenkian found other ways of putting Royal Dutch-Shell in France's 'good books'. He helped develop plans for an oil import monopoly. He presented a temporary shortfall in oil deliveries by Standard as an attempt to force the French into dropping this plan.[44] Meanwhile Deterding placed 1 million francs at the French government's disposal. Gulbenkian ensured that this and the Hôpital Hollandais that Royal Dutch-Shell generously endowed at Pré Catelan received plenty of attention in the French press, countering claims that the company was in league with 'les Boches' (the Germans).[45]

In July 1916 Gulbenkian had been briefly detained by the British authorities during a Channel crossing, on the suspicion that he was still acting as financial adviser to the Turks – in other words, the enemy.[46] As his MI5 file shows, some officials viewed Gulbenkian as 'an unsatisfactory sort of person', sometimes found in the company of the equally undesirable Madeline Robert, a 27-year-old lady. Working his contacts, Gulbenkian saw to it that the officials responsible were (in their words) 'jumped on by the D.M.I.', that is, the Director of Military Intelligence. Thereafter Channel crossings were easier.[47]

Work as liaison between Shell and the French also involved Nubar, who had recently graduated from Cambridge with a second-class degree in law. Alongside Bénard and Bérenger, after 1917 Calouste and Nubar found much of their time taken up with the day-to-day routine of coordinating the movements of tankers and the sale of their cargoes to various agencies of the French government and armed forces.[48] Every little helped. In June 1918 Deterding agreed to grant Gulbenkian a 1 per cent commission on all Royal Dutch-Shell's sales to France, including those made anywhere in the world to the French navy and the Messageries Maritimes shipping line. As Royal Dutch-Shell was now providing almost half of France's oil imports, this was a profitable arrangement.[49] It was extended to Italy and the Italian navy and empire from 1 January 1919.

The war years brought surprisingly little change to Gulbenkian's daily life. Relations with Nevarte did not improve. There would be no more talk of divorce, however. In the City several of Gulbenkian's London office staff entered the armed forces; one, Herbert Pannell, sent his employer regular reports from the front and, later, from a German POW camp.[50] With so many of Pannell's colleagues absent, Gulbenkian's landlord at St Helen's Place found himself having to provide extra lavatories for female staff (still a novelty).[51]

Many Ottoman Armenians and many sons of the Armenian diaspora served in the British and French armies. The French created special units for Armenian recruits. Some made the journey east to join the Republic of Armenia's forces, led by the charismatic General Antranik. But there is no evidence that Calouste or Nubar himself ever considered that the latter might fight. Instead he entered Trinity College, Cambridge, where he passed Part I of the natural sciences course and Part II in law.

At Cambridge Nubar struggled to make the 'desirable friendships' his father demanded. 'Practically everyone who is at all worth knowing has gone off to the war,' Nubar reported, leaving 'practically nothing but Hindus and other black people and foreigners'.[52] Meanwhile Rita, at school near Ascot, passed her senior certificate exams in French, history and English in February 1916. Nevarte and Calouste began thinking of suitable Armenians for their children to marry; in Nubar's case, this was largely out of a desire to stop him gambling.[53]

Writing one of his near-daily letters to Nubar from his suite at the Ritz in Paris in the summer of 1918, Gulbenkian refused to be put off by 'Big Bertha', the long-range cannon then shelling the city. After noting the discovery of a new oil horizon at Tarakan (in Borneo), Calouste simply pauses. 'Boom!! Just when I am about to start writing again – it shakes!! But I shouldn't mention such things – one shouldn't allow oneself to be put out by those barbarians and idiots.'[54] He did, however, have forty cases of artworks moved from his Paris apartment to the safety of Biarritz.[55]

The news from Tarakan might have been good, but prospects for Gulbenkian's interests in the Caucasus dimmed towards the end of the war, thanks to successive invasions by Turkish and British forces, as well as uprisings incited by Bolsheviks and Georgian, Chechen, Azeri and Armenian separatists. British capital had played a large part in the Caucasian oil industry for more than two decades, and by 1917 38 per cent of the capital (171 million roubles) invested was British; French and German capital represented a mere 7 per cent and 3 per cent respectively. Gulbenkian's own investments were concentrated in three companies, all of which he had entered alongside Royal Dutch-Shell, taking 13 per cent of Ural Caspian, 18 per cent of North Caucasian and around 5 per cent of New Schibaieff. Thanks to new wells, improved plant and wartime demand, North Caucasian increased production from 22 million *pudi* (111 million gallons) to over 30 million (166 million) in a year.[56]

By October 1917 the Grozny region was descending into chaos. Field managers for North Caucasian reported that 'native outlaws depredate the country killing people and stealing live stocks, derailing trains and killing and robbing passengers'. Any equipment that could be moved was stolen. That which could not be moved, including tanks and pipelines, was shot or blown up. Russian as well as foreign managers faced increasing danger: 'This antagonism finds vent in wheeling such persons off the property in wheelbarrows and threats of more serious physical violence in case of return.'

Managers had previously hired local Cossacks to guard their properties. Now Colonel Michaeoloff, the Cossack commander at Vladikavkaz, declared himself unable to help.[57] On 17 December the Chechens attacked, setting many of North Caucasian's wells on fire, while the local Bolshevik

Revolutionary Committee demanded 1 million roubles in protection money. Only with the triumph of these 'Red' Russians over the 'Whites', led by Generals Wrangel and Denikin, in 1920 would stability return to the Caucasus. But by then North Caucasian and all the other companies (including the giant Nobel) had been nationalised by the Soviet regime.

The Armenian Genocide

For the Armenians the war years brought unimaginable suffering. In April 1913 Gulbenkian had invited Boghos Nubar (leader of the western Armenian community) and Cavid for lunch at 27 Quai d'Orsay, to discuss yet another set of Armenian reform proposals: special administrative measures intended to guarantee the security of Ottoman Armenians in the eastern *vilayets* from the depredations of their Kurdish and Turkish neighbours. Many previous reform schemes had seen the western powers demand the appointment of western observers or officials, demands which only exacerbated the Sultan's fear that the 'Armenian Question' had become a humanitarian smokescreen for the break-up of his empire.

Boghos and Gulbenkian proposed that the 'Armenian' *vilayets* be placed under a governor and civil agents to be nominated by Britain or France, and approved by the Sultan. Although Cavid felt Boghos to be a 'frank man', he did not think much of his plan, concerned that Russia was bound to foment agitation if any such protectorate was established by Britain and France. Privately he noted that Boghos's claim to lead the Armenian 'nation' was being challenged by the pro-Russian initiatives of other Armenian leaders.[58]

Another long-standing problem lay in the tendency to present the six *vilayets* of eastern Anatolia as 'Armenian provinces', when Ottoman Armenians were not, in fact, the largest ethnic group in those regions. Like the Ottoman Kurds, the Ottoman Armenians were dispersed among other populations. From the Kurdish perspective, the only difference between the two lay in the fact that the Ottoman Armenians could draw on a wealthy and influential community in the West in demanding a 'national home', whereas the Kurds did not have such a resource.

After the Turkish cabinet signed the Temporary Relocation Law in April 1915, persecution of Ottoman Armenians quickly developed into organised mass deportations of Ottoman Armenian communities in central and eastern Anatolia. German army officers and *Bagdadbahn* officials lent their assistance, packing victims onto carriages intended for sheep.[59] In 1915–16 between a third and a half of the world's Armenians died on forced marches to camps in the Syrian desert around Deir ez-Zor. Those who did not die of exhaustion, starvation or disease were shot by Ottoman army soldiers or the Ottoman Kurdish irregulars who had been deliberately set upon them in a callous attempt to distract the Kurds from their own irredentist agenda.

As president of the Paris-based Armenian delegation, Boghos gathered relief funds and called on Britain and France to issue joint declarations holding Turkish ministers personally responsible for the atrocities. By July 1915 he was pushing an 'autonomous and neutralised' six-*vilayet* 'Armenia' under joint British, French and Russian protection. A joint declaration was made, though the Foreign Office had reservations, noting that the 'personal responsibility' threat had been wielded once already and would only be rendered less effective by being repeated. Indeed, it might even incite more anti-Armenian violence.[60]

Though both France and Britain promised in 1917 to secure the Armenians a national home free from the Turkish yoke, these promises would later be broken.[61] Gulbenkian does not appear to have lobbied French or British officials in support of an autonomous Armenia, and was presumably unsurprised that the initiative went nowhere. For an Ottoman Armenian of his pedigree, election to the Armenian delegation would have been a foregone conclusion. Yet he did not stand for election, despite repeated invitations.[62] Gulbenkian's apparent lack of interest in an 'Armenian National Home' would lead to charges that, like other *amiras*, he was only a token Armenian.

There is something tokenistic about the Armenian benefactions stipulated in the will Gulbenkian drew up in November 1916. Bequests of £5,000 (£2.7 million) were to be paid to Surp Pırgiç Hospital in Istanbul (where his parents were buried) and to Armenian orphans. But the Society for the Prevention of Cruelty to Animals and the Royal Horticultural Society were to receive similar sums. While half the residual estate was destined for Nubar under various conditions, the rest was to be given to the Palace of Versailles, with instructions to spend it so as to encourage 'beautiful and singing birds ... to choose the Park as their abode'. The bequest would have filled a lot of bird baths with Évian.[63]

Svengali

The war cemented the alliance between Gulbenkian and Henri Deterding. Their relationship was never stronger than in 1918. But a relationship with Deterding was not quite the same thing as a relationship with Royal Dutch-Shell, thanks to Deterding's dysfunctional relationship with fellow executives, such as Robert Waley Cohen in London and Hendrikus Colijn in The Hague.[64] Gulbenkian regularly found himself having to remind Deterding's colleagues of sales commissions, share pools and other arrangements which Deterding had agreed with him in one-on-one meetings or in personal correspondence. Often it emerged that Deterding had neglected to inform his fellow Royal Dutch-Shell directors of these agreements. Over time Deterding's colleagues came to see Gulbenkian as something of an annoyance, as an accomplice to Deterding's fly-by-night activities, rather than (as Gulbenkian himself saw it) the 'fatherly eye' that kept the brilliant Deterding in line.[65]

For the time being, however, the arrangement worked: Gulbenkian made a great deal of money and Royal Dutch-Shell managed to keep hoovering up oil companies in the United States, Venezuela, Russia – and, as we shall see, Mexico as well. In 1918 Gulbenkian also began negotiations for a loan-for-oil deal which would have given Royal Dutch-Shell and the Pearson group access to the Comodoro Rivadavia field, Argentina's richest.[66] The more concessions Gulbenkian bagged and dressed for Royal Dutch-Shell to consume, the more concession-holders beat a path to his hotel door. The more shares he helped the company to float on the stock markets of New York, London, Paris and Amsterdam, the more acquaintances badgered him for tips on whether to buy, sell or hold. 'Shells and Royals are my pets,' he wrote in one letter to Lane. It was his business 'to know how they are going to jump'.[67]

At the start of the war there had still been a question mark over the loyalty of Royal Dutch-Shell. In June of 1914, for example, Winston Churchill had stated in the House of Commons that His Majesty's Government had always found the firm willing to help Great Britain out, 'for a price'. These three words stung Gulbenkian, who told Churchill's brother 'frankly that the attitude of his brother was anything but "chic"' towards the firm.[68] The war saw Royal Dutch-Shell succeed in persuading both Britain and France that they could be sure of Shell.

Royal Dutch-Shell had a number of well-informed executives based in

London able to advise and at the same time lobby the British government. In France the company had only Gulbenkian. Gulbenkian's role was even more important because of the French state's dilatoriness in developing an oil policy. Despite his best efforts to interest them, French banks had shown scant interest in TPC before the war.[69] French policy towards the Middle East during these years was strikingly ineffectual, if it can be said to have existed at all. Whether the issue was access to Mosul oil reserves, Arab nationalism or Zionism, the French were adrift.[70]

The war had brought many changes to the international oil business, the most important being greater state intervention. It had become clear to all powers that they could not rely on the market to supply their needs in wartime. To remain a 'power' one needed access to one's own areas of production as well as tame national oil companies to ensure security of supply. Rationing, the corralling of rivals into syndicates and measures intended to rationalise tankerage spawned new government directorates, offices and administrations in the United States, France and Britain. Far from being resisted, the oil companies saw the opportunity to coopt these agencies. Lobbying became more important than ever before. Gulbenkian proved to be as gifted in this work as he was in finance.

Instructed to trail Gulbenkian and find out whom he was dining with, agent C.T. of MI5 provided a pen portrait of a man in motion:

> Age 49, height about 5' 6" or 7"; black closely cropped hair (bald on top) dark eyes and eyebrows, clean shaven; sallow, oriental type of complexion, beard shows black under skin, rather full face. Almost invariably dressed in black morning coat, and striped trousers and bowler hat. Always moves about quickly. He usually occupies the same table for lunch at the Carlton every day.[71]

EIGHT

TALLEYRAND, 1918–20

Under the Foreign Office Agreement of March 1914 the British government had levered Anglo-Persian into Gulbenkian's Turkish Petroleum Company and lent its support to a joint Anglo-German effort to extract the Mesopotamian oil concession from the Sultan. This policy had born fruit in the *Lettre Vizirielle* of June 1914, which promised the concession to TPC. With the outbreak of war, however, this architecture had collapsed. The Foreign Office disavowed the Foreign Office Agreement and Deutsche Bank's 25 per cent share of TPC was sequestered as enemy property.[1] Deutsche Bank parked its *Bagdadbahn*-related oil interests in Switzerland, secure from post-war reparations.[2] In Turkey the vestigial government in Istanbul and consortia of self-described 'Sultan's Heirs' had also taken steps to protect their competing claims over the oil lands of Mesopotamia.[3] In the years after 1918, therefore, it was very far from clear whether TPC held a valid concession. Even if it did, from whom did it hold it? The Turkish government in Istanbul? Or Mustapha Kemal's Nationalist regime in Ankara?

Legal arguments were one thing, physical control another. The British and Ottoman empires had signed an armistice at Mudros on 30 October 1918, under which hostilities were to cease the following day. Having failed to grasp the significance of Mosul until the eleventh hour, British forces in Mesopotamia raced north as fast as they could, and only managed to occupy Mosul on 1 November.[4] Britain received a League of Nations mandate for the region in November 1920, charged with building up a new country named Iraq. At the Cairo Conference of March 1921 they decided to place the Hashemite leader, Faisal, on a new Iraqi throne. In August 1921 he was duly crowned in Baghdad, ruling under a constitution which earned 96 per cent approval by the Iraqi nation in a (rigged) plebiscite. Meanwhile Faisal's brother Abdullah became emir of neighbouring Transjordan, itself part of the British mandate for Palestine. It wasn't the 'Arabistan' promised by T. E. Lawrence, but it was enough to annoy the French, who had evicted Faisal from their mandate of Syria after a popular Arabist movement had proclaimed him king of Syria.

It now fell to the British mandatory authorities to create a unified and stable Iraq. Shortly after British forces arrived in Basra, the Belgian consul observed that while the locals were happy enough to be free from being pillaged by Ottoman troops, 'the people here are essentially venal in character and very divided by faith and local interest'. There were no 'cohesive elements' around which an identity could be formed.[5] The Mosul region was rocked by a Kurdish revolt, while to the west the Druze were also restless. British proconsular officials like Arnold Wilson (Civil Commissioner for Iraq) recognised that if Iraq was to be put on its feet it would need all the oil royalties it could get. Though they received little thanks, these men (drawn from the Government of India) took their responsibility seriously – more so, perhaps, than His Majesty's Government back in London did.

The Settlement of the World

During the war the British and French agencies in charge of oil policy had been partly staffed by oil company executives on secondment, men like Robert Waley Cohen, Georges Bénard and Nubar Gulbenkian. Such men were unlikely to sit on their hands while the diplomats deliberated the new post-war order at Versailles, San Remo, Sèvres, Genoa and Lausanne. Indeed, in May 1919, one month before the main Versailles Treaty was signed, they secured the Long–Bérenger Agreement, which committed France and Britain to a policy of share-and-share-alike in oil, as well as the cession of the German quarter of TPC to French interests. To the ministries which formally oversaw the petroleum agencies, such agreements could seem suspicious. Were these agencies implementing government policy? Or were they being used by oil companies to create it?

As a disgruntled Foreign Office mandarin noted in a memorandum discussing the agreement, 'in the settlement of the world at the Peace Conference, both the British and French Governments are anxious to obtain a large share in the oil interest of Middle Europe and the Middle East.' But the process of obtaining that share seemed to be poorly coordinated. The Foreign Office had not been invited to participate in the Long–Bérenger talks. 'Instead of this the FO is presented with a cut and dried agreement.' At this point in the memo Curzon pipes up, writing in his distinctive green ink. 'Do we [the Foreign Office] approve?' he enquires. 'And how comes it that the thing has been done in this hole and corner way[?]'[6]

Nothing better illustrates the way in which the First World War had forged an oily military-industrial complex than the diplomatic squabbles over whether oil surveyors were to be granted permission to travel to Syria and Iraq to prospect. Thanks to the principled stand taken by Wilson, representatives of the American firm Socony were kept out of Iraq.[7] Gulbenkian's war service had given him excellent contacts among Allied forces' supply divisions, however, and he now made effective use of them as scouts able to pull rank (and strings). He secured the services of US Brigadier General Avery D. Andrews in Mexico, of French General Charles Payot (former chief of army supplies and communications) in Romania and of British General Sir John Cowans, GCMG, KCB, MVO, in the Middle East.[8] After Cowans's death in 1921 Gulbenkian replaced him with Lieutenant-General Sir George Macdonogh, GBE, KCB, KCMG, former Director of Military Intelligence.

In one letter Cowans wrote to Gulbenkian from Paris promising to find out if Mesopotamia was about to be discussed by the allies. After calling on Sir George Clerk at the Astoria (the British delegation's hotel) and getting an update on Foreign Secretary A. J. Balfour, Cowans decided to pop over from Paris to London and 'look in on Cadman [at the Petroleum Executive] and ask myself to dine with Harcourt or Curzon if they are in town and will also look in at the War Office or Downing St and generally see what is going on.'[9]

These were connections even a Gulbenkian might envy. As he put it to Deterding, 'I never expected [Cowans] would be such a propagandist for us in every direction.'[10] Cowans was equally impressed with Gulbenkian, whom he addressed as 'Talleyrand'. As far as Cowans was concerned, the unreliable Lloyd George, self-important diplomats like Curzon and jumped-up Government of India officials like Wilson needed to stand aside and let men of action take the decisions that needed to be taken, men like Gulbenkian and himself. In December 1919 Cowans wrote plaintively to 'my dear old Talleyrand', reporting on the agreement apparently reached on how the 'Mesopotamian Company' would be divided up:

> I miss you very much – <u>really</u> – as you do get things done – Things have gone fairly well with Mespot. Hamar Greenwood [at the Board of Trade] is a good man and I am sure Cadman runs straight and is <u>most</u> keen to get things settled. I fancy they have given the French 19 per cent local Gov[ernmen]t 20 Home Govt 2 and our share was 34 so that only leaves 26 for Anglo-Persian but I haven't heard anything <u>final</u> – Our agreement with Govt is through I think – I do wish we could get on with orders and arrangements I never saw such ridiculous and unnecessary delays ... Winston Churchill and [Chancellor of the Exchequer Robert] Horne are coming on Monday – I will give them a bit of my mind over all their delays, of course Winston looks on the Anglo-Persian as his invention.[11]

Even if Cowans's numbers didn't quite add up (the percentages total 101), there was no doubting that this was a good deal for Royal Dutch-Shell. In lieu of 50 per cent of TPC, Anglo-Persian was now to get just a quarter, while Royal Dutch-Shell would be the dominant partner, and would also have the management.[12] The 'local government' – that is, the mandatory authorities in Mesopotamia – were also taken due notice of, in a way calculated to pacify Wilson (whom Cowans referred to as 'an old lady').[13]

In 1919 the industrious Cowans also made it out to Basra and Baghdad, having got his former private secretary (still at the War Office) to arrange the necessary permissions. 'Everything is working out well for us so far,' he reported, 'but if I owned Basra and Hell – I would let Basra and live in Hell.'[14] Meanwhile, having found that State Department protests got them nowhere, Jersey Standard decided to take a leaf out of their rivals' book. As the Foreign Office reported in a memo:

> The Shell Co. having succeeded through the W[ar]O[ffice] in smuggling out a British general (Sir J. Cowans) to Mesopotamia to spy out the land for them there, – the Standard Oil Co, not to be outdone, now proposed to secure through the Adm[iral]ty a British Admiral

to perform a similar service for them. There is humour in this, but it should not be allowed.[15]

To Curzon's dismay, this 'hole and corner way' continued to characterise oil diplomacy. 'My dear Talleyrand the great' flourished in these holes and corners.[16]

Gulbenkian used his generals, diplomats and other forces to secure control of Mexican, Persian, Romanian, Russian and Mesopotamian oil for Royal Dutch-Shell. Rather than intervening directly, he had these men coach the leaders and diplomats who sat around the negotiating table at international conferences. Though the oil companies' unofficial delegations at Versailles and other conferences were frowned upon by diplomatists like Curzon, their presence could not be ignored. 'An unpleasant smell of oil continues to pervade Genoa,' noted *The Nation* in May 1920.[17] The same was said of Versailles, San Remo, Sèvres and Lausanne.

The oily stench was everywhere because, for all their proclivity to wriggle around regulations, the leaders of Jersey Standard, Anglo-Persian and Royal Dutch-Shell recognised that state intervention in the oil industry was here to stay, and could be harnessed to advance their own interests. Oil import monopolies were particularly tempting prospects: intended to protect a country's consumers from the oil octopus, for the oil company lucky enough to secure the contract they afforded ample opportunities to fix prices and dish rivals. Governments would also determine who got to exploit the oilfields that had been under the control of Germany and the Ottoman Empire. Above all, governments would determine whether they would be divided up according to pre-war spheres of interest, or the more liberal 'open door' system championed by that newcomer to international diplomacy, the United States.

The stakes of the post-war settlement were high, but Gulbenkian's spirits were higher still. When his old friend Frederick Lane wrote to him in the summer of 1918, expressing doubt about the future of Royal Dutch-Shell, Gulbenkian gave a revealing if unpunctuated reply:

> I have read somewhere that if there was no America, God would have created one to recompense the faith of Christopher Columbus. As you know the whole of the moral system of the world is centered on faith, which one draws from healthy principles, moral or material. I emphasise the word HEALTHY principles because I don't want you

to think that I place faith on flimsy grounds. You must draw faith from intuition, and you get intuition by experience ... I have no doubt that after the war we shall have immense openings and I shall stick to my system of faith, based on an healthy architecture.[18]

One of the most tempting 'openings' lay in Mexico, the world's second-largest oil producer. During the war Germany overran Romania, Russia was knocked out by the Revolution, Persia was in a mess and Mesopotamia was decades away from coming on stream. If 'the Allies had floated to victory upon a wave of oil', as Curzon put it, this had partly been a Mexican wave.[19] The head of the second-largest Mexican oil company, El Águila (The Eagle), was a sixty-two-year-old Yorkshireman named Weetman Pearson. Fearing Águila's wells could turn to salt, Pearson was looking for a way out of a business he had entered by accident.

Mexican Eagle

The engineering firm Samuel Pearson and Sons had drifted into the oil business on the back of a series of large infrastructure projects it undertook in Mexico in the 1890s under the *Porfiriato*, the seven-term reign of President Porfirio Díaz. Samuel Pearson's grandson Weetman Dickinson Pearson became a close friend of Díaz, and the firm created the massive canals that allowed the expansion of Mexico City, as well as the Tehuantepec Railway, which linked the Atlantic and Pacific shores. Ennobled in 1910 as Baron Cowdray, Pearson began searching for oil to fuel his railway and eventually discovered the Dos Bocas field on the isthmus of Tehuantepec itself.[20]

The Mexican petroleum industry began as an offshoot of the Californian one, with the American Edward Doheny's Pan American Company leading the way, drilling its first Mexican well at Tampico (on the Gulf of Mexico) in 1901.

Fearful of American influence, Díaz recognised the value of playing British and American interests off against each other. Águila's production derived from the 'golden lane' running south from Tampico through Portrero del Llano, a series of fields that proved so rich that Mexican production increased more than sixfold between 1914 and 1920.[21] Águila struggled to develop the refinery, transport and marketing capacity necessary to keep pace with its runaway production. During the First World War this was not a problem, however, as the only customers, the Allied states, were desperate for supplies.

During the war Cowdray had drawn up plans for a state-controlled 'Imperial Oil Company', which would, he hoped, take Águila off his hands as well as buying (with bonds) Anglo-Persian and all other British oil companies at cost price plus 10 per cent.[22] Deterding was happy to play along, as a way of checkmating Anglo-Persian. In May 1919 the British cabinet approved an agreement whereby Royal Dutch-Shell accepted various conditions intended to ensure that the firm would always remain British-controlled. With his characteristic ingenuity, Deterding proposed to make the Britishness of his firm clear by taking control of Anglo-Persian.

For both Gulbenkian and Deterding this would have been sweet revenge. In 1914 His Majesty's Government had then taken the unprecedented step of injecting £2.2 million of public funds into Anglo-Persian, ostensibly to save it from the 'Shell menace' but really to rescue it from its managers' incompetence. Anglo-Persian's contribution to the war effort had been far smaller than that of Royal Dutch-Shell – a company Charles Greenway, chairman of Anglo-Persian, had claimed was 'under the control of the German Government itself'.[23] If even more reassurance of Royal Dutch-Shell's Britishness was required, the company was happy to buy a controlling stake in Anglo-Persian. Fortunately, the Burmah Oil Company was keen to be rid of its large holding in Anglo-Persian and so the necessary shares were available. It would have been nice to have Greenway dance to Royal Dutch-Shell's tune for a change. Though an agreement was initialled in 1919, however, it was never implemented, for reasons that remain unclear.[24]

Gulbenkian was more successful when it came to acquiring control of Águila for Royal Dutch-Shell. The inspiration for this coup was Philippe Bunau-Varilla, the French military engineer and company promoter notorious for his role in creating Panama (both the canal and the country). In September 1918 he approached Gulbenkian at Biarritz, proposing some sort of cartel agreement for Mexican oil between Royal Dutch-Shell, Doheny and Águila. Though Gulbenkian would have nothing further to do with Bunau-Varilla, the latter gave him the idea of 'a straight deal in shares' between Cowdray and Deterding, under which the latter would 'assume the management and leave Lord Cowdray with a perfect peace of mind'.[25] Under the final agreement of 7 February 1919, Royal Dutch-Shell bought 1.5 million Águila shares at £4 18s a share.

Rather than paying Cowdray cash, however, Royal Dutch-Shell paid 5 per cent interest on the unpaid purchase money. The company held on to 500,000 Águila shares, but placed the remaining 1 million together in a share pool to be managed by Gulbenkian. Royal Dutch-Shell gave a subsidiary, Bataafse Petroleum Maatschappij (BPM), a twenty-one-year contract to manage Águila. Cowdray placed another million Águila shares in the same pool. Under a separate agreement, Gulbenkian received a fat brokerage fee of 20 per cent.[26] He sold shares through his favoured brokers in London (Panmure Gordon, Vickers DaCosta), as well as selling to himself and his friends, including Edmond de Rothschild and Frederick Lane. He sought to get the shares quoted on the stock markets of New York, Paris and Amsterdam. The 'sale' of Águila to Shell thus depended on Gulbenkian's ability to use his contacts in Paris (Fray, Émile Francqui), New York (Kuhn Loeb) and Amsterdam (Hendrik Braat, Labouchere Oyens) to drain what was an exceptionally deep pool of 'Eagles'. It helped that Gulbenkian had been dealing in them since 1912.[27]

Initially the pool seems to have worked to everyone's satisfaction.[28] Gulbenkian succeeded in introducing 'Eagles' to Paris, shuttling between Paris and London, sometimes making the journey by aeroplane, a very novel form of business travel.[29] By early 1921, however, strains were appearing in Gulbenkian's relationship with Cowdray and Deterding. Gulbenkian suspected that Royal Dutch-Shell was using Águila as a source of cheap production and (thanks to new share issues) cheap capital, rather than implementing the programme of investment in tankers and marketing facilities that had been agreed prior to the 'sale'. He badgered both Deterding and Cowdray to agree to appoint an advisory committee to encourage BPM to do a better job of making Águila work as an integrated company.

Cowdray admitted that Águila's numbers were disappointing, but admired Deterding and did not want to rock the boat and risk attracting Royal Dutch-Shell's ire.[30] He still had large oil interests in the United States (through Amerada) and his Whitehall Petroleum was exploring new ventures all over the globe. Only after Cowdray's death in 1927 did Pearson and Sons begin to appreciate that Gulbenkian might have been correct.[31] Gulbenkian's unhappy position in Águila, caught between Cowdray and Royal Dutch-Shell, resembles that which developed around the same time in Venezuelan Oil Concessions (this episode is considered in Chapter 10).

Another source of friction common to Águila and VOC was financing.

In early 1921 Gulbenkian saw recent issues of Eagle shares on London and a proposed $50 million Eagle issue in New York as characteristic of Deterding's arrogant attitude towards his shareholders, who faced a drought as far as information about their company's performance and prospects went, but a flood of new shares that watered their holdings (including dividends paid in bonus shares rather than in cash). 'All our shareholders, both big and small, are saturated with our paper,' Gulbenkian informed Royal Dutch-Shell's Colijn in March. 'I get the impression that you are always relying on getting money at any time by the issues of shares at par. We have repeated this formula so often that we have overdone it.'[32]

Thanks to his role running share pools and as portfolio adviser to a raft of small-time investors (ranging from West End starlets to the prime minister of Persia and the art dealer Joseph Duveen), Gulbenkian gave his fullest attention to the 'digestion' of oil shares on world markets.[33] His aim was to avoid a situation in which 'undigested' shares ended up sloshing around the market long after the original issue. He sought to sell to investors who would hold them long-term rather than dumping them at the first sign of panic. He recognised that different investment vehicles appealed to different kinds of investors, regularly urging Royal Dutch-Shell's leaders to issue bonds or debenture notes at long maturities in lieu of shares, and to issue dividends in cash rather than in bonus shares. When he deigned to respond, Deterding simply insisted that shareholders had to trust him.[34] He admitted to watering VOC's shares. 'Quite so, but when you find very big production the water becomes gold.'[35]

An Oily Entente

These activities were making Gulbenkian something of a name in Paris. As *Le Figaro* noted in April 1920, he had become 'one of today's high-profile personalities'. 'Everyone claims to know Mr. G... . or a friend of a friend of his.'[36]

At the same time as Royal Dutch-Shell was polishing its 'British' credentials, Gulbenkian cultivated the close relations he had established with Bérenger and other French officials. Plentiful supplies, as well as generous credit facilities and other gestures, had seen Royal Dutch-Shell come to France's aid in her hour of greatest need. This was recognised with the offer to both Gulbenkian and Deterding of membership of the Légion d'honneur, which Deterding accepted.

Gulbenkian had not courted this celebrity. Although the habit seems showy today, it is worth remembering that Gulbenkian had been living in hotels since he was a teenager, and continued to do so for the sake of comfort and convenience. Far from attention-seeking, such behaviour protected his privacy, even (or especially) from his own family. Though formal, little about Gulbenkian's wardrobe or entourage was flashy. He hid in the plain sight of journalists and paparazzi, who regularly failed to recognise 'one of today's high-profile personalities' as he scuttled out of the Ritz. His decision to refuse membership of the Légion d'honneur was characteristic, therefore. When pressed, he proposed that the decoration be offered to Nubar. Cut of a very different cloth from his father, Nubar jumped at the offer. He duly became one of the youngest *commandeurs* – and never let anyone forget it.

Bérenger's secret November 1918 report on French oil policy and the peace negotiations identified four areas to focus on: Romania, the Caucasus, Mesopotamia and Persia.[37] Gulbenkian helped with all of them. Discretion was crucial, as Royal Dutch-Shell's rapid expansion was making it appear less like the scrappy challenger to the American hegemon, Standard Oil of New Jersey, and more like one of *les trusts anglo-saxons* intent on enslaving France. Gulbenkian presented an alliance with Royal Dutch-Shell as an opportunity for a war-weakened France to punch above its weight on the world oil stage, rather than as a threat to its energy independence. For Deterding, an entente offered the chance to secure French diplomatic support in Romania and the Middle East (areas where the Foreign Office was committed to supporting Anglo-Persian), as well as an opportunity to wrest the French market from the Americans.

Given Deterding's indifference to public relations and tin ear for the finer nuances of French amour propre, however, it was evident that Royal Dutch-Shell needed someone else to act as liaison if the firm was to retain French goodwill. Someone able to reassure both sides that they stood to benefit, rather than being exploited. Someone with a personal stake in the entente, but without exclusive ties to one or other partner. It was a situation which played to Gulbenkian's strengths as a back-room fixer of no fixed abode, or rather of so many abodes as to make his loyalties appear reassuringly blurred. Gulbenkian bearded French officials inside the corridors of the Quai d'Orsay, while Nevarte charmed them at receptions in their apartment, at 27 Quai d'Orsay.

Gulbenkian in London in 1892: barely in his twenties, already shifting his attention away from his family's import-export business.

LEFT: Gulbenkian's parents Dirouhi and Sarkis were the first generation of the Gulbenkian clan to pose in European dress.

RIGHT: But little Calouste (at left) was used to seeing cousins in local costume, such as the Kouyoumdjians of Baghdad, shown here.

RIGHT: *Gulbenkian with his tutor Setrak Devgantz in Marseille. A beloved family retainer, 'Dev-Dev' would later find Gulbenkian's son Nubar a less tractable pupil.*

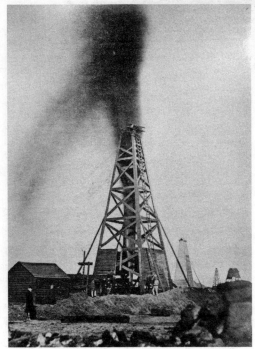

LEFT: *In 1888 Gulbenkian visited Baku. He would never visit an oil field again.*

LEFT: *Even by the standards of the time, Nevarte and Calouste's 1892 wedding photo was somewhat stern.*

RIGHT: *In Paris ten years later, Nevarte appears confident. To her irritation, Calouste put her skills as a hostess to work for his business.*

LEFT: Nubar aged five, looking every inch the spoilt child.

RIGHT: Nubar with his sister Rita – trying, as ever, to keep up with her precocious brother.

ABOVE: Gulbenkian was far from vain. This 1912 portrait by Charles Joseph Watelet is the only one he ever commissioned.

RIGHT: At one time or another Gulbenkian held Ottoman, Armenian, British and Iranian passports. This photo from his First World War-era British passport captures the bowler-hatted, Channel-hopping oil diplomat.

ABOVE: Iranian prime minister Timurtash (at centre in light suit, with cane) arrives in London in 1931, backed (on his right) by a bespectacled Nubar and (on his left) Calouste, who would rather not appear at all. At far right stands a nervous John Cadman, chairman of the Anglo-Persian Oil Company.

LEFT: Until a squabble over Venezuela tore them apart, Henri Deterding was Gulbenkian's closest friend. Together they made Royal Dutch-Shell an oil giant.

TOP: *As he put it to Kenneth Clark, Gulbenkian's palace at 51 Avenue d'Iéna in Paris was 'built like a battleship'. 'Fortress' would have been more accurate.*

BOTTOM: *Like the rest of the house, Gulbenkian's ground-floor office was not really meant for use. Business was done elsewhere.*

LEFT: *From Gulbenkian's private penthouse suite you could see the Arc de Triomphe ... if it wasn't for the hedges and screens in between.*

RIGHT: *Here Gulbenkian could enjoy the company of his beloved peacocks. Until the neighbours complained of the noise.*

TOP: *Gulbenkian had a fine bedroom at Avenue d'Iéna, complete with single bed. He never slept in it, though, returning to the Ritz every night.*

BOTTOM: *Meals were taken surrounded by Brussels tapestries of cherubs cavorting in trees. Gulbenkian and his family ate at separate sittings.*

LEFT: *Rodin's bronze of a chained burgher of Calais (at right) and Houdon's Apollo (silhouetted at rear) guarded the main foyer.*

RIGHT: *An admirer of eighteenth-century French architecture, Gulbenkian studied all the great staircases before settling upon a design for his own. Few visitors ever swept up it.*

Even in a collection as great as that of the Hermitage, Houdon's life-size marble of Diana had enjoyed a privileged position. In 1930 Stalin sold her to Gulbenkian.

LEFT: A rare snap of a smiling Gulbenkian on holiday in Fez in 1932, surrounded by his curator, secretary and doctor.

BELOW: The Hotel Aviz in Lisbon. In 1942 Gulbenkian took five of its thirty-three suites; in 1955 he died there. Designed to look like a Manueline fortress, its defences unfortunately did not always keep prying journalists out.

LEFT: *In stark contrast to his father, Nubar courted the press: for journalists, Nubar's divorces, plane crashes, fox hunts and taxis were gifts that kept on giving.*

BELOW: *Calouste and Nevarte celebrate their sixtieth wedding anniversary in 1952 with their children Rita and Nubar. Within a few weeks Nevarte would be dead.*

LEFT: Ian Fleming had at one time worked for one of Gulbenkian's brokers. In wartime Lisbon, Fleming was probably too busy spying to notice a fellow British exile: a reclusive millionaire famed for his love of white cats.

BELOW: An elderly Gulbenkian awaits the arrival of Cyril Radcliffe at Lisbon airport in 1953, guarded by the ever-faithful Isabelle Theis.

Three figures who played a central role in shaping Gulbenkian's testamentary plans: his beloved (if suspect) son Nubar (top), lawyer-turned-confidant Cyril Radcliffe (centre) and the man who ensured that the Foundation would become 'a gift to Portugal': José de Azeredo Perdigão.

As in his pre-war dealings with Mantashev, here again Gulbenkian sometimes found himself struggling to keep both sides on board. When, in December 1919, Colijn of Royal Dutch-Shell hesitated to maintain supplies to the French state (such supplies being paid for using a £2 million credit line Royal Dutch-Shell had extended in June), Gulbenkian warned him:

> it will be a very black day for us if you determine not to support the French Government ... It has been everywhere decided that the French shall have an equal call with England in all petroleum matters. Whereas in England we have to meet severe competition, in this country we shall be able to seize upon every opportunity of benefit to ourselves, and we shall have Government support through thick and thin which is the end for which I have been labouring for so many years.[38]

Gulbenkian negotiated a further credit line of £5 million (200 million francs) with Bérenger in January 1920. In his report to the Finance Minister, Bérenger acknowledged 'the direct and personal intervention of M. Gulbenkian' and noted that Standard had threatened to withdraw its credit line if France passed the proposed monopoly law.[39] To the raft of French refiners and distributors allied to Royal Dutch-Shell, however, Gulbenkian seemed *plus royaliste que le roi* in representing Royal Dutch-Shell's interests.[40]

The vehicle for this entente was the unimaginatively named Société pour l'Exploitation des Pétroles (SEP), founded in July 1919 with a capital of 40 million francs, half of which was subscribed by a Royal Dutch-Shell subsidiary. Gulbenkian sat on the board along with Lucien Villars and Frédéric François-Marsal, powerful figures within the Banque de l'Union Parisienne (BUP), as well as Émile Deutsch, of the refiner Deutsch de la Meurthe.[41] SEP was Gulbenkian's baby. He drafted the company's Articles of Association and had a 31 per cent stake in it (again, carried by Royal Dutch-Shell, to keep it secret).[42] He took great pride in having secured a fine Louis Seize building, the Hôtel Coislin on the Place de la Concorde, as its headquarters. 'The most magnificent in the whole of Paris', this palace was built in 1770 to designs by Ange-Jacques Gabriel, and was part of an ensemble with the Hôtel de Crillon and the Hôtel de la Marine.[43]

Gulbenkian nonetheless sought to make SEP appear the brainchild of the French government, stage-managing a meeting at which a senior official at the French Finance Ministry apparently asked Villars when he was going to form an entity to take France's share of TPC.[44] But SEP was about more than getting control of the 25 per cent of TPC which had formerly belonged to Deutsche Bank: it was designed to implement that policy of Anglo-French collaboration in petroleum production Bérenger had proposed in November 1918, enshrined in the Long–Bérenger Agreement of May 1919. Unfortunately, the mercurial British prime minister David Lloyd George had disavowed the agreement five days later.

However, a new agreement was negotiated along similar lines the following December, and confirmed by the San Remo Oil Agreement of April 1920. A milestone in the history of the French oil industry, under its terms France and Britain agreed to share equally any oil concessions gained or already held by either partner. France would get the 25 per cent of TPC that had belonged to Deutsche Bank. As France held few cards of any value, this was quite a coup. Deutsche Bank's other UK-based oil interests had been sequestered and then sold by the Public Trustee to Anglo-Persian.[45]

The Foreign Office struggled to explain why Britain would sell TPC shares to France 'without getting anything tangible in return, – not even a formal renunciation of the French claims to Mosul', under the Sykes–Picot Agreement of 1916.[46] Lloyd George had in fact got the French premier, Georges Clemenceau, to renounce Mosul the previous December. It would seem that Clemenceau agreed in exchange for Lloyd George's support for a 'buffer republic' in the Rhineland, separating France and Germany. Clemenceau, in short, offered to trade Mosul's oil for the Rhineland's coal.[47] It was a characteristic step for a man who disdained to show any interest in oil and failed to grasp its significance. 'When I need oil,' Clemenceau sniffed, 'I ask my *épicier*' (*épicier*, or grocer, being the pejorative term for any small-time businessman).[48]

Establishing what exactly Lloyd George and Clemenceau agreed on 1 December 1918 is impossible, as this was an unminuted Sunday meeting held at the French Embassy in London. Nobody at the Foreign Office seemed to know of the agreement until June 1919 – that is, six months later.[49] Nor did they know much about Lloyd George's plan to exploit Mosul's oil riches without enriching Marcus Samuel (whom Lloyd George despised) or his company, Royal Dutch-Shell. Instead of collaborating through TPC, Britain and France would work through an entirely state-owned entity. Curzon's view of the 'Welsh Wizard''s latest wheeze was clear: 'This is great nonsense.'[50]

As if inter-ally rivalries were not enough, Gulbenkian also had to handle interpersonal and inter-ministerial rivalries. He was bemused by the demands of coaching those who in turn briefed the British and French prime ministers. He wrote to Hendrikus Colijn in January 1920 of a meeting between Lloyd George and Clemenceau, held a few days before the Versailles negotiations commenced, at which the pair

> seemed quite mystified – the omnipotent ones of this world seemed to be ignorant of what they had met to discuss. Their understudies made valiant effort to explain the situation, but the two Great Ones did not seem to grasp, and so the matter was put off until the following day (Monday). I understand that at this meeting the French claimed 50% in Mesopotamia on the ground that they had given over Mosul.

Gulbenkian had, he claimed, seen this demand coming and arranged things so that the 'political side of the question' would be carried over to another meeting. He coached the French to accept 25 per cent of TPC in lieu of this demand for 50 per cent.[51] He also tried to manage Lloyd George's dislike of Samuel. 'I have the greatest sympathy for Sir Marcus,' Gulbenkian assured Deterding, 'but if he could be induced to take a voyage around the world, I think the Mesopotamian question and many others pending would very soon be settled.'[52]

Alongside Mesopotamia Gulbenkian also sought to acquire new concessions for SEP – that is, for Royal Dutch-Shell and the French – in Persia. With Bérenger's help, he got the French government to ask Tehran to appoint Gulbenkian *conseiller financier* to the Persian Legation in Paris. The appointment duly came in May 1920.[53] Gulbenkian once again enjoyed diplomatic status, which he retained (with one short interruption) until his death thirty-five years later. He helped the Persian Finance Minister, Prince Firouz Mirza Nosrat Al Dowleh, and other officials invest in Royal Dutch-Shell shares. The capital came from bribes paid to them by the British in exchange for signing the 1919 Anglo-Persian Treaty, which effectively made Persia a British protectorate.[54]

The Qajar Shah's authority barely extended beyond Tehran, which was itself guarded by Norperforce, a small British expeditionary force. Given the weakness of the Persian state and its subservience to Britain and Russia, a concessionaire with little diplomatic heft in the region was appealing. Unfortunately for Gulbenkian, American companies such as

Sinclair Oil and Jersey Standard met this criterion as much as French ones such as SEP did. Sinclair was also prepared to offer a $5 million loan. Gulbenkian lost the fight for the north Persian concession, named after a Georgian, Arkady Khostaria, who had secured the rights in 1916.[55] Sinclair Oil emerged the winner, only to implode shortly after, a victim of the Teapot Dome bribery scandal, which landed both Harry Sinclair and the US Secretary of the Interior in jail.[56]

Meanwhile Soviet shelling of the Caspian port of Bandar-e-Anzali and the declaration by Jangali rebels of a Soviet Socialist Republic of Persia suggested that north Persia was doomed to end up back inside a Russian sphere of interest. When Gulbenkian returned to the north Persian question seven years later, he wisely went through Russia. In the intervening period the Qajar Shah was eased off the throne and replaced by a cavalry colonel, Reza Khan, someone the British officers of Norperforce thought would do a better job of holding the line against the Russians. It would not be the last regime change imposed in Tehran.

SEP also stumbled in Romania, another area where the San Remo Agreement committed the British to collaborating with the French. Deutsche Bank had invested heavily in Romanian oil production before the war. Now their Romanian subsidiaries were up for grabs, just as Deutsche's 25 per cent of TPC was.[57] The new post-war 'Greater Romania' was more than twice the size of pre-war Romania. Politically it was still dominated by the Bratiano family, who had been providing its prime ministers since the 1880s. Even before the war the Bratianos had been under pressure at home to 'romanise' the Romanian oil industry, leading to post-war moves to nationalise subsoil rights, create an internal sales monopoly and restrict inward investment.[58] Vintila Bratiano resented seeing his country's oil shared out at San Remo, which he considered 'yet another manifestation of a desire to return to the old days, when the Great Powers treated Romania as a second rate Balkan power'.[59] At the same time he recognised his country's need for a loan and for weapons, both of which could be secured in exchange for Romania's oil.

Deterding instructed Gulbenkian to take advantage of SEP, applying French diplomatic support to protect Royal Dutch-Shell's Romanian subsidiary and secure the Romanian State Lands concession. A £40 million loan could be dangled as a sweetener. If the French didn't do as they were told, they could forget about another credit line from Royal Dutch-Shell.[60] After Villars lobbied the Quai d'Orsay, a French mission under

General Payot was sent to Bucharest to secure a lowering of export duties and an arms-for-oil deal. Payot being one of Gulbenkian's generals, this was a promising start.[61] Unfortunately, Payot found himself obstructed by a Canadian adventurer, Joe Boyle. Boyle had made his fortune in the Klondike before serving the British Secret Service in Bessarabia during the war, rescuing both the Romanian crown jewels and a group of leading Romanians from the Bolsheviks. He had secured a massive Canadian loan for Romania and was allegedly pursuing an affair with Queen Marie.

Sadly for Gulbenkian, the plan for SEP to secure significant stakes in both Romanian and Mesopotamian oil fell foul of French inter-ministerial rivalry in the years 1919–21. This rivalry between the French Finance Ministry and the Foreign Ministry had its equivalent in the rivalry between BUP, which had close links to the former, and the Banque de Paris et des Pays Bas (Paribas), which was close to the Quai d'Orsay, as well as Jersey Standard. Paribas resented BUP's move into petroleum finance, as well as Royal Dutch-Shell's success in garnering powerful support within the French state.[62] It successfully lobbied President Raymond Poincaré to abandon plans for a French oil import monopoly (plans Royal Dutch-Shell had supported).

Gulbenkian had played the Finance and Foreign Ministries against each other during the 1910 Ottoman loan negotiations. Now, however, the junior banking partners in SEP changed sides, including Georges Bénard. Gulbenkian was surprised to be let down by 'those in whom, as man to man, you thought you could place trust – at least to a certain extent'.[63]

False Dawn

Gulbenkian's brothers spent the war in relative safety, Karnig in Neuilly and Vahan in Algiers. Both continued to receive their monthly stipends from Calouste, although Calouste felt it was high time the forty-two-year-old Vahan began 'to earn a decent living and render himself useful in the community'.[64] From now on both brothers wrote only when there was a delay in payment or when they wanted a raise in their allowance, and even then they corresponded (as per instructions) not with their elder brother, but with Calouste's secretary.

With the end of hostilities, Calouste's more distant relatives re-established contact. In 1920 Calouste received a letter from his cousin Parsegh's daughter Matilda, in which she described how in July 1915 the Turks rounded up 1,200 Ottoman Armenian men and boys in Angora (Ankara), marched them to the edge of town and there shot them. Matilda herself had been transported to Konya, where friends managed to hide her. The rest of the womenfolk were sent on a death march to Deir ez-Zor.[65]

Another cousin, Roupen Selian, had been in Mersin, taking care of the Gulbenkian farms at Guerdan and Dikilitash, when war broke out. Five years on, Roupen wrote from Aleppo. He had managed to avoid deportation to 'the killing places', first by hiding in Mersin and then by fleeing to Birecik, near the Syrian border. Thanks to his engineering skills, Turkish officers spared his life, putting him to work organising the manufacture of limbers for artillery. When the British Army came, they set him to repairing roads. Now it was time to get back to business: 'If you have any friend at Manchester who sends one steamer full of Manchester good[s] between Beirouth and Mersina, no doubt it will be sold to very good prices, and steamer can take back goods which will bring just as good as the imported goods.'[66] While Calouste was relieved to hear that his cousin was still alive, Roupen's proposition must have seemed positively quaint, a throwback to his father's way of doing business.

With the collapse of the Ottoman Empire it had become much safer for Armenian *amiras* like Boghos Nubar to use their wealth and influence in the service of the Armenian cause, whether that was by raising funds to arm Armenian forces or by making representations to diplomats at Versailles. Unfortunately, the Armenians struggled to speak with one voice, with two Armenian delegations: one, the Délégation Nationale Arménienne, associated with western Armenians and the other, the Délégation de la République Arménienne, associated with eastern Armenians and the Armenian Republic, declared at Yerevan in 1919.[67]

Gulbenkian and the leader of the Délégation Nationale Arménienne, Boghos Nubar, did not agree on how to respond to the Armenian crisis. Gulbenkian's focus was economic. He assisted with plans for a new National Bank of Armenia.[68] He proposed forming an 'Armenian Repatriation and Reconstruction Committee', looking to encourage British inward investment in the region and to fund the return of ethnic Armenian refugees. Boghos, by contrast, wanted to fund an Armenian army to defend the republic against the Turks and the Russians.[69] Gulbenkian grew frustrated with 'inefficient, uneconomical and unbusinesslike' Armenian philanthropy, which he felt was more interested in issuing propaganda than offering practical assistance.[70] Many fellow Armenians expected Gulbenkian to be their community's equivalent of the Ottoman Greek arms dealer Basil Zaharoff – that is, they expected Gulbenkian to bankroll an independent Armenia the same way Zaharoff had bankrolled Greece. Coming as he did from a great Armenian family, the role was Gulbenkian's birthright. 'No individual should refrain from action when the good of the Nation is at stake,' wrote the Armenian patriarch of Istanbul, 'but in your case the responsibility is greater. The very name "Gulbenkian" is both trust-worthy and trust-building for our Nation.'[71]

Gulbenkian continued to give generously and regularly to a wide range of philanthropic causes: American, Dutch, French and British as well as Armenian. When asked to contribute towards a new Armenian church in London, he volunteered to pay for the entire church himself and establish an endowment to pay for the priest's salary. Designed by Charles Mewès and dedicated by Calouste 'to the everlasting memory of his beloved parents', St Sarkis was built in Iverna Gardens, near Kensington High Street. It was consecrated in 1923, in a ceremony recorded by a Pathé film crew. The church's chief fundraiser and first *vardapet* (celibate priest), Abel Nazarian, repaid Gulbenkian's generosity by eloping to Paris with the wife of his cousin, Nerses Gulbenkian. Nazarian travelled to Moscow and joined the Cheka (secret police), who gratefully accepted his offer to work for them in Yerevan, 'liberating the masses' from the grip of the same Church which had recently defrocked him.[72]

The dream of an Armenian sovereign state, something last seen in 1375, proved short-lived. 'Red' Soviet forces pushed south, driving White Russian forces out of Ukraine and picking off the divided Caucasian republics, nationalising the oilfields of Grozny and Baku for good measure. As noted above, they then turned to Persia. Caught between this Red Army and the Kemalists, the forces of the Armenian Republic stood little chance. The Soviets entered Yerevan in November 1920, and the republic signed a peace treaty with Turkey in December, accepting the loss of territory including Mount Ararat, where the Armenians' forebears had, so the legend ran, first disembarked from the Ark. These territories had been promised to the Armenians just a few months earlier by the Treaty of Sèvres. In 1922 Armenia was bundled with Georgia and Azerbaijan into the Transcaucasian Socialist Federative Soviet Republic, and remained under Soviet control until 1991.

As for President Wilson's proposed 'Greater Armenia' to the west, in

May 1920 the US Senate refused to accept a League of Nations mandate over it. Hopes of a sovereign Armenian national home vanished for the remainder of Gulbenkian's lifetime, or rather were invested in turf wars between the Dashnak and Hnchak parties. In addition to targeting each other, Dashnaks and Hnchaks assassinated ex-Ottoman Turkish officials they held responsible for the genocide. Gulbenkian's cousin Gullabi was gunned down outside his Broadway carpet showroom, presumably for having failed to making his 'patriotic' contribution to one or other party. In the face of all these events Gulbenkian remained unmoved.[73]

NINE

OPEN DOOR, CLOSE RANKS, 1921–3

In 1921 steps were finally taken to revive TPC, which Gulbenkian had struggled to keep ticking over since 1914. The 1914 Foreign Office Agreement had assigned Anglo-Persian 50 per cent, Royal Dutch-Shell 25 per cent and Deutsche Bank 25 per cent. Anglo-Persian finally took up its shares, and appointed one of its own, Henry Nichols, managing director. Under the Foreign Office agreement Gulbenkian's 5 per cent share was carried jointly by Anglo-Persian and Royal Dutch-Shell. As this was a personal rather than a corporate interest, however, it was unclear if these shares would have to be sold to his TPC partners on his death. Under the company's Articles of Association, any shareholder wishing to sell had to give the others first refusal. In July 1921 Gulbenkian persuaded Nichols and Deterding to waive their right to exercise this purchase option on Gulbenkian's death.[1] This was a decision Anglo-Persian and Royal Dutch-Shell later forgot having made, a decision they came to regret.[2]

Under the terms of the (secret) Anglo-French oil agreement signed at San Remo, Deutsche Bank's sequestered 25 per cent shareholding was to be sold to the French. Gulbenkian had been grooming the French on Royal Dutch-Shell's behalf for almost ten years now, and had created a company, SEP, intended to take the TPC shares. In July 1922 the British ambassador urged prime minister Raymond Poincaré to nominate a company to receive these shares. Yet the French government did not do so until 1924.[3]

Poincaré and his predecessor Aristide Briand had apparently taken a dislike to Gulbenkian, fed up with bumping into him in the corridors of the Quai d'Orsay. Briand even queried whether TPC had a valid concession in Iraq.[4] After 1920 (when Poincaré became president) Gulbenkian was short of allies to make his case. Bérenger was pushed off the Commissariat Général aux Essences. Gulbenkian found a more than satisfactory replacement in the secretary-general of the French Foreign Ministry, Philippe Berthelot. Berthelot was disgraced in the 1921 crisis surrounding the Banque Industrielle de Chine (BIC), however, exposed as having abused his position to issue statements denying that BIC (led by his brother, André) was on the verge of bankruptcy.[5] Although Gulbenkian still had influence at the Finance Ministry, for the French the BIC scandal only lessened the appeal of an alliance with Royal Dutch-Shell.[6]

Gulbenkian felt uncomfortable playing on his contribution to France's war effort, performed 'with the object of rendering an affectionate service to France'.[7] It was hardly chic to be seen seeking a quid pro quo. Yet the longer the French waited, the more opportunity there would be for the Americans to intervene, causing 'difficulties and diplomatic shilly-shally which will ultimately be to our serious disadvantage'.[8] The US State Department's principled stand against cartels like TPC encouraged both the Standard Oil companies and the French to toy with alternative schemes, encouraged by a resurgent Turkish regime. The Franklin–Bouillon Agreement, which had seen the French cosy up with Kemal in 1921, had, Gulbenkian knew, been 'lubricated' by the Standard companies.[9] The French hoped to reap a 'moral reward' of American goodwill, something which might be traded for access to any new regions the Americans secured through their famous 'Open Door'.[10] It was a case of trying to keep this door open without losing any benefits to be derived from the 1920 San Remo Agreement, which committed the French to collaborating with the British.

Turkish Typists at the Beaurivage

From Gulbenkian's perspective, the Lausanne Conference that opened in November 1922 was a colossal inconvenience. Royal Dutch-Shell had refused to reduce its 25 per cent to make room for any new TPC partners, proposing that Anglo-Persian's 50 per cent be cut in half to allow a four-way split: 25 per cent each to Anglo-Persian, Royal Dutch-Shell, the

French and the Americans.[11] Gulbenkian welcomed this idea. Unfortunately, the conference put negotiations for French and American entry to TPC on hold, as all sides waited 'to see which way the cat would jump' (to use one of Gulbenkian's favourite phrases). Events in Anatolia had changed the balance of power in the Near East, necessitating a new diplomatic settlement. The 1920 Treaty of Sèvres, signed by a vestigial Ottoman Empire, was a dead letter.

Under Kemal's leadership, Turkish Nationalists had repelled a Greek invasion in the west, established a new National Assembly at Ankara, humiliated the French in Cilicia and restored the old 1878 border in the east, making friends with the Soviets and cutting the Republic of Armenia in half. Their brinkmanship over the Dardanelles Straits (placed under international administration in the Treaty of Sèvres) helped push Lloyd George out of office in the crisis over Çanakkale (Chanak) in October 1922. Now the Turks wanted Mosul. They also wanted TPC stripped of any rights it claimed under the 1914 *Lettre Vizirielle* – that is, the Sultan's promise to award the oil concession for the *vilayets* of Mosul and Baghdad to TPC.

At Lausanne, the *Daily News* reported, the world's leading oilmen haunted the corridors of the Hotel Beaurivage, disguised as Turkish typists.[12] The 'typists' and the diplomats were in turn pursued by financial soldiers of fortune with questionable claims to Turkey's oil lands, some built on the abortive 1909 Chester Concession, others on rights claimed by various heirs of Sultan Abdülhamid II. While the American government initially viewed them as diplomatically useful, Gulbenkian had no time for such 'Yankee charlatans'.[13] He was acutely embarrassed when it emerged that one of these speculative syndicates included his own cousin, Nevarte's brother Yervant Essayan.[14]

Gulbenkian did not attend Lausanne, but could still draw on his links to the former Young Turk Finance Minister, Cavid Bey, who was part of the Turkish delegation. In January 1923 Cavid contacted Gulbenkian from Lausanne, seeking to consult him regarding Mosul. Ismet (head of the Turkish delegation and future prime minister) had demanded Mosul early on in the conference, meeting with firm resistance from Curzon, who argued that it belonged to Iraq solely on grounds of geography. Pushing the border south would deprive Iraq of natural mountain defences. Further diplomatic notes were exchanged. Curzon proposed to put the matter to the League of Nations for arbitration; Kemal considered invasion.[15] Cavid asked Gulbenkian if Curzon might let Turkey have Mosul if the Turkish government promised to give TPC the Mosul concession. Gulbenkian's reply was cagey: he was not qualified to offer a view, he insisted, being 'a very bad politician'. Instead Gulbenkian asked Cavid what kind of terms Ankara might offer TPC. Cavid replied gnomically that Gulbenkian already knew the answer to his own question. Clearly the pair no longer trusted each other and the discussion hit a dead end.[16]

As no one was able to reach a settlement, the Mosul question would be referred to the League of Nations. British influence at Geneva was strong enough to make a favourable (to TPC) settlement likely. For the American diplomats in attendance at Lausanne, Richard Child and Joseph Grew, Ismet's attempt to stand up to Curzon over this Mosul question had been a disappointment: 'It was a Greek temple against a dish of scrambled eggs.' They encouraged Ismet to resist attempts to insert a clause mentioning TPC in the treaty. This time Ismet succeeded, despite 'treatment which would make the third degree in a Harlem police station seem like a club dinner'. Though these American diplomats denied that oil had played any part in their thinking, after Lausanne it was difficult to imagine how TPC would be able to proceed without an American participation.[17] Feeling himself betrayed by both the French and the Americans, Curzon was disgusted. 'The end of the Lausanne Conference is indeed a sordid anti-climax', agreed one British diplomat, 'squabbling over money and rights of capitalists, with an America fouled by oil in the background and the spirit of an insolently triumphant Angora government over all.'[18]

In Washington Congress had been spooked by US Secretary of the Interior Franklin Lane's claim that US oil reserves would run out in 1937, leaving American consumers at the mercy of the British.[19] The publication of the secret 1920 San Remo Agreement by *Le Temps* on 25 July fuelled suspicions of a vast British conspiracy to corner the world's oil.[20] It was therefore unsurprising that the State Department contended that TPC had no *droits acquis* – diplomatic argot used to denote rights acquired before hostilities began.[21]

The only way to stop the Americans upsetting TPC, it seemed, was to bring them inside. This was preferable to having the Americans try to enter Mesopotamia alone. Happily, the State Department was privately inclined to such a solution, recognising how little diplomatic heft they had in the region, as well as the potential of American concession-hunters to embarrass them.[22] Sir John Cadman encouraged the Americans to view TPC as an opportunity, rather than a threat. Cadman had recently resigned from the Petroleum Executive to become technical adviser to Anglo-Persian, the firm he would later lead. His goodwill tour of the United States in 1921 scotched rumours of a British 'Petroleum Octopus'. Soon Anglo-Persian and Jersey Standard reached an agreement: they would work together in north Persia, while in Mesopotamia Jersey would stop undermining TPC's claims, in return for a participation.[23] The size of this American participation, however, was yet to be determined.

Melodramatic Cutthroats

Central to the deliberations at Lausanne had been the relationship between the new Turkish and the old Ottoman regimes, and whether the financial obligations entered into by the *ancien régime* should be honoured by the new. Similar questions were raised, albeit with regard to Russia, at the Genoa Conference of 1922. This conference would, it was hoped, reach a basis for economic cooperation with the Bolshevik regime in Russia, one that would satisfy holders of Tsarist-era debt and investors in expropriated industries. The Soviet regime had yet to be officially recognised by Britain, France or any other major power. Yet it acknowledged a role for western capital and technology under Lenin's New Economic Policy, as part of the proposed mixed economy of public and private enterprises.

Other than matches, Old Master paintings and various ores, petroleum was the only thing the Russians could sell in return for the tractors, turbines and other items they urgently needed. From 1921 to 1932 Gulbenkian would help the Russians to export them all: petroleum from Grozny, Rembrandts from the Hermitage, gold from Lake Baikal, lead and zinc from Siberia's Pacific Rim – everything but the matches. Accusations that such goods were 'stolen' from pre-Revolutionary proprietors, produced by slave labour or 'dumped' on western markets to undermine capitalism could not be ignored. At Genoa the People's Commissar for Foreign Affairs, Georgy Chicherin, and Commissar for Foreign Trade Leonid Krasin appeared 'dressed in a quite incongruous manner', like 'real melodramatic cutthroats' straight out of *Babes in the Wood*.[24] Patronised by other delegates, the commissars continued their policy of setting the powers against each other by signing bilateral agreements, this time with

Germany. Krasin dangled tempting deals in front of Anglo-Persian, Jersey Standard and Royal Dutch-Shell, deftly sowing mutual suspicion.[25]

At home the Russian state oil agency, Neftsyndikat, struggled to impose a coherent oil policy. Nationalisation of the oil industry secured the Soviet regime a vast array of equipment and infrastructure, the legacy of more than forty years of largely foreign investment, not to mention the oil sitting in tank farms or underground. But the circuitry was unsuited to central control. Even worse, the managers who understood how it worked had fled or been killed. Many facilities in the Caucasus had been damaged in the course of the Russian Civil War.

The system could not simply be repaired and reprogrammed. New investment and new technology were needed, both of which were in short supply, as well as the authority to command the managers of an equally confusing array of new state agencies with offices thousands of miles apart, in London, Baku or Vladivostok: foreign trade delegations (such as Arkos in Britain), central storage (Vato) and pipeline entities, as well as production entities, organised geographically (Grozneft for Grozny, Embaneft for Emba, and so on), each of them keen to strike its own deals. Indeed, Azneft and Grozneft had both established competing sales offices abroad.[26] With a staff of just fifteen, Neftsyndikat struggled to maintain control.

As its Berlin representative wrote in October 1922, Neftsyndikat suffered from a big disadvantage in not having a distribution and marketing network in western Europe. With the exception of Russian Oil Products in Britain, it had no way to sell direct to the consumer, so had to choose between selling to firms who did, or not selling at all. As almost every firm was tied to either Royal Dutch-Shell or Jersey Standard, its options were further limited. To use Russian supplies to create a third oil giant was possible, but would require a lot of financing.[27] In 1922 this option was unthinkable. Five years later, Gulbenkian would set about making it happen.

For those like Royal Dutch-Shell who were too financially committed to Russia to sell out, the reputational risk of striking deals with the Soviets was more than balanced by the fact that Jersey Standard was already doing it.[28] The prize was to make oneself the sole channel by which Russian oil products reached foreign markets. There was also the prospect of exploiting oilfields which had not been sold or leased before, and of financing a much-discussed pipeline from Grozny to Novorossisk – and getting repaid in oil. 'Stolen' oil looked and smelled the same as the regular kind. The 'thieves' would always find someone in the West willing to buy.

Deterding took a two-pronged approach to Russia. On the one hand, he sought to secure control of all the Caucasian oil companies he could and establish a lobby group (the 'united front' or Front Uni) so that the expropriated interests spoke with one voice. On the other, he negotiated directly with the Soviet authorities, trying to prevent supplies going to Jersey Standard, even if this necessitated Royal Dutch-Shell buying 'stolen' oil itself. Gulbenkian and his associates, including Nubar, were key to the first prong in 1921–3, buying controlling stakes in yet more Russian firms with fields around Grozny.[29]

Cash today when tomorrow seemed so uncertain certainly appealed to Alexander Mantashev's heirs, propping up the White Russians' favourite bars in Paris.[30] Gulbenkian's intermediary with them and other Russians was a fellow Armenian, yet another exile from Soviet Russia, named Moïse Adjemoff. A lawyer who had sat in the Russian duma as a member of the Constitutional Liberal (or Kadet) Party, representing the Don Cossacks, Adjemoff arrived in Paris in 1918. In 1919 he sought French assistance for the provisional government the Kadets led in the Crimea.[31] A physically small man, by Nubar's account Adjemoff 'knew how to play on people's weaknesses', and used this to secure a hold on Calouste, Deterding and Nubar himself. Adjemoff introduced Deterding to a series of aristocratic fellow exiles, who included Lydia Koudoyaroff, who became Deterding's second wife in December 1924.

Adjemoff led the twenty-two-year-old Nubar astray in the fleshpots of Paris, much enlivened by White Russians wildly splurging on whatever their pawned jewels, defunct noble titles or questionable oil shares could get them by way of cash or credit.[32] For both Nubar and his sister, Rita, now eighteen, the self-indulgent sentiment of *après moi le déluge* was novel. It was not what was being consumed, but how. There was champagne and caviar at 27 Quai d'Orsay, their Paris home. But here such luxuries were enjoyed without the constant reckoning of the sort Calouste demanded: what Rita called 'your "spare time game" of comparing the different [accounts] rendered by the different members of the family!'[33] It was Rita's and Nubar's first taste of hedonism. Both were enthralled by the experience.

Two Weddings

Calouste sought to tame his children by marrying them off. Rita and Kevork Essayan wed in 1920. Kevork was the son of Nevarte's cousin Vahan, and the twenty-three-year-old grandson of the impecunious Meguerditch, who had sued Gulbenkian back in 1910. Quiet, self-effacing and with little experience of life outside Istanbul, 'Kev' soon became a fixture of the London office: a reliable drudge set to work keeping the books on £100 (£3,600) a month.[34] Later on his familiarity with Armenian made him useful in fielding begging letters from the Church or self-styled 'cousins' in need.[35] The marriage was not a love match.

Nubar eluded his father's matchmaking efforts, becoming engaged in May 1920 to a Cuban Roman Catholic *oddar* (Armenian for 'non-Armenian'): Herminia Elena Josefa Maximina de Feijóo. Both sets of parents disapproved. Parental consent being required in the case of children under thirty, there was no question of a marriage taking place in France. When Nubar began showing signs of nervous strain, it was decided that he should be sent to Egypt to recover, and hopefully forget Herminia. After his uncle Yervant refused, the task of accompanying Nubar fell to a friend from university, George Ansley, scion of the Ansbacher banking family.[36]

A few days after arriving in Cairo (having transferred 1.5 million francs' worth of securities into Herminia's name en route, at her insistence) Nubar suffered a fit, during which he threatened Ansley with a loaded revolver. The pair returned to Paris in January 1921, whereupon Calouste informed his son that 'relations of father and son had ceased'.[37] Nubar began working as an independent concession-hunter, apparently earning enough money to satisfy Herminia – who threatened to break off the engagement unless he gave her another $500,000 – but not really knuckling down to any fixed employment.

As Cambridge undergraduates, Ansley and Nubar had revelled in student jinks, pursuing Gaiety Girls on regular jaunts to London. Both ended up with second-class honours degrees in Law.[38] Now Ansley urged his friend to leave his 'unhealthy life' behind and 'go and do some work', warning Nubar that his 'natural qualities and inherent ability [were] slowly but surely dwindling away', to the extent that 'unless you pull yourself together there can be only one end the gutter'. Nubar had found George 'a bit pompous at times at Cambridge', and does not seem to have paid much heed.[39] Herminia and Nubar married in a register office in Westminster in March 1922, suffering a serious road accident near Lisieux on the way back from their honeymoon. As Nubar later noted, 'There have been more auspicious beginnings to a marriage.' The shock of reading about the crash in the newspapers did, however, jolt Calouste into re-establishing contact with his prodigal son.[40]

Ever since Nubar was a child his father had preached the value of 'independence'. As his sister, Rita, jealously noted, Nubar had been given a range of experiences and responsibilities far earlier than other boys of his rank. In his teens he was entrusted with carrying (and accounting for) large sums of money, for example, and occasionally sent abroad on his father's business. After Nubar left the University of Bonn (where he had been the youngest-ever undergraduate), Calouste had toyed with the idea of sending his eighteen-year-old son up to Glasgow, to work for North British Diesel, a factory he and Lane had established to produce marine engines under licence from Krupp. Alternatively, he suggested, Nubar might research a dissertation on solar or tide power.

Whatever Nubar ended up doing, the aim was not to punish him but to encourage him to 'make his own way and be dependent upon his merits'.[41] Yet Calouste had failed to practise what he preached. Nubar's accounts were rechecked by his father, he was peppered with countless letters of paternal advice and told whom he could and could not marry. After his Cambridge studies, Nubar was set to work in his father's office, rather than being pushed out to make his own way in the world.

In 1922 it seemed that all this might change. Though reconciled, Calouste was still not prepared to have Nubar work directly for him, and instead arranged with Deterding for Nubar to work in the London offices of Royal Dutch-Shell. Deterding made Nubar secretary to the Front Uni, giving him a front-row seat at its occasionally tempestuous meetings. Encouraged by his second wife, Deterding had become a fire-breathing anti-communist, insisting that the Front Uni's oil embargo would acceler-ate the inevitable collapse of the Soviet regime. Yet Deterding also bought oil from the Soviets, claiming he did so to prevent the oil being sold to others. Front Uni members wondered if Deterding was really fighting their corner or wrapping them in a pretty bow before selling them out to his new friends in Moscow.[42]

At Royal Dutch-Shell Nubar was paid a salary, freed at last from financial dependence on an allowance from his father. He experienced a side of the oil industry his father knew little about. Apart from a short visit to Baku in 1888, Calouste had no first-hand experience of oil exploration or field operations. Nubar accompanied Deterding on an important American tour in late 1923. After discussing Russian matters with Jersey Standard at their New York headquarters, the pair travelled to Texas and on into Mexico, inspecting Royal Dutch-Shell fields and installations at Tampico. On the way back they stayed with Jersey president Walter Teagle at his massive quail-hunting estate in Florida. Nubar got to know several American oil executives who had never met Gulbenkian senior. At twenty-six, he was beginning to emerge from his father's shadow.

TEN

THE END OF THE AFFAIR, 1924–6

As one of his staff later recalled, Gulbenkian's health was 'one of his greatest and most constant preoccupations'. He followed a strict dietary regimen: plenty of fruit and raw vegetables, malt extract, unrefined sugar, curds. Though he was constantly moving from one hotel to another, his valet always carried a wide range of lotions, gargles, creams, powders, salts, oils and pills. Even when his health was good he still medicated himself, 'to stimulate appetite, to aid digestion, to ward off disease or other illnesses'.[1] Nevarte, Nubar, Rita, Deterding and even secretarial staff like David Young received a barrage of unsolicited instructions and advice on how to take proper care of themselves – or were simply given orders to visit Dr Mahokian or one of the many other doctors Gulbenkian patronised, in order to have suspicious symptoms checked out, at Gulbenkian's own expense.

As a young man in 1890s London Gulbenkian had regularly ridden in Hyde Park and even took the odd fencing lesson. He forbade Nubar games at Harrow, however, and constantly fretted over Nubar's and Deterding's fondness for point-to-points. Fox-hunting was a reckless indulgence, its snobbish appeal no excuse for self-endangerment. When Deterding broke his pelvis in a riding accident in February 1923, therefore, Gulbenkian was deeply shaken. The accident occurred at Deterding's country estate near Melton Mowbray, Leicestershire, where he now spent every spare moment he could on horseback. Should the two halves of Deterding's pelvis be wired together or simply left alone? Gulbenkian discussed the options with Deterding's brother (a doctor) and Deterding himself. Rather than worrying about Royal Dutch-Shell, Deterding's main concern was that he might only be allowed to hunt two days a week, instead of his usual six. He nonetheless welcomed Gulbenkian writing to him about business matters, and he soon had Waley Cohen on hand to deal with routine affairs. Waley Cohen, however, could not be trusted with handling one piece of unfinished business.

At the time of the accident Deterding had been on the verge of cutting ties with his mistress, a certain 'Countess W.' 'W.'s letters to Deterding increasingly combined declarations of affection with demands for money. 'All she wants is continually money and sentimentality and rhino goes [*sic*] badly together,' Deterding observed. 'I felt I had become or was likely to become a sort of preferred stock yielding good dividen[d]s.'[2] The metaphor and the City slang ('rhino' meaning cash) harked back to the good old days of Frederick Lane, before the war. Deterding forwarded 'W.'s letters to Gulbenkian, who agreed to pay her off. And that was that.

Another piece of unfinished business proved to be less easily resolved. This concerned a sale contract between a Royal Dutch-Shell company and yet another major American oil company that Gulbenkian had helped it acquire back in 1913: Venezuelan Oil Concessions. Over the next two years disagreement regarding the terms of this contract continued to fester, before erupting in early 1926 into a very public contest for control of the company. The stakes were high, in more ways than one. Venezuela was now the third-largest oil producer in the world and VOC controlled just under half of the country's output.[3] The crisis had a profound personal and professional impact on both Calouste and Nubar.

Yo, Ho, Ho, and Another Barrel of Oil

The contract between VOC and the Royal Dutch-Shell company BPM had been made back in 1920, at a point when Deterding had taken a six-month sabbatical to recover from overwork. Under it BPM was appointed to manage VOC. VOC agreed to sell its crude to BPM on terms which were, Gulbenkian observed in 1923:

a model of greed and squeeze. Under the cloak of purchasing 1000 barrels per day, the [Royal Dutch-Shell] Combine gets hold of the VOC by the throat and, at a FIXED PRICE OF FIFTY CENTS PER BARREL gives unto itself the option of buying any production the VOC may have. So, if the market price goes up the Combine can buy 100,000 barrels a day; if the price goes down, it is only bound to take 1000 barrels a day ... [the deal] reminds me of an old English pirates song 'Yo, Ho, Ho, and another bottle of rum' though in this case the appropriate rendering would be: 'Yo, ho, ho, and another barrel of oil.'[4]

Another contract between VOC and Eagle Transport, the shipping arm of Águila, saw VOC being charged above-market rates for transport of its crude.

Although these were sweetheart deals for BPM, the contract bound VOC for twenty-one years in a fashion harmful to VOC's minority shareholders, who included Gulbenkian and General Aranguren (the original concessionaire). As described in Chapter 7, Gulbenkian had managed Royal Dutch-Shell's relations with Aranguren and kept an eye on various court cases which saw VOC's concession challenged, as well as running share pools.[5] Gulbenkian was once again concerned that these issues had watered VOC's capital, which had been raised from £225,000 to £3.1 million.[6] Privately he suspected Deterding of plotting to drive down the share price so that Royal Dutch-Shell could buy the minority holders out cheap.

Alongside VOC, Gulbenkian had also brought Royal Dutch-Shell control of another firm with valuable concessions in Venezuela: Colón Development Company. Together Colón and VOC had Venezuela's most promising oilfields around Lake Maracaibo and in Zulia State sewn up. In the early 1920s the country's president, Gómez, and Jersey Standard sought to break Royal Dutch-Shell's grip. A reforming minister of development, Gumersindo Torres, introduced a series of new oil laws intended to limit squatting, create a national reserve and prevent the flipping of concessions by speculators. In April 1920 Jersey Standard offered both Gómez and Torres $1.3 million each in return for allowing them to survey plots held by VOC and Colón.[7] Royal Dutch-Shell paid 10 million Bolívars to have its concessions confirmed. By 1928 Royal Dutch-Shell's near-monopoly had become a duopoly: together Royal Dutch-Shell and Jersey Standard controlled 92 per cent of the country's production.[8]

On 14 December 1922 a well that had been abandoned in 1918, Barroso

No. 2, suddenly became a gusher, running out of control for ten days. Whereas VOC had previously made little or no profit, the situation had now changed radically, bringing the unfavourable nature of the 1920 contract into focus as never before. In May 1923 Royal Dutch-Shell's Andrew Agnew agreed as president of VOC's board to commission a report on the contracts from the parent company's legal counsel, H. van Blommestein. The report was favourable to Gulbenkian's position, yet Deterding refused to share it with Gulbenkian, insisting that 'it is all nonsense and it is misleading'.[9]

Gulbenkian was, as ever, caught between his fellow minority shareholders and the Royal Dutch-Shell Group. As he wrote in his reply to Deterding, 'All I have been doing is simpl[y] to soothe the feelings of dissenting shareholders and to press matters forward with [the company] on the other hand.' He made yet another appeal to Deterding to focus his attention on the relevant paperwork and reach his own conclusions. Deterding grew impatient with his friend's appeals to this other Deterding, 'a supreme judge, unbiased and uninfluenced ... [with] the big wig and the Ermine Robe'.[10]

After his accident Deterding had been perfectly willing to concede to Gulbenkian that 'circumstances are so totally different to what they were at the time of the action' (that is, the signing of the contract). Yet he did nothing to revise the contract.[11] Deterding was annoyed by Gulbenkian's ambivalent position as financier-cum-'oilman'. On the one hand Gulbenkian accused Royal Dutch-Shell of failing to run VOC profitably, and on the other he refused to take his 5 per cent of TPC production in crude, on the basis that he was 'a financier and not an Oil man and would not know how to get the best price for his Oil. This is what one would call trying to have it both ways, which is really at the bottom of all the disputes with Mr Gulbenkian of late.'[12]

Things might have turned out differently had Gulbenkian had any other allies in Royal Dutch-Shell. Had Cowans not died in 1921, he might have served as peacemaker. To directors like Hendrikus Colijn and August Philips, who had not been around in the very early days, the Gulbenkian–Deterding relationship was problematic. Time and time again Gulbenkian had to remind them of commissions or participatory interests Deterding had granted him without Deterding taking proper notes. Naturally these managers queried the matter with Deterding, who almost always confirmed Gulbenkian's account of what they had agreed.

Such questions often touched on the sensitive yet still obscure connection between Chairman Deterding, who acted on behalf of Royal Dutch-Shell, and the other Deterding, the private investor, who had, like Lane and of course Gulbenkian, made deals on his own individual account. These deals served as unpleasant reminders of the swashbuckling pace at which Deterding had expanded the company, a legacy which continued to make it almost impossible to establish how much money they were actually making. While Deterding was making noises about his own retirement, here was a near-contemporary, Gulbenkian, with no intention of retiring.

In 1918, at the height of their friendship, Deterding had been willing to discuss his own character, its strengths and flaws. Although his accident rewound the clock to some extent, if the episode served to remind him of how much he stood to lose by alienating Gulbenkian, he either forgot the lesson or concluded that he had overcommitted himself. The Gulbenkian–Deterding relationship had been close, but also somewhat one-sided: apart from his claims to be 'more of a poet and dreamer than a maker of memoranda' (which belied his relentless eye for detail), the former did not reveal much of his own inner character. Gulbenkian's obeisances to Deterding's sense of justice may not have been as self-effacing as they initially appear. Gulbenkian's admiration for and friendship with Deterding were nonetheless genuine. 'You are my only friend,' Gulbenkian wrote, 'besides the old tutor of my son [Devgantz] whom you know.'[13] Gulbenkian's decision to push the dispute into the open was not lightly taken.

Having exhausted other options, in early 1926 Gulbenkian prepared to confront VOC's management at the next shareholder meeting. He joined forces with brokers Cull & Co. (in London) and Fray (in Paris) in gathering as many VOC shareholder votes and proxies as they could, intending to demand that the firm spend £1 million building up its own ocean terminal and shipping facilities. In the meantime he wanted the BPM and Eagle Transport contracts revised, so as to free VOC to find a more competitive rate for shipping, as well as better terms for its oil. Such a proxy battle had been seriously considered in 1923 and 1924, but Gulbenkian had been restrained by a friend, the mining magnate Alfred Chester Beatty, and Hermann Marx of Cull & Co.[14] Like his father, Nubar was frustrated by the willingness of Marx and Beatty, as well as Cowdray, to be bullied by Deterding. 'All your people get very weak at the knees when they get sworn at by Deterding,' he wrote to his father, 'and need someone of whom they are even more frightened, i.e. <u>you</u>, to keep them straight.'[15]

Now Gulbenkian and his allies went all out, including a press campaign. The opposition was gearing up as well. From Paris Gulbenkian's assistant, D. H. Young, reported that Royal Dutch-Shell's London office had sent over 'a special Director ... for the purpose of getting votes', a sign that 'they are treating this in the same way as political candidates treat voting'. Rather than trying to get letters published in *The Times* and issuing pamphlets, Young urged Gulbenkian to hire their own 'propagandist': 'VERY FEW people will bother to read a pamphlet,' he noted, whereas 'when you get the ear of a person and talk properly it's 95% success'.[16] The best Gulbenkian and his allies could expect, however, was to get their proposals put to a vote. It was unlikely that they would win, as Royal Dutch-Shell could flood the room with a crowd of clerks to whom small qualifying packets of shares had been transferred. 'This kind of thing is often done in rotten companies where the directors expect trouble,' Gulbenkian noted.[17]

'Oil Feud in the City: Sensational Meeting Anticipated' ran the headline in the *Daily Express*, describing Gulbenkian as 'a man of mystery'. 'He has long posed as a great inscrutable figure, ever in the background, exercising enormous influence on the world's oil market. When Mexican Eagles or Royal Dutch rise or slump the stock exchanges ask "What is Gulbenkian doing?"' After three and a half hours of 'heated argument' (during which Marcus Samuel stated that his honour was being impugned), Royal Dutch-Shell won the vote convincingly.[18] Waley Cohen was cock-a-hoop: 'In the whole history of great affairs in the City I do not think there has ever been a finer story than that ... of the way in which the Shell Co. has acted towards the V. O. C.,' he wrote to Lionel de Rothschild, 'and guided it to its present sound position, notwithstanding the hampering disturbances of Gulbenkian and his soviets.'[19] The London financial press criticised Royal Dutch-Shell for giving its shareholders 'the barest of reports and the baldest of accounts', but preferred to trust them rather than the minority which, they noted, was 'not composed of practical oil experts'.[20] Defeated, Gulbenkian and his allies resigned from the board of VOC. A few months later Gulbenkian resigned from Águila as well. He had had enough of the Pearsons' failure to stand up to Royal Dutch-Shell (Pearson held a larger stake in Águila than Royal Dutch-Shell did).[21]

As the authoritative history of Royal Dutch-Shell notes, Gulbenkian had been a 'constant source of creative schemes and new opportunities' for more than twenty years. Though he was now fifty-seven, there were plenty of 'schemes' still in his head. Now, thanks to the VOC dispute, Royal Dutch-Shell had 'acquired a powerful enemy'.[22] Over the following years the world's press built up what might otherwise seem a minor disagreement into an epic feud, adding the unfounded claim that Gulbenkian and Deterding had been rivals for the hand of Lydia Koudoyaroff. While Gulbenkian had been a good friend to Deterding's deceased first wife, Katherina Neubronner, there is no evidence that he knew Lydia, who clearly resented Gulbenkian's relationship with her husband.[23] With Lydia's help, 'Bolshevik thieves' and 'Gulbenkians' fused into a single obsession in Deterding's increasingly paranoid mind – and in his correspondence with colleagues. When asked about the relationship after Deterding's death, however, Lydia Deterding claimed that her husband had never mentioned Gulbenkian's name.[24]

The Crown Prince

At twenty-seven Nubar was earning a hefty £3,000 (£154,000) a year working for Royal Dutch-Shell and seemed to have a glittering career ahead of him. He knew that he could count on his father's support and so was able to stand firm in the face of Deterding's explosive temper in a way few of his colleagues dared. In December 1925, however, it all fell apart: when Nubar refused orders to head up Royal Dutch-Shell's Spanish operations Deterding blew up, dismissing him on the spot.[25]

In a parting letter to his employer, Nubar wrote that the way Deterding had 'used' him was 'scandalously unfair'. He claimed to have been warned at the start that he had been hired with malice aforethought: the plan supposedly was for Nubar to replace his father on the boards of the various Royal Dutch-Shell firms; once in place Nubar himself would be dismissed, thus ridding the company of meddling from either Gulbenkian. 'You also threatened me that you would do your utmost to prevent my obtaining my means of livelihood elsewhere.' This last accusation was fair. Jersey Standard's European chief, Heinrich Riedemann, had got to know Nubar well during the American trip and jokingly referred to him as 'the Crown Prince'. Within hours of Nubar's dismissal he wrote Nubar a curiously stilted letter informing him that 'if the impossible should happen and you should break with Sir Henri, you could not work with the Standard'.[26]

In October 1925 Nubar had indeed taken his father's place on the

boards of several Royal Dutch-Shell-controlled companies. He now submitted letters of resignation to Tampico Panuco, Geconsolideerde, Astra
Romana, Jupiter and Nafta.[27] Were the rumours of a Machiavellian plot on
the part of Deterding correct, therefore? Or did this step suit his father,
who avoided attending board meetings whenever possible? The vehe-
mence of Deterding's denial is suggestive: not only did he deny any plot,
he vowed to dismiss any other employee who repeated the accusation.[28]

On the other hand, if Nubar's rise within Royal Dutch-Shell was to
continue it was natural to expect him to accept a foreign posting, where
he might prove himself capable of handling greater individual responsibility. Before Spain a posting to Venezuela had been discussed. In both
cases Calouste had refused to let his son go, fearing that Nubar was being
set up as a 'scapegoat' and that his health would suffer.[29] Though Nubar
was up for the experience, his father insisted that he stay near, and Nubar
complied.

Putting Calouste's suspicions to one side, it is clear that Calouste
would have struggled to cope without his son. His son-in-law, Kevork, was
not up to the job of advising and assisting with what were going to be difficult negotiations over TPC. Calouste had others on his clerical staff, of
course, but had yet to hire anyone more senior, like the extremely capable
team of lawyers who would later form a kitchen cabinet of trusted advisers.

Calouste may have had his own motives for placing Nubar in an office
next door to Deterding's. The divide between the London and The Hague
offices that had yawned during the war had not closed: Waley Cohen (in
London) and August Philips and Frits de Kok (in The Hague) were still
trying to persuade Deterding to delegate and identify each director's area
of responsibility. Reminding these challengers that 'there was only one
Pope' and 'that that Pope was myself', Deterding repeatedly threatened
to resign.[30] Early 1924 found him writing Gulbenkian a series of letters in
which he raged at colleagues and the world in general.

'I want to write to you, to you only,' Deterding began. 'I could write
pages and pages ... if it only could show you, what I have inside me which
wants to burst.' He wondered if he might be dying. The only certainties
in this maelstrom were his own divine genius for guiding the fortunes of
Royal Dutch-Shell and the jealous perfidy of his self-seeking colleagues,
'low class animals who parade as human beings!' Deterding revealed to
Gulbenkian his dream of a new world 'where vanity is punished and ban-
ished', which might be planted in Russia 'when nothing is left and when

we find virgin soil to start anew'. This world would house 'a new race, no jews or their descendants'.

> I <u>do</u> feel a devil and still I feel so well and kindly disposed. That is not bad, is it Calouste? I hate nobody, but pity so many and give myself where others want my labour's outcome. Just these lines put me a bit right. I had such a high steamer-pressure but now the safety-valve does [not?] whistle anymore. I talk a great deal with Nubar and I can see in his eyes that he pities me and that <u>is</u> a great reward because he knows, [that] I mean well to all those who hate me so.[31]

Sensing their compromising nature, Gulbenkian sealed these letters in their original envelopes, but did not destroy them. The letters suggest that Calouste's policy of 'cultivating friendship and joining the armies' while defending Deterding may have been impossible to achieve.[32]

In his final letter to de Kok, Nubar ruefully recalled Philips warning him that the Gulbenkians were 'backing the wrong horse'.[33] The wrong horse was Deterding. Not only did Deterding not win the race, he bucked his rider. But perhaps it is better to see the Gulbenkians as the trainer, rather than the jockey. Calouste claimed to know and understand Deterding's 'great genius' as well as his 'most childish and most dangerous weaknesses'.[34] He sought to tame Deterding's genius and channel it into effective leadership. Whether this was in fact possible is an open question. What is clear is that the Gulbenkians, senior and junior, were both heavily punished for trying.

The cost was higher for Nubar than for Calouste. The break-up restored Calouste's precious independence. He was now free of the suspicion of being a fully owned subsidiary of Royal Dutch-Shell. That made him all the more sought after as an oil adviser to oil-producing states. The break-up ended Nubar's independence, however. 'For quite a long time I felt that I had given up my independent career,' Nubar would write later, 'which had a reasonable prospect of taking me to the top, only because of my duty to, and perhaps because of my fear of, my father.' This relationship

> was based on the fact that I was the apple of my father's eye and all he wanted was my welfare – according to his lights. In practice, this meant that I had to endure a great deal of interference by him. He justified this on the ground that, first, he was older and more experienced than

I was and therefore knew better than I did what was good for me and what I ought to want and, secondly, that we were an Oriental family, which meant it was not only his duty to interfere, even in the smallest details of the lives of his family and particularly that of his beloved only son, but also his undoubted right.[35]

Calouste's powers of judgement were apparently confirmed when his son's marriage to Herminia collapsed and she petitioned for divorce in October 1925. The 'oriental' father intervened with Nubar's divorce lawyer in an attempt to ensure that she did not receive a penny more than £500 in settlement. Herminia's venal intentions were obvious, he intimated, from the fact that her 'closest adviser' was Almina Dennistoun, the former Countess of Carnarvon. The previous year Almina and her second husband had been the focus of a scandalous divorce case which went to the High Court.[36]

Nubar's divorce proceedings dragged on through 1926 and 1927. Nubar was cited as co-respondent in Alexander Freeland's petition for divorce from his wife, the music hall starlet Doré Plowden (who subsequently became Nubar's second wife). Herminia's allegations of abuse at Nubar's hands must have made painful reading for the whole family. It cannot have been easy for Calouste, Nevarte and Nubar's uncle Yervant to give evidence in court emphasising Nubar's mental incapacity during the original engagement. A divorce was finally secured in January 1928. Legal fees added up to an eye-watering £13,157 (£715,000).[37]

A House is Not a Home

In his memoirs, the American diplomat Richard Child expressed frustration at the media's obsession with oil. 'In the main, recent diplomacy of the world has had less to do with oil resources than the average man supposes,' he claimed. Yet even Child could not deny that the rumours which swirled around him at Genoa and Lausanne had a certain allure. 'I used to feel sometimes a kind of appetite for intrigue and almost a wish that I might be involved in oil. It gives a man a sense of importance, but alas, I never struck it.'[38]

These years saw Gulbenkian's emergence as a celebrity, albeit one not famous for being famous, but rather famous for being mysterious. The

Sunday Express's society correspondent named Gulbenkian as one of the habitués of London's Embassy Club, one of those influential individuals 'whose reputations are whispered [about] all over the world'. 'I should like to know what he really thinks,' the correspondent mused, 'whether he has a home; whether he plays golf or has any other interest outside money-making.'[39]

Though Gulbenkian would never have dreamed of telling a journalist from the *Express* as much, he certainly did have an interest outside money-making: his art collection. The early 1920s saw the collector at his most active. He expanded the chronological parameters of his paintings collection, acquiring his first fifteenth-century (Stefan Lochner) and Impressionist works (Claude Monet). Around two-thirds of the paintings he would later bequeath to his foundation were acquired before 1925. So was the majority of his small (fifty-three items) collection of Egyptian antiquities, as well as his collection of Roman gems.

Gulbenkian appears to have been inspired by visiting a 1921 exhibition of Egyptian antiquities at the Burlington Fine Arts Club, which included a fine obsidian head of the pharaoh Senwosret III. When the head and other items from the collection of the Reverend William MacGregor went to auction a year later Gulbenkian had the great Egyptologist Howard Carter bid for him. Carter later scouted out similar items (including a bronze cat and a gold mummy mask) in Cairo.[40] In 1924 Gulbenkian acquired a fine set of medals by the fifteenth-century artist Antonio Pisanello.

Gulbenkian also expanded his collection of Greek coins, a field where he claimed personal expertise. He liked to tell a story of how his father, Sarkis, had once tested him as a fourteen-year-old, giving him fifty piastres as a reward for doing well at school and then sending him to an Istanbul bazaar to see what he could get in exchange. Young Calouste returned with two electrum staters from Kyzikos. Sarkis reprimanded him, so the tale went, not appreciating the coins' true value.[41] As a coin collector Gulbenkian favoured the 'austere' style of fifth-century-BC Sicilian issues. He regularly sought the advice of curators at the British Museum; in exchange they regularly sought (and received) contributions towards acquisition funds. 'Mr. G.' was a regular Saturday afternoon visitor to the Medal Room, 'with his quick tripping step, always in a hurry but himself unhurried ... with half-a-dozen carefully packed coins in his pocket'.[42]

Gulbenkian was a challenging client for Joseph Duveen, Otto

Gutekunst, Arthur Ruck and the other leading art dealers of the inter-war period. He expected 'friendly prices' and special terms, notably the right to return works of art he had purchased for a full refund (including commission). Although the many demands on him made it a challenge to find the time to inspect pieces in country house collections outside London, he nonetheless blamed his dealers when other collectors snapped up these treasures. Yet the dealers put up with such treatment, partly in the hope (constantly deferred) of striking bigger deals with Gulbenkian later on, partly because Gulbenkian brought them other wealthy clients. More importantly, all these dealers had invested in Mexican Eagle and other oil shares and relied on Gulbenkian for advice on when to buy, sell and hold. In 1920 Gulbenkian wrote to Duveen remarking that he knew exactly how much profit the latter had made following his investment advice. In return he expected 'a very prominent Work of Art, one in which I shall see increasing value and in any case, on which, when I look at it I shall exclaim with great joy "this is from Joe."' At the end of the letter he put it more simply: '<u>Stick</u> to your shares and find something very fine for me.'[43]

Though he was portrayed as a possessive 'oriental' who kept his 'harem' of objects close, in reality Gulbenkian was happy to leave recently acquired items with dealers, on loan to museums, or even in storage, sometimes for years at a time, without the need to inspect them himself.[44] In 1922 he finally took steps to build an appropriate setting for his collections, purchasing the Paris *hôtel* (palace) of Rodolphe Kann, which enjoyed a corner site halfway along Avenue d'Iéna, which runs south from the Arc de Triomphe to the river. A Gulbenkian would arguably have been more at home in one of the *hôtels* by the Monceau park, where bankers and merchants settled around 1900, among them the Ottoman Jewish Camondo family. The park's eighteenth-century follies were the perfect foil to wealthy men who shared Gulbenkian's love of eighteenth-century French bibelots, and who established 'house museums' that would serve as perpetual reminders of their taste, notably the Musée Nissim de Camondo and the Musée Jacquemart-André.

Built in 1897, Kann's *hôtel* at 51 Avenue d'Iéna was an exercise in French Neoclassicism by Paul-Ernest Sanson. Despite admiring this style, Gulbenkian had the building gutted and largely rebuilt around a structure of steel girders; this took four years, from 1923 to 1927. As architects he again chose the Anglo-French practice Mewès and Davis. An extraordinarily demanding client, Gulbenkian scrutinised the plans closely and brought in the services of other artists and designers, such as Edgar Brandt and his friend Lalique, who designed the remarkable master bathroom on the top floor. As Kenneth Clark later recalled, Gulbenkian 'knew every great staircase in Paris' and he took particular care about this element at Avenue d'Iéna.[45]

Those who sought entry by the discreet main door were immediately confronted by a porter. Two short flights of stairs led up to the hall: one for important visitors, the other, linked to a waiting room, for the less important. Gulbenkian's own office was on this ground floor, along with rooms for secretaries and archives, as well as a small round salon in which to discuss business. The various stairs and hall were eminently suited for the display of sculpture, and would come to house two life-sized Houdon figures of *Apollo* and *Diana*. Those left waiting immediately inside the front door could commiserate with *Jeanne d'Aire*, one of Rodin's *Burghers of Calais*, chained yet defiant.

Very few people were fortunate enough to climb the gently curving marble stairs to the *piano nobile*, which contained a library, dining room, grand salon and two more intimate salons, one lined in sycamore panelling, the other in Beauvais tapestries. The dining room was designed around a set of sixteenth-century Mantuan tapestries acquired in 1920, showing putti disporting themselves beneath trees. Although this room had a whiff of the Renaissance palazzo about it, otherwise the taste on display was overwhelmingly French Louis Seize. Gulbenkian's modern and Islamic artworks were carefully displayed, but in less important rooms such as the library (where a vitrine contained the collection of Lalique beneath Edward Burne-Jones's *Mirror of Venus*) and the private staircase, whose walls were inset with panels made up of Iznik tiles. The so-called 'Assyrian Room', containing the Egyptian artefacts from the collection, served as antechamber to the large, top-lit picture gallery, dominated by eighteenth-century paintings by Largillière and Canaletto.

Calouste had a lift to take him straight from the ground floor to his private suite of rooms on the top, third floor. Here a bedroom (with a single bed), office and Lalique's art deco bathroom overlooked a terrace, designed as a haven of privacy, with trellises and hedges blocking off any views. A pump and hose complete with pressure gauge stood at the bathroom's centre: from here the valet directed the hose while his master stood, naked, in a niche lined in silver leaf. When it came to one's ablutions, Calouste and his son were in agreement: there was no call for modesty in the presence of servants.[46]

Apart from Calouste, the only beings allowed to sleep at the top of the house were the valet, who had his own bedroom and pantry, and a collection of exotic birds, which inhabited an aviary at one end of the terrace. The latter included a peacock, whose morning cries drove the neighbourhood to distraction (it was eventually packed off to the Jardin des Plantes).[47] Nevarte, Rita, Kevork and Nubar had rooms on the floor below, the second floor. Although these rooms were somewhat more homely, the family constantly complained of feeling as if they were camping out in a museum. If this was a museum, its director was often absent. Though he ate, worked and showered at the house, Gulbenkian still preferred to sleep in his suite at the Ritz, where he could dine and bed the parade of young women discreetly provided for his pleasure. Even when he did eat at Avenue d'Iéna, the servants had strict instructions to serve Calouste's lunch an hour or two after the rest of the family sat down, so that he could dine alone.

Gulbenkian's eye for detail ranged well beyond the decorative. The servants formed part of an impressive array of machinery, most of it located in one of the building's three basement levels. As well as a garage, a generator (the building was heated by electricity) and a suite of safes, including one exclusively for the storage of Nevarte's furs, the basement housed a series of large tiled chambers with sodden sheets of cloth hung on racks: an early form of air conditioning and humidification. In its way the building's basement was as 'artistic' as the upper floors.[48] For all its refinement, 51 Avenue d'Iéna was lovingly over-engineered. 'Built like a battleship,' as Gulbenkian put it to Kenneth Clark.[49]

Whether 51 Avenue d'Iéna was engineered for his family's comfort and convenience was moot. It was the Ideal House, not a home. From the works on the walls to the invisible yet exquisitely conditioned air, the house was made for contemplation by a man who lived elsewhere. The carefully thought-through arrangements held out the promise of a perfect life lived amid beautiful things, an existence Gulbenkian's restlessness placed beyond his reach, except, perhaps, as a series of solitary moments of 'consolation and relief' which left few traces.[50]

The contemplation of 51 Avenue d'Iéna and its contents reinvigorated Gulbenkian, helping him through periods when others might have become dispirited. He tried to infuse some of his spirit into his son, to teach Nubar to view their work the same way he did:

I rely on you to put more soul into your work and not do it because you are obliged to or to please me; if you do not love work educate yourself to love it. Everything in life is bound up with will-power and thus you get to see things in a totally different light. I have no doubt that both of [us] are completing the other and that, with my experience, will enable us to form a combination for all kinds of initiative and we shall be only too thankful for what has happened in that we are rid of connections where dignity and honesty were set at defiance. I was rather amused at your saying that we are hated by everyone and are unpopular in the world. You must not allow yourself to be carried away like that; whenever you feel that way bring into play your reasoning and do not let yourself be the slave of a passing moment.[51]

Eight busy years after writing in similar terms to Lane, much had changed in Gulbenkian's life. Lane was dead. Gulbenkian had broken with Deterding. But Gulbenkian's faith in his own 'will-power' was as strong as ever, and was now combined with a new faith in his beloved if prodigal son. 'Hated by everyone', the pair now set about defending their 5 per cent from all comers.

ELEVEN

FIGHTING OR MAKING LOVE, 1926–8

The break with Deterding left Gulbenkian exposed. Deterding nursed his feud, making it clear to everyone that they had a choice to make: Deterding or Gulbenkian. When it came to working out how to adapt TPC so as to admit the Americans and their open door, Deterding held that everyone 'could go ahead and treat Mr. Gulbenkian as non-existent'.[1] The situation was rendered even worse for Gulbenkian by the state of international oil markets, glutted by new discoveries in east Texas, Oklahoma and Venezuela. These more than compensated for a decline in Mexican and Romanian production and the ongoing failure to work out some long-term arrangement under which Soviet-controlled oil could be brought to market.

A glutted market led Anglo-Persian, Royal Dutch-Shell and Jersey Standard to cartelise. They introduced 'short-haul' shipping programmes, 'as-is' agreements on market quotas and joint marketing entities to end wasteful competition in tanker transport, to put a floor under crude prices and otherwise to limit competition.[2] The centrepiece of these arrangements was the Achnacarry Agreement, named after the Scottish castle to which Deterding invited Teagle and Cadman (now chairman of Anglo-Persian) in September 1928. As Teagle's top man in Europe, Heinrich Riedemann noted, 'our road in all our business outside the United States is converging more and more into a parallel course with Deterding's.'[3] This explains why Riedemann told Nubar there could never be a job for him at Jersey

Standard if he was dismissed from Royal Dutch-Shell. What chance did Calouste have of keeping his 5 per cent in TPC from the hands of his far more powerful partners, now they were so cosy with one another? Even if he got to keep it, how could he prevent his partners from sitting on TPC's concession rather than developing it?

Where Nubar saw only the negative aspects of a situation in which 'everybody hates us', Calouste recognised the opportunities in being independent, if despised. Free of ties to Royal Dutch-Shell, Gulbenkian's years of experience were now available to the French, the Russians and the Persians (or rather the Iranians, as they now called themselves), all justifiably concerned about being stitched up by the majors. In the oil industry it could be hard to distinguish between displays of affection and aggression. 'Oilmen are like cats,' Gulbenkian liked to observe, 'one never knows when listening to them whether they are fighting or making love.'[4]

Architect and Landlord

Initially reluctant, after the Lausanne Conference Gulbenkian recognised that room would have to be made in his 'house' for the Americans. But they would have to honour TPC's house rules, including the self-denying clause. This clause prevented any TPC shareholder from seeking oil anywhere within the former Ottoman Empire, except through TPC. Could such a restrictive clause be reconciled with the American principle of the open door and American law, which forbade anti-competitive practices? The State Department struggled to work out what the practical implications of this much-discussed open door were. Allen Dulles of the Near East Department wondered 'how the [State] Department can in all instances rigidly oppose monopolistic enterprises' when 'there are certain situations in which they are an economic or political necessity.'[5]

In the end Secretary of State Charles Hughes decided that, while the US government did not formally approve of how TPC had been set up, it would not prevent American firms from participating in it.[6] Official negotiations with TPC could now begin, led by Jersey Standard on behalf of the Near East Development Company, the vehicle through which the American firms agreed to participate in TPC. In order to avoid double taxation, the Americans wanted TPC to produce as little profit as possible. They wanted to take crude, rather than profits. The other groups participating in TPC were amenable to that. But Gulbenkian did not have the means to store, refine or sell oil. He wanted TPC to develop into an independent, integrated oil company, and take dividends on his 5 per cent participation. Finding a solution to this conflict of vision – the Red Line Agreement – would take four years, far longer than anyone had imagined.

In July 1924 Jersey Standard's president, Walter Teagle, met with Gulbenkian to discuss the problem. In a report to Allen Dulles he described Gulbenkian as

> a particularly able and crafty oil man, the holder of the largest individual interest in the Shell Company and a naturalised British subject of Armenian origin and reputedly very wealthy, probably worth several million pounds ... Mr. Gulbenkian made clear his position to Mr. Teagle that he was not an oil man, that he did not wish to trade in oil, that he was not interested in the international viewpoint of the question, and that he was interested simply from the standpoint of his own personal business interests and profit. He stated that, as a minority stockholder, he could not agree to the Company's operating on the basis proposed except by agreement of the other interests to certain terms. He stated that, as a minority stockholder, he had certain rights under British law, which his attorney advised him would entitle him to apply to the courts for an injunction restraining the Turkish Petroleum Company from operating on basis other than for profit or along any lines other than those ordinarily followed by other oil producing companies; i.e., he claimed that the Turkish Petroleum Company should produce oil, transport it to seaboard or refinery, refine it and market it.

If his partners wanted to proceed to operate TPC as a non-profit-making body, they would need to pay the calls on his 5 per cent share, give him a seat on the board and pay him a one shilling royalty. Gulbenkian was a business architect: he had '"built the house" ... although the other four interests were now "in the house which he had built", they could only "live in it" by accepting his terms'.

Teagle boiled this metaphor down to one sentence: '"Pay me my price or I'll upset the show."'[7] After three days of talks Teagle emerged with nothing, except the realisation that Gulbenkian was a far more serious problem than he had been led to believe. Gulbenkian was 'in a position where he absolutely dominated the situation'. Teagle accused his TPC partners of trying to keep this inconvenient truth from the Americans. How, he wanted to know, could TPC even think of sending a representative to Baghdad to negotiate a concession while this Gulbenkian question remained unresolved?[8] The others probably agreed, but thought such criticisms rich, coming as they did 'whilst the American Group remains so adroitly poised on the TPC fence'.[9] Were they in or were they out?

While the lawyers locked horns in London and the leaders of the world's leading oil companies bombarded each other with letters, memos, wires and telephone calls, TPC geologists in Iraq drilled exploratory wells. One of the most promising areas lay near Kirkuk, at a site known locally as Baba Gurgur ('Daddy Fire') on account of its natural seepages of oil. At 3 a.m. on 14 October 1927 the drilling team reached a depth of 1,521 feet, where they met an oil horizon under considerable pressure. The gusher flooded the surrounding wadi, running out of control for over a week at a constant flow of 90,000 barrels of 'sweet' (low-sulphur) crude a day. Two American and three Iraqi workers were asphyxiated by the gas cloud that formed.[10] TPC had discovered the world's largest oilfield.

The Gulbenkian Knot

In the immediate post-war years Gulbenkian had coached French diplomats on how to claim the quarter-participation in TPC that had formerly belonged to Deutsche Bank. He had established a French firm to take those shares. In 1924 Poincaré had given them to a separate entity, which became the Compagnie Française des Pétroles (CFP, known today as Total). To placate the powerful French refining lobby, CFP was restricted to 'upstream' activities: it was prohibited from refining and marketing. Poincaré entrusted CFP to Ernest Mercier, who had cut his teeth running Omnium, a French firm with large interests in Romanian oil.

Foreign observers assumed that CFP was the tool of the French Foreign Ministry, the Quai d'Orsay. In fact, French oil policy was and would remain 'a continuous tug of war' between the Foreign and Finance Ministries (themselves associated with competing banking groups), as well as between the well-established cartel of domestic refiners and rival, integrated oil companies.[11] Although the French state took a 25 per cent stake in CFP in 1928, the rest of the shares were distributed among various French banks, refiners and oil companies (even SEP got a slice). While CFP focused on Iraq and North Africa, a rival 'national champion', Pétrofina, sought Persian and Russian supplies. A state agency, the Office Nationale des Combustibles Liquides (ONCL, established 1925, in succession to the Comité Générale aux Essences et Pétroles), tried to keep them from getting in each other's way. Gulbenkian had good relations with ONCL's head, Louis Pineau, as well as with the head of Pétrofina, Léon Wenger. He was less close to Mercier.[12]

In November 1924 CFP finally joined the board of TPC, paying £8,924 (£460,000) for 40,000 shares. Like the Americans, the French initially tried to claim that Gulbenkian was not their problem, only to find themselves drawn into discussing what form a settlement with him might take. CFP informed TPC in January 1925 that they were willing to reduce their 25 per cent to 23.75 per cent, thus giving Gulbenkian 1.25 per cent. If the other three groups did the same, this would equal 5 per cent. But CFP insisted that Gulbenkian's 5 per cent should be only a life interest.[13] TPC's managing director, Henry Nichols, explained that what he called 'the Gulbenkian knot' could not be unpicked so easily. Although Gulbenkian had only a life interest in his 5 per cent under the 1914 Foreign Office Agreement, in 1919 it had been agreed that he had a permanent one.

It seemed as if the only thing to do was to liquidate TPC and start over again without Gulbenkian. Yet as Nichols pointed out, to start over was not the same thing as rewinding the clock. Any revamped, Gulbenkian-free TPC would be negotiating in a far harsher climate.

> In the San Remo days there was no such thing as an Iraq Government, and, as Mandatory, one had the right to assume that one could promise much. We are now face to face with a fully-fledged Iraq Government and if we go into liquidation we automatically tear up the 1914 Grand Vizier's letter; all our 'droits acquis' fall to the ground, and we represent ourselves to Iraq, humbly begging for a Concession.[14]

King Faisal's interest lay in developing his country's oil as quickly as possible. The 1925 concession agreement signed between TPC and the Iraqi state committed TPC to starting to drill within two years. It made no mention of the 20 per cent 'native participation' allowed for in the 1920 San Remo Agreement. The Iraqis would not, in other words, become a sixth lodger inside Gulbenkian's house: they would receive royalties, but no equity (shares).[15] The only concession was made not to please Faisal, but the open door. Instead of a blanket concession for the whole of the two provinces of Mosul and Baghdad, TPC was to select twenty-four plots of eight square miles each, leaving the remainder free for others to lease.

In early 1925 the Organic Law intended to replace the provisional government in Iraq with a fully fledged government answerable to an elected national assembly had already been postponed several times. It was crucial that the TPC concession agreement be signed with the provisional government, before this Organic Law was passed, so that the assembly could be presented with a fait accompli. Thus while Teagle conceded to Mercier that Gulbenkian's demand for a royalty (paid in gold, to avoid the risk of depreciation) of a shilling a ton on TPC's production was excessive, speed was of the essence.[16] Once convened, an Iraqi assembly would insist on scrutinising any concession agreement, with all that entailed, including (if the Persian parliament was any precedent) massive bribery of assembly delegates by rival oil companies.

In March 1925 it seemed as if Mercier had managed to get Gulbenkian to agree to a modified version of the so-called 'Heads of Agreement', under which TPC would operate at a small profit, providing all partners with oil and binding the groups either to supply Gulbenkian with his 5 per cent in oil at a deepwater port or to pay him a one shilling per ton royalty. Gulbenkian would have to pay the calls on his 5 per cent, contributing his share of the costs of building pipelines, a refinery and so on. He would also have the right to nominate a director to the board of TPC. Nichols was in Cannes when Mercier informed him of the settlement.

When these terms were relayed to the American group, however, Teagle objected to the fact that Gulbenkian was to receive his shilling royalty on oil produced by TPC outside their twenty-four Iraqi plots. Gulbenkian took his stand on the Foreign Office Agreement of 1914, which stated that TPC's area of operations comprised 'the Ottoman Empire in Asia'. Nobody was quite sure of where the edges of that empire had been in March 1914, but it doubtless included large swathes of the Arabian peninsula, vast areas that might or might not contain oil. Persuaded that Gulbenkian was simply being greedy, CFP agreed with the other groups that preparations should be made to proceed without him.

Nichols was therefore instructed to prepare a new set of draft working agreements, which would be put to Gulbenkian with an ultimatum in July. Apart from the question of concession area, the parties to the negotiation were close at this stage and one wonders why they did not settle.[17]

Instead they walked back from the relatively minor concessions CFP had offered in March. Gulbenkian refused to sign the Heads of Agreement and instructed his lawyers to get the writs ready.

The groups blinked. Though they had agreed on 17 July 1925 to proceed without Gulbenkian, instead they dithered, and back-room negotiations continued in August. This time it was Montagu Piesse, Socony's general counsel, who volunteered to negotiate one on one with Gulbenkian. Negotiations with Gulbenkian followed a cycle. First a representative of one of the groups thrashed out a promising set of terms with him. Once they read what had been agreed, however, the other groups began finding fault, while privately speculating on what conspiracy might lie behind the new arrangement. Suitably chastened, the group responsible for the latest démarche was brought into line, concessions were whittled down and a less generous set of terms presented to Gulbenkian. After some more negotiating, Gulbenkian would be confronted with an ultimatum, at which point he would call the groups' bluff.

Officially negotiations would break down, along with the health of the negotiators, who would be shipped off to French watering holes in the hope of restoring their nerves. Those left behind endeavoured to get their version of events through to their respective Foreign Ministries, hoping for diplomatic support. 'The negotiations between the American Group and the Turkish Petroleum Company are approaching a critical stage,' Dulles noted in November 1924; '(they have, however, been through so many critical stages that it is difficult to know how seriously to take the present information).'[18] The Quai d'Orsay and Foreign Office became equally jaded. Eventually some other representative of one of the other groups would volunteer to go and meet with Gulbenkian, whereupon the process would begin all over again.

This was the pattern followed by TPC negotiations from 1924 right through to the early hours of 31 July 1928, when the Red Line Agreement was finally signed. Gulbenkian was perhaps guilty of seeing a conspiracy to 'whittle him down' behind every move his TPC partners made. The latter were certainly guilty of attributing the drawn-out nature of negotiations to Gulbenkian's stubbornness, rather than to mutual distrust or the sheer complexity of the questions involved. As Gulbenkian was an individual, rather than an oil company, negotiating with him was always going to present unique challenges.

When the Foreign Office Agreement became public knowledge (in

1924) *The Economist* remarked on the oddity of finding Gulbenkian and his 5 per cent referred to. Like many at the time and since, it assumed that this was a commission awarded to Gulbenkian for putting TPC together, rather than an investment on his part:

> It is to be hoped, for the sake of the other shareholders, that the price of his mediation is not always a shilling in the pound sterling. But it would be strange if his 5 per cent. interest is allowed to remain in the Turkish Petroleum Company when competition for participation is so severe.[19]

Only in December 1927 did Gulbenkian set up a company, Participations and Investments (Canada), to hold his 5 per cent participation. Pandi would be joined by fifteen other shell companies with similar names. One of them, Participations and Exploitations (Partex), continues today as an upstream oil company, fully owned by the Gulbenkian Foundation.

Negotiating Tactics

Gulbenkian insisted that his negotiating position was consistent, being founded on fixed moral principles. We know that he took these principles seriously because he preached them to his closest relations: to Nevarte in the 1890s, to Nubar in the 1920s and, later still, to his grandson, Mikhael. Such principles were not only ethically sound, they were 'healthy' principles, embracing the private as well as the public sphere, the care of one's business interests as well as one's own body. Not drinking or eating to excess was one principle. Otherwise, however, Calouste never spelled out exactly what he meant by 'principles'; the key thing was to hold on to them, even if those around you did not.

With business associates Gulbenkian paid due respect to a similarly unwritten code of practice, couched in the argot of the Edwardian London stockbroker. It was not 'chic' (Gulbenkian put the word in quotation marks) for Churchill to have bad-mouthed Royal Dutch-Shell in Parliament in 1914, and Gulbenkian had told Churchill's brother as much.[20] Nor was it 'chic' when friends kept profitable deals to themselves, without allowing Gulbenkian 'to taste a slice of it'. 'I always like the satisfaction of solidarity and not the egoistic love of self materialism,'

Gulbenkian told one associate.[21] He nonetheless recognised that in the oil business materialism was to be expected, observing, 'The oil crowd are not exactly possessed with refined feelings.'[22] Observing their moral failings brought out the 'philosopher' in Gulbenkian, a world-weary pose he clearly enjoyed adopting.

A similar tension between the 'philosopher's' passivity and the visionary's passion characterised Gulbenkian's view of his own role in TPC. At times he complained that the entry of the French and then the Americans was damaging the 'architecture' of his 'house'. At other times he claimed credit for having the foresight and wisdom to fashion a vehicle apparently designed for such international collaboration, 'for having always wanted to bring in other people and been contented with a small whack of a large thing rather than a large whack of a small thing', as one Anglo-Persian executive put it.[23]

Gulbenkian told Riedemann in 1923 that he had forty years' experience of oil negotiations – a ludicrous claim (twenty years would have been closer to the mark).[24] His role in TPC also increased in the telling. Gulbenkian had played little part in securing the *Lettre Vizirielle* of 1914. Inattention had almost seen him left out of the Foreign Office Agreement. While he had certainly encouraged the French and Americans to join TPC, did either really need to be invited to do so? Although Anglo-Persian did challenge this account internally, it was Gulbenkian's version which entered the history books.[25]

An excellent network of contacts gave Gulbenkian ample opportunity to make his case privately and discreetly. At the Foreign Office he had the ear of Sir William Tyrrell, who had been Private Secretary to Foreign Secretary Edward Grey before the war. As Permanent Undersecretary from 1925, Tyrrell was the highest-ranking civil servant at the Foreign Office, as well as the one charged with liaising with Britain's intelligence services.[26] He became a semi-official intermediary between Cadman and Gulbenkian.[27] Gulbenkian's friendship with Philippe Berthelot of the French Foreign Ministry and Louis Pineau of ONCL helped him to coach CFP. Pineau told Mercier that the Foreign Office Agreement (which Royal Dutch-Shell and TPC itself had declared invalid) was 'one of the essential documents on which France's interests in the Middle East rest, and which must be fully defended'. Berthelot drummed the same 'thèse française' into Mercier.[28]

The launching of court proceedings in London by CFP against TPC,

Royal Dutch-Shell and Anglo-Persian in February 1927 was very much Gulbenkian's idea, therefore, and CFP's case was built on the claim that the Foreign Office Agreement was valid and that CFP and Gulbenkian were party to it (even though neither had signed it). Gulbenkian supplied CFP's London lawyer, Leslie Burgin, with documents relating to the early history of TPC that proved crucial to making this case. He dug out Deterding letters from 1914 which proved that, contrary to his protestations, Deterding had then interpreted the Foreign Office Agreement in exactly the same way as the French were doing in 1927.[29]

Gulbenkian also made use of the influential editor of the *Morning Post*, Howell Gwynne. The precise nature of this relationship is unclear, but the run of secret memos they exchanged between 1925 and 1928 suggests something deeper than a social relationship, founded on a shared interest in policy towards Soviet Russia. Imperialist, conservative die-hard and anti-Semite, Gwynne viewed journalism as an invitation to influence events as much as report on them. In 1923 he had collaborated with Gulbenkian's friend William Tyrrell in scheming to persuade Stanley Baldwin's government to enter a formal alliance with France, an extraordinary plot which saw them conniving with Poincaré to oust Curzon as Foreign Secretary.[30] Gulbenkian's insights into the 'psychology' and 'machinations' of the oil industry piqued Gwynne's appetite for the inside track, as well as pricking his imperial conscience.[31] Gulbenkian's travails at the hands of Anglo-Persian and Royal Dutch confirmed Gwynne in the belief that the time had come to take these oil barons in hand, before they caused any more damage to Britain's reputation, particularly in the eyes of Russia.

In his exchanges with Gulbenkian, Gwynne repeated the phrase 'unless the state controls oil, oil will control the state.'[32] Gwynne lobbied Foreign Secretary Austen Chamberlain, Home Secretary William Joynson-Hicks and others on Gulbenkian's behalf. His intervention stymied an attempt by Lords Inverforth and Beaverbrook to collude with the Turks, Americans and Paribas in snatching the Mosul concession from TPC.[33] Gwynne also lobbied for a Russian oil embargo. 'When you ask me how we should hit back at Bolshevism,' Gulbenkian wrote, 'I would say that before thinking of hitting back at the Bolsheviks, you should endeavour to hit back in the domestic circle against so many abuses causing demoralisation, intrigue and lack of scruple and resulting in absolute lack of consistency.'[34] In a sense Gwynne and Gulbenkian were advocating a kind of moral rearmament.

Though Gwynne did have influence, the tone he struck in his letters to Gulbenkian often suggests a self-important fantasist, a type Gulbenkian normally steered clear of. It remains unclear what lay behind a mysterious scheme to which the pair made coded allusions. This was to be carried out by Gulbenkian on the understanding that 'if the thing is successful ... the British Government would stand firmly behind you', while if it failed 'it will be a private failure'. Although Gwynne did ensure that Gulbenkian received some favourable coverage in the *Morning Post*, full-blown attacks on Inverforth and Royal Dutch-Shell never materialised.[35]

At the opposite end of the spectrum from such discreet string-pulling, Gulbenkian also recognised the value of sustained, one-on-one negotiation, in the absence of lawyers and intermediaries like Tyrrell and Gwynne. Between 1924 and 1928 he had sustained bouts lasting several days apiece with Walter Teagle, Ernest Mercier, John Cadman (twice) and Montagu Piesse (also twice). Although Gulbenkian was always the older party, he seems to have had no problems when it came to stamina. Indeed, he liked to get started early: as a peeved Cadman noted in his diary, 'Gulbenkian was calling on me before I was up.'[36]

Exactly what went on during these intense negotiations is unclear. Neither party took detailed notes, apparently at Gulbenkian's request. This suggests that Gulbenkian used these opportunities to rehearse his moral case, perhaps illustrating the un-chic nature of the other side, using examples drawn from his excellent memory. The general nature of discussions also spared Gulbenkian the appearance of haggling over precise phrases and figures. Such details could, it was suggested, be left to the lawyers to settle. What really mattered was that Gulbenkian and his interlocutor saw eye to eye on the big picture. For the man who loved to relax by going over his children's household expenses, whose office mantra was 'check, check, check', this was a studied pose. Inevitably problems emerged when it came to pinning down the precise terms that had been agreed – whether as a result of one or other party repenting a momentary weakness, or genuine confusion.

Whatever the outcome, Gulbenkian always managed to charm and impress his opposite number with his own patient good nature in the face of attempts to chip away at his position, one founded on equity and justice. He never, ever, lost his temper, as Deterding and Waley Cohen were wont to do. But Deterding and Waley Cohen also knew Gulbenkian of old, and had frequently dealt with him face to face. For everyone else a one-on-one meeting with the elder Gulbenkian would have been a rare occurrence: they would have been more familiar with Nubar and Calouste's various lawyers.

'Oriental' origins, reclusiveness and the rumours surrounding him lent Gulbenkian an aura of mystery. But when one actually met him, Gulbenkian turned out to be someone rather different. Physically he was shorter and thinner than expected. A young graduate of the École du Louvre, Marcelle Chanet, had been hired to install Gulbenkian's art collection in 51 Avenue d'Iéna, and was kept on as curator. She later recorded her first impressions:

> The most striking thing about his physiognomy were those extraordinary eyes, surmounted by thick eyebrows of a very particular shape. His gaze, which bore into the very depths of you, was unforgettable. Of middling height, his whole person radiated such power, such magnetic force that one knew straightaway that this was an exceptional man, a man made to dominate others.[37]

Gulbenkian's magnetic aura was particularly effective in the case of Piesse. Nubar reported to Calouste that Piesse had 'impressed on Teagle that in dealing with you, he had to deal with a really great personality, whose operations were dictated by real qualities of statesmanship'.[38] Piesse wrote in similar terms to Mercier:

> I think great credit is due to him for the broad minded way in which he has faced the situation, and for making, what he considers a considerable sacrifice to meet the above mentioned desire. My negotiations with Mr Gulbenkian have been on the most friendly basis and we have both worked hard to bring about a settlement of all outstanding points which existed between him and the Groups, and this, I think, we have now done. I am writing you this letter as I wish to put these facts on record with the French Group.[39]

The reaction of Mercier and CFP was to take this letter as evidence that Piesse and Gulbenkian were conniving together to do CFP out of its rights. 'As if G. and Piesse hadn't agreed ages ago how they wanted this comedy to play out!' wrote Louis Tronchère of CFP. 'As if G. himself didn't write the terms himself!'[40] These kinds of suspicions made it difficult for the groups to present Gulbenkian with a united front. At this point CFP thought Gulbenkian was in cahoots with the Americans and the British thought he was in cahoots with the French.

Back-room lobbying and these set-piece negotiations played to Gulbenkian's skill in the arts of one-on-one persuasion. Unfortunately, very few accounts survive of his manner of addressing those who found themselves alone with him. In 1926 one old business associate with plenty of experience in this regard, Georg Spies, published his memoirs, which offer some clues:

> Back when I first came into contact with him Gulbenkian was a relatively small player. One or two years before he had moved to London from Constantinople with £10,000, dealing in carpets and other Turkish exports. He came from a distinguished Armenian family, and combined a cultivated mind and a deep understanding of art with cleverness, exquisite manners and oriental deviousness. Whenever he sketched out the benefits of some syndicate or other he always did so in such a refined, ingratiating way that, to use an oriental phrase, he could slip a camel through the eye of a needle.[41]

Gulbenkian did not perform well in group settings. Instead he relied on Nubar, his son-in-law, Kevork, Adjemoff and the best lawyers his money could buy to attend the countless meetings which occurred in London during the four-year negotiation process. Alongside Sir William McLintock, Gulbenkian had retained the services of the barristers Wilfred Greene and Sir John Simon. Sir John Simon's opinion of February 1927 held that Gulbenkian had been a party to the Foreign Office Agreement (being represented by NBT), and that the agreement remained binding on all parties, including the self-denying clause (which prevented partners from exploiting independently any oil found within the red-line area).[42] Greene confirmed that Gulbenkian would have a strong case against the others if they entered a working agreement without him.[43]

For what it was worth, Simon's former partner Sir Douglas Hogg also agreed: 'The use of their power by a majority of the shareholders to acquire an advantage over others at the company's expense is a fraud on the minority which the Courts will intervene to prevent.' As the working agreement was designed to reduce TPC's profits to an artificially low level, it certainly did come 'at the company's expense'. Admittedly, Hogg was no longer retained by Gulbenkian in 1926. But he had remained a friend and one worth having: Hogg was now Attorney-General.[44]

Collecting legal opinions and sounding out eminent legal minds was one thing, going to court was another. Gulbenkian recognised the opportunities his solicitors and barristers offered to negotiate at arm's length, to relay messages to parties with whom he was not in official communication and, where absolutely necessary, to intimidate by threatening writs and injunctions. Even when legal proceedings were started, deadlines for the presentation of arguments could be manipulated to beneficial effect. With Gulbenkian's help, CFP's case against TPC and their TPC partners was kept ticking over until the very day the Red Line Agreement was signed, much to the frustration of Justice Astbury of London's Court of Chancery, who had vowed not to offer any more deferments.

Discussing business matters in open court, however, came at the cost of publicity. His experience of VOC had not changed Gulbenkian's distaste for publicity. In a case with CFP and Gulbenkian on one side and the Americans, Royal Dutch-Shell and Anglo-Persian on the other, however, the costs of publicity were higher for the latter side. The Foreign Office recognised that if the case went to court the French would drag them in too and pushed Cadman to settle.[45] CFP and Gulbenkian were the underdogs, the others were 'the trusts', with a well-established reputation for anti-competitive practices. Once the decision was taken to go to court, Gulbenkian believed, it was important to 'hit and hit hard', exposing 'as much dirt as possible', 'so that, if we lost (if they deny that they are [g] oing to do these things) we shall have them by the throat if they attem[p] t anything in the future'.[46]

In the United States the likes of Jersey Standard and Socony faced opposition from domestic independent producers with strong congressional support. Gulbenkian sent one of his lawyers, Louis Levy, to New York with his own ultimatum to Teagle: either Teagle should get on a boat to London to come and negotiate or Levy 'will diplomatically create such a stir through the Senate as will give Teagle to think [*sic*]'.[47]

The 1928 Red Line Agreement saw Gulbenkian abandon whatever hopes he still had of TPC developing into an independent, integrated oil company. Instead it would be run so as to provide its shareholders with cheap oil, making the smallest profit possible, so as to avoid British taxes. This important concession aside, otherwise Gulbenkian did rather well. There was no more doubt surrounding the question of whether his was a life interest, rather than a permanent one. He would contribute his 5 per cent share of TPC's drilling, pipe-stringing and other costs. CFP promised to take his 5 per cent crude and pay him a price set by an impartial expert, in a fashion sufficient to protect Gulbenkian from currency devaluations. Should TPC lease any of its Iraqi territories to outsiders, Gulbenkian would also receive his 5 per cent of those profits.

Thanks to the French (who drew the red line as broadly as they could), Gulbenkian would also be able to claim his share of the risks and rewards should any of the TPC partners seek concessions outside Iraq too. In signing the Red Line Agreement, the French and the Americans thus promised to abide by the self-denying principle which Gulbenkian had laid down in 1912, and which Anglo-Persian and Royal Dutch-Shell had signed up to in the 1914 Foreign Office Agreement. According to this, they undertook 'not to be interested directly or indirectly in the production or manufacture of crude oil ... otherwise than through the Turkish Petroleum Company' in all of the Middle East, except Kuwait and Iran (which had not been part of the Ottoman Empire in 1914 and hence were outside the red line). In 1928 none of the major partners in TPC thought there was oil in the Kingdom of the Hejaz (as Saudi Arabia was then known) or the Gulf. Had they suspected just how much there in fact was, they probably would not have signed the 1928 agreement. Nor would they have signed had world markets not been glutted. Gulbenkian's survival as a minority interest in TPC was as much down to this good timing and good fortune as it was to his negotiating tactics.

Our Man in Tehran

One of the less persuasive claims made by Gulbenkian during the four-year red-line slog was that he was fighting to protect the Inland Revenue from an attempt to defraud it of its rightful share of TPC profits.[48] Gulbenkian himself, of course, was a tax exile. In 1928 someone at the British Home Office noticed his extended absence from the UK and considered stripping him of his British citizenship. Although he held quasi-diplomatic status at the Persian Legation in Paris, Gulbenkian did not hold a Persian passport. He had misplaced his old Ottoman passport, and the Armenian passport he had acquired in 1919 would probably not have been recognised. Had the Home Office had its way, therefore, Gulbenkian would have been left stateless.

While such non-nationality would have been appropriate, it would have made travel something of a challenge. Fortunately, the Home Office consulted the Foreign Office, which pointed out the possible repercussions. A 'deeply offended' Gulbenkian would, Undersecretary of State Lancelot Oliphant predicted, find 'a variety of ways, probably through the Quai d'Orsay ... to get his own back'. In his own letter to the Home Secretary, Tyrrell was forthright: 'It would be very prejudicial to our interests commercial and even political to offend Mr Gulbenkian.'[49]

Had Gulbenkian restricted his activities to TPC and Iraq, the costs of offending him would have been affordable. It was Gulbenkian's ties to Iran and Russia which made the difference. Anglo-Persian needed to maintain good relations with Iran, for obvious reasons. Its chairman, John Cadman, joined the chorus urging the Home Office to allow Calouste to retain his British citizenship. Cadman probably knew that 'Isa Khan (Persia's Oil Commissioner), Timurtash (prime minister), Sardar Assad (chief of the Bakhtiaris) and other Persian leaders all consulted Gulbenkian, not least to have him check that Anglo-Persian was paying them the correct royalties.[50] When Reza Shah cancelled Anglo-Persian's concession in 1932, Gulbenkian again sought to play honest broker.[51] Cadman supported the proposal that Nubar be appointed commercial attaché to the Persian Embassy in London. Nubar thus came to enjoy a status similar to that his father had enjoyed in Paris since 1920. Nubar's name was entered in the 'social' list of London's corps diplomatique, however, not the official one.

Nubar's naturalisation and appointment as attaché were part of a renewed effort by his father to secure the oil concession for northern Persia and develop it with Russian cooperation. The concession was first claimed by Anglo-Persian and then the American company Sinclair, but neither had been able to work it. With the accession of Reza Shah in 1925, the reign of the Qajars had given way to that of the Pahlavis. Not that Gulbenkian's boss at the Paris embassy, Prince Samad, paid much attention, 'behaving in a very stupid manner' by allowing the embassy to remain 'full of portraits etc of the former Shah which cannot be very tasteful to the new regime'.[52] Gulbenkian moved with the times, sending the new Shahanshah a pair of Purdey shotguns and some Louis Vuitton luggage – coronation presents a Persian shah might actually find quite useful.[53]

Though the Shah had changed, the overall political situation continued much the same. 'We have out there several friends who sometimes come on to the top and at other times, owing to Bolshevism and other movements, are cast into prison,' Gulbenkian noted. Ministers changed as frequently in Tehran as they did in Paris, though the consequences of falling from favour in Reza Shah's Iran could be very serious. Sometimes Iranian 'friends' holding diplomatic posts abroad even refused to return to Tehran to take up ministerial office. Gulbenkian was philosophical, noting that 'these are factors we knew all about when we decided to go into this business'.[54] In addition to payments to Samad and other diplomats to cover 'postage costs', Gulbenkian footed the bill for fixing up the London embassy. It was a small amount to pay for diplomatic status, which offered certain tax benefits in peace and rather more protections in war. While Calouste found the taste for such things *rastaquouère* (flashy and arriviste), Nubar delighted in the other benefits: the right to wear court dress (with the cross of the Légion d'honneur he had received earlier), attend state dinners and add 'CD' (corps diplomatique) plates to one's car.[55]

Although 'Golbangian' ('Gulbenkian' in Farsi) had had a sideline in trading Persian rugs and antiquities back in the early 1900s, he never visited Persia and his Persian connections are challenging to reconstruct. His mother's branch of the Gulbenkians is said to have hailed from Persia. Gulbenkian was certainly close to Hovhannes Khan Massehian, an Armenian who served as Persian ambassador to London from 1917.[56] Born in 1846, he had served the Qajar court as translator, diplomatic envoy and adviser. In 1925 he returned to Tehran for the coronation of the first Pahlavi Shah, Reza, and presented Gulbenkian's gifts to him. 'The Armenian people have displayed their talents in all areas,' the Shah observed politely; 'they are an intelligent and energetic nation, and I like them very much.'[57] That was all well and good, but would the Shah's influential Court Minister, Timurtash, do anything to implement the big scheme Gulbenkian had prepared?

TWELVE

THE BIG SCHEME, 1928–30

Having failed to build his Turkish Petroleum Company into an integrated oil company, Gulbenkian started over, without, of course, ceasing to defend his minority position within TPC. His 'big scheme' proposed to piece together a new oil major. An international network of specialist investment banks was formed to finance the acquisition and development of oilfields in north Persia, Russia, the United States and Venezuela. Although the plan drew on French diplomatic support, otherwise the aim was to avoid identification with any single national interest. Gulbenkian's syndicate, known simply as 'the International Corporation', was to be 'free from any political tinge, i.e. free of influence from the British, French or any other government'.[1] The linchpin was Soviet oil: Gulbenkian's plan proposed to give Russia a seat at oil's big table, where it could negotiate its own share of world markets. With his help it could join the world oil cartel, as a partner of Anglo-Persian, Royal Dutch-Shell and Jersey Standard, rather than being the despised outsider those majors used when they wanted to cheat on each other.

Gulbenkian's main collaborator in the 'big scheme' was Chester Beatty, the mining magnate who had attempted to serve as honest broker in disputes over VOC's management. Beatty's work as 'doughty champion and defender' of minority shareholders had impressed Gulbenkian. So did his knowledge of manuscripts. In London Beatty travelled to work on the tube and, like Gulbenkian, was conspicuous for always dining alone.

Writing to thank Beatty in June 1924, Gulbenkian expressed a hope that the pair might one day 'combine together to build something big of our own together'.[2] The big scheme afforded an opportunity to do this.

The pair began by securing control over two of the most important foreign concessions granted in 1925 under Lenin's New Economic Policy: Lena Goldfields and Tetiuhe Mining Corporation, which extracted gold, silver and other metals from mines in the Urals and the Pacific coast of Siberia respectively. Lena and Tetiuhe struggled under Soviet currency and export restrictions, agitprop by local party figures and assaults on non-Russian staff. Meanwhile, in London and Paris, public opinion and official foreign policy towards the Soviet Union posed equally serious problems. In an attempt to resolve the situation in March 1927 Gulbenkian held a series of meetings in Paris with Georges Piatakoff of Gosbank, the Russian State Bank.[3]

In November 1927 the People's Commissar for Foreign Affairs (that is, the Russian Foreign Minister) Georgy Chicherin instructed his staff to keep a close eye on the progress of Gulbenkian's talks with Piatakoff. 'Gulbenkian is a very important figure,' Chicherin observed, 'a former ally of Deterding, who subsequently turned against him. He is the best card we hold. All those who know him from England are talking about him as a strong financial and political power.'[4]

Throughout the 1920s Gulbenkian and others invested in Russia were sent mixed messages by both sides: a muddled cocktail of ideology, prestige, concern for human rights and a desire to foster employment and wider economic growth.[5] In the late 1920s the Foreign Office was concerned that encouraging Russian exports might lead to charges of indirectly funding slave labour within Russia. As far as any communist was concerned, of course, there was never any doubt that western capitalists were slave-drivers, oppressing the proletariat.

Yet both sides also felt that economic ties could bring wider benefits; each felt that trade might end up not only benefiting them, but undermining the opposing economy, including its fundamental principles (be they capitalist or communist). Gulbenkian's friend Gwynne, for example, certainly believed that decisions over how to admit Russian exports to world markets would influence the future of Bolshevism inside Russia itself. Economic relations had the potential to change the broader course of history.

Laying the Foundations

Suspicious that his letters were being read, Gulbenkian was loath to commit his 'big scheme' to paper in all its ramifications. He confessed to Nubar that the scope and ambition of the scheme exhilarated him, and Calouste may also have felt that, properly laid out, the 'big scheme' might appear fantastic to others. The ground needed to be prepared and trust established through various small-scale experiments. Putting the pieces of the puzzle together, however, an overall plan does emerge. Persian oil from the Semnan concession south-east of Tehran was to be exploited through an existing Soviet–Persian joint venture, Kevir-Khurian, in collaboration with the Franco-Belgian oil company, Pétrofina. Majlis deputies in Tehran would vote for a broader concession on favourable terms, having previously had their palms greased with shares in Kevir-Khurian. The oil would be loaded at the Caspian port of Enzeli, carried to Baku and then via pipeline to Batumi, on the Black Sea.[6]

Although the financing would come from a largely American syndicate of investment banks (the International Corporation itself), this would be hidden from the State Department. This was necessary not only because the department might feel beholden to support Sinclair or Jersey Standard's prior claims to north Persia, but because the United States did not formally recognise the USSR until 1933. France recognised the USSR in 1924 and was the most 'pro-Soviet' of the western powers. The International Corporation would thus draw on the Quai d'Orsay and the French ambassador in Tehran, Lucien Bonzon (whose share portfolio Gulbenkian was also managing).[7]

After building up mutual trust through this joint venture, the International Corporation would finance Venezuelan concessions owned by another associate, the German-born banker Alfred Meyer, who claimed to have good relations with the dictator, Gómez. The International Corporation would also acquire control of a second-tier American oil firm. Thus the Soviets would get hard currency, the French and Persians a supply of oil and royalties free from meddling by *les trusts anglo-saxons*, and Gulbenkian and the fellow investors in the International Corporation would make money. The latter included brokers and banks in New York (Kuhn Loeb, Hayden Stone, Blair & Co.), Paris (Warburgs) and Amsterdam (Lippmann Rosenthal), as well as Darmstädter Bank and the Wallenberg family of Sweden.[8] Société Générale joined later, in 1928.[9]

While Gulbenkian tackled Mortimer Schiff of Kuhn Loeb in Paris, the job of persuading Hayden Stone to join the International Corporation fell to Beatty. In January 1927 he wrote to Charles Hayden in New York, sketching out Gulbenkian's qualifications and motives in putting the 'big scheme' together:

> I think that Gulbenkian understands the Eastern psychology and the Russian and far eastern conditions probably far better than any man in Europe. In fact he is really the brains that built up the Shell Royal Dutch Combination as regarding getting hold of the raw material in the way of concessions like the Turkish Petroleum, the V.O.C., etc... . He is very anxious to build up a big situation – I think to be his last big work. He is a man of the most unbounded energy and I think he is keen to build this up for his son so he has an added incentive besides simply that of making money.[10]

Deterding of course saw things differently. The idea that Gulbenkian was now obstructing his own Russian plans for Royal Dutch-Shell and Jersey Standard infuriated him. So did Gulbenkian's success in peeling away Deterding's associates, including Gustav Nobel and former Royal Dutch-Shell director Hendrikus Colijn, who agreed to head the International Corporation.[11] Deterding lashed out in letters to Teagle, president of Jersey Standard:

> Mr. Gulbenkian having no longer any interests in the oil world, is now trying to become the petroleum expert for the French Government in order to lead them directly into the petroleum business. I am sorry to say that Gulbenkian's trading as a petroleum expert is backed by our mutual friend, G[ustave] Nobel. Mr. Nobel has the erroneous idea that in regard to finance nobody can surpass Mr. Gulbenkian's ability of putting matters right. In this way he is doing a great deal of harm to all the big petroleum companies.

Nobel had an inflated sense of Gulbenkian's importance, Deterding argued. 'He never was anything else than a financier, and was only employed by us as such until we found that loyalty was a thing which was not very well known to Mr. Gulbenkian, seeing that we paid him well for all he did and that, had it not been for me, he would not even [have] had a participation in the TPC.' Gulbenkian was such a regular presence in the Quai d'Orsay, Deterding sneered, 'it has been asked whether he has his sleeping quarters there'.[12]

Both Deterding and Teagle were in the uncomfortable position of having invested very large sums in buying up Russian oil facilities that were now being operated by state-run Soviet entities like Grozneft and Azneft. In 1920 Jersey Standard had been confident enough of the imminent collapse of the Soviet regime that it had paid Nobel more than $6 million for half of Nobel's vast Russian operations. In November 1924 Teagle had agreed to collaborate with Deterding in negotiating for a Soviet oil export monopoly. Given the opprobrium Deterding had received after buying Russian crude in 1923 (breaking the Front Uni embargo Deterding himself led), going in with Deterding in this way carried significant reputational risks for Jersey Standard. One of Teagle's executives warned that 'the first use that the Royal Dutch will make of this association will be to divide with us the odium of purchasing stolen goods'.[13]

In late 1924 Louis Pineau had negotiated a contract with Neftsyndikat (the Russian oil agency) on behalf of the French state. This supplied the French navy's fuel oil needs for three years.[14] Pétrofina took over this contract and a few months later secured Russian supplies as well as a sales monopoly for France, her colonies and protectorates – in other words, Neftsyndikat was prohibited from selling into these areas except through Pétrofina.[15] This relationship grew closer in 1928, when a joint venture named Pétronaphte was established that continued importing Russian oil into France until 1935. What Pétrofina and Neftsyndikat had established for the French market – that is, a Russian export monopoly run through a jointly owned holding company (Pétronaphte, in this case) – was exactly what Deterding and Teagle had been trying unsuccessfully to negotiate for other, larger markets since 1924.

Given Gulbenkian's existing ties to Pineau and Léon Wenger of Pétrofina, as well as the Quai d'Orsay, one might wonder if Deterding and Teagle were wise in allowing the Gulbenkians to guide their joint negotiations with the USSR in 1925 – that is, before the breakdown in relations between Gulbenkian and Deterding. Gulbenkians senior and junior held that the best strategy was to wait until anti-Soviet feeling aroused by reports of communist agitation in the Balkans subsided. Teagle was persuaded not to buy Russian oil.[16]

In a letter to Riedemann, Teagle declared himself 'at a loss to understand what is in the back of Gulbenkian's mind'. 'Has it ever occurred to you that what he has in mind is that if he can postpone the actual negotiations between the Shell and ourselves it might be possible for him to so arrange matters with the Russians as to be in a position somewhat similar to the position he is today occupying in the T[urkish] P[etroleum] Co. matter?'[17] Calouste was delighted that Nubar was serving as unofficial liaison between Royal Dutch-Shell and Jersey Standard on Russian questions. It was a position 'I have always been wishing for you', he wrote, adding in Armenian, 'May God grant you success!'[18]

Calouste felt himself to be the best intermediary with the Russians and had resented Royal Dutch-Shell sending Joe Boyle and others to negotiate for them.[19] It is difficult to work out what he was up to in 1925.[20] Whatever his role was, the collapse of his relationship with Deterding did not sweeten relations between Royal Dutch-Shell and Jersey Standard. In November 1925 Socony negotiated the purchase of 60,000 tons of Russian kerosene at rock-bottom prices. This went ahead despite Teagle's opposition and a direct appeal by Deterding to John D. Rockefeller Jr himself. 'Such money instead of being used as means of trading is used to promote revolution and murder,' Deterding wired. 'The Soviet regime is an anti-Christ regime.'[21]

When Socony subsequently 'dumped' this Russian kerosene on Far East markets Royal Dutch-Shell viewed as 'theirs', Deterding launched a price war in the region.[22] When Teagle thrashed out a Russian export monopoly scheme Deterding sabotaged it: revenge for Teagle's failure to rein in Jersey's 'sister', Socony.[23] Deterding's poor negotiating skills nonetheless continued to stymie his own efforts to secure a monopoly. As one British diplomat noted, his tendency to try to charm the Russians into an export monopoly, then 'blow up' when he failed and make unrealistic threats (vowing that he would see that Russians did not sell a drop of their oil to anyone), represented 'an utterly stupid and at the same time thoroughly characteristic thing for him to do'.[24]

The Persian Connection

Although Gulbenkian met with Chicherin and other Soviet leaders on occasion, his main Russian contact was the chairman of the national bank, Georges Piatakoff, 'the one man I know in that crowd, up to the present, who I can trust'.[25] Son of a wealthy Ukrainian sugar refiner, Piatakoff had been exiled to Siberia by the Tsarist regime in 1912 for Bolshevist activities. He returned to Kiev during the Revolution, where he helped organise the formation of Red Army units in 1918–19. Gulbenkian probably first met him in 1925, when Piatakoff visited Paris as a member of the USSR's Supreme Soviet of the National Economy. Piatakoff later joined the Paris branch of Gosbank, the state bank of the USSR. In 1928 he moved to Gosbank's headquarters in Moscow, becoming president the following year.

In his letters and in memos sent to Piatakoff, Gulbenkian was nothing if not forthright in his criticism of the way Neftsyndikat had been negotiating with various non-Russian oil firms. Neftsyndikat's poor grasp of tactics had diminished rather than enhanced the Russian position in international oil:

> I wish to profit by the unique opportunity your petroleum offers to lay down the law to the trusts, by making them feel the full strength of the finance company [i.e. International Corporation] which will stand by your side. In my opinion the action you have taken is very dangerous because you have, by dint of sacrifices begun to adopt a certain strategic importance for the Trusts. You must not give up these advantages for the sake of small side-agreements, but rather find ways of leveraging this position so as to draw the greatest possible advantages from it.

He enclosed with his letter confidential Front Uni memoranda which were, he insisted, just bluff on behalf of Deterding, the Front's leader. 'I can demolish this association any time I want, but I won't do so willy-nilly, without having first come up with some practical scheme with you.'[26] For Gulbenkian, this was a rare example of swagger.

Gulbenkian was sending similar memos to Timurtash, de facto prime minister to Reza Shah of Persia. The pair had 'a long chat' in October 1926, when Timurtash visited Paris, during which Gulbenkian sketched out his plan for Soviet–Persian collaboration in the development of north Persia's oil reserves. Timurtash asked Gulbenkian to prepare a report, which he duly did, with the assistance of Gustav Nobel.[27] Trade agreements and a neutrality and friendship treaty had seen relations between the USSR and Persia warm somewhat in 1924 and 1925, to the benefit of their joint venture for oil, Kevir-Khurian. In 1924 this firm had purchased the north Persian concession from that irrepressible Georgian concession-hunter,

Arkady Khostaria. Khostaria had already sold the rights granted under this firman (concession grant) of 1880 once (to Anglo-Persian) and possibly twice.[28] He retained a 20 per cent stake in Kevir-Khurian. The USSR held 65 per cent and the rest belonged to the Shah, Timurtash and other Persian notables.[29]

Even more promising, in February 1925 the Russian ambassador in Tehran was pushing Chicherin to invite French capital into this business, in order to keep Jersey Standard out.[30] In 1926 Timurtash paid a visit to Moscow, during which time the Supreme Economic Council took Kevir-Khurian's affairs into its own hands. Chicherin and Commissar for Trade Anastas Mikoyan also pushed the French to get involved. Pineau advised them to approach Pétrofina and Gulbenkian.[31] Gulbenkian negotiated two protocols with Piatakoff, under which the latter agreed to sell half of the Russians' 65 per cent of Kevir-Khurian to a French syndicate, presumably subject to Persian approval.[32]

Piatakoff realised that for Gulbenkian the question of Persian oil was only one part of a much larger scheme. 'From a small issue it grows into a very big question,' he noted, 'which should be treated with the utmost seriousness.'[33] It was time for his superiors to decide how to respond to the deal Gulbenkian had offered them: a complete monopoly on Russian oil exports for four or five years (the oil to be sold at a fixed price), in return for a £10 million investment in developing the USSR's oil facilities. In May 1928 Chicherin submitted a memo to the Politburo weighing up Gulbenkian's proposal and assessing the interests he had brought together in the International Corporation.

Chicherin noted that the International Corporation 'does not have any government behind it'. Though much weaker than the British and American 'trusts', it was probably up to the job. But how could Gulbenkian claim to get better deals selling Russian oil abroad when he didn't have his own marketing company? Creating a new Royal Dutch-Shell-style entity would be difficult, given that any such entity would face competition not only from the trusts but from the state entities which placed the markets of Spain, France and Italy entirely off limits or allowed only limited access. 'At best, he will be able to create new marketing subsidiaries in some countries, which will strengthen our existing apparatus somewhat, but this is something we were planning to do ourselves.' Gulbenkian's skill set lay in mediation, Chicherin observed, not in running a large enterprise, and if the Politburo were minded to make use of him for anything, they should draw on 'his financial power and his value as an intermediary'. Neftsyndikat would sooner or later have to reach some global settlement with the 'world trusts' regarding its oil exports, which represented 35 per cent of Russia's total oil production. Chicherin valued the oil annually available for export at £50 million. He questioned, however, whether it was right to give Gulbenkian the lead in negotiating the aforementioned settlement in exchange for a £10 million investment.[34]

The Politburo's response was mixed, suggesting a lack of consensus on a broader strategy. 'Who else, if not Gulbenkian, would be the mediator between us and the trusts?' asked one commissar. Other commissars felt that 'independent management of our oil exports' was 'something which we can not possibly give up', at least not without significant loss of international prestige.[35] In the absence of any other ideas, the Politburo instructed Piatakoff to keep negotiating with Gulbenkian, and to play him off against Deterding, spinning both along in order to extract as much intelligence as possible about the 'world trusts'' resources and intentions.[36]

Shopping at the Hermitage

In the summer of 1928 Gulbenkian added a further strand to his negotiations with Piatakoff: Old Master paintings and other art treasures. Rembrandts and Houdon sculptures were now included on the diverse shopping list of Ural gold (Lena Goldfields), Siberian zinc and lead (Tetiuhe Mining), north Persian oil (Kevir-Khurian) and Russian oil (Neftsyndikat). Despite Piatakoff's reminders that he was not an art expert, between 1928 and 1930 they negotiated four consignments of works from the Hermitage in Leningrad (now St Petersburg). Gulbenkian became the first of the select group of art collectors and dealers permitted to acquire masterpieces from this prestigious institution.

When the Soviets determined that Gulbenkian was not, in fact, their trump card in negotiations with the 'world trusts', the art sales stopped. Sales to others, however, continued until 1935. By that point more than 24,000 works had been lost from the Hermitage, including 2,880 paintings.[37] Many of its finest paintings were sold via the dealer Knoedler to the American banker turned Treasury Secretary Andrew Mellon. They now hang in the National Gallery Mellon endowed in Washington, DC. While Gulbenkian and Mellon went for quality, Americans with existing mining concessions inside Russia such as Armand Hammer (asbestos) and Averell Harriman (manganese), as well as the second American ambassador to the USSR, Joseph E. Davies, went for quantity, exporting vast amounts of diamonds, furniture and other *objets d'art* to the United States. Consignments were sold through the Berlin auction house Rudolf Lepke and even a New York department store, Lord & Taylor.[38] These efforts did not realise nearly as much hard currency as one might have expected, and the Great Crash of 1929 only made things worse.

Years after the 1917 Revolution the fate of the royal palace-turned-museum was still a mystery. When the British art expert, explorer and MP Martin Conway received special permission from Krasin to visit Leningrad and look around the Hermitage, therefore, there was great interest in what he would find. He arrived in Leningrad on 1 June 1924, was warmly welcomed by officials and spent two whole days in the Hermitage, 'which is opened to me at any and every hour and where in the afternoon I am left absolutely alone – the whole place empty, silent, – and me like the last survivor left in an empty world'.

Conway sent this report in a letter to his wife while he was still in Leningrad, where, as he well knew, he was being closely watched. A less happy picture emerges from a letter sent a few days later from Stockholm, during Conway's return journey: 'I can now tell you that two professors asked by [the British ambassador] to meet me at dinner were arrested that same afternoon, and one of them promptly committed suicide.'[39] In the years following his return to Britain Conway published articles and gave lectures on 'The Art Treasures of Russia' which reassured readers that the Hermitage's masterpieces had survived and were being well treated. In private Conway encouraged British museums to purchase these same treasures.[40]

In January 1928 the Soviet authorities set each state collection a sales target, including the Hermitage. Its director, Sergei Troïnitsky, was demoted and replaced with a party functionary who had never worked in a museum before.[41] Gulbenkian began leafing through published catalogues of the Hermitage, marking up the items he liked, just as he did with sales catalogues from Sotheby's and Wildenstein. He began preparing lists of individual paintings (Leonardo da Vinci's *Ginevra de' Benci*), sculpture (Houdon's *Diana*, to go with the *Apollo* he already owned), furniture, silver, Assyrian gold cups, Byzantine jewellery. He was interested in Armenian and Persian manuscripts and illuminated French and English manuscripts of the fifteenth and sixteenth centuries. Fine bindings also appealed. Was Giorgione's *Judith* available? Botticelli's *Adoration* and Rembrandt's *Danaë* were quite nice, too.[42]

As one might expect, the first list Gulbenkian handed to Piatakoff in 1928 was quite long, and the latter asked him to cut it down. He reduced it to nine paintings and fourteen pieces of silverware. Gulbenkian wanted them as a job lot, but was prepared to deal for the Giorgione *Judith* or Rembrandt's *Pallas Athene* and *Prodigal Son* separately. He sent the Paris jeweller Marcel Aucoc to Moscow and Leningrad in October to inspect these and other works. After receiving Aucoc's report, he sent Karl Fehrmann to Berlin to negotiate with the officials at Antikvariat, the Russian export agency for antiquities. When those negotiations went nowhere Gulbenkian became involved directly, negotiating with Antikvariat's chief, A. M. Ginzburg, in Paris. A deal was eventually agreed in April 1929, whereupon Aucoc returned to Leningrad to oversee delivery to Paris via rail.

For £54,000 (£2.9 million) Gulbenkian secured a mixture of items from his short and long lists as well as totally unrelated items. He got twenty-four of the twenty-five pieces of gold- and silverware by the eighteenth-century French master François-Thomas Germain. He also acquired Dirk Bouts's *Annunciation*, an eighteenth-century French desk and two paintings of the gardens of Versailles by another eighteenth-century French artist, Hubert Robert.[43] Gulbenkian remained fond of the gardens of Versailles, which had been among the intended beneficiaries of his 1916 will. The Robert paintings do not, however, show the gardens in their pomp. Instead they show tree-felling and clearing undertaken in 1774, as part of Louis XVI's abortive plans to redesign the park along more naturalistic, 'English' lines. Far from celebrating a masterpiece of landscape architecture, they seem to suggest its destruction.

Negotiations were not straightforward. Gulbenkian's offers were considered too low, something Gulbenkian attributed to the unwillingness of some Soviet officials (or curators) to have any sale go forward. He was happy to appeal to independent experts, and provided evidence in support of his bids drawn from his earlier purchases and recent auction prices. When Ginzburg failed to respond, Gulbenkian appealed to Piatakoff, who in turn appealed to Commissar Mikoyan. 'We really need to act more decisively,' Piatakoff noted, or else Gulbenkian might lose interest in their oil discussions.[44]

When negotiations seemed stuck, both Ginzburg and Gulbenkian tried adding other works to sweeten the deal. The Bouts, for example, was not on any of Gulbenkian's original lists. Gulbenkian was also offered the entire Stroganoff collection and the Pavlovsk library.[45] Whether as a result of Gulbenkian's pressure or sheer disorganisation, the staff of Antikvariat repeatedly found decisions taken out of their hands by superiors in Gostorg (the main USSR export body), the Foreign Ministry and the Concessions Committee.[46]

Gulbenkian claimed that 'the passion of the collector' was leading him to make offers which were, if anything, overly generous. Piatakoff was lucky, Gulbenkian wrote, to be immune to this 'disease'.[47] Some in the Russian trade delegation in Paris had indeed noticed this 'disease', and wondered why Ginzburg was not taking advantage. One unidentified official knew exactly what approach to take:

> The difficulty is that the people who know their way around this business are opposed to selling, and put up as much resistance as they can to prevent it. Me, all I'm interested in is results, that we get more money. Of course, it is better to take 50 than 15, but if you want to get 50 for the painting which costs 15, you get nothing. This Gulbenkian I spoke to is the greatest obsessive of them all. I met with him several times and he kept telling me 'For God's sake, sell me a painting.' He wanted to buy all our junk. These paintings – they're nothing but a load of rubbish.

Negotiations should only be entrusted to people who knew nothing about art. Otherwise 'the sabotage of the intelligentsia' would continue. It was worrying that Ginzburg's knowledge of art had grown on the job: 'he can now tell his Raphaels from his Rembrandts.'[48]

This hard-nosed attitude seemed to gain the upper hand in January 1930. When Mikoyan sent Troïnitsky the list of eighteen works Gulbenkian proposed to buy for 10 million roubles, Troïnitsky cited the attention given to Conway's visit as proof that the Hermitage was considered among the top rank of world collections. If Gulbenkian got his paintings the Hermitage could drop to the second or third rank.[49] In the past curators like Troïnitsky had managed to use discussions over valuations of works to draw out sale preliminaries. Now the selection and valuation of works were entrusted to 'shock brigades' sent by Narkompros (the Education and

Culture Ministry). Works actually on display (rather than in storage) were no longer exempt.[50]

With curatorial staff sidelined, the next three consignments were negotiated quickly. In February 1930 Gulbenkian secured Rubens's *Hélène Fourment* and fifteen more pieces of silver for £155,000 (£8.8 million). Then came Houdon's life-sized marble figure of *Diana* along with two Rembrandts (*Titus* and *Pallas Athene*) and three other paintings. Curators managed to salvage a *Lady and Her Cook* by the seventeenth-century Dutch master Pieter de Hooch, substituting Gerard ter Borch's *Music Lesson*.[51] Leblond, Gulbenkian's agent in St Petersburg, struggled to find the tools and staff necessary to pack up these works. In the end they were packed at night, by the light of candles.[52]

Bought from the artist by Empress Catherine the Great in 1784, Houdon's *Diana* had stood guard in the inner hall of the imperial palace at Tsarkoe Selo before being transferred to the palace-museum of the Hermitage in the early nineteenth century. At the Hermitage it was prominently displayed, serving as 'a kind of greeting card and invitation' to the museum as a whole.[53] Leblond accompanied the two-ton *Diana* on the steamer *Dzerzinsky*'s voyage to London, where he was instructed to inform Gulbenkian of her health immediately upon their arrival. Gulbenkian duly received word that a certain lady had arrived in the Pool of London 'a little tired', code for 'minor damage'. Happily this damage to the goddess of the hunt's bow represented an old injury and was easily made good.[54] All deliveries ended up at 51 Avenue d'Iéna, and travelled, if not literally by the diplomatic bag, then at least under the seal of the Persian Legation. Thanks to Gulbenkian's diplomatic status, customs officials were barred from opening the cases and no duty was paid.[55]

Gulbenkian was candid enough to acknowledge that such sales might come to haunt the USSR. In one 1930 memo he reminded Piatakoff:

> I have always been of the opinion that those things which have been held in your <u>museums</u> for many years should not be sold, not just because they represent your nation's birthright, but as a great educational resource and a source of great national pride. If word of their sale were to get out it would harm your government's credit. The conclusion drawn would be that things must have come to a pretty pass for one to be obliged to sell things in order to realise sums which, for a country like yours, are hardly significant.

He had always told Piatakoff and his representatives that if they insisted on selling, they should keep him abreast of their plans and allow him first refusal. Instead these same representatives were selling objects to American collectors behind Gulbenkian's back. Whereas Gulbenkian was the soul of discretion, these other sales were high-profile and harmed Russian prestige. 'How I laughed when one of your intermediaries told me that during the French Revolution the revolutionaries had sold Versailles. How naive can you get, and how ignorant of history!'[56]

The fourth and final sale was agreed three months later.[57] This consignment consisted of a single Rembrandt, *Old Man*, for which Gulbenkian paid £30,000 (£1.7 million). All in all, Gulbenkian bought three out of his original list of nine masterpieces, as well as a third Rembrandt, plus a range of items which complemented his existing collections of silver and furniture. The Hermitage acquisitions stepped his collecting up a gear. Gulbenkian was beginning to consider the make-up of his collection as the director of a public gallery might, concerned that each great master be represented by a characteristic masterpiece.

The Scheme Comes Apart

In Paris in October 1928 Gulbenkian, Chester Beatty, Carl Melchior of Warburg and Piatakoff thrashed out a set of terms for an oil sales monopoly which Piatakoff agreed to take back to Moscow, promising to return in a few weeks with their response. In December Piatakoff reported that his superiors had refused to consider long-term sales arrangements. Gulbenkian was frustrated that 'all our discussions ended in nothing', concluding that the change in policy had been forced on Piatakoff.[58] He was probably correct. A member of the Trotskyite Left, Piatakoff's position in Moscow was shaky. In August 1928 he had been sent on a 'holiday' by the Central Committee, and was only reinstated after being vetted by the feared Rabkrin (Workers' and Peasants' Inspectorate).

Originally created by Lenin to allow peasants to police government agencies from below, the Rabkrin was becoming part of the machinery by which Stalin intimidated his Trotskyite rivals, tightening his own grip on power. A former stoker, Rabkrin member Boris Royzenman opposed the Hermitage sales (clearly it wasn't just the intelligentsia who did). The unnamed official who had been so gung-ho about selling Hermitage 'junk' to Gulbenkian had sought to calm Piatakoff. Piatakoff should not allow 'scary Royzenman' to frighten 'people by saying that we are accepting low offers or that we are tearing pictures off the walls'.[59] Though he held senior office, Piatakoff was not in a position to throw his weight around. Nor were the other Paris-based diplomats and trade representatives Gulbenkian knew, most of whom were also Trotskyites. Piatakoff was hauled in again in 1937. This time he was executed. Royzenman followed in 1938.

In such a climate it is perhaps unsurprising that the Russians stuck to playing Gulbenkian against Deterding.[60] The Russians did not join oil's top table. All they got was a series of 'as-is' agreements, under which they agreed to rest content with a small market share and sell their oil to the 'world trusts' below cost price.[61] The 1929 crash and new oil discoveries in east Texas a year later only served to confirm this policy, by driving down demand. In 1930–32 Gulbenkian and Beatty gave up trying to mine inside Russia: Piatakoff brokered a settlement under which they were bought out of Tetiuhe Mining by the Soviet government (Lena Goldfields proved less easy to resolve).[62] As for north Persia, the French syndicate Wenger had created in 1927 sent a survey party to Semnan in 1929–30, but made little progress.[63] In 1932 Timurtash visited Moscow again, where he reportedly initialled a further agreement on Kevir-Khurian. By this point Reza Shah's suspicions of Timurtash had got the better of him, however, and Timurtash was thrown into prison, where he died of 'food poisoning' in 1933.[64]

Without Russia, Gulbenkian's 'big scheme' was high and dry. The Venezuelan element had involved plans to exploit National Reserves that had been established under Venezuela's 1920 Oil Law.[65] Having agreed terms with former oil minister Gil Fortoul in Paris, Gulbenkian sent E. H. Keeling to Caracas to negotiate with President Juan Vicente Gómez.[66] When it emerged that Fortoul lacked the influence he had claimed, Gulbenkian tried again, this time through the Société Pétrolière de Caracas, a firm established in 1928 with support from Gustav Nobel and Wenger's Pétrofina. Unfortunately, Gulbenkian was unable to secure the French Finance Ministry's formal approval (the *côte*) necessary to float this firm on the Paris stock market. The scandalous collapse of Banque Oustric had led to a freeze on new *côtisations*.[67]

The American part of the 'big scheme' focused on Tidewater Petroleum, a firm with concessions in Texas, Oklahoma and Alaska. Here Gulbenkian's proposed partners were the investment house Blair and Co., whose staff included his old Paris friend Georges Bénard, as well as Jean Monnet, who would later be the driving force behind the European Economic Community. Blair & Co.'s Henry Lockhart agreed that, despite the consolidation of the American oil industry, 'it would be possible ... to more than duplicate the success of Shell Union from material which might be made available in this country, adding foreign sources of supply, and combining with a group on your side with a view to ultimately controlling the widest possible profitable distribution.'[68]

Might the 'big scheme' have come off had circumstances been different? Meyer's concessions proved profitable enough to establish an integrated oil company, Ultramar, which operated until 1991.[69] In the late 1930s Tidewater was acquired by a playboy-turned-oilman who used it to build what would become an even larger integrated oil company with valuable fields in the Saudi-Kuwaiti Neutral Zone as well as Mexico and the United States. His name was not Gulbenkian, however, but Getty.[70] Though John Paul Getty's multiple marriages smacked more of Nubar, in his notorious miserliness and general approach to deal-making he strongly resembled Calouste. Getty's success suggests that, had the Great Crash not intervened, Gulbenkian could well have pulled off his 'big scheme'. A negotiator and deal-maker rather than a manager, however, one wonders if Gulbenkian could have run the resulting oil company successfully.

In the end, after so many years of wire-pulling and negotiation, the only export monopoly Gulbenkian managed to get out of the USSR was for another form of 'black gold': caviar. Starting in 1924, Gulbenkian had advanced the Soviet caviar export agency hard currency in return for the monopoly. But even here the Soviets proved difficult business partners. After a few successful deals the main Soviet export agency suddenly turned the tables, holding back enough caviar to undercut Vanetzian, the ethnic Armenian caviar merchant Gulbenkian bankrolled. Gulbenkian was landed with two tons of caviar he could find no market for. Having failed to make a dent in supplies by eating it themselves, the Gulbenkians gave away vast quantities to their friends. 'So generous were we,' Nubar would later recall, 'that almost the first question we put to anyone we met was, "Do you like caviare?" If the answer was "Yes", we made an immediate present of a one- or two-pound tin.'[71] Calouste's 'big scheme' ended as a potlatch of caviar. It was magnificent, but also somewhat farcical.

THIRTEEN

MR PRESIDENT, 1930–34

The first biography of Calouste Gulbenkian appeared in 1930. Although written by a relation, Aram Turabian, *Calouste Gulbenkian: Le milliardaire arménien et sa vie* was anything but friendly.[1] It contrasted the opulence of Calouste's lifestyle with the 'democratic' modesty of his father, Sarkis. Sarkis's death had, Turabian claimed, allowed his eldest son to indulge 'his innate egoism' to the full. Calouste had humiliated and impoverished his brothers, Vahan and Karnig, now languishing in Algiers and Neuilly. He had failed to support not only his own family, but the cause of the Armenian *patrie*, collaborating with Cavid. Turabian's conclusion was damning: 'Family! *Patrie*! Race! For [Calouste] all are eclipsed by one sole thing: money-making.'[2]

The biography was not so much a hatchet job as blackmail, Armenian-style. Turabian had previously asked Calouste for money to cover medical expenses for his sick mother, then his daughter and latterly for himself. Calouste and Nevarte had sent money. Back in 1914 Turabian had rallied Armenian volunteers to the French flag, served alongside them and then raised funds for injured veterans.[3] He had also served the Armenian *patrie* as a journalist, publishing pro-Armenian propaganda. Having given his life and fortune to the *patrie*, Turabian was (in his own eyes, at least) owed larger sums by Gulbenkian. He was prepared to use threats as well as entreaties to get the 20,000 francs' capital he wanted to start a business.[4] The biography was Turabian carrying out one of his threats.

To be fair, Turabian had made his personal connection to Gulbenkian clear in his biography, claiming that he had been reluctant to publish it and expressing a hope that his relation might yet repent of his many sins. Turabian included in his text a description of his own mother's deathbed, 'a moving and distressing scene'. Having appealed to her 'cousin' (Gulbenkian was in fact her sister-in-law's nephew) for help with medical expenses, she had apparently waited in vain for the postal order to arrive. Driven mad by despair, her last words were, 'Calouste! Calouste!' Had she not been driven out of her mind by this *idée fixe*, Turabian suggested, she could easily have lived another fifteen years.

As it happens (or, rather, as it was recorded – an important distinction), similar deathbed vigils had previously been kept by both Calouste's mother, Dirouhi, and Calouste's nephew (Karnig's son) Sarkis, in 1908 and 1914 respectively. Apparently little Sarkis was fixated on shaking Calouste's hand before he died. This repetition suggests a certain amount of dramatic licence.[5] The important point is that Turabian's charges were not unique: Calouste had been facing accusations of egoism and neglect of 'patriotic' duty for years. Though lurid, Turabian's 1930 biography prompts consideration of whether these charges were fair.

Turabian quoted British press reports estimating Gulbenkian's wealth at 1.2 billion French francs (£530 million). In 1931 Gulbenkian's main share and bond portfolio was vested in a Liechtenstein entity named Anstalt Vega, which ensured that he paid a mere 100 Swiss francs per year in tax, on a portfolio valued at £4.6 million (£288 million).[6] Considering the depressed state of the New York and London stock markets at the time, this was a very large fortune indeed. Although the break with Deterding had ended the 1 per cent and 2 per cent commissions on Royal Dutch-Shell's sales into various European markets, Gulbenkian continued to make money selling VOC shares. In 1930, however, it was clear that Gulbenkian would need to realise a significant part of this portfolio in order to pay the calls on his 5 per cent of TPC – that is, to pay his 5 per cent share of the cost of constructing a pipeline from Baba Gurgur to the Mediterranean, about 400 miles as the crow flies. For 1933 alone (when construction costs peaked) this represented a sum of around £264,000 (£16.9 million).[7]

This order of financial commitment was manageable for oil majors like Anglo-Persian and Jersey Standard, each with thousands of shareholders relatively comfortable with the associated political risk. For Gulbenkian, it was a matter worth careful consideration. Power in Baghdad remained in the hands of a small Sunni landowning elite, frustrated by mandatory tutelage by British officials and eager to accelerate Iraq's entry into the League of Nations as a sovereign state, yet reluctant to forgo the protection of British armed forces. This elite was wary of nationalists, yet frequently at odds with King Faisal. Ministerial office provided its members with ample opportunities to pilfer estates from Iraq's Department of State Lands.[8]

Iraqi ministers' attitudes towards TPC were characterised by similar ambiguities. Nationalist sentiment was about tactics, not strategy or ideology. In London in March 1928 Interior Minister Muzahim al-Pachachi warned John Cadman (who served as chairman of TPC as well as Anglo-Persian) that on his return to Baghdad he would take 'an ultra-nationalistic policy as regards politics, [but] as regards economical matters, and specially as regards the development of the TPC, he will be very friendly to foreign enterprise'. To make the company appear less foreign they agreed that Muzahim would take with him a letter inviting the Iraqis to suggest 'a more Irak sounding name, such as Irak Petroleum, or Mossoul Petroleum, or something like that'. In 1929 TPC duly became the Iraq Petroleum Company (IPC).[9] In September 1929 the new Labour government in London suddenly announced that it would support Iraq's entry into the League of Nations in 1932.

Strikingly, Gulbenkian had hardly any contacts in the Iraqi government.[10] With Iraq on the verge of independence, it was important to get some. When prime minister Nuri al-Said visited London in 1929, Nubar threw him a party to get better acquainted with 'the various Iraq notabilities'. After dinner Nuri's Minister of War (also his brother-in-law), Ja'far al-'Askari, explained how the Iraqis viewed IPC: 'He said it was like a woman married to four husbands and that was very difficult for the woman and for Iraq. I asked him where Gulbenkian comes in that simile and he told me that Iraq considers Gulbenkian the "Amant" [lover].'[11]

Nubar was not reassured by this. He encouraged his father to sell out to the Spanish or Italians. Seen as 'a cold business matter', Nubar noted, it was obvious that they should liquidate their position. 'But [if] you think that you can afford to lose half a million of pounds for a question of pleasure and personal interest, that is another matter.' Calouste replied that he would only sell for a 'truly enormous value'. 'I am very stubborn and I have decided to lose even more than what you name but will have the benefit of the T. P. C.'[12]

Publicity, Propaganda, Philanthropy

Gulbenkian was now sixty-one, feeling his age (thanks to neuritis in his legs) and starting to think about his legacy. As always, Nubar was first in his thoughts.[13] Calouste still hoped that his son would one day run IPC as managing director, and took comfort from Cadman and CFP's 1929 proposal that Nubar tour Iraq as IPC's representative, in another effort to warm up relations between the company and the Iraqi government.[14] Calouste also welcomed Nubar's election to the board of the Armenian General Benevolent Union (AGBU).

'It is a duty for all Armenians with a heart and with feelings to bring their activity for the defence of this Union,' Gulbenkian noted, and address 'the poverty and misery of tens of thousands who are hungry and homeless'.[15] Gulbenkian's decision to accept nomination as president of AGBU in 1930 was nonetheless striking. He had previously shown little interest in the administration of such Armenian organisations. Here again Gulbenkian may have been thinking of his son, as it was suggested that Nubar might take over the presidency from his father after a few years.[16] Calouste's plans for a smooth handover of his commercial and philanthropic responsibilities would not be realised quite so easily.

Although AGBU had been established in Cairo in 1906, in 1930 it had until then only known one president: the Egyptian-born Boghos Nubar, son of the four-times prime minister of Egypt, Nubar Nubarian, after whom Nubar Gulbenkian had been named.[17] AGBU had been founded as a technocratic organisation for agricultural improvement. Confronted with war, genocide and the resulting refugee crisis, Boghos transformed it into an organisation focused on diplomacy and propaganda as much as philanthropy. Administratively, AGBU was run by a series of committees that struggled for control. Donations and bequests often came bound with conditions restricting their use to benefit Armenians from the donor's home town or village. Thanks to the genocide, the community in question had often vanished. Even where funds could be used to fund resettlement, here again Armenian parochialism held sway, demanding that new villages be named after the old village (or the donor) and be populated with survivors from the donor's home village or region.

Like its American equivalent, Near East Relief, AGBU had been effective when it came to offering short-term assistance, meeting the immediate needs of those refugees who found themselves in refugee camps in Port Said or on the Shatt al-Arab near Basra. Unlike Near East Relief, however, AGBU found it difficult to work out what to do when orphans outgrew orphanages and risked falling into destitution and prostitution for want of skills. In 1922 AGBU established contact with the Soviet authorities who ran what was left of the independent Republic of Armenia. As if the war had not been bad enough, famine had struck the region in 1921–2. Diseases like malaria were rife. The following year the foundation established by Calouste's cousin Badrig, the Gullabi Gulbenkian Foundation, funded an AGBU delegation to Armenia intended to identify projects suitable for funding. Plans were made for a new settlement to be built on 7,400 acres south-west of Yerevan, to be named 'Nubarashen' in Boghos's honour.

The first convoy of Armenian refugees left Jaffa for Batumi (the nearest Black Sea port to Armenia) in October 1924. But the authorities in the Armenian capital, Yerevan, turned back the majority of a second convoy sent three years later. It was becoming clear that Yerevan saw AGBU as a cash cow to be milked for hard currency and machinery, and was giving those refugees it did admit a far from warm welcome. Refugees used to practising their trade or craft in cities struggled to make a home in a country where four-fifths of the population lived off the land. Others found the unfamiliar communist ethos stifling. Some even fled to Beirut, refugees from their 'national home'.

The Yerevan authorities drove a hard bargain, taking any excuse to lower the number of refugees they admitted and increase the quid pro quo in financial support they demanded for accepting them. While the Soviets recognised that AGBU was the best-endowed philanthropic organisation in the Armenian diaspora, they were jealous of AGBU's grip on that same diaspora, and hoped in time to build up its rival organisation, Hay Oknutyan Gomide, into a vehicle for both inward investment and the diffusion of pro-Soviet propaganda among the diaspora. As the executive secretary of Near East Relief noted, 'the Communist Armenian government visualises something like an Armenian Zionist movement, which will result in constant contributions of all kinds to the educational and social welfare work of the Armenian Government.'[18]

AGBU's general director, Vahan Malezian, and other AGBU officers had probably hoped that Gulbenkian would be an absentee figurehead with deep pockets. Instead, staff at head office in Paris discovered that their new president expected them to work just as hard as he did himself.

Gulbenkian abolished the Propaganda Committee and introduced a log in which staff had to record the times they clocked on and off.[19]

Drawing on his strengths in financial and legal questions, Gulbenkian focused his attentions on leveraging AGBU's £709,000 (£43 million) endowment by means of 'a new Holding Company or Armenian Charity Trust'. Under this proposal a company would be created which would issue shares in exchange for donations. Existing funds' portfolios could be replaced with such shares. The holding company would, one presumes, never issue a dividend, but rather devote the interest on its portfolio to charitable projects.[20] AGBU's finances would be centralised. Assets would be leveraged further by focusing less on outright gifts to refugees and more on microlending. Here Gulbenkian may have been following the lead of the Norwegian explorer and humanitarian Fridtjof Nansen, who in 1926 had developed an abortive 5 per cent bond scheme to support projects within Soviet Armenia (only for Yerevan to object).

There proved to be legal hurdles to realising AGBU Holding in the United Kingdom or United States. Charitable entities or trust funds would not, Gulbenkian was advised, be allowed to hold shares in an entity like AGBU Holding.[21] Happily, Canadian laws were different, though there was always the chance that 'Bolshevik or Ultra-Socialist legislation' might get passed in that country. On consideration Gulbenkian concluded that 'we can all take the risk of Bolchevism in Canada.'[22]

Lacking the romantic visions of an Armenian national home full of happy shepherds playing their *duduks* (Armenian flutes), Calouste was far less willing than his colleagues within AGBU to tolerate the extortion-ate relationship with Yerevan. He was also, of course, a far more skilled negotiator. In September 1931 he persuaded the chairman of the Soviet Armenian Council of Commissars, Sahak Ter Gabrielian, to accept 6,000 refugees currently in Greece and Bulgaria, with another 4,000 to follow. With the assistance of the Nansen International Office for Refugees, Cal-ouste launched a campaign to fund transfer costs, priming the pump with his own large donation. And 6,242 refugees actually made it to Yerevan, twice as many as had been managed in two previous convoys.[23] This success would not go unpunished by Soviet Armenia.

Soviet Armenia also resented Gulbenkian on account of his support for the settlement of Armenian refugees in Syria and Lebanon (rather than in Armenia). This scheme had been started back in 1927 by the Nansen Office, which bought up large plots of land on Ashrafiye Hill, on the edge of Beirut. Under this scheme refugees received loans to help them purchase new homes, not only in Beirut but also in Aleppo and Damascus. Almost all the loans were repaid, and in terms of the number of houses built and refugees resettled (23,000 by 1933) the Nansen scheme was far more successful than Nubarashen, AGBU's ill-advised adventure in Yerevan.

Unfortunately, Gulbenkian's fundraising appeal for his Syrian resettlement scheme met with a feeble response, partly owing to the German banking crisis.[24] Calouste turned to his cousins in New York. In 1928 the Gullabi Gulbenkian Foundation established a maternity hospital in Aleppo, named after Badrig Gulbenkian's wife, Virginie.[25] In 1931 the same foundation contributed $15,000 towards two new neighbourhoods on the outskirts of Beirut. Completed in 1932, 'Gullabashen' housed 750 refugees by 1935.[26]

Gulbenkian's plans for AGBU eventually fell victim to infighting in Yerevan between Ter Gabrielian and Aghasi Khanjian, First Secretary of the Central Committee of the Communist Party of Armenia. Khanjian took Ter Gabrielian's apparent weakness in negotiations with Gulbenkian as evidence Ter Gabrielian was an imperialist agent. A speech by Khanjian published in the newspaper *Soviet Armenia* on 16 October 1931 claimed that Gulbenkian preferred to settle refugees in Syria so that he could use them as slave labour constructing the IPC pipeline.[27] It was a ludicrous accusation. Far from seeking to pack the company with fellow Armenians, Gulbenkian told Armenians who wrote to him soliciting IPC jobs that 'the only thing that counts is individual merit'.[28]

In September 1932 Gulbenkian resigned the AGBU presidency. His frustrations had been mounting since he was nominated in 1930. The AGBU board had kicked the proposal for AGBU Holding into the long grass.[29] A culture of pettifogging self-importance and patronage had proved unshakeable. As Gulbenkian wrote to Devgantz in Nice, 'everyone on the board wants to shine.'[30] Khanjian's lurid accusations were the final straw. But Gulbenkian was self-aware enough to admit that 'my temperament is that of a lone worker'.[31] He was not cut out for committee work. AGBU now fell back into old habits. Yerevan even persuaded it to buy luxury Ford cars for party apparatchiks, with funds intended to build Nubarashen. This dysfunctional relationship continued until 1937, when Stalin's purges reached Yerevan, claiming Ter Gabrielian as one of their many victims.[32]

From Kirkuk to the Sea

Under the 1925 convention agreed with the Iraqi government, IPC had until November 1928 to survey the two *vilayets* of Baghdad and Mosul and decide on the location of its twenty-four plots of eight square miles each. The unwieldy nature of the international consortium made it difficult for IPC to take decisions, however, even when they weren't distracted by trying to negotiate a working agreement. Absent or impassable roads, mountainous terrain, disease, tribal unrest and the vast distances involved made operating in the region particularly challenging. It had taken Anglo-Persian four years and a thousand men to string a six-inch pipeline the 138 miles from its Masjid-i-Sulaiman field in south-west Persia to the Gulf. Kirkuk lay more than 500 miles from the Mediterranean.

Gulbenkian looked to Nubar and his son-in-law, Kevork Essayan, to represent his interests at IPC meetings. In Nubar's words, their duties involved:

a) taking an intelligen[t] part in the proceedings
b) helping the French against the others
c) not being unfriendly to Cadman [of Anglo-Persian] and the others.

Nubar concluded that 'the practical way' to achieve these occasionally contradictory instructions was 'for Kev[ork] and myself to sit in our corner with our mouths tightly closed, which Kev always does'.[33]

The question over which route the IPC pipeline to the Mediterranean should take brought all these questions of high diplomacy and statecraft into focus in the years between 1928 and 1935 – that is, between the Red Line Agreement and the point at which the IPC pipeline came on stream. The cheapest and most direct route to the Mediterranean lay across Syria. Ever since Clemenceau's 'gift' of Mosul to Lloyd George in 1919, the French had taken comfort from this. Mosul's oil would have to cross their mandate, giving them leverage. Unfortunately, their eviction of Faisal from Damascus in 1920 had not been forgotten and Faisal insisted that the pipeline run south-west, through Transjordan (another British mandate, with a fellow Hashemite on the throne) to the Palestinian port of Haifa. The added cost of the longer, southern route was estimated at between $8 and $13 million above the $45 million cost of the shorter, northern route.[34] Even worse, under the 1925 Convention the Iraqis had insisted that any pipeline be a 'common carrier' – that is, leave at least 30 per cent of its capacity for rival firms' oil.

Irritated by IPC's dilatoriness in selecting its plots, in 1928 Faisal indicated that he also wanted them to build a railway to the Mediterranean. The king was able to make such demands thanks to the arrival of a rival would-be concessionaire: British Oil Developments (BOD). In December 1928 a BOD director arrived in Baghdad bearing gifts, or at least, promises of them. According to reports he gave to the *Baghdad Times*, alongside a railway to the Mediterranean and a £2 million loan, BOD would build a permanent bridge at Baghdad, replacing the existing pontoon bridge, as well as a long-awaited barrage on the Euphrates at Habbaniya, which would improve river navigation by raising water levels. All BOD wanted in exchange was IPC's concession.

Sixty-four-year-old former Admiral of the Fleet Rosslyn Erskine Wemyss, 1st Baron Wester Wemyss, had probably got to know Faisal during his days working in the Arab Bureau in Cairo during the First World War. Well connected at the court of King George V as well as that of Faisal I, Wemyss had been left off the list of admirals granted money awards by His Majesty's Government at war's end. In need of cash, in 1925 he followed the example of other admirals and entered the service of an oil syndicate.

The brains behind BOD was the adventurer Francis W. Rickett. Rickett traded heavily on Wemyss's name and sent him to Baghdad twice in 1928. In June 1929 Wemyss visited Rome and, working through a General Mola (Italian military attaché in London), persuaded Mussolini's state oil company, AGIP, to take a 40 per cent participation in BOD. Rickett dropped by the Gulbenkians' London office three times to stir the pot, inviting them to negotiate some kind of agreement between BOD and IPC.[35] Meanwhile speculation about who was really behind BOD was rife. The State Department thought it was Royal Dutch-Shell; CFP thought it was Anglo-Persian. John Paul Getty, who passed through Baghdad in October 1930, told the State Department it was Sinclair Oil. Former Iraqi prime minister Muzahim al-Pachachi thought BOD was in fact IPC.[36]

BOD eventually secured a seventy-five-year concession in western Iraq in 1932 and AGIP's small team of technical staff even found some oil. Babes in the wood of international oil policy, AGIP took several years to realise that the powerful British interests supposedly behind BOD existed only in Rickett's imagination. Faced with financial pressures linked to Italy's 1935 Ethiopian War, AGIP sold out to IPC.[37] After Wemyss's death in 1933, his widow sought to track down her husband's 20,000 BOD shares, only to find herself chasing shadows: behind the British part of BOD lay nothing but a mysterious entity named 'The Far & Near Development Syndicate'. Like Mussolini, Wemyss had been sold a pup.[38]

Where his IPC partners were willing to consider buying off such entities, Gulbenkian recommended standing firm.[39] As for the pipeline, he supported the idea of a forked line, one sixteen-inch line to run to Haifa, another to Tripoli. After much diplomatic wrangling, this was the option agreed in October 1930. Under the new IPC–Iraq agreement signed on 24 March 1931, IPC swapped its twenty-four plots for a blanket concession on all of Iraq east of the Tigris (35,000 square miles), an end to the 'common carrier' requirement and other concessions.[40] Once it bought out BOD, therefore, IPC had the whole country to itself. So much for the open door. For the Iraqi state, however, the 1931 agreement was a lifeline: though royalties would only appear when the pipeline was completed, in the meantime IPC undertook to pay a 'deadrent' which saved the country from bankruptcy.

Heirs and Russian Bears

Throughout the pipeline negotiations Nubar in London and Calouste in Paris had been working together fairly peaceably. Nubar was now thirty-five years old and understandably resented not having a salary. He was no longer a young man chipping in around the office. As of 1928 he had a wife to support, the actress Doré Plowden, whom he had met at the tables in Monte Carlo. Nubar was also concerned at the growing influence of his brother-in-law, Kevork.

Kevork's character was very different from Nubar's: quiet, reserved and somewhat nervy.[41] In the early years Calouste had treated Kevork ('Kev') as something of a drudge, taking full advantage of his Stakhanovite love of accounts. Calouste may have hoped that Kev's good habits would rub off on his daughter, Rita. The pair had had a son, Mikhael, in 1927. Married twice, Nubar remained childless, and was doomed to remain so, having suffered a childhood attack of mumps, which had left him infertile. Could Calouste really have forgotten this? It seems that he chose to, for he continued to chivvy Nubar on his failure to provide an heir.[42]

In early 1931 Calouste invited Nubar to spend time with him at

Cannes, where Calouste thought they had reached a modus vivendi. But Nubar would not be charmed out of his demands. 'Don't try to pull a fast one using your soft voice,' Nubar added in Armenian at the end of one letter. When the pair next met in person, in Paris on 16 April 1931, there was a confrontation, the only occasion on which Calouste is reported to have used violence. According to Nubar's account, father struck son in the face and shouted (in Armenian) 'Clear out!', adding that, as far as he was concerned, his son was as 'dead' to him as his brothers were. Calouste instructed Kevork and all his staff to cease communicating with Nubar, whose allowance was also stopped. When Calouste wrote to his son a few months later, inviting him to 'return with heart and love to your father's work and receive and enjoy your usual allowance', Nubar refused.[43]

By October 1931 father and son were able to discuss things more calmly. 'I want to live a decent and respected life as a useful member of the community,' Nubar wrote, 'and especially I want to work and earn a living in congenial surroundings.' A 'regularised Trust Fund' would guarantee what they both wanted: 'For me, a congenial and worthy occupation. For you, a life according to your preference.'[44] With the help of Cadman and a trusted associate from Águila, J. H. Macdonald, a trust fund was established, along with an agreement stating the hours Nubar would work in London, his annual allowance (£10,000) [£600,000] and holidays.

What happened between the April 'scene' and this rapprochement would be a mystery, had Nubar's second wife not serialised her memoirs in the *News of the World*. 'With Nubar I never knew what was in the kitty,' Doré recalled, describing finding herself with him in Biarritz in September 1931, unable to pay their hotel bill. Doré's appeals to her mother-in-law, Nevarte, drew a non-committal if candid reply.

> My dear, neither of you should think that we have a poor opinion of Nubar – he is exceedingly clever – tender-hearted and kind – but my! he is strong-headed ... and it is a great pity! The money belongs to my husband – he can give it to his parrot – or buy *antiques* – he can even buy me an emerald tiara or a diamond necklace (alas! no such luck). He is an exceedingly generous man (no doubt you both know it), but he wants to give money *his own way*. I don't approve or disapproved [*sic*] [of] him – but we either accept his money and do our best for him – or we refuse £ s. d. and just are our own boss! There is no real freedom, my dear, one has always some sort of boss on top of one ...

and if one has no boss – one is so overwhelmed with responsibilities
that there is still less freedom and independence![45]

The letter displays Nevarte's characteristic combination of a light-hearted
(*tetevsolik*) approach to life with profound insight. Like Rita, Nevarte had
learned to approach Calouste as an original, inscrutable force of nature,
something one had to come to terms with, something which could not be
reasoned or bargained with.

In October 1932, while negotiations between father and son were still
under way, Calouste was invited to join in a speculative attack on Royal
Dutch-Shell. Two shady stock market operators linked to Société Pétrolière de Caracas, a certain Goulin and a Levy-Grunwald, asked Gulbenkian
to collaborate in a 25-million-franc syndicate to 'bear' both CFP and Royal
Dutch-Shell – that is, to sell borrowed shares in the latter companies in the
hopes of causing a panic, then buy the shares back later at lower prices, so
making a profit. Goulin and Levy-Grunwald held Mercier and Deterding
responsible for the failure of Société des Pétroles Française de Caracas to
secure a listing on the Paris bourse. Royal Dutch-Shell looked weak after
Shell's price on the London exchange dropped in May 1932 to just over
10⅛, having stood at 26⅞ in 1931.[46]

'If we sham the credit of the R[oyal] D[utch] by bringing down the
price of their shares,' Levy-Grunwald predicted, 'there will be an outcry in
Paris and Pineau will not dare to take up an attitude hostile to the Caracas
as he will be attacked for acting on behalf of Deterding.' A 'bear' attack
on CFP would harm its planned debenture issue, piling on more pressure.
While Kevork was keen to go in with them, Nubar struck a note of caution.
Both Goulin and Levy-Grunwald had been implicated in recent French
banking scandals, surrounding Banque Oustric and Banque Industrielle
de Chine respectively. They also had links to Marthe Hanau, a notorious
company promoter who had recently been convicted of defrauding gull-
ible investors of millions of francs, many of them sunk in 8 per cent bonds
Hanau issued herself.

Even if his father had sunk £100,000 into the Caracas venture, Nubar
noted, the risks to their reputation and to their relationship with CFP
were just not worth the rewards. To associate oneself with Hanau and 'her
crowd is not only hardly distinguished, but also can end up in unpleasant
enquiries and publicities'. Such a scheme would irritate Royal Dutch-Shell
without 'doing them any great harm or bringing any benefit to ourselves'.[47]

Calouste seems to have backed off, and persuaded Hermann Marx and Léon Wenger to do so as well.

Once she had served her prison sentence for fraud, Hanau decided to go straight, setting up a newspaper, *Forces*, in which she revealed yet more about her shenanigans and the complicity of various highly placed officials. She turned on Goulin and Levy-Grunwald, publishing a piece entitled 'Sinister Trinity' in which she revealed their plans to attack Royal Dutch-Shell. 'Goulin, Levy-Grunwald ... that's already quite a pair,' she noted. 'But behind them lurks the shadow of Mr Gulbenkian, about which we will reveal more later. For now, though, we are pleased to have put a stop to their plans, thanks to our revelations.'[48]

Although any press coverage was unwelcome to Calouste, this piece probably had little effect, thanks to the far greater media speculation earlier in the year, claiming that the sudden drop in Royal Dutch-Shell's price back in April had been part of another plot by Gulbenkian and the Soviets to seize control of the combine. As the *Vossische Zeitung* noted:

> What we are seeing unfold is not the long-awaited cleansing of the stables at Royal Dutch, the departure of Henri Deterding and his cronies. It is rather the latest episode in the long-running, bitterly fought struggle between Royal Dutch and the Armenian oil magnate Gulbankian [*sic*], a struggle whose outcome is far from clear. Gulbenkian plays a role in the oil industry similar to that of Sir Basil Zaharoff in the arms industry. He is the 'man in the shadows,' whose web extends almost everywhere and who has been Deterding's sworn enemy for some time now, ever since the Dutchman succeeded in pushing the Armenian to the wall in the Venezuela Oil Concessions Company.[49]

Deterding hired Pinkerton's detective agency to investigate. Agent Gerhardt pinned the blame on various media figures (including the editor of the *Vossische Zeitung*) in the United States, France and Germany, who were all supposedly following orders from Piatakoff in Moscow. Gerhardt did not finger Gulbenkian. Deterding continued to suspect him, and probably did so right up until his death in 1939.[50]

The Grand Tour

Gulbenkian spent most of the 1920s continuously moving around the same circuit of hotels, largely in France. Though the names of the resorts are synonymous with luxurious leisure, this was not a life of relaxation. Gulbenkian made a list in his pocketbook of all the things he needed to have with him when he travelled: passports, stationery, telegraph code-books, wines and champagnes, medicines, coffee, honey (a special kind), sunglasses, binoculars (for bird-watching).[51] Accompanied at all times by his valet and a secretary, Gulbenkian was never free from the mountain-ous traffic of cables, letters and reports generated by his London and Paris offices. He was regularly hounded by concession-hunters and *brasseurs d'affaires* of all nations. It was a struggle to find the time to read catalogues and keep up with the *Burlington Magazine* and other art periodicals, let alone experience actual objects on display in museums or auction houses.

In 1928, however, Gulbenkian set out on the first of a series of tours, the nearest thing he ever had to holidays. They lasted between ten days and a month, and culminated in a trip round Egypt and Palestine in January 1934. Gulbenkian kept a diary in which he recorded (in French) brief impressions beside long extracts from museum catalogues. At the end of each trip he added a conclusion and had his notes typed up and bound in ring binders, together with the postcards he had collected. These were organised so as to be easily consulted later, should that be necessary. The diary of Gulbenkian's 1929 Italian tour even has an index.

Wherever he went, be it in Spain, Italy, Germany, Egypt or Pales-tine, Gulbenkian kept up a fearsome pace, sometimes accompanied by art experts, such Leo Planiscig of the Kunsthistorisches Museum, Vienna. With the help of Planiscig and others, Gulbenkian notched up four to six art collections a day during his Vienna tour. Though he had visited some of these already, he noted, he had been eager to return, on account of 'my art studies'.[52] Several days might be devoted to a world-class museum, such as the Alte Pinakothek in Munich or the Egyptian Museum in Cairo, as Gulbenkian worked his way through the collection, recording his views room by room. As ever, gardens (Boboli in Florence, Kitchener's Island at Aswan) formed another strand of Gulbenkian's tourism. The Jardín del Retiro outside Málaga inspired a rare personal aside: 'There are two great life objectives that have eluded me (poor me, whom everyone envies): to be a scientist, and to be a dreamer in a garden designed just the way I want it.'[53] As we shall see, Gulbenkian was already taking steps to realise the latter objective.

Valet-masseur, chef, physician and secretaries aside, Gulbenkian toured alone. In April 1930, however, Rita was permitted to join him on the hired yacht *Narcissus*. The pair embarked at Cannes for a month's cruise, visiting the archaeological sites of Sicily and the Ionian Islands. Despite bad weather and trouble securing provisions, he was persuaded to go on a second cruise (on the *Ausonia*) along the North African coast in 1932, this time accompanied by both Rita and Yervant.[54] Gulbenkian got sick from eating Majorcan strawberries right at the start, and was disappointed by the antiquities he saw, including the remains of Carthage. He did not call on his brother Vahan in Algiers. Although Calouste had increased the monthly allowance he paid Vahan, to fund the education of Vahan's children, he had no interest in meeting any of them.[55]

Hearing a chorus of nightingales in the harbour at Cattaro was a delight, but was not enough to redeem cruising for Gulbenkian. He had been roused at 4.30 that morning by his valet, Pierre, to inform him that the ship was in a fog and advise that the captain was going to sound the foghorn:

> This morning passed very disagreeably for me. Stretched out on my bed, I reflected that the appeal of yachting is snobbery. My personal view is that it is an enormous waste, without any rewards, moral or physical. On land it is hard to resist the apparent attractions, but on further consideration the illusion soon wears thin.[56]

Gulbenkian did not go on another cruise.

During his 1934 trip to Egypt Gulbenkian made a quick excursion to Jerusalem, an important pilgrimage site for all Armenians. Those who had made the journey to Jerusalem bore the title *mahdesi*. In 1877, aged seven, Calouste had travelled to Jerusalem with his father, Sarkis, brother Karnig and several other family members. A painting of the Resurrection donated by his family in 1896 hung prominently in the Church of the Holy Sepulchre, where it remains to this day.[57] Like other leading Ottoman Armenian families, the Gulbenkians had many philanthropic ties to the Armenian patriarchate of Jerusalem, based in the Convent of St James in the Old City. Calouste's cousin Badrig had continued this tradition.

Badrig had agreed to act as president of the Turian Jubilee Committee, charged with organising celebrations for the fiftieth anniversary of the ordination of His Beatitude Archbishop Yeghishe Turian, who had been elected ninety-ninth patriarch of Jerusalem in 1921. Funds were raised to erect a two-storey manuscript library within the convent. Unfortunately, both Turian and Badrig died before this plan could be realised. Calouste inherited the project from his cousin, generously offering to fund it himself in its entirety. The Gulbenkian Library had duly opened in 1932.[58]

Gulbenkian had not attended the opening, and in 1934 he did his very best to keep his visit as short and low-profile as possible. He did not inform the patriarchate of his plans until the very last minute. Patriarch Torkom Kushakian nonetheless managed to turn the tables on this master negotiator, subjecting Gulbenkian to the same surprise morning assault Gulbenkian was wont to spring on others. Early in the morning, while the train was still hours away from Jerusalem, the patriarch boarded Gulbenkian's carriage to welcome him. Gulbenkian only got round to visiting his library at 10 that evening. Though he noted in his diary that he 'would never forget this mysterious nocturnal visit', his second visit to Jerusalem (which lasted less than forty-eight hours) was a snatched, hurried affair, hardly a pilgrimage.[59]

Gulbenkian's experience of trying to coordinate the ramshackle AGBU surely informed his subsequent deliberations on the shape of his own philanthropic legacy. At the very least it taught him the importance of allowing one's trustees wide powers of discretion, rather than laying down strict terms which might be overtaken by events. It may also have confirmed Gulbenkian's sense that the best philanthropy was that performed in private. The Armenian model, however, emphasised philanthropy as a way of raising the status of one's clan. Payments to editors of Armenian-language newspapers, as well as grants to scholars writing the history of Armenian communities, were part of this system. Calouste had never been interested in playing this game and scorned the *chan-chan* (gossip) circulating about him. It is unusual, therefore, to find him writing to his lawyer in Istanbul in early 1930, instructing him to give donations to the editors of that city's three Armenian-language newspapers. Calouste was tired of reading gushing accounts of philanthropic donations by Nubar Paşa, Kelekian and others that were, he pointed out, much smaller than his own donations, which the same editors passed over with little or no comment.

After his resignation from AGBU, Gulbenkian came to regret this moment of weakness. As he wrote to Devgantz, 'All the ravenous dogs of the press are busy writing articles against me, claiming credit for having driven me to resign from AGBU, and so trying to get me to increase the size of the subsidies we were foolish enough to give them last year.' When it came to the press, it was best to remember Gulbenkian's favourite Turkish proverb: *It ürür kervan yürür* ('The dogs bark, the caravan passes').[60]

FOURTEEN

POOR POP PAYS, 1935–8

Back in 1894 the twenty-five-year-old Gulbenkian had compiled a report for the Ottoman Minister of the Civil List, explaining how Mesopotamian oil could be exploited in commercial quantities. Forty years later, Mesopotamian crude finally came to market. On 16 October 1934 the first crude reached Haifa, having travelled the length of the 622-mile IPC pipeline from Kirkuk to the Mediterranean.[1] The line could carry 3 million tons a year. As IPC chairman John Cadman observed, it was a remarkable example of the 'tenacity of a private individual … having waited some 40 odd years to reap the benefits of this venture and his faith in having sunk so much money in it'. While Gulbenkian was pleased to hear such comments from a man he admired, he recognised that they were intended as much to bury as to praise him.[2]

The official opening of the IPC pipeline was held at Kirkuk in January 1935 and presided over by King Ghazi of Iraq, who had succeeded his father, Faisal, two years before. The arrangements smacked more of British imperialism than anything else. Cadman's portrait, rather than that of the king, took the place of honour in the glossy commemorative leaflet. As one American diplomat noted:

> The distribution of compartments on the train discriminated against the Iraqis. They were put in the smaller and less desirable compart-ments – usually two together, while the Americans and most of the

Europeans had compartments to themselves. The predominance of the British among the non-Iraqi guests gave the whole affair the aspect of a British jubilee rather than that of a show put on by an international company for the purpose of entertaining and impressing the Iraqis.[3]

Given his dislike of formal occasions, it is unsurprising that Calouste did not accept the invitation to attend the ceremony in Kirkuk. Instead he sent Nevarte and her brother Yervant Essayan. The pair travelled via Jerusalem, where the Armenian patriarchate lavished on them the hospitality Gulbenkian had been so careful to duck during his visit earlier that year. At Jerusalem Nevarte discovered that female guests were not going to be allowed to travel beyond Baghdad, owing to a shortage of seats on the plane. She elected not to proceed any further, but stayed in Jerusalem with the Waley Cohens. As she wrote to Nubar, Yervant was 'no more use than a sick headache – he just looks well and is a gentleman'.[4] The choice of family representatives was limited, however, owing to a crisis in Calouste's relations with Nubar, as well as with his daughter, Rita.

The tendency for son and daughter to get into scrapes and require bailing out reminded Nevarte of a music-hall song whose refrain ran 'And then poor Pop pays.'[5] Starting in 1932, Rita had taken to disappearing for long periods of time, leaving her husband and young son in order to indulge her taste for the bohemian lifestyle. Though a source of upset and shame to her parents, Rita's misbehaviour could at least be hushed up. The same could not be said of Nubar's infidelities. A former actress, his second wife, Doré, was happy to wash dirty linen in public in a way Nubar's first wife, Herminia, had not been. Divorce proceedings crawled through the courts for more than five years until 1940. Although these drew to an amicable conclusion when 'poor Pop paid', Nubar's subsequent decision to take his father to court demanding a share of the famous 5 per cent represented a nadir in the family's public fortunes.

'Poor Pop' clearly viewed his son's infidelities very differently from his own. By his lights, this was not hypocritical. As Nevarte had candidly admitted during their courtship, husbands of their class took mistresses 'all the time'. It was silly to get worked up about such things, let alone seek a divorce. Divorce remained disreputable, especially when it involved court battles, as Nubar's divorces did. Years before, Calouste had been advised by his Ottoman Armenian physician, Dr Kemhadjian, to have sex regularly with young women, as a rejuvenating tonic. He followed this advice, and continued to do so, on into the 1930s. Although the women concerned were wined and dined (the right kind of dress was provided), they were regularly changed. Neither prostitutes nor high-class escorts, they were probably the daughters of shabby genteel familes who valued discretion as much as Calouste himself did. It was all very transactional.

The arrangements were sure to have been as efficient as those governing any other aspect of Calouste's life. Not a shred of paper, not a single letter or account entry survives to shed light on these arrangements, however, leaving us to rely on the unreliable and sometimes embittered recollections of Nubar and Calouste's secretary D. H. Young. The former claimed that Madame Soulas, Calouste's Paris housekeeper, managed her employer's 'carefully selected and changing harem'. Young claimed that his former employer 'took girls from the gutter', which was highly unlikely, given Calouste's concern for his own health. Nubar was fond of a story in which one young lady, nervous and perhaps overcome by the lavishness of her surroundings, overindulged in the fine food and wine before being violently sick.[6]

Correspondence between Calouste's brother-in-law Yervant and the British entomologist Malcolm Burr provides less lurid evidence for this practice. In 1928 Burr wrote of how effective what he called the 'Rich Turks Method' had been: 'after a few weeks of this treatment, everybody told me that I was markedly rejuvenated. But it has its dangers, for men over 60 frequently die of it.'[7] Gulbenkian's doctor was not alone in prescribing such 'treatment', therefore. For Rita and Nubar, however, educated in Britain, it probably seemed rather rich for 'poor Pop' to undergo the 'Rich Turks Method' while condemning them for pursuing more meaningful relationships.

The neglect of maternal and filial responsibilities on the part of his beloved children so distressed Calouste that he seemed unable to frame a coherent response. Instead of speaking or writing, he simply ordered that all communication cease. No letters to Rita or Nubar from Calouste survive from these five years, though Calouste corresponded with his grandson, Mikhael (Micky), and sought to protect him as far as he could. In practice, however, Calouste was not incommunicado. Instead he relied on Nevarte, as well as close friends such as Cadman and J. H. Macdonald, to negotiate with his errant children. Calouste disappeared into his business affairs, and began constructing his ideal garden near Deauville, a garden he had no intention of sharing with anybody else. Now in his sixties and with all hope of collaborating with his beloved son lost, his affairs reduced in scope. There would be no more 'big schemes'. Five per cent would have to be enough.

The Rita Question

As a child it had always been made clear to Rita that she was far less important than her brother. Nubar was royally spoilt by his parents and their staff, and managed to persuade little Rita that any treats that may have happened to come her way were somehow in his gift, reflections of his magnanimous nature. When they were given two peaches, Rita asked her brother to teach her how to peel hers. He graciously did so, then ate the peach. Appearing one day holding a dish of blancmange, Nubar cut her a generous portion, then urged her to eat it quickly before the grown-ups saw. The blancmange was soap.

'Yet', as she reflected in a poem written many years later, 'I loved him just the same.'[8] In 1921, when Nubar's infatuation for Herminia had been at its most feverish, Rita had agreed to get out of bed and listen (for five shillings an hour) as Nubar gave vent to his feelings 'with Herminia's photograph in front and your revolver to the left'. Recalling this episode in 1935, in the midst of her own crisis, Rita emphasised their sibling bond. 'Comparisons are odious – whether you or I have been the greater fool – we must not judge – we must <u>believe</u> in each other or not – I believe in you absolutely – you might return the compliment.'[9]

In the 1920s Rita seems to have found family life in the house at 38 Hyde Park Gardens satisfying enough. Gulbenkian made the house over to her and Kevork. But when Calouste had them join him in Paris in 1930 things seemed to fall apart. The couple settled around the corner from 51 Avenue d'Iéna, in a slightly smaller house in Rue Émile Menier that had originally been intended for Nubar.[10] Quiet, hard-working and 'without authority' (according to Nevarte), able to read Armenian but without any patriotic Armenian axe to grind, Kevork was well suited to be Calouste's chief clerk, but not to be Rita's husband.

To judge by the few letters which survive, mother and daughter shared a number of characteristics – too many, perhaps, for comfort. Both were acute observers (including of Calouste) with a gift for the pithy aperçu, usually delivered in a combination of languages (French,

English and Turkish) and with scant regard for grammar or syntax. Both were socialites and craved novelty. Separated by twenty-five years, it was inevitable that Rita found her mother's idea of good company (diplomats) dull. It was not enough for her to follow the annual progress from Paris to Baden Baden, Aix, Deauville and back. Rita's passionate nature sought other outlets, in a sometimes scattergun manner. She was a stubborn, unrepentant individualist.

Perhaps Nevarte's preoccupation with avoiding 'scandal' masked resentment at her daughter's attempt to do what she herself had nearly done in 1914 – that is, walk out on her pampered if restrictive lifestyle and be free. Even if Nubar hadn't gone to the trouble of pointing it out to his mother, the parallel was there.[11] In her letters Rita tended to refer to '51' and 'Nevarte' interchangeably, but in reality Nevarte was hardly the *châtelaine* of 51 Avenue d'Iéna. Calouste gave his wife 'no authority to deal with the smallest item' regarding the household.[12]

Both Rita and Nevarte needed to find other places if they wished to meet friends and have some amusement. Hence Rita's famous drinks parties, convened on the bench in the street outside 51, where Calouste's servants served guests she was not permitted to welcome inside. Unfortunately, these servants were not above telling Calouste of such antics, making 51 Avenue d'Iéna feel even less comfortable. 'I live in a <u>house of vipers</u> who try to make trouble for me with your father,' as Nevarte put it to Nubar.[13] This explains the competition between Nevarte and Rita for the use of 30 Rue Émile Menier.[14]

Rita's 'scandals' (as her mother called them) began in 1932, when she was thirty-two, and continued until 1937. Her 'boy friend Mack' (as Rita usually called him) was the Russian émigré portraitist and miniaturist Paul Mak. At the Revolution Mak and his wife had escaped to Tehran, where he mastered the technique of Persian manuscript illumination and became court painter to Reza Shah. Leaving his wife and child in Athens, Mak later moved to Paris. He probably arrived with an introduction to Gulbenkian: as a collector interested in Persian art who was also attached to the Persian Embassy, Gulbenkian was well placed to help him become established in the city.

Calouste probably did help in getting Mak his one-man show, at the Bernheim-Jeune Gallery in the Rue du Faubourg Saint-Honoré. He certainly purchased a miniature from Mak that same year (1932).[15] A photograph of the *vernissage* shows Rita and Nevarte standing next to Mak, in front of a large full-length portrait of Rita which Calouste may have commissioned.[16] A remarkably handsome and talented man, Mak choreographed every movement and gesture impeccably; his performances started a flamenco craze in Paris. As Rita put it many years later, Mak was 'a special number', an original who could not be judged by everyday standards, particularly given his heavy drug use.[17]

By 1936 Mak was struggling financially. To support herself and help Mak, Rita took on secretarial work for Pour Que l'Esprit Vive, a Paris-based charity supporting artists and intellectuals.[18] Mak's close relationship with the film star Jeanne de Hérédia (who lived in Avenue Kléber) did not faze Rita. When this or that friend was in funds life was one long round of good food and wine, drugs and nightclubs, with evenings occasionally culminating in a spell in a police station.[19] Holidays were spent camping out with other, largely Russian exiles in their country houses. In a letter to her uncle Yervant, Rita described a house party at which the sole sanitary arrangements consisted of a single cold-water tap and the surrounding woods. 'All charming sauced by LLLLLOVE but in the circumstances unsavoury.'[20]

In 1938 Nevarte and Calouste worked their contacts in the Quai d'Orsay, Préfecture de Police and Renseignements Généraux (the secret police) to have Mak expelled from France as an 'undesirable alien'. Rita managed to pull strings of her own with a *député*, Marcel Massot, and this was stopped. Had he been sent back to his family in Athens, Mak would have been paid a monthly allowance for a year by Calouste.[21] Instead he made his own way to Brussels, where he spent the rest of his life.

'At present nothing – not her son, not her husband, not her family – has any hold on her – only this man,' reported Nevarte in 1938. Shocked by 'her deplorable and <u>bohemian</u> mode of living', Nevarte insisted that even five minutes of 'her way of talking – her movements' would spell 'terrible harm' for the eleven-year-old Mikhael.[22] Steps were taken to keep the location of his schools a secret from his mother. At the first sign that Rita might be contacting lawyers with a view to divorce and custody, Nevarte pulled her grandson out of his French preparatory school and had him brought to 51 Avenue d'Iéna, noting that 'possession is nine points of the law'.[23]

In January 1936 Rita drew up a memo entitled 'What each person wants in the Rita Question'. Dividing the page into columns for Nubar, Calouste, 'Kev' and her mother, Rita gave her version of their respective

wishes. At sixth place in her mother's wish list is 'Rita to have no more fun
than she did!!' Her father's list is the longest:

1) No one to want any money
2) No one to touch injuriously or tire in any way his Kev
3) His Kev to be like a 'corpse' in a Jesuit college
4) If boy friends must be had by his women folk then let them not
    a) want jobs
    b) want to sell antiques
    c) borrow money.[24]

It is revealing, forthright, even witty – if in a very dry way. Above all,
it is on the nose as regards Calouste's view of his close relatives and their
demands. As the phrase 'his women folk' indicates, Calouste's attitude
combined an 'oriental' possessiveness towards his female relations with a
business-minded indifference to their goings-on, provided said goings-on
did not cost money or create a scandal. This was clearly a scenario in which
Calouste was on one side and everyone else, including his own wife, was on
the other, trying to make poor Pop pay.

In July 1937 Calouste agreed to rent Rita her own apartment at 62
Rue Lauriston, and to give her an increased allowance. It was a first step
towards reinstatement, conditional on her behaviour satisfying certain
conditions (such as keeping away from Mak, a condition she did not keep).
Rita was also allowed to have her son write to her once a week. Nevarte
refused to be her daughter's keeper, so the job of chaperoning her fell to
Madame Soulas, whose efforts only stoked Rita's irritation with constant
'spying' and 'interference'.[25]

On the morning of 14 January 1938 Rita was walking down Avenue
Kléber when she spotted her son on the same street. Had Nubar not had
the kindness to go against orders and send her a recent photograph, she
might not have recognised her eleven-year-old son, several years having
passed since they last saw each other. 'I nearly bumped bang into him this
morning,' she reported to Nubar, 'luckily he didn't see me ... but it is too
nerve wracking [*sic*]. Mack [*sic*] in the Avenue Kléber and Mike in the
Avenue d'Iéna I can't leave my fastness in security now ever.'[26] The war
would trap Mikhael in London and Rita in Paris, bringing another six
years of separation.

Just as he had taken Rita to Regent's Park to look at the monkeys, so Calouste took his grandson to the zoo in the Bois de Boulogne. The sixty-six-year-old Calouste would hide in the bushes, wait for 'Micky' to walk by, then spring out, roaring like a lion, to his grandson's terrified delight. When other visitors complained, Calouste roundly put them in their place.[27] Although Mikhael still slept at 30 Rue Émile Menier, he spent many happy days at 51 Avenue d'Iéna, where the resident electrical engineer, Dufretin, was always on hand to repair his toy trains. Christmas morning 1935 found the eight-year-old in bed at 30 Rue Émile Menier, his bed surrounded with presents placed there in the night – by Miss Rae, his beloved governess.[28]

Loyal Kevork was never in disgrace and was present in Paris throughout these years. It would seem that he was happy to let his father-in-law take the decisions regarding his son's upbringing and education. Here again, Calouste took advice from Nubar and Nevarte (Kevork does not seem to have had a view), deciding to send Micky to Orley Farm School in 1937, the same feeder for Harrow that Nubar himself had attended.[29] Reaching a consensus on the boy's name was less straightforward: was he 'Mikhael', 'Mik', 'Mike', 'Micky' or 'Mickey'? The boy had signed himself 'Mik', later 'Mikäel', but for Nevarte 'Mik' was too much like 'Mak'.[30] His mother referred to him as 'Mike'. In a doubly revealing letter Nubar reported to his mother how 'I took Kev. this morning to see Mick (?) Mike (?) Mickey (?)– I have forgotten by which exact denomination you wish to refer to your grand-son and my nephew.' In the margin Nevarte has written: 'His name should be Mikhael or Mickey – (Taboo! Taboo! Mick or Mike!).'[31] Happily, the boy himself seemed far less concerned about such questions. Whether at home in Paris, away at school or on holiday (spent in hotels at Saint-Germain-en-Laye and Fontainebleau), Miss Rae was ever-present: a constant source of affection and reassurance.

Gulbenkian v. Gulbenkian

Having married in 1928, in the early 1930s Nubar and his second wife, Doré Plowden, settled into a comfortable life divided between a series of Mayfair apartments and country houses in Berkshire, all rented. Rounds of golf, country house parties and other entertainments formed an important part of Nubar's activity as his father's chief London representative and as commercial attaché to the Iranian Embassy. When a new

Petroleum Department official asked to meet him, therefore, curious to hear about Calouste, Nubar saw him and went through his spiel, doing 'a little propaganda on the usual basis – big house [that is, IPC], reduced to attic, determined enjoy attic; whole cake, indigestion; invite international partners, only 5 per cent left, but good cake – all on the approved and stereotyped lines.'[32] Nubar had his father's core message down pat.

Indiscretions with a fellow fox-hunter, Lady Diana Gibb (young-est daughter of the Earl of Lovelace), soon put Nubar's marriage to Doré under pressure. In June 1935 Doré filed for separation. A few weeks later Nubar had a narrow escape when the De Havilland Dragon biplane he and a group of friends had chartered to view the naval review crashed and burst into flames shortly after taking off from Heston Aerodrome.[33] Hearing the news, Nevarte rushed over, only to find Doré out at a bridge party.

Nevarte and Calouste had never been keen on Doré, and were even less enthusiastic when Doré confronted Nevarte 'like a coster-woman from Les Halles', shouting, 'you will all see what it is to be dragged into English law courts.'[34] One reason for the drawn-out nature of divorce proceedings was the issue of whether Nubar had been domiciled in Britain or France when he married Doré. Justice Langton of the King's Bench eventually determined that Nubar had been domiciled in Britain, which meant that he had married Doré bigamously, as his first marriage to Herminia was still in force in the United Kingdom.[35] 'Pop paid' under a settlement reached in 1939.

Nubar's fondness for appearing 'clever' gave a relish to the cat-and-mouse game of establishing his domicile. Justice Langton duly noted the family's 'idiosyncrasy of forming a limited liability company upon any occasion upon which they propose to acquire a real estate'. This, as well as Nubar's Iranian nationality, seemed to be intended solely 'to secure the family and himself from the unwelcome attention of the Revenue authorities'. The press made much of Calouste's fabled millions and par-ticularly appreciated his son's melodramatic account of his last-minute escape from Istanbul in 1896. A steeple-chasing, cigar-chomping heir to a fabled fortune who had cheated death as a babe by fleeing in a Gladstone bag: it was *One Thousand and One Nights* meets *The Importance of Being Earnest*.

Yet as one headline in *Paris-Soir* noted, 'It's not always fun being a millionaire's son.'[36] Behind the glamorous press copy of feasts at Claridge's, caviar and mishaps involving hunters and planes, 1938 found Nubar at his lowest ebb. Without a wife to keep house, he struggled to find and hold on to suitable domestic staff, sending pitiful appeals to his mother as well as to Rita, asking them to come over and literally put his house in order.[37] A new trust settlement had been reached, revising that agreed in 1929. But Nubar refused to comply with its requirements, alleging that the terms of settlement sent to his lawyers for signature differed from those his father had originally proposed. A similar problem had arisen in the Red Line negotiations.[38]

Nevarte came over to meet Nubar and John Cadman in September, but Nubar disavowed the latest settlement, built on the understanding that Nubar would leave the city and be set up by his father as a farmer.[39] With payments from the 1929 trust at an end, Nubar sold his beloved Rolls, let his faithful chauffeur Wooster go, and began looking for a new job.[40] Having reached the milestone of forty, he was deeply unsatisfied with his situation.

He regretted having taken the decision back in 1926 to work for his father. He noted the harsh way in which his father addressed him, needling about the cost of the lunch Nubar had ordered in to the London office – and how much more affectionately his father had written to him fifteen or ten years before. Now it was all too late:

> Mr N. S. G. has willingly sacrificed the best years of his life and, which is more important, his chance of obtaining an independent and respected position in life, for the sake of helping Mr. C. S. G. amass a few hundreds of thousands of pounds more and finds himself in his present position. He quite admits that he has lost most of his self-respect and has sunk down very low in his relations with Mr. C. S. G.; the oriental strain in our blood has made it easier to do that for his Father, but there are limits below which even the greatest filial affection cannot push him.[41]

Feeling himself sidelined, Nubar seems to have entered a kind of stupor.

Nubar's refusal to come to a settlement with his father regarding his income was combined with a profound inertia when it came to settling other matters. Should he divorce Doré or patch things up with her? Should he marry Mary Cadman, John Cadman's daughter, or spend more time with Marie Samuelson (who in fact became his third wife)?[42] Where should he live? He waited for someone else to take the decisions, indifferent to the consequences. Nevarte was distraught to find her son in such a pathetic state, and felt that she and her husband bore some of the blame.

> I feel terribly guilty for the hopeless way we have brought you up – our misguided love and appalling weakness have made you to-day at 40 – a man with no responsibility – no ideal – no aim – tired of himself and tired of others – no wish for any respect – material comfort at any cost and with the minimum of effort to yourself seems to be your motto – I am terribly unhappy!![43]

Left by Calouste to deal with Nubar's crisis as well as to find a resolution to the 'Rita Question', Nevarte was near breaking point. 'I am so tired,' she wrote in June 1937, 'I wish I was dead!'[44]

A Garden Near Deauville

Back in 1922 Gulbenkian had dreamed of retiring to a large garden in Istanbul, 'on the sea [where] I could sit beneath my big pine trees at lunchtime and gaze at the sea while being caressed by langorous winds from off the sea.'[45] The Kemalists had put paid to that hope, by refusing to return properties confiscated from Gulbenkian and other Ottoman Armenians. Now, fifteen years later, Chester Beatty tried to persuade his sixty-eight-year-old friend to slow down. Writing from the Breakers in Palm Beach, where he was enjoying the sun and fishing, Beatty set his 'pupil' Calouste some homework: to step back from his business affairs for set periods of time and try to cultivate a less anxious attitude. When Beatty returned to Europe in April, Gulbenkian would have to 'report how many hours per week you have spent in studying your collections and in reading interesting books'. Beatty urged him to follow his own example in commissioning illustrated catalogues of his collections. Supervising such scholarly projects was one way 'to cultivate a spirit of tranquility and enjoy each day as it comes along without losing tranquility'.[46]

Gulbenkian had acquired the estate of Les Enclos in 1927, adding further parcels of land in 1931. He now set about consulting landscape architects and hiring workers to develop it into his ideal garden, creating a special company, the Société Horticole et Foncière, as a tax-efficient means of managing it. The estate was situated on a ridge behind Mont Canisy, just outside Deauville. The higher parts were wooded, the rest parkland and fields. A two-storey house stood at one end, a set of farm buildings at the other. From the start it was clear that Les Enclos was intended for the exclusive enjoyment of Gulbenkian and the birds. As with 51 Avenue d'Iéna, so here Gulbenkian issued the Armenian retainer in charge of the project with numbered *feuilles d'instructions*. *Feuille* number one ordered him to 'take all steps to prevent hunting on the property. Encourage the birds to make their nests on the property.'[47]

Though dubbed 'the Napoleon of *paysagistes*' (landscape architects) and held to be one of the founders of the profession in France, Achille Duchêne met his match in Gulbenkian, who proved a demanding client at Les Enclos. Duchêne's father had helped design the squares and public parks of Haussmann's new Paris, seeking to revive that great tradition of highly architectural landscape gardening that began with André Le Nôtre in the seventeenth century. Gulbenkian felt that he knew and understood this tradition well, and did not appreciate receiving long screeds in which Duchêne expanded on his historicising vision or his particular understanding of the term *romantique*. 'In all modesty I think that my knowledge of art is extensive enough to spare me the need to receive such lessons,' Gulbenkian wrote in April 1938. 'It is high time that you made your mind up and began following my wishes, rather than your own.'

Nor did he welcome Duchêne's somewhat personal probing. In seeking to make 'the garden of your dreams', Duchêne claimed that he needed to know all about his client's 'psychology', as well as the specific places on the estate Gulbenkian found particularly appealing. Gulbenkian did not want to waste time or ink discussing such things with a stranger. He was not interested in hearing about the Swiss-style chalet Duchêne had made for himself as a place to meditate.[48] Duchêne eventually got the message, although his design for a pavilion intended to provide Gulbenkian with a place to sleep, eat and read was not carried out. Duchêne's design of a Trianon-style house was on far too grand a scale for a building Gulbenkian planned only to spend the odd weekend in, 'most of the time on my own'. The entrance and ground-floor plan looked like a poky 'office layout', when 'I have always held that the best buildings are like books, which reveal themselves chapter by chapter.'[49]

Gulbenkian was happier with Duchêne's ideas for the rest of the estate, which closely followed his own vision. The central *allée* was designed to offer pleasant shade. Here Gulbenkian would be able to pace up and down, pausing now and then to dictate yet another letter to a secretary waiting at a small folding desk – a practice he had developed back in Paris, in the Parc de Saint-Cloud.[50] Below the *allée* was a formally arranged *roseraie*. These two features took up only a fraction of the estate. Otherwise Gulbenkian was eager to complement the natural declivities of the site by planting rhododendrons and flowering trees.[51] The fields to the south and east were to be made into a large *potager* (kitchen garden), an orchard and meadows with gently snaking carriage paths, while the *basse-cour* of service buildings was to be complemented by a concrete duck pond and a series of pavilions intended for Gulbenkian's peacocks, hens and other birds. Duchêne's design for a peacock house survives, though it is unclear whether it was built.[52] Much of the scheme was still being hammered out at the outbreak of war, whereupon material and labour shortages presented new problems.

Calouste's idyllic weekend retreat, his '*weekend glorifié*', was still a work in progress in January 1939, therefore, when Nubar took the momentous step of taking his own father to court. Nubar claimed that his father had promised him a 5 per cent participation in the famous 5 per cent.[53] This step profoundly shocked and hurt Calouste. Although he had cut ties with his son on previous occasions, this time he did so with unprecedented fierceness. Nevarte was banned from communicating with Nubar, Nubar was banned from attending St Sarkis Church in London and was made to hand over his archive of IPC- and Iranian-related files.[54] Nubar's friend George Ansley (formerly Ansbacher) advanced him funds to pay his lawyers, Elvy Robb and Co., who sought to make the process as painful for Calouste as possible, by using the principle of 'discovery' to make him submit several tons of private records to the court. This was the same weapon Calouste had held at the throats of his TPC partners in the late 1920s.

The squabble over whether or not these 'dangerous documents' (as the *Daily Herald* dubbed them) would be produced or not kept the affair in the public eye and ensured that proceedings dragged on until 1941.[55] Otherwise, however, Nubar's issuing of a writ against his own father lost him any sympathy his parents, Cadman, Macdonald or others may have had for him. Even Manns, senior clerk at Elvy Robb, felt compelled to send Nubar some unsolicited words of advice, words which could easily have got him dismissed (as Manns himself acknowledged) had Nubar shown the letter to Manns's principal.

A father himself, Manns had tried to imagine what Calouste would have felt when served with his son's writ 'and I must confess that it nearly chokes me'. Calouste was 'a very hard man who has been very successful in life and he has had two main interests in life namely his money and his son'. Considering that Nubar 'never at any time had a dog's chance of winning your action', why on earth did he keep instructing his lawyers to do 'some of the most outlandish things it is possible to conceive ... good or bad, whether it is in your favour or not ... just to show how clever you are'?[56]

In Nubar's childhood and youth his father had taken great pride in his precociousness, which he took as indicative of great talents. In the 1920s Calouste had chalked up any of his son's shortcomings to the supposedly depraved environment to which he had been exposed at Royal Dutch-Shell.

As Nevarte observed to Nubar in 1938, subsequent events had finally disabused this proud father of his illusions. During his childhood, she noted, Calouste

allowed you to 'bully' every body – your mother and sister were made your slaves – your word was law – <u>crazy fuss</u> for your health and welfare – <u>and exaggerated solicitude</u> were for years l'ordre du jour – and one day you got '<u>surfeited</u>' and your only thought has become '<u>to get away</u>'! – in the meantime your <u>private doings</u> against your father's wishes your <u>arrogance</u> towards him began to open his eyes – he realised that you were <u>not</u> the 'surhomme' [superman] he thought you to be! And here is all the reason of the trouble!

In Nevarte's view Calouste was simply 'reaping what he sowed'.[57] In having her son taken away from her, Nevarte believed that Rita, too, was reaping what she had sowed.

Outside Concessions

Though they welcomed the opening of the Kirkuk–Mediterranean pipeline, the Iraqis were well aware that IPC could have acted more swiftly to develop their country's reserves. IPC had got a reputation for being 'anxious to obtain Concessions with the purpose of not working them'.[58] Anglo-Persian, Royal Dutch-Shell and the Americans were wont to blame Gulbenkian for this dilatoriness. This was unfair. While they had plenty of oil production elsewhere in the world, Gulbenkian and CFP did not. While the majors were happy to keep Iraqi oil underground (as a reserve), Gulbenkian, CFP and the Iraqis all wanted Iraqi oil lifted and brought to market as soon as possible.

IPC's 'Outside Concessions Committee' was charged with concession-hunting outside Iraq. The opportunities were vast, as the red line embraced all of the Arabian peninsula. In 1927 Gulf Oil had taken an option on a concession in Bahrain. Gulf was one of the American companies which participated in Near East Development Company, the holding company through which the Americans held their 23.75 per cent of IPC. Gulf honoured the Red Line Agreement's self-denying principle and offered the option to IPC. Unfortunately, the committee dithered, leaving Gulf no option but to sell to Standard Oil of California (Socal).[59] In 1932 Socal struck oil on Bahrain. Socal also secured the concession to eastern Saudi Arabia, outspending and outmanoeuvring IPC's concession-hunter.[60]

Socal was a newcomer to the region, however, and lacked the infrastructure necessary to refine and sell any oil it did find in the Middle East. Crucially, it had no sales network in the Far East, the natural market for Persian Gulf oil. Jersey, Socony, Royal Dutch-Shell and Anglo-Persian had well-established arrangements to divide up the Far East market among themselves, and had no desire to see Socal acquire its own refining and sales capacity in that region. They needed to find some way of taking Socal's Bahrain oil off its hands. If they did not buy it, this oil might end up being freely traded on the 'spot market'. The members of the international oil cartel wanted to set prices themselves, not allow them to be set by the free action of such a market.

From 1932 to 1939 the major IPC partners (Royal Dutch-Shell, Anglo-Persian, Jersey and Socony) tried to find a way to collaborate with Socal: either by devising a way for IPC to buy Socal's crude or, more ambitiously, by bringing Socal into IPC – in both cases, without falling foul of the 1928 Red Line Agreement. In 1935 they almost managed to redraw the red line, cutting out the part south of a line drawn between Suez and Baghdad. This would have allowed them to join Socal without having to bring Gulbenkian or CFP with them. The quid pro quo was a reduction in the price IPC charged for its crude from its artificially high level (which suited the major partners). Gulbenkian somehow managed to get the price reduced without redrawing the line.[61]

Frustrated by the difficulty of negotiating with Gulbenkian, in February 1937 Royal Dutch-Shell proposed that IPC proceed to purchase Socal's crude in a manner which would have prevented Gulbenkian from exercising his 5 per cent participation in such purchases. Gulbenkian responded by threatening legal action against his IPC partners. For Jersey, this was a step too far: to test the Red Line Agreement in the courts would not only reveal that such a monopolistic agreement existed; it might trigger 'a series of disclosures which, in our business interests, we might wish to avoid'. The partners backed down. When a sales agreement between IPC and Socal was finally agreed in 1938, arrangements were made for CFP to sell 5 per cent of the crude on Gulbenkian's account.[62]

In hindsight these long-winded negotiations cannot help but seem a wasted opportunity. Gulbenkian could have worked harder to renovate his 'house', making room for Socal and Texaco (with whom Socal struck an alliance in 1936) within IPC, and so secure his 5 per cent of Saudi Arabia's oil riches.[63] Even after Socal struck oil at Dammam in 1938, however, it was far from clear that Saudi Arabia held much oil. Ibn Saud's grip on his kingdom, gained partly by conquest and partly with the help of an Islamic revivalist movement, still seemed shaky. As one Royal Dutch-Shell director noted in 1933, 'political security is nil.'[64]

IPC was successful in acquiring and developing other 'Outside Concessions', including that to western Saudi Arabia (in 1936, surrendered in 1941). In May 1935 it signed a seventy-five-year concession for Qatar with Shaikh Abdullah bin Qasim al Thani. It also secured exclusive concessions for the emirates of Dubai and Oman (both 1937) and Abu Dhabi (1939).[65] Kuwait was outside the Red Line area, and went in 1932 to a joint venture of Anglo-Persian and Gulf.

In the ten years since 1928 the significance of oil for the region and the wider world had gradually become clear. Oil production was no longer a two-horse race between Iraq and Iran, between IPC and Anglo-Persian. The centre of world oil production was beginning to shift, from the Gulf of Mexico to the Persian Gulf. So was the balance of power. Though the Persian Gulf remained a British lake for the time being, the British Foreign Office no longer sought to resist growing American investment in the region, and even welcomed it as a way of strengthening the line against the Soviet menace.[66] The events of 1939–45 caused all these trends to accelerate alarmingly.

FIFTEEN

FOR THE DURATION, 1939–42

It had been predicted that London and Paris would be incinerated in a massive German bombing raid within hours of war starting. By the time Britain and France declared war on Germany on 3 September 1939, therefore, children as well as works of art had been on the move for several days. Gulbenkian's grandson Mikhael Essayan followed his school to Wiltshire. The British Museum and National Gallery were responsible for the Egyptian artefacts and paintings that Gulbenkian had lent them several years before. These Gulbenkian collections joined the rest of the nation's treasures in storage, initially in remote country houses, before being relocated underground in abandoned quarries. Gulbenkian's London office moved to the White House in West Humble, near Dorking. In Paris Madame Soulas kept the flags flying, much as she had in 1914. Gulbenkian once again used his diplomatic status to protect his personal possessions: 51 Avenue d'Iéna was designated 'the Chancellery of the Economic Attaché to the Iranian Legation'.

Instead of mass destruction Gulbenkian was confronted with the *drôle de guerre* ('Phoney War'), known in Germany as the *Sitzkrieg* ('Sitting War'). The bombs did not fall, the tanks did not roll west. In February 1940 Gulbenkian travelled to London, summoned to appear at the court of King's Bench in *Gulbenkian* v. *Gulbenkian*, his son's attempt to secure the share of IPC profits which had supposedly been promised him. Nubar's lawyers had successfully secured 'discovery' of more than

987,000 documents detailing all aspects of Nubar's work in the service of his father's IPC interests. Naturally these documents contained much else besides, material Gulbenkian and his IPC partners did not want in the public domain.

In later years Nubar claimed that his father had been impressed by this manoeuvre. 'Isn't my son clever to have thought of this idea?' Calouste is supposed to have remarked to one of his counsels, John Foster, QC. 'He's getting tough, he's a chip off the old block.'[1] As Calouste had himself used the threat of 'discovery' in his battles with his IPC partners, perhaps imitation was a form of flattery. It seems more likely, however, that Calouste considered Nubar's approach far from 'chic'. Indeed, the prospect of having to encounter his own son in a public courtroom seems to have enraged Calouste, who turned on Nevarte. This on top of her worries about Rita led Nevarte to consider separation. She appealed to her brother Yervant either to intervene between her and her husband or to help her to 'abdicate'.

Yervant had always been the philosopher among the five Essayan siblings, a bookish and, by his own account, somewhat cynical looker-on. Having settled into a rentier lifestyle in Nice, he was happy to serve as a straw man on the board of Calouste's holding companies and to keep an eye on Devgantz, that faithful old retainer, now advanced in years and also in Nice. In the 1930s Devgantz and Yervant became a two-man Greek chorus on the fringes of the tragedy. They were happy to provide a listening ear, but were not prepared to go further. In February 1940 Yervant's response to his eldest sister's quandary was strikingly candid:

> can you hope to abdicate, abandon your <u>title of Madame 5%</u> and still retain the friendship of Ministers and ambassadors and *le reste*? Surely you know enough of the world to have no such illusions. You have starred too long as Mme 5% to be able to put up with honest mediocrity. No, the stigmata of 5% is branded on your forehead, you can not efface it. <u>And CG knows it</u>.

However short-tempered Calouste might be with her,

> it cannot be compared with Nubar's attitude towards his father. <u>Nubar has broken his father's heart.</u> (CG has certainly not broken yours) – and nothing but <u>true repentance</u> can mend it. Whereas all broken

hearts can be mended with *cavalerie de St Georges* [i.e. money] – I do not want to insinuate that people in other circumstances are mercenary but in the rupture of CG's heart even that monetary consolation is denied, hence the Tragedy.[2]

Nevarte elected not to 'abdicate'. A few days before Calouste was due to take the stand she sent her son a final appeal by telegram: 'Extremely upset beg of you remember family ties are more precious than money – Mama Gulbenkian.'

Three days later, on the morning of his father's planned appearance, Nubar relented: 'Received your telegram mother dear have followed your wishes and withdrawn case this morning without cross examining dear poppa.'[3] Having washed his hands of the situation in late September 1939, J. H. Macdonald once again attempted to reach a settlement. It remained a challenging task, as Nubar claimed to have been on the point of winning the case against his father.[4] In March 1940 Macdonald thrashed out terms under which Calouste would pay his son a certain sum in lieu of the 1938 settlement. With the invasion of France, however, the agreement was left unsigned, and so the dispute rumbled on until December 1941.[5]

A Gulbenkian Gallery at Trafalgar Square

Calouste had a second, more cheerful reason for visiting London in February 1940: to view a model of the proposed Gulbenkian annexe to the National Gallery in Trafalgar Square. As his annotated National Gallery catalogues show, Gulbenkian knew the collection well from his many years in London.[6] For a largely self-taught student of art history, eager to learn but with limited time on his hands, the National Gallery was a more welcoming prospect than the Louvre. With just thirty-two galleries, it housed a relatively small collection of masterpieces, of all European schools, dating from the fourteenth century right up to Cézanne.

Gulbenkian also admired its director, Kenneth Clark, whom he had first met in the summer of 1936. Clark and his fashionable wife, Jane, visited Paris that summer and secured an invitation to view the collection at 51 Avenue d'Iéna. 'He was short and dense like a mole,' Clark later recalled, 'but one did not think of him as either small or fat, because one's eyes were concentrated on his magnificent head. It was bald, with a deeply cleft chin, bushy eyebrows, and eyes as menacing as those of Mr J. P. Morgan.' Clark was as attentive to Gulbenkian's Islamic and Egyptian art and to the furniture and decorative art as he was to the European paintings.

Clark had spent part of his apprenticeship under the sway of the Edwardian art critic Roger Fry, whose approach to art was heavily theoretical. Clark also worked under the great art scholar Bernard Berenson, renowned for his skill at the equally dry game of attributing Italian paintings. In subsequent years, however, Clark had drifted away from both approaches. When Gulbenkian first met him, therefore, Clark would have come with a reassuringly scholarly pedigree, particularly thanks to this link to the great Berenson. Gulbenkian may have visited Berenson at his famous villa at I Tatti near Florence in 1903 – when Clark was just a baby.

Rather than being a specialist or theorist like Berenson or Fry, however, Clark espoused a catholic openness to all forms of beauty. This approach captured Gulbenkian's attention, and explains the uncharacteristic speed with which Gulbenkian subsequently acted. Within days of that first meeting at 51 Avenue d'Iéna Gulbenkian offered to lend thirty-four of his finest paintings to the National Gallery. He confided in Clark a hitherto unarticulated desire to 'decentralize my works of Art' until such time as he reached a final decision on where his collection would finally rest. 'I am most anxious they should have happy surroundings,' he added, 'and procure public enjoyment. No one will understand me better than yourself and for this I am very grateful.'[7]

This project would keep the pair in regular contact until 1945, when Clark resigned from the gallery to focus on his writing. 'It would be foolish of any man to say that he had been Gulbenkian's friend,' Clark later observed, '[but] I think I can claim that, during the next ten years, I came to know him as well as almost anyone outside his family circle.'[8] By early 1937 twenty-nine paintings from the Gulbenkian collection were on display at Trafalgar Square, while twenty-six Egyptian statuettes and other artefacts were on loan at the British Museum, where they were exhibited in the entrance hall.[9] Gulbenkian began pushing Clark to recommend new purchases. If anything, this pressure only increased as the international situation darkened, and would be maintained right up to 1942, when restrictions on currency movements began to limit Gulbenkian's purchases. Once acquired, works such as François Boucher's *Madame de Pompadour* were delivered straight to the National Gallery. Thanks to the war and subsequent ill-health, Gulbenkian never saw them himself. Yet he does not appear to have minded this. Given his fondness for describing his relationship to his paintings in 'oriental' terms, referring to them as his 'children', this is striking.

As with his other advisers on Greek coins and Egyptian antiquities, Gulbenkian constantly impressed on Clark his desire that his collection should consist exclusively of works of the highest quality. Whether dealing through such advisers or direct, Gulbenkian also kept an eagle eye on the prices he was paying. When the art dealer Wildenstein quoted him a certain amount for a Monet landscape in February 1940, Gulbenkian reminded him that he expected *un prix amical* (a friendly price) rather than *marchandage* (hard bargaining).[10] His concern for the material well-being of his art was almost obsessive. Though he did not inspect himself, he regularly sent Rita, Nubar, Kevork or members of the London office staff to do so, in obedience to his mantra 'check, check, check'.

In July 1937 Clark informed his trustees of Gulbenkian's intention to bequeath his collections to the National Gallery and endow an annexe to house them, 'the whole to be known as the G[ulbenkian] Foundation'. 'It was to be under the Trustees of the National Gallery, but with a separate curator, and endowed to make purchases and occasional publications – a sum of £20,000 [£1.2 million] a year for this purpose had been mentioned.' Clark informed prime minister Neville Chamberlain, who welcomed the proposal.[11] Clark also consulted the Treasury, seeking answers to Gulbenkian's questions about death duties and other tax implications of his proposed gift. In January 1938 Clark reassured his trustees that these legal and testamentary challenges were for the most part resolved, so as 'to make the possibility of a bequest almost a certainty'. This endowment was the richest the National Gallery had been offered since its foundation in 1824, although as the trustee Walter Samuel (son of Shell founder Marcus Samuel) somewhat primly observed, it would be exposed to fluctuations in the oil price.[12]

Alongside Samuel, the National Gallery board included the art dealer Joseph Duveen (to Gulbenkian, simply 'Joe') and others who would have known Gulbenkian in rather different capacities. Now Viscount d'Abernon, Sir Edgar Vincent had been director-general of the Imperial Ottoman Bank during the 1896 massacres in Istanbul. The Conservative MP and Minister for Air Philip Sassoon was descended from a great Ottoman Jewish trading dynasty. Sassoon's grandfather had regularly transacted business with Gulbenkian's father. For these trustees, Gulbenkian's insistence that his 'children' be kept together in a semi-detached part of their institution was problematic. Not that such conditions were in any way unusual: earlier benefactors to the National Gallery had occasionally done the same – as happened, for example, with the Mond Bequest of 1911, left by the chemicals magnate Sir Ludwig Mond. The long-term risk of accepting gifts under such conditions lay in compromising the legibility of the collection as a whole, organised along art historical lines.[13] The prospect was so tempting, however, that the board instructed Clark to proceed.

Clark warned them that Gulbenkian had 'definite ideas' when it came to architecture, though he was careful to add that these were based on 'real knowledge' of the subject.[14] Gulbenkian certainly had a clear idea of what he wished the Gulbenkian Foundation to look like. Having admired the US Embassy building on the corner of the Place de la Concorde as 'the best example of the architecture of modern times I have seen', he asked Clark to find out who had designed it and commission plans from him. 'Our building, particularly the entrance and the ground floor', was to be 'exactly the same as the Consulate'. There was to be no quarter given for the architect to indulge in what Gulbenkian described as that profession's tendency 'to experiment and carry out new ideas'.[15]

The Chancery of the US Embassy was constructed in 1931, on a site next to the Hôtel de Crillon. It had been designed by William Delano of Delano and Aldrich, designers of club-, country and town houses for the Rockefellers, Vanderbilts and Astors. In 1938 Delano was busy with designs for the New York World's Fair, as well as the Marine Air Terminal, still in use today as New York's LaGuardia Airport. After meeting Clark in New York and Gulbenkian in Paris, Delano came up with a 'Gabrielish' scheme – that is, in the style of the eighteenth-century French architect Ange-Jacques Gabriel, whom Gulbenkian admired – for a two-storey annexe to be built onto the west end of the National Gallery, where the Sainsbury Wing stands today.[16] Visitors would be able to access the main, first-floor suite of top-lit painting galleries from the main floor of the building. There was also a ground-level entrance leading directly onto the north-west corner of Trafalgar Square. Here the visitor would find a grand foyer and staircase surrounded by side-lit galleries for the Near Eastern, Egyptian and Greek collections. As at 51 Avenue d'Iéna (which it resembled), so here Houdon's *Diana* would stand guard.

Gulbenkian admired the model and asked Clark to secure a full estimate from Delano. Delano and Clark shared a certain bemusement at

Gulbenkian's refusal to acknowledge the deteriorating international situation. 'He is not naturally an optimistic man,' Clark noted in one letter to Delano, 'but I suppose has more belief in the continuity of the capitalist system than we have.'[17] Although the government had had other plans for the site, Clark secured the approval of the Office of Works.[18] While pushing Clark to hammer out the details for a gallery-focused foundation, Gulbenkian was also instructing one of his lawyers, Harold Brown, to explore an alternative plan, whereby Pandi (Participation and Investments, Gulbenkian's main holding company) would be transferred to a 'Trust to be for the advancement of Art, Architecture and Science'. This remit was broader than the art-focused philanthropic organisation which formed the basis of Gulbenkian's discussions with Clark.

A transfer of Pandi to a trust would be free of tax, Brown noted, provided Gulbenkian lived at least a year after making the transfer and retained no beneficial interest for himself or his children. Even then, it would be at the mercy of 'confiscatory' legislation. 'It is a serious risk,' Brown noted, 'as all sorts of people are devising and making these schemes and the Government is continually legislating to make them more difficult.' Gulbenkian also needed to face the risk that his heirs might seek to apply French testamentary law, under which they could have contested such a trust. For his part Brown urged Gulbenkian to abandon the attempt to hold on to some form of residual rights. He also asked for more detail on Gulbenkian's plans for the foundation. 'Are you content to leave all details to the Trustees, including the allocation of the Funds as between the three subjects [that is, art, architecture and science], or do you wish to lay down rules and regulations for the guidance of the Trustees?' It was a question that Gulbenkian consistently failed to answer.[19]

Trading with the Enemy?

On 13 May 1940 the Germans invaded France. British forces evacuated Dunkirk. Now bombs did indeed fall on Paris. At the Ritz the basement was tidied up for use by guests as a bomb shelter, with Persian rugs, army beds and sleeping bags by Hermès. Though Gulbenkian normally slept at the Ritz when in Paris, it is unclear whether he availed himself of these facilities. Perhaps he remembered working in his room to the music of 'Big Bertha' in 1918 and decided to remain upstairs.

On 10 June the French government announced its plans to leave the capital for Bordeaux, unleashing panic in Paris and driving even more people onto clogged roads leading south. On the 14th the Germans entered Paris. Two days later the hero of Verdun, Marshal Pétain, assumed the presidency, signing an armistice six days later. In July a new 'État Français' based at Vichy took the place of the Third Republic. Wherever the government went, the diplomats accredited to it tried to follow, roads and hotel capacity permitting. For over thirty years the Gulbenkians had been constantly on the move, their largesse ensuring a smooth passage wherever they went: two dozen bottles of port for His Majesty's Customs Officers at Croydon Aerodrome, a box of caviar for the concierge at the Majestic ... as the *chef de gare* at Boulogne put it in his thank-you letter, the Gulbenkians were 'our favourite clients', admired for their 'delicacy and exquisite simplicity'.[20] If you had the misfortune to find yourself in France in June 1940, chasing a disintegrating bureaucracy as it fled before a German *Blitzkrieg*, the Gulbenkians were useful people to know. The Iranian ambassador, Anouchiravan Sepahbodi, certainly thought as much. He ordered Gulbenkian to join him and the four other members of the legation.

Gulbenkian struggled to cope. He had never taken his legation duties very seriously before, but diplomatic immunity was too precious in wartime not to heed Sepahbodi's summons. On 11 July Gulbenkian wrote to his doctor from Pau describing how

> my official legation duties have necessitated successive decampments ... If possible we are going to rejoin the government immediately in Vichy, if we can find room there to settle ourselves comfortably – otherwise we will wait in Cannes. There are crazy crowds everywhere, it is difficult to find supplies, petrol is hard to get hold of, lots of refugees, soldiers.[21]

On 15 July the Iranian Legation officially arrived in Vichy. Calouste and Nevarte installed themselves at the Hôtel du Parc et Majestic.[22] They would remain until March 1942. Meanwhile on 19 July a train pulled out of Baghdad headed for Istanbul – the first ever to do so. Kaiser Wilhelm II's dream of a Berlin–Bosphorus–Baghdad railway had finally become reality. Almost nobody noticed.[23]

Under the terms of the Armistice, France was divided into zones: some were fully integrated into Germany, some occupied, some left unoccupied.

Paris and northern and western France were directly administered from Paris by the German military authorities. A coastal zone between ten and twenty kilometres wide was created in 1941. The heart of France was left unoccupied and administered by the Vichy regime. Movement between these zones was difficult and Calouste did not see Paris again until after the liberation. Kevork and Rita remained in Paris, living at 51 Avenue d'Iéna. Les Enclos was stranded in the coastal zone. Nearby Mont Canisy's importance for coastal defence had been recognised by the French, who had built an artillery emplacement there. Now the Germans expanded it, building an anti-aircraft battery on Gulbenkian's land. Homesick gunners cut down his specimen pines to use as Christmas trees. On the morning of D-Day HMS *Warspite* bombarded the area, knocking out the guns, but causing yet more damage to Les Enclos.[24]

Direct communication with the London office was now impossible. The office was headed by a sixty-five-year-old Armenian of Persian extraction, Avetoom Hacobian, whose family had been wealthy *amiras* in 1870s Istanbul. Hacobian and his brothers were general merchants on Java until 1921, when Avetoom moved to London to set up a new branch of the business. In the 1920s he had been one of the leading activists of the Armenian diaspora in London. He joined the Gulbenkian office in 1931, presumably because the family business had failed in the Depression and he had no other means of supporting himself. He was fiercely loyal to Calouste, if lacking in initiative and imagination. Unless someone was around to give him orders, he was of little use except in routine matters.[25]

Fortunately, one of the rising stars of Freshfields (Gulbenkian's lawyers) happened to live close to the relocated office in Dorking.[26] Charles Whishaw was soon playing an active role defending Gulbenkian's interests within IPC. Whishaw kept a wary eye on Nubar, who had been banned (by his father) from visiting the office, but whose counsel was still sought. For his part, Nubar admired Whishaw's talents, but feared that his lack of experience of the oil industry left him prone to be far too trusting of Pandi's IPC partners. As Nubar put it, Calouste 'knew the people with whom [they] were dealing and that they were, in fact, "Man-eating tigers"'. It was therefore unsettling when Whishaw 'insisted on treating them as harmless "ginger tom cats"'.[27]

After the fall of France, Gulbenkian had become a 'technical enemy' in the eyes of the British authorities, under the terms of the 1939 Trading with the Enemy Act. Gulbenkian's IPC interests were taken over by the

Custodian of Enemy Property. In late July Wilfred Greene (Master of the Rolls) drew Gulbenkian's situation to the attention of Rab Butler at the Foreign Office, noting that Gulbenkian was an old client and friend of his, as well as 'a thorn in the side of the big oil interests'. 'It would now appear that these interests are trying to oust him on the ground that he has been caught in France and ought to be treated as an enemy. This looks to me like a racket of the worst kind.'[28]

Butler pointed out that enemy status was given by the Trading with the Enemy Department and had not been the result of lobbying by Gulbenkian's IPC partners. 'Mr Gulbenkian is a man who has done services to this country,' Butler noted on the memo. 'I trust that I shall be kept informed of developments.'[29] The status of the 1928 Red Line Agreement was unclear: while the Americans as well as IPC's managing director, John Skliros (originally an Anglo-Persian man), acted as if the Red Line Agreement were still in force, the UK Petroleum Department considered it 'possibly null and void'.[30] Although Gulbenkian took his enemy status as a personal affront, he was not treated that badly: his representatives were allowed to continue attending IPC meetings and contribute to discussions, though their presence was not formally minuted.

CFP's 23.75 per cent share of IPC had also been sequestered. It seemed reasonable to assume that the German occupation of France would continue for some time, and that the Germans would reclaim Deutsche Bank's 25 per cent of IPC, the share which had been sequestered during the First World War and subsequently sold to the French. Goering did indeed come up with a plan to turn back the clock to 1914, reclaiming Deutsche Bank's former stakes in Mesopotamian as well as Romanian oil companies. These were to be placed under the control of a holding company, Kontinental, formally established in March 1941. With Operation Barbarossa (the German invasion of the Soviet Union), Goering's mind turned to the oilfields of Maikop, Grozny and even Baku. Kontinental received exclusive rights to those Caucasian fields as well.

Given their lack of experience in the oil industry it is perhaps unsurprising that Kontinental turned to Gulbenkian for advice. Dr Otto Wittrock met with Gulbenkian at Vichy in February 1941. Gulbenkian began by rehearsing the story of how he had come to be the first to draw the Sultan's attention to Mosul oil. He then spoke of TPC and expressed frustration at the fact that Deutsche Bank's share had been taken during the First World War: 'G. deeply regretted this development as he had always been of the opinion, both theoretically and practically, that all oil-consuming countries and other interested parties should participate in [TPC], in order to rule out economic competition that might prove harmful to the enterprise.' Gulbenkian had ceded the majority of his 40 per cent of TPC to Royal Dutch-Shell, he stated, in order to stymie British attempts to monopolise the fields. The forked IPC pipeline balanced French and English interests, he observed, and should 'be taken as confirmation of Gulbenkian's oil policy and of that policy's influence'.

Gulbenkian held it to be 'both possible and necessary' for the Germans and Italians to enter IPC, 'regardless of the war's outcome', and was himself ready to help bring this about. He acknowledged that in wartime it was justified and necessary for the Germans to secure control of Romanian and Russian oilfields. But to build an oil policy around the needs of a single state was 'no way to go about establishing dominance in the international oil industry'. He cited the 'narrowminded policy of "grocer" Pineau and Wenger' as evidence of how such an approach could backfire, causing France to lose 'her position in international oil politics, even with her share of Iraqi oil production'. Gulbenkian clearly saw Kontinental as an embryonic CFP, with some justification.[31] He urged the Germans to take up concessions in Venezuela and north Persia, and Wittrock suggested that Gulbenkian would be an appropriate intermediary for any attempt to explore north Persia.[32]

Despite their close relations before and after the war, Gulbenkian does not seem to have had any influence on CFP policy under Vichy. That said, identifying a coherent CFP policy in the war years is difficult, as some executives fled, while others remained in France. In July 1940 Mercier met with the Vichy authorities to discuss their options vis-à-vis their new German masters. They could maintain a low profile, with the risk that the Germans would simply ignore them and exploit CFP's Romanian and Middle East interests for themselves. Any attempt by CFP to collaborate in a more active manner, however, carried the risk of alienating the British or their American partners in IPC.[33]

CFP decided to keep a low profile, leaving Vichy officials in France as well as in Syria free to develop schemes to wrest physical control of IPC facilities for joint exploitation with the Italians and Germans.[34] These schemes came closest to succeeding in 1941. In January of that year the pan-Arabist prime minister of Iraq, Rashid Ali al-Gaylani, put out feelers to Hitler, offering to fight Britain if Germany recognised Iraqi independence.

When the pro-British regent, 'Abd al-Ilah, and the former prime minister, Nuri al-Said, pushed for Rashid's resignation, the colonels came out in defiance, surrounding the palace and forcing the regent to flee to Amman.

By the end of April 1941 the Iraqi capital was in rebel hands and the linchpin of British power in Iraq, the RAF base at Habbaniya, was besieged by an armed mob. Twenty-one Luftwaffe fighter-bombers were on the tarmac at Mosul, awaiting fuel to enable them to fly sorties. The Vichy High Commissioner sequestered IPC assets within Syria, including pumping stations on the northern fork of the pipeline as well as the Tripoli terminus and refinery. Following an agreement between Ribbentrop and Vichy's General Darlan, the latter agreed to join the Germans and Italians in sending materiel to support the Iraqis. The colonels failed to capitalise on this support, however. In May the British regained control. The regent returned to Baghdad and hanged the colonels. IPC's oilfields were saved for the Allies.[35]

Escape

Once the Persian Legation was established in Vichy, Gulbenkian's diplomatic duties were probably minimal. Calouste and Nevarte knew Vichy well and both had friends among the diplomats gathered there. The climate was pleasant. In October 1940 Nubar even managed to visit from London, though he had to travel by a roundabout route, via neutral Lisbon and Madrid. As he reported on his return, Nubar had tried to persuade his father to follow his London lawyers' advice and leave Vichy,

> which he can easily do any moment he wants to. He, however, categorically refuses on the ground that at the age of 72 years he is not going to leave France where he made his home for over 30 years, and to settle either in Portugal where he does not know the language or in England where he dislikes the climate and the taxation. The Gestapo had been making exhaustive inquiries about him ... but even this does not affect him as of course his attitude having been perfectly correct throughout, he has nothing to fear from any inquiries.[36]

Calouste was also put off by reading Nubar's account for his short stay in Lisbon, noting that the cost of living there was 50 per cent higher than in Vichy. This as well as Nubar's troubles with Portuguese immigration authorities led Calouste to abandon plans to leave Vichy with Nevarte for four weeks of 'sun and relaxation' in Lisbon.[37] In April 1941 Gulbenkian reconsidered, and arranged visas and transport for Portugal, only to cancel in May, owing to rumours that Franco was going to invade the country. It was clear that Portugal was not a safe refuge. Gulbenkian began thinking of the United States.[38]

Events in Iran took the decision out of Gulbenkian's hands. After the Anglo-Soviet invasion of August 1941 it had been hard to maintain the pretence that Iran was a sovereign state or that it was neutral. Reza Shah was perceived to be pro-Axis by the Allies and was deposed in favour of his son, Mohammad Reza Shah. In January 1942 the latter signed a treaty with the Soviet Union and Britain, agreeing to lend them logistical support for the 'Persian Corridor', a major route by which Lend-Lease aid reached the Soviets. Although Iran did not declare war on Germany until 1943, diplomatic relations between Persia and France now ceased. Gulbenkian and his fellow Iranian diplomats were asked to leave Vichy. Gulbenkian applied for visas – first for Switzerland and then, when that failed, for the United States. He would, of course, travel via Madrid and Lisbon. Nubar advised him to try to secure permission to remain in Lisbon for a few weeks, to improve his health before embarking for New York.[39]

Leaving Vichy on 30 March, it took Calouste two weeks to make the journey to Lisbon, where he checked into the Hotel Aviz. Nevarte had suffered an attack of pneumonia and had remained in France to receive medical treatment. Although she arrived in Lisbon later in May, her pneumonia returned and became much more serious. Calouste summoned the children to Lisbon, warning them that Nevarte was not likely to live much longer. Though she recovered, events had taken their toll on Calouste. 'You can appreciate how at sea we feel,' he wrote to a fellow Iranian diplomat in late July, 'finding ourselves in a foreign land, where we don't know the language.'[40]

The State Department having refused him a diplomatic visa, Gulbenkian now applied to the British for a visa to travel to New York on his British passport.[41] In London the Passport Control Office referred this application to the Ministry of Economic Warfare, who were curious to know more about Gulbenkian and the motives behind his proposed trip to the United States. As an official at the ministry noted:

Gulbenkian disliked portraits of women he considered mannered or sentimental. Acquired in 1929 through the art dealer Joseph Duveen, Domenico Ghirlandaio's Young Woman *(c. 1490) was neither.*

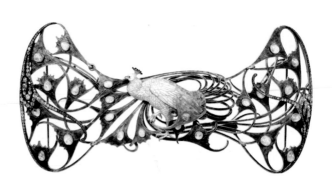

When not on loan to public exhibitions, Gulbenkian's outstanding collection of jewellery by René Lalique was displayed in vitrines at his Paris palace at 51 Avenue d'Iéna. Nevarte could admire the masterful use of opal, diamonds and other precious stones in items such as this choker (top) and pectoral (bottom) – but was on no account allowed to wear them.

'My first impression of Degas is one of curiosity,' Gulbenkian admitted in 1918, 'as I am not accustomed to that school, and being ignorant I must be educated.' He acquired Degas's The Artist in his Studio *(c. 1878) the following year.*

In 1930 Gulbenkian went through a published catalogue of the Hermitage, noting in pencil the works he wished to buy. A small tick appears next to Rembrandt's Pallas Athene *(c. 1657), which Gulbenkian purchased that same year.*

Gulbenkian expected full-length portraits such as Thomas Gainsborough's
Mrs Lowndes-Stone *(c. 1775) to 'flirt' with him. He 'divorced' a similar lady by*
John Hoppner when her charms wore off.

Alongside his masterpieces, Gulbenkian also enjoyed collecting what he called 'decorative' pictures, such as Hubert Robert's Le Tapis Vert *(top, c. 1776) and Stanislas Lépine's* L'Estacade *(bottom, c. 1882). Such acquisitions reflect his love of the park at Versailles and of Paris, the city he knew best.*

Gulbenkian drove his son-in-law Kevork Essayan hard, at least until the Second World War stranded them on different sides of the conflict. Unable to receive orders from Gulbenkian, Kevork had free time to paint works such as this self-portrait (bottom), while his wife Rita (right) shivered in a frigid 51 Avenue d'Iéna.

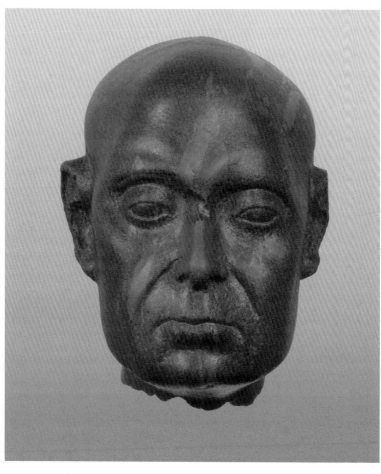

The great archaeologist Howard Carter was one of the agents Gulbenkian employed to scout the market for Egyptian antiquities. Alongside remarkably expressive heads such as this one of an official, Gulbenkian also acquired several statuettes of cats.

Calouste is one of the richest men in the world, and the sum derived from the Iraq Petroleum Co royalty must exceed £500,000 [£21 million] a year, I should have said. He has always been much concerned to avoid taxation in any country in which he was classed as a 'resident', or where he had other business interests. He is a great picture collector, and his house in Paris was full of treasures. There is a dossier for him I find, but there is little about him in it.

The many intercepts of Gulbenkian's cable traffic by British Intelligence did not add much to this picture. This was hardly reason enough to refuse him a visa.

The British decided to let Gulbenkian travel to the United States, but at the same time to take steps to ensure that the Internal Revenue Service there were given 'a hint to pay special attention to him on arrival'. The Passport Control Office would 'authorize this journey on the lines of the obsolete code word "CERBERUS" taking care to see that he is eaten by the US tax authorities on arrival'. On Gulbenkian's file another official has admiringly written, 'Machiavellian!' immediately below this proposal.[42]

Gulbenkian did not travel to the United States in 1942, though he tried again in 1943, securing visas for himself, Nevarte, his secretary, Isabelle Theis, and two other French servants. He may have been tipped off about the plan to hand him over to the IRS. The British and American authorities in Lisbon used their joint control over international currency movements to keep Gulbenkian on a tight leash, hoping thereby to flush out the precise nature of his business interests. In 1943 the US Treasury asked the financial attaché in Lisbon, James Wood, to investigate Gulbenkian's affairs. Soon Wood became uneasily aware that, as he investigated Gulbenkian, his supposed subject was also investigating him. The great diplomat and political scientist George Kennan was then a lowly counsellor at the Lisbon embassy, handling intelligence matters. Wood wrote to Kennan, stating, 'I am disturbed over the fact that Mr Gulbenkian is well acquainted with my investigation of him.' Wood asked Kennan to work out where Gulbenkian was getting his information from. Gulbenkian's own intelligence service was still working, even in a foreign land.

Wood subsequently confessed to Kennan that his investigation was getting nowhere. Gulbenkian's business interests were so 'ramified' that Wood could not establish clearly where his loyalties ultimately lay. 'It seems reasonable to assume that a person with the vast resources and extensive contacts such as those possessed by Mr Gulbenkian is very likely to manage his affairs in such a way as to give evidence of supporting either side in the war,' Wood concluded, 'the direction of the main support at any time being dependent upon which side appears to be moving towards victory.'[43] In many ways neutral Portugal was a highly appropriate place for a man like this to shelter in 1942.

PART III

ANACHRONISM, 1942–55

'CSG when I knew him was like a Rip van Winkle, a survivor from
another age and one who didn't know that things had changed.'
N. M. Ekserdjian

'In his inner personality Mr Gulbenkian is a man of
rare nobility. He is like a king constantly fighting for the
protection of his kingdom. It is so sad he fights alone!'
Alexis Léger

SIXTEEN

PAYS DE COCAGNE, 1942–4

For wealthy exiles like the Gulbenkians, wartime Lisbon afforded an escape from the privations of life in London, Paris and Vichy. Despite their wealth and the ever-present black market, Calouste, Nevarte, Nubar, Rita and Kevork could not escape rationing, which would continue well after the end of the war. Nevarte would recall having to survive at Vichy with 'no milk – no butter – no eggs – no poultry – no fish – no meat'. Nubar, by contrast, found 'plenty of food' in Lisbon during his 1940 stopover. As he wrote to Rita, 'Portugal in general and Lisbon in particular are a regular Pays de Cocagne to anyone coming from a war scarred England.' Once installed at Lisbon's Hotel Aviz, Calouste soon began sending care packages to Britain. Friends who had politely acknowledged gifts of caviar five years previously now wrote gushing letters of thanks for a box of Elvas plums. A land of sun, peace and plenty (at least for the rich), Portugal seemed a very paradise in 1942.[1]

Gratitude was not the only response, however. A certain resentment was present as well. Trapped inside the 'mausoleum' of 51 Avenue d'Iéna, Rita and Madame Soulas took turns standing in the interminable queues which formed daily outside the bakers and other shops. The building's state-of-the-art electric heating system was a serious liability, now there were only a few hours of electricity a day. Kevork, however, was happy enough: released from bondage to his father-in-law, he could practise his oil painting.[2] In London Nubar was exposed to a different set of indignities (such as having to stand in packed trains), but nonetheless shared Rita's increasing frustration with Calouste's failure to recognise just how much the times were changing.

Nubar warned his father that the standard of living which Calouste considered to be 'an elementary frugal existence' was no longer possible in Britain, France or Spain. Not only was it no longer possible, it was positively frowned upon. This was more than a case of temporary patriotic belt-tightening. Nubar and Rita recognised that Calouste's 'frugal existence' was gone for good. At Harrow boys were even learning to type. Maybe his grandson, Mikhael, should learn, too?[3]

Portugal's neutrality not only made it easier to find food in Lisbon, but also caused the city to blossom into a cosmopolitan interchange. Thanks to its illustrious history as an imperial power, the city already possessed scenery befitting this drama, even if, as Nubar somewhat snootily noted, the national gallery's paintings could not match his father's collection. One part of this empire, the Azores, had crucial significance to the Allies, as a transatlantic refuelling base for airborne supplies. Northern Portugal also possessed Europe's only reserves of tungsten (then known as wolfram), a heavy metal that the Allied and Axis armies both used to tip the armour-piercing shells they were busy firing at each other's tanks.

President of the Council as well as minister of war, foreign affairs and finance, in 1942 Dr António de Oliveira Salazar had been in power for ten years. A former university professor of economics with a notoriously frugal lifestyle, in 1939 Salazar had opted to ignore the treaties tying Portugal to Britain and remain neutral, on the grounds that Britain had refused to play her part by guaranteeing Portuguese sovereignty. Salazar also faced the threat of invasion from Franco's Spain, whose armed forces were far stronger than Portugal's. With the entry of the United States into the war in December 1941, Salazar realised that the Allies were likely to win and began moving away from his previous position of strict neutrality. A month after Calouste's arrival in Lisbon, Salazar cut off tungsten sales to the Axis. Reluctant to be seen moving too quickly, however, negotiations for Allied use of the Azores only began a year later.

In the meantime Lisbon and the nearby Atlantic resort of Estoril became the haunt of spies and adventurers, as well as wealthy exiles hedging their bets. All available hotel rooms were filled, and hotels were loosely divided between 'allied' and 'axis' establishments. Nevarte installed herself in the Palácio at Estoril; like the Aviz, this counted as an 'allied' hotel. There she would have crossed paths with a former clerk of Gulbenkian's London stockbrokers Cull & Co., now working for His Majesty's Secret Service. Ian Fleming had checked in in May 1941, and was busy with Operation Golden Eye: a network of 'stay-behind' agents against the expected Spanish invasion. Fleming had found the business of handling Gulbenkian's share trades dull. History does not record whether he took any notice of his former client at the Aviz – now a balding, publicity-shy man of mystery and fabulous wealth, with a fondness for white Angora cats.

The arrangement whereby Nevarte spent most of her time at the Palácio in Estoril and the Buçaco Palace Hotel while Calouste remained in Lisbon at the Aviz suited both parties well. Each autumn Nevarte usually moved to the Aviz for a month or two. She knew to be 'very quiet', recognising that her husband didn't 'like people – so I don't "receive" – I lunch and dine out but I ask no one at Aviz'. 'It is fair,' she wrote, 'and I am quite content and happy – In marriage one must give and take.' At the Aviz she came down to dine an hour before Calouste, dining separately in obedience to the routine established at Avenue d'Iéna. Like Nubar, she appreciated the good food available in Lisbon, though she sometimes found herself 'dying for a [smoked] haddock!!!'[4]

From Palácio to Prison

At Estoril, by contrast, Nevarte could be 'quite free'. She cut a swathe through diplomatic circles just as she had in Paris, charming ambassadors, generals and other officials. When it came to the tightly knit local elite, she recognised that Portuguese society was far more conservative than that of Britain or France. Nevarte acknowledged that aristocrats, diplomats and other functionaries – who included the Duke of Palmela, Marcello Mathias and the head of the PVDE (secret police), Agostinho Lourenço – gave her licence to behave in ways they might not tolerate in a Portuguese.

When Nubar warned his mother that rumours of the Gulbenkians' dining rituals had reached London Nevarte reflected on what this said about Lisbon society:

When one does not lead in Portugal an absolutely conventional life – husband – wife – communicating bedrooms!! – out together – in

together – slippers – bezique or bridge – people get amused and <u>talk</u> –
one must be careful not to do an <u>outstanding</u> thing <u>different</u> to anyone
else to the l[e]ast degree – with our age – our position – our outward
'tenue' – I mean I don't dye my hair or give 'rastaqu[ou]ère' parties
– we are allowed certaines <u>originalités</u> i.e. not being always together –
meals – drives etc.

Nevarte was nonetheless grateful to Nubar for keeping her informed of
what was being said about her. She needed to know if she was overstep-
ping the line. 'It is <u>useful</u> to know l'opinion publique,' she wrote. 'What
one could do <u>with impunity</u> in France – one cannot do it here.' At the end
of the day, she concluded, when it came to the Portuguese elite, 'I seem to
please them as <u>I am not too modern</u> altho' cheerful – and always ready for
a bit of fun.'[5]

Nevarte's friendship with secret police chief Lourenço began in June
1943, when she was seated next to him at one of the many diplomatic
luncheon parties she attended. Noting that he was 'the great and most
important man of Portugal', Nevarte recounted that 'we got on like a house
on fire'. Lourenço laughed heartily when Nevarte told him of the contrast
Rita had drawn between her life in Paris and her mother's in Lisbon.
While the former was the life of 'the Salvation Army', Rita claimed, life in
Lisbon was *One Thousand and One Nights*. 'I told him one or two of my
funny stories – and asked no favours!!!!'[6] Nevarte's success with Lourenço
of PVDE is striking, as just six months before Lourenço had thrown her
husband in jail.

In December 1942 Gulbenkian had five of the thirty-three suites at
the Hotel Aviz, a mock castle designed in the famous Manueline Gothic
style. This was not simply a case of vanity. In addition to himself he needed
a suite for his private secretary, Isabelle Theis. His son-in-law, Kevork, had
arrived the previous month for an extended stay. Whishaw was expected to
arrive, and there was always Nevarte to think of. When the manager asked
Calouste on 14 December to vacate a suite, therefore, Calouste refused.
Clearly one suite was nonetheless taken, as when Whishaw showed up he
had to be put in a servant's room. On the 17th the manager asked Kevork
to vacate his suite, claiming that it had been requisitioned for government
use. Calouste again made his objections clear. What happened next was
truly remarkable.

At 7.50 p.m. Calouste and Kevork were forcibly taken to a police station. Calouste's diplomatic passport was confiscated, he was separated from Kevork and told that he was now a prisoner, even though he had not been placed under arrest. Calouste never learned Portuguese and yet when he asked for someone who spoke French he was rudely told to sit and wait. After an hour he was interrogated and told to sign a statement in Portuguese, which, again, he could not understand. Although he initially refused to sign, on being threatened he did so.

At 10 p.m. he was taken to the Central Prison. Permission to make a phone call was repeatedly refused. Some regard was being paid to his social and diplomatic status, however, as he was kept waiting a further three hours while a 'first class cell' was prepared for him. There was no Iranian Embassy in Portugal, so Kevork appealed to the Egyptian ambassador, Fakhry Paşa, who arrived at the prison an hour later and negotiated Gulbenkian's release. Apart from a single memorandum drawn up by Kevork, this incident was never referred to by anyone, even in private correspondence, until *Life* magazine reported it in 1950.[7] This silence served to cover what must have been a deeply humiliating experience for Calouste.

It is difficult to imagine this drama playing out in Vichy or London. It accurately reflected the PVDE's disdain for the niceties of due process, diplomatic immunity and civil rights. Despite the language barrier, Calouste had received an instructive lesson in the less attractive side of Lourenço and his minions, and indeed of the Salazar regime itself. He was careful to include Lourenço's officers in the long list of Portuguese charities he supported, and acknowledged the excellent service they provided, above all by keeping reporters away from the Aviz.[8] It seems fair to assume that Gulbenkian admired the emphasis Salazar's regime placed on tradition, family and hard work.[9] The pair shared a disdain for communism and trade unions, though Gulbenkian would not have supported Salazar's corporatist approach to the national economy. At the end of the day, Portuguese politics was not very important to Gulbenkian. He had no investments in Portugal, did not intend to stay long and had many more pressing matters to occupy him.

The Siege of Avenue d'Iéna

Meanwhile, from the safety of New York, William Delano continued to work on the projected Gulbenkian annexe for the National Gallery. He couldn't help but wonder privately to Kenneth Clark at Gulbenkian's optimism. 'Where now are the objects to go into it,' he enquired in July 1942, '– in Berlin?'[10] It was a reasonable question to ask. A week before, two officials had pushed their way into 51 Avenue d'Iéna while Mme Soulas was out and spent half an hour wandering round the building. They then left, promising to return. In anticipation, Soulas had the house's resident electrician, Dufretin, put a heavy chain on the door.

Two days later Colonel Baron Kurt von Behr of the Einsatzstab Reichsleiter Rosenberg (ERR) appeared at the door with two high-ranking German officers and a woman. Named after the Nazi racial theorist Alfred Rosenberg, the ERR had been charged by Hitler with the task of confiscating cultural property belonging to Jews, as well as the looting of national archives and collections across Europe. Its French headquarters was just down the street, at 54 Avenue d'Iéna. Behr's party insisted that if Soulas did not remove the chain, they would force their way in. Soulas relented and they entered, giving instructions that nobody attempt to use the telephone.

The officers insisted that the owner of the *hôtel* was an Egyptian Jew; indeed, an unnamed individual had denounced Gulbenkian to them as such. Soulas's assertion that the premises were the chancellery of the Iranian Legation, and the Swiss *lettre de protection* attesting to this fact, were dismissed as '*louche* excuses'. Although the high-ranking officers are not named in Soulas's report, the presence of a woman suggests that 51 Avenue d'Iéna was being inspected as a prospective residence for a senior German official. A similar Rothschild-owned *hôtel* on Avenue Marigny had been confiscated for just such a purpose. As Behr toured the premises, the Paris police were beginning a massive round-up of more than 13,000 Jews, who were held for the next five days in unspeakable squalor and distress at the Vélodrome d'Hiver in the west of the city, before being sent to a camp at Drancy. Most were then sent on to Auschwitz, apart from a few set to work sorting the lorryloads of private possessions looted from Jewish homes across Paris. The very best items, such as Vermeer's *Astronomer* from the Rothschild collection, were sent to the ERR facility at the Galerie Nationale du Jeu de Paume, to which Hermann Goering paid regular visits to pick out pieces for himself.

Behr's party declared themselves satisfied with what they had seen: 51 would do them nicely. Soulas was to hand the keys over at 54, and send the *gardien* for questioning. Instead she contacted the Iranian consul-general in Paris, Abdol Hossein Sardari, who halted proceedings and even got the German Embassy to phone Soulas with an apology.[11] Goering was interested in a number of items from Gulbenkian's collection, but had the courtesy to make offers through Prince Andrei Youssoupoff, offers which Gulbenkian refused.[12] Houdon's *Diana* did not go to Berlin.

In Lisbon, however, restrictions placed on his currency movements by the British and American authorities continued to tie Gulbenkian's hands, making it difficult to acquire new items for his collection. It took over a year for him to make arrangements to pay Henri de Rothschild for his portrait of the astronomer Pierre-Simon Laplace by Lépicié and for another portrait by Nattier. Henri's grandmother had formed a renowned collection of works by Chardin and other eighteenth-century French artists, which Gulbenkian had admired at La Muette in Paris thirty years before. At the outbreak of war these paintings were moved to London, where the majority were destroyed in the Blitz. Gulbenkian tried to buy several of Rothschild's Chardins and add them to all the other paintings he planned to give to the National Gallery, but was again unable to release the funds.

Gulbenkian acquired some Portuguese escudos in 1943 by selling his 3 million Reichsmarks' worth of Reichsbank shares for 1.4 million Swiss francs. Acquired in 1925, these shares represented 2 per cent of the German central bank's share capital. The American and British authorities facilitated the sale to the Germans. This seemed to herald a thawing of previously icy relations between the American Embassy and Gulbenkian.[13] Although the British Embassy remained suspicious, American officials came to value Gulbenkian as a useful source of information. The appointment of Herman Baruch as US ambassador in 1945 only confirmed this rehabilitation.

Gulbenkian hailed Baruch 'as being more like a New York broker than an Ambassador', a comment he clearly intended as praise.[14] Baruch was the same age as Calouste, and had indeed been a partner in the New York brokerage house Baruch Brothers. Calouste knew the brothers from Versailles-era oil negotiations.[15] Now Herman and Calouste shared many 'confidential talks'.[16] According to Baruch:

> The view expressed by officers of the Embassy here is that Gulbenkian has given valuable information on the oil situation in the Near East and in the world in general, that in so doing he has performed a valuable service to the United States, and that if properly handled he can in future prove to be of unique service to our Government.

The State Department was particularly appreciative of Gulbenkian's open-ness in showing them documents relating to Iranian oil. In 1944 Tehran was eager to have Gulbenkian serve as an intermediary between the Iranian government and western oil companies interested in North Persia. Gulbenkian was ready to help, but unwilling to travel and reluctant to make deals while the war was still ongoing.[17]

In July 1943 the British Custodian of Enemy Property returned control of Pandi. But Gulbenkian wanted more than this: he wanted a letter from the Foreign Office stating not only that he was no longer an enemy, but that he had never been one. Those who had formerly held enemy status were subject to increased currency restrictions. Here again Gulbenkian had placed his hopes in Kenneth Clark's lobbying, even as he insisted to Clark that his philanthropic plans be kept strictly separate from the question of his enemy status. 'Playing with my future intention in this particular instance would make me feel extremely humiliated,' Gulbenkian noted. Although Gulbenkian's insistence that his philanthropy should not be seen as buying favours is admirable, there was also something naive about it.[18]

Clark went to the top, discussing the matter with Foreign Secretary (and National Gallery Trustee) Sir Anthony Eden. 'Mr. Gulbenkian is a man of somewhat suspicious temperament,' Clark informed Eden, 'and he believes, rightly or wrongly, that his colleagues in Irak Petroleum ... are profiting by his enforced absence from England and by the high positions which many of them occupy in Government service, to deprive him of what he considers his rights.' Add in the fact that one of Gulbenkian's IPC partners was Anglo-Iranian (as Anglo-Persian was now known), in which the British government had a large stake, and 'the train of thought which such a situation would arouse in the Oriental mind is easily imagined.'[19]

A Foreign Office mandarin looked into the matter and drew up a briefing memo for Eden. Even if the Trading with the Enemy Department was willing to consider a 'mammoth exercise in whitewashing' and made a statement that Gulbenkian had not been an enemy within the meaning of the Enemy Acts, it probably would not secure him his lost income, which the Petroleum Executive estimated at £200,000 ('a mere flea-bite for Gulbenkian'). This was the income Gulbenkian should have received from sales of his 5 per cent IPC oil in 1940–42 – that is, during his sojourn at Vichy. The whole issue for Gulbenkian was probably more a matter of honour than anything else, the memo argued. He was therefore:

using every method of pressure on H[is] M[ajesty's] G[overnment] that he can think of, and his threat not to leave his pictures to the nation is probably his strongest bargaining counter. What he is in effect claiming is that the question of his diplomatic status should be interpreted in such a way that his commercial profits are safeguarded – a line which it seems hard to countenance.

'I agree' wrote Eden next to this, using his ministerial red pen.

Diplomatic *officiers de carrière* were not supposed to have personal 'commercial' interests. As for Gulbenkian's supposedly 'enforced' residence in Portugal, the memo continued, the only factor doing the 'enforcing' seemed to be Gulbenkian's desire to avoid British residence on grounds of taxation. Eden underlined this point and drew a conclusion: 'Mr. G would seem to have been treated pretty generously.'[20] Another factor which prevented such a 'whitewashing' was fear that the Americans would notice. In Lisbon American Embassy officials like James Wood had been working hand in glove with the British Embassy to put the squeeze on Gulbenkian. If the British suddenly changed tack, the Americans would wonder why they had done so. As the British Ministry of Economic Warfare noted, 'we do not wish the Americans to gain the impression that we are appeasing him for our own oily ends.'[21]

The British Foreign Office's view of Gulbenkian had changed. When Wilfred Greene had lobbied Eden's predecessor, Rab Butler, in 1940, Butler had minuted that Gulbenkian was 'a man who has done services to this country'. Four years later the British Embassy in Lisbon minuted that Gulbenkian was 'not a citizen of whom the British can be proud'. Charitable giving to the Red Cross and other British charities supposedly veiled an 'ulterior motive'.[22] Meanwhile the State Department had warmed to Gulbenkian. Though Gulbenkian only began seriously exploring the possibility of establishing his foundation in America in 1950, the seeds of that decision were sown in 1944.

A Second World War

Gulbenkian managed to keep his humiliation at the hands of Salazar's PVDE a secret, at least for the time being. Designation as an enemy under the British Enemy Acts, by contrast, was a matter of public record. For

Gulbenkian this was an insult he never forgot, an insult which would later influence plans for his art collections and foundation. In the short term it was also a matter of business: IPC partners used his enemy status to justify their refusal to pay him his 5 per cent on IPC oil. After the fall of France the Allies closed the Mediterranean to commercial as well as enemy tankers. Gulbenkian was left unable to take his 5 per cent in cash or in crude. Even if he had not had enemy status, he would not have been permitted to charter a tanker to lift his 5 per cent of IPC crude from the pipeline terminal.

With Gulbenkian and CFP out of the game, Anglo-Iranian, Royal Dutch-Shell and the American members of the Near East Development Company (Jersey Standard and Socony) did very well for themselves. This was partly because production ceased or was run down elsewhere in the Middle East, and partly because of their shared interest in a refinery at Haifa, which they enlarged to meet the massive wartime demand of the British armed forces. From the fall of France in June 1940 to the lifting of the sequester in July 1943, well over 5 million tons of crude had been lifted from IPC's fields and 5 per cent of this rightly belonged to Pandi. The closure of the Mediterranean, however, allowed Gulbenkian's partners to argue that it was inappropriate to pay IPC a 'world market price' for its oil. By controlling the only accessible refinery, Gulbenkian's IPC partners had been able to fiddle with 'cost' and 'world market prices' to their own advantage.[23] The Petroleum Executive's 'flea-bite' estimate of £200,000 was one product of this fiddling. In this, as in the Great War, national oil policy bodies were led by executives seconded from the very same oil majors who were denying Gulbenkian his share of oil sales.[24] In the oil industry it made sense to be paranoid, especially if you did not have a Great Power behind you.

In May 1943 it was clear that Gulbenkian would soon have his IPC interests restored to him by the Custodian of Enemy Property. But it was equally clear that, rather than marking a return to a familiar status quo ante, this was just the beginning of another epic struggle for survival. As Nubar observed to his father:

> I feel that we are now inevitably on the threshhold of the second 'World War', whereby our associates will take every opportunity to squeeze us out. Having lived through the first 'World War', which culminated in the 'Peace' and the agreements of 1928, and having had the

benefit of your guidance and experience in those battles, I cannot help feeling that similar pitfalls, which we then successfully avoided, are being prepared for us.

When it came to oil policy, Calouste's four-strong kitchen cabinet was divided. Nubar and Whishaw were more assertive and arguably more capable than Kevork and the aged Hacobian, both of whom preferred to be told what to do by Calouste. The loyalty of Kevork and Hacobian to Calouste was beyond doubt, however, which was not the case with Nubar and Whishaw. While Whishaw was working in Gulbenkian's London office full-time, he was still a partner at the law firm Freshfields. Calouste admired Whishaw and wanted him to resign the partnership and become a Pandi employee. But, as Nubar reported to his father, Whishaw 'dislikes our outlook, especially mine, and attached importance to working in a congenial and happy atmosphere'. Thanks to Nubar's bullying, the London office was far from a 'happy atmosphere'.[25]

Picking Sides

As Nubar noted, 'the cardinal point' of his father's policy in the 'first "World War"' – that is, 1924–8, ending in the 'Peace' of the Red Line Agreement – had been to 'divide and rule' his IPC partners.[26] Once again Gulbenkian elected to side with the French against the other IPC partners: Anglo-Iranian, Royal Dutch-Shell, Jersey Standard and Socony. Once again the Americans suspected the British of using the war to strengthen their grip on the world's oil, and sought to control neo-imperialism through international agreements enshrining the open door. A US–UK petroleum agreement prepared (but not signed) in 1921 was even dusted off and became the 1944 Anglo-American Petroleum Agreement.[27]

There the similarities between 1945–8 and 1924–8 ended. This time around the United States was not going to retreat into post-war isolationism: it now championed the Atlantic Charter and the United Nations, and would pump billions of dollars of aid into Europe through the Marshall Plan, inoculating it against communism. This time around Middle East oil was no distant pipe dream: indeed, the focus of the world oil industry was shifting from the Gulf of Mexico to the Persian Gulf. Where that focus went, American economic, diplomatic and military investment followed.

Imperial thoroughfare no more, thanks to Indian independence, the region was on its way to becoming a Cold War frontier of client states. Saudi Arabia epitomised this process.

Having beaten IPC to the east Arabian concession in 1932 and struck oil in 1938, Socal was eager to secure the State Department's support in managing relations with Ibn Saud. With his Mecca-based pilgrimage revenues reduced owing to the war, Ibn Saud was struggling to pay the subsidies needed to keep the vast peninsula's tribes in line. Yet when Socal first urged President Roosevelt to shoulder the burden of subsidising Ibn Saud (which the British government had been carrying up until then), it was said that Saudi Arabia was 'a little far afield' for the United States to take an interest.[28] In February 1943 Roosevelt changed his mind and declared that the defence of Saudi Arabia was a vital US interest. The United States now paid Ibn Saud his subsidies. Roosevelt and Ibn Saud met at Great Bitter Lake (on the Suez Canal) in February 1945. Thereafter US subsidies took off, starting in 1946 with a $10 million soft loan from the Export-Import Bank and a $4 million airfield at Dhahran. Twenty-three years after the humiliating end of the Admiral Chester concession at the Lausanne Conference, the Americans were in the Middle East to stay.

An important figure encouraging Roosevelt to invest in the region was Harold Ickes, head of the US Petroleum Administration for War. As far as Ickes was concerned, 'we were gradually losing our pants to the British in the Near East.'[29] He established the Petroleum Reserves Corporation in July 1943, 'an American holding company created for the purpose of acquiring sizeable governmental oil reserves in the large producing areas of the world'.[30] He developed plans for a $200 million, 1,000-mile-long Trans-Arabian pipeline (Tapline), running from the Persian Gulf to the Mediterranean. For Ickes, Tapline was a 'weapon with which to beat the British over the head'.[31] He even proposed that the US government should take control of Aramco's concession, exploit it themselves and pay Socal and Texaco a royalty.

Socal and Texaco were pleased to have their government's attention, but this was too much.[32] They invited Jersey and Socony to join them in Aramco, helping spread the cost of Tapline and enabling them to put Ickes's vision of a public-private partnership back in the box it had come in. As Saudi Arabia lay within the red line area, however, Jersey and Socony would have to bring their IPC partners into Aramco with them, under the self-denying clause.

Experience suggested that this would be difficult. They had tried unsuccessfully to bring IPC and Socal together in the 1930s. While the Red Line Agreement had served 'the very useful purpose' of giving the American companies access to the oil reserves of French- and British-mandated regions, for Harold Sheets (Socony) it was now redundant.[33] For the British government, defending the red line was less important than securing American loans and American collaboration in the Middle East.[34] That left the French.

Gulbenkian as well as the French appreciated the benefits of having a strong American commercial, diplomatic and military presence in the region, particularly given the supposed Soviet menace. Both opposed the 1944 Anglo-American Petroleum Agreement, however. Gulbenkian lobbied Wood and Baruch against it, and even collared Ickes himself during a stopover in Lisbon.[35] The State Department contended that it could form the foundation of an international oil body which France, Russia and other nations might join. To Gulbenkian this was idealistic claptrap, not worth the risk of encouraging oil-producing nations in the Middle East to form a matching body – to form an OPEC, in other words.[36] There were already signs that oil-producing nations were learning from each other.

The Venezuelan government's introduction of a 50 per cent tax on production profits under a new Petroleum Law in 1943 captured the attention of Arab nations. Soon they began to lobby for their own share of profits, in lieu of earlier, tonnage-based royalties. Their oil revenues had stalled in the 1930s and 1940s; a fixed four shillings per ton (Iran) or 13 cents per barrel (Kuwait) royalty did not capture anything of the increase in the market price that Anglo-Iranian and Gulf Oil received when they sold that ton and that barrel of oil.[37]

Gulbenkian's new entente with CFP was built on his friendship with René de Montaigu, a CFP executive who spent much of the war in Lisbon. In December 1944, four months after the liberation of Paris, Gulbenkian invited Montaigu to return to Lisbon to discuss how CFP and Pandi might work together. By that point Gulbenkian had already resisted two attempts by the other IPC partners to buy him off, first by offering to pay what was owed to him for the period after his move to Lisbon, and then by offering to increase his IPC holding to 6.25 per cent.[38] In resisting these offers, Gulbenkian had shown loyalty to CFP, refusing to betray their long-standing alliance. But this was the oil business, where loyalty bought you few favours. What else did Gulbenkian have to offer CFP?

During the 'first "World War"' over the Turkish Petroleum Company (as IPC was then known) in 1924–8, CFP had drawn on Gulbenkian's legal team, archives and long experience. In the intervening years these had lost none of their appeal. Like the Americans, the French were also intrigued by Gulbenkian's contacts in Tehran. In addition to an invitation to advise Iranian premier Mohammad Ali Foroughi on who should get the north Persian concession, Gulbenkian had also been invited to lead a proposed new Iranian National Oil Company.[39] As ever, it was clear that the best way to exploit North Persian oil was in collaboration with the Soviets, who were again pressing Tehran for the concession. Stalin's dismissive view of de Gaulle did little to revive French hopes of securing Iranian oil.

On his return from visiting Gulbenkian in Lisbon in January 1945, therefore, Montaigu was initially sceptical. He wondered if CFP should get mixed up in Pandi's case against its IPC partners. While 'Iranian matters are in suspense, we have no need of [Gulbenkian's] services'. A few days later in London, however, Montaigu was struck to hear IPC's managing director remark that, of the IPC partners, only CFP and Pandi seemed interested in increasing Iraqi production by constructing new pipelines.[40] Unlike CFP, Royal Dutch-Shell, Anglo-Iranian and the Americans had little incentive. They all had plentiful supplies elsewhere and were happy to keep Iraq a swing producer.

The Americans' lack of interest was, Montaigu concluded, linked to their desire to escape the red line's self-denying clause and accept Socal's and Texaco's invitation to enter Aramco and Saudi Arabia. On 25 January CFP wrote to Gulbenkian agreeing that they should work together. The French Foreign Ministry, it noted, placed a high value on Gulbenkian's counsel and would follow it.[41] Meanwhile in London Nubar, Whishaw and the others stood ready to serve Calouste, well aware that 'nothing any of your advisers here could do would stop you from a fight'.

Nubar couldn't help but feel that at the ripe old age of seventy-six, it might be better for Calouste to sit back and take things easy. If his father decided to fight, Nubar rightly observed, it would not be on account of the potential gains, which were small relative to Calouste's existing, 'not inconsiderable fortune', but rather for 'your principles (e.g. always be careful never to take anything for granted and always to look out for the snags and loopholes)'.[42] Against the advice of his son as well as Whishaw, Calouste Gulbenkian decided to fight. He had decided which side he would take in IPC's 'second "World War"'. Battle over Iraq and Saudi Arabia commenced.

Unsurprisingly, therefore, the thirty-two-page memoir Gulbenkian dictated around this time smacked more of propaganda than autobiography. Copies were distributed to the Foreign Office, State Department, Quai d'Orsay and other influential parties.[43] Not only were the 'Memoirs' carefully read at the time, they were preserved and would later serve as source material for historians of the oil industry. Gulbenkian's version entered the history books.[44]

In these 'Memoirs' Gulbenkian shared the three important lessons experience had taught him. The first was that his policy 'to keep myself entirely free' from ties to this or that company was bound to elicit jealousy. The second was that there were no limits to 'what the oil groups can do through the ropes they control to influence Government circles', even if such string-pulling 'ultimately ... work[ed] against their very interests'.

For Gulbenkian the Anglo-American Petroleum Agreement of 1944 was an insider's cartel masquerading as an inter-governmental trade treaty,

> a grandiose scheme to serve as a sounding board for internationally ambitious men [with] no real teeth to force the various companies to comply with its idealistic views of cooperation ... the result will be conferences, publicity and grand dinners for the directors of large corporations and state officials while the real oil operators continue their extravagant and piratical practices as in the past ... only firm regulations by government, forced on the companies, could bring any semblance of order and cooperation.[45]

The final lesson followed naturally. It preached scepticism whenever oil companies expressed any desire to serve the greater good. The famous open door which the Americans had made such a fuss about in the aftermath of the First World War, Gulbenkian noted, had been 'hermetically sealed' once US companies entered TPC. It had all been 'eyewash'. Now the Americans were at it again, with their idealistic visions of co-prosperity spheres and the calibrated development of the world's natural resources, all in support of democracy.

> To a philosopher – particularly one who is interested in oil matters – what an amount of reflection would there be for him in the fact that to-day the same oil groups, forgetting all their former traditions, are offering themselves to carry out the spirit of the Atlantic Charter,

of the bold declarations of the Washington Oil Conferences, and to become the apostles of World welfare and interests in oil economics. It may be a miracle, but my personal opinion, as a Scotsman would say is 'I hae me doots about it.'[46]

SEVENTEEN

THE DOGS BARK, 1945–8

In late 1944 Gulbenkian's only grandchild, Mikhael Essayan, began his final year at Harrow. After years of enforced separation, his mother was finally able to cross the Channel and see her son. Other boys' parents were pulling strings to secure commissions for their sons in fashionable guards regiments. Seventeen-year-old 'Oiley' (as Mikhael was known to his peers) was eager to join them, but unsure whether his grandfather would allow him to serve, in any uniform.[1] Although he had been born in London and largely educated in England, it was evident that 'Oiley''s family was different from those of his friends. It was Armenian. But what did that mean in 1944? For Mikhael himself the question of military service was tied up with the broader question of his future career. For his parents, Rita and Kevork, for his uncle, Nubar, and for his grandparents, however, it was merely the latest manifestation of an ever-present family dilemma surrounding identity and loyalty. Rita called it 'the pasdeurma question'.

'Tell me what you eat,' wrote the famous nineteenth-century culinary writer Brillat-Savarin, 'and I will tell you what you are.'[2] Pasdeurma is a form of dried beef, a speciality of the region around Kayseri in central Anatolia, where the Gulbenkians' ancestors settled around 1700. As anyone who has eaten it can attest, pasdeurma's effects on one's breath and digestion make it a pungent messenger of identity. As a metaphor it suggests a visceral identity resistant to assimilation, rendering it impossible for Armenians to pass as anything but exotic 'orientals'.

Armenian names could be changed – 'Badrig' could become 'Patrick', 'Mikhael' can and did become 'Micky'. When it had been suggested that Mikhael might have extracurricular tuition in Armenian while at Harrow, his family had decided against it. A former Harrovian himself, Nubar recognised his nephew's desire not to 'be made to appear "a freak" by unusual activities on the part of those responsible for his upbringing'. When it came to religious observance the family concluded that 'a good Protestant is better than an ignorant [Armenian] Orthodox'.[3] After all, none of the family attended an Armenian church regularly, not even St Sarkis, the church Calouste had built in Kensington.[4]

Rita felt that Calouste and Nevarte had used a token Armenianness to avoid the responsibilities which came with allegiance to a nation. In a long letter written to her parents in December 1944, she sought 'to clear up once and for all this "pasdeurma question" that pops up every 25 years with each war'. 'If you take the view that in life one must avoid all unpleasant responsibilities at all cost then any argument is pointless,' she noted, but if one wanted to claim that the Gulbenkians were Armenians, then one needed to shoulder the responsibilities which came with that identity. Had her father ever done so? What if, back in 1919, Nubar had expressed a wish to travel to Zangezur and fight for the Republic of Armenia under the great General Andranik? Would Calouste have let him go? 'If you are honest you will admit that you would have found it silly and over the top.'

Rita was determined that Calouste and Nevarte would not repeat with Mikhael the mistakes they had made in her own upbringing,

> which can all be summed up quite simply by saying that ever since I was a child I was never allowed to do what the others did. We were a law unto ourselves, without any basis of comparison and I remember how unhappy I was to be stigmatised by my chums because I didn't do any war-work. Daddy is a Genius, a Special Number, he can permit himself to do everything in his own way, he has that right, but Mikhael and I want to do as those around us do, as it happens the English are an admirable race which one cannot help but admire. Naturally, with our looks it would be silly to try to pass ourselves off as real English people. I will never call myself anything other than an Armenian. But, being in complete ignorance of the Armenian religion I feel a need to give my loyalty to the country where I was raised, and *a priori* Mikhael must feel this even more.

While Calouste may have felt he had had little at stake in earlier wars, the current war was different, Rita insisted:

> The outcome of this war is vital, not only for mankind but also for our personal and material interests. I say 'our' when I mean 'your:' it's about your return, your house, your belongings, your material and moral comfort. I don't see why other mummies and daddies' little Mikhaels, just as precious to them as Mikhael is to us, should sacrifice themselves, for you and for him.

Friends and other relations of Armenian extraction had, Rita noted, enlisted in the Royal Air Force, the French Army – even the Australian Army.[5] Just a few years older than Mikhael, Calouste's nephew Robert (son of Vahan) had joined the French Army and won the Croix de guerre (with *étoile*).

In 1945 Mikhael entered the Royal Artillery, where he served for three years, including a year in Palestine. Rita's letter may have helped to overcome Calouste's unwillingness to see his grandson in uniform. Traces remain elsewhere in the archive, however, that suggest Calouste was already in two minds on the question. He had extracts from Robert's citation for bravery typed on small slips of paper, which he kept in his pocketbook along with other slips giving quotations that had captured his fancy. Under the Ottoman *ancien régime* military service had been something the wealthy bought themselves out of, and Calouste's attitude continued to reflect that mind-set. But that did not prevent him from admiring the bravery of family members who chose to fight. Indeed, Robert's citation led Calouste to offer him a job working in his Paris office.[6]

The View from Baghdad

Although the British had quickly intervened to quash Rashid Ali's coup in 1941, with the restoration of peace in 1945 they gently nudged the Iraqi prime minister, Nuri al-Said, to liberalise, granting greater press freedom and fostering a form of multi-party democracy. It was hoped that such parties might encourage a secular polity, rather than one operating along familiar racial or sectarian lines. The 'Old Gang' around Nuri marginalised the Kurds in the north (where, of course, most of the oil was), as well as the majority Shiite community. The only real opposition ideology present in Iraqi politics was communism. The nationalism of Rashid Ali and others had done little to create a true national feeling. 'In the Near East, there is no patriotism, no spirit of democracy,' Calouste wrote in 1947; 'these are empty words for people who are dominated by a fanatic hatred of the Christians, and are influenced by their selfish interests, intrigues and envy.'[7]

One of the few Iraqi political parties to have a mass following was the leftist Hizb al-Watani al-Dimuqrati (National Democratic Party). Its vice-president was the Mosul-born, LSE-educated Mohammad Al Hadid, whose daughter Zaha Hadid would become an internationally recognised architect. In August 1946 Al Hadid commented that 'the history of petrol concessions in Iraq reminds one of those films in which one sees how "the white man" sallies forth into the remote corners of the world and trades toys with ignorant tribes for considerable resources'.[8] This kind of rhetoric had been heard in other oil-producing countries for several decades: a gambit employed by outsiders who wished to join the ranks of insiders enriching themselves at their country's expense. Apart from Russia (arguably a special case), the only oil-producing state to nationalise its oil industry and set up a 'national champion' had been Mexico in 1938.

As urban populations grew, trade unions formed and mass political parties emerged in oil-producing countries, rhetoric like Al Hadid's took on greater significance. 'The people' could no longer be dismissed as a fictional entity, nor could their governments be treated as if they were colonies 'to which you simply dictated orders'.[9] Gulbenkian recognised this in a way other oilmen never did.

The Iraqis should, Gulbenkian believed, be encouraged to become informed stakeholders. With a seat on the board, access to minutes and further measures to let daylight through the proconsular façade, leaders like Al Hadid might appreciate that, far from having got oil for 'toys', IPC's investors had been obliged to invest vast sums inside Iraq before seeing a single drop of oil. The more Iraqi elites understood the oil industry the more they would appreciate the importance of long-term thinking. 'They will not resort to extreme steps such as confiscation, nationalization,' Gulbenkian contended, 'when they are witnessing a gradual development.'[10]

Gulbenkian thus welcomed the demands for an Iraqi shareholding in IPC made by successive Iraqi Ministers of Economics between 1946 and 1948. The Iraqis initially suggested that IPC might become a public company, with the partners agreeing to sell 10 per cent of the company's shares to outsiders (under the company's articles of association any IPC shareholder wishing to sell had first to offer their shares to the other holders). That 20 per cent 'native participation' promised under Article 8 of the 1920 San Remo Agreement would finally become reality. The IPC partners were hardly likely to agree to a step which would oblige them to run the company as an independent, profit-maximising concern, however, rather than as a means of getting cheap oil and avoiding British tax.

Unfazed, Gulbenkian suggested that the Iraqis could be allowed to buy shares in an Iraqi holding company that would itself participate in IPC, in return for a lower royalty. IPC's managing director, John Skliros, supported the plan and welcomed other measures intended to break years of trying to keep the Iraqi government in the dark. It was high time IPC's partners 'understand that the days are past when such things were possible', Skliros noted. It was better to act now rather than end up negotiating in a crisis situation.

Though Gulbenkian won round René de Montaigu, the others involved refused to take these proposals seriously.[11] In the short term they were let off the hook by the Red Scare. For Middle East leaders the fear of Soviet invasion or infiltration was so strong, it trumped complaints about oil royalties and even western support for Israel, which declared independence in May 1948. Persuaded (like many others) that 'world war three' was around the corner, Nuri al-Said backed down. Iraq needed its allies more than it needed IPC shares.[12] Gulbenkian found solace in his 'philosopher' pose, bemoaning to anyone who would listen his partners' tin ear for 'psychology'.[13]

The Big Inch and the Big Stick

Back in 1939 the IPC partners had agreed to double the capacity of the IPC pipeline to the Mediterranean, but failed to sign the agreements before the onset of war. In view of Saudi Arabia and Tapline, the Americans within IPC did not view this project as terribly urgent in 1945. Gulbenkian managed to politely decline any interest when the Americans proposed to construct a new line on the cheap using army surplus. At five inches diameter, this was an almost insulting offer.[14] The old line completed in 1934 was sixteen inches. Gulbenkian and CFP wanted a firehose, in the shape of a thirty-inch line, known in the industry as 'The Big Inch'. They had been offered a used cocktail straw.

With the European steel industry either in ruins or focused on domestic reconstruction, it was evident that, whatever its diameter, any new pipeline would have to come from the United States. To export American steel one needed a government permit. American domestic oil producers resisted any attempt by Washington to 'conserve' their oil and pump foreign oil instead. Their congressional representatives thus challenged export permits linked to the construction of foreign oil installations. Meanwhile the US government used export permits to influence the development of Middle East oil. As Ickes's adviser Max Thornburg noted, controls over steel exports gave them the power 'to paralyze oil developments in all countries which look to us for such supplies'.[15] In August 1945 the Americans refused IPC a permit for steel needed to add a second sixteen-inch line, citing the ongoing war in Japan.[16]

As if Tapline was not enough of a rival, in December 1946 Jersey Standard and Anglo-Iranian signed a twenty-year sales contract, to include a jointly financed pipeline from Iran to the Mediterranean planned for completion in 1951. IPC's proposed new line from Kirkuk to Banias (on the Syrian coast) threatened to be squeezed between two rival pipelines, and pushed to the back of the queue for any American pipe.[17] For Gulbenkian, this must have stung. Back in September, when the American consortium in IPC (Near East Development) informed their partners that they considered the Red Line Agreement to have been abrogated by something called 'supravening illegality', it had been something of a comfort to have Anglo-Iranian declare that it considered the agreement still in force.

Now Jersey had peeled Anglo-Iranian away, and Anglo-Iranian also declared the Red Line Agreement dead. To spare its blushes, Anglo-Iranian had secured a legal opinion concurring that the agreement had been 'ipso facto abrogated and avoided' when Gulbenkian had been declared an enemy. Gulbenkian's lawyers by contrast found 'strong evidence of a new agreement entered into between the parties on the terms of the old agreement' in the fact that Anglo-Iranian had observed the agreement's terms once the sequester was lifted.[18] The remaining major IPC partner, Royal Dutch-Shell, had held back from getting too involved in the dispute, but finally joined the others in declaring the Red Line Agreement a dead letter on New Year's Eve 1946. It, too, had been coopted by the Americans, through a long-term sales contract with Gulf.[19]

Throughout 1945 and 1946 Gulbenkian and his IPC partners had batted back and forth proposals for a revised working agreement as well as a new pipeline. Although the American partners came out in support of the Big Inch in September 1946, such was the climate of uncertainty and suspicion that Gulbenkian was careful not to appear overly enthusiastic. He recognised that such a thirty-inch line would take longer to string than one that was sixteen or twenty-four inches, owing to supply issues, and did not trust the Americans to stay the course. Aiming high, he demanded a Big Inch line in addition to a narrower one.[20] CFP and Royal Dutch-Shell wanted to build in 'Flexibility Clauses' that would allow them to pay their partners to 'overlift' – that is, to pump more than their 23.75 per cent share of IPC's production.

The Americans insisted that, whatever they had signed up to in 1928, they could not sign an agreement that included clauses (such as the self-denial clause) which might expose them to antitrust prosecution under the Sherman Act. Just because this or that party had a legal opinion denouncing the Red Line Agreement did not, however, prevent the same parties from continuing to negotiate a revised agreement 'without prejudice'. To declare the 1928 agreement void was not, in other words, a declaration that the 1928 agreement was void. Instead it was a means of indicating that the proposed new IPC working agreement presently on the table had yet to take a satisfactory form. As the Jersey–Anglo-Iranian sales deal indicates, all parties to these negotiations were playing on more than one table.

Then there was the question of whether Ibn Saud would allow non-Americans to enter Aramco, when this had been forbidden under a secret rider to the original concession of 1933. Ibn Saud told Loy Henderson of the State Department in January 1947 of his concern at 'the possibility that the Red Line Agreement may still be in force, or if not actually in force will still be honored in some way'.[21] This ban seems to have been somewhat flexible, however, as four days later the Saudi Foreign Minister told Ambassador Baruch that the way the American companies in IPC were treating the French was 'hardly fair'.[22]

The Saudi minister was accompanying Ibn Saud's son on a mission to President Truman when bad weather forced their plane to divert from Paris to Lisbon. Gulbenkian being Gulbenkian, he was the first to hear of the surprise visit, and immediately rushed to the city's new Portela Airport, where he was photographed with the royal party shortly after it touched down. He also informed Baruch (who was unaware of the visit), securing gratitude for saving what might have been an embarrassing incident. The Foreign Minister's comment to Baruch suggests that Gulbenkian also used his advance knowledge to bend the ear of the Saudis. Considering he had no diplomatic or personal ties to Saudi Arabia, it had been a stretch, but the press and diplomatic coverage doubtless served to scotch any rumours that Gulbenkian was a spent force.[23]

Even had Gulbenkian been allowed into Aramco on the coat-tails of Jersey–Socony, there is the question of whether he could have afforded the price of admission.[24] Aramco shares came with matching obligations to fund Tapline (built 1947–50). There was no question of the French being able to afford it, being effectively bankrupt: in 1947 half of French crude imports were paid for using US Interim and Marshall Aid dollars.[25] Gulbenkian's 5 per cent of the Jersey–Socony's 40 per cent Aramco holding represented a $22.5 million ($221 million/£170 million) commitment. The only way he could have stumped up this cash, as well as the estimated £500,000 (£16.4 million) needed to cover his share of the new Iraqi pipeline, was if he had liquidated a significant chunk of his investment portfolio.[26] Yet Calouste viewed the latter as a reserve purely intended to guarantee his family's quality of life.

Another option was to sell his 5 per cent. Nubar repeatedly urged his father to sell his IPC stake, which Jersey valued at between $60 and 70 million ($640–740 million/£490–570 million) in 1947.[27] Why on earth would Calouste want to touch 'our investments for our *train de vie* [that is, living expenses] for the sake of the I.P.C. gamble', doubling down in the Middle East when the future seemed so uncertain?

> To what extent are we in such a violent hurry to sink £450,000–500,000 more into this venture in order to draw profits therefrom three years hence? Will profits at that time still be £1 a ton? To what extent will inroads be made somewhere on such profits at that time? Will there be an unrestricted scramble for markets and slashing of prices and profits? Or will there be Cartelisation and international oil agreements, and if so will these international agreements maintain profits and will they allow unrestricted production from Iraq?[28]

Calouste never seems to have viewed selling his famous 5 per cent as a serious prospect. Or perhaps he was never offered the right amount. What is certain is that the 'price' only rose the harder he pushed to get into Saudi Arabia.

For both Gulbenkian and CFP, therefore, demanding their right to enter Aramco was not really about Saudi oil, but rather about securing some other form of compensation for Arabian oil which neither could, in fact, have hoped to secure had they been treated 'fairly'. Faced with Anglo-Iranian's betrayal of the 1928 agreement, in January 1947 the French Foreign Ministry made a démarche through their ambassador in Washington, Henri Bonnet, culminating in a formal note dated 13 January. Bonnet protested to Dean Acheson that the State Department had been party to the Red Line Agreement and should therefore intervene to prevent French interests from being harmed by American oil companies. Bonnet also claimed that, in striking long-term sales contracts with Anglo-Iranian, Jersey and Socony had bought off the British government as well. Privately Bonnet and the French Foreign Ministry conceded that this was bluster intended to salvage something from 'a position which has been irrevocably lost'. As Harold Sheets of Socony put it, it was 'essentially an effort to extort some kind of pay-off under threat of reprisals'.[29]

As he had in the 'first "World War"', in the second Gulbenkian used the threat of legal action to intimidate, and as before he coordinated these threats with CFP and the French government. By exposing the behaviour of Jersey Standard and Socony in the British courts he ran the risk, admittedly, of losing his court battle. But though defeat would carry costs, the costs for the winners were potentially greater than those borne by the losers. Robert Cayrol of CFP warned the Americans that the French public would be 'very angry' to discover 'how French interests had been hurt, how France was considered an enemy'.[30] Jersey and Socony were hardly worried about hurt feelings; threats to restrict their access to French markets were more effective.[31]

Above all, Gulbenkian realised, it was 'the trouble which is being raised in the Senate' that would cause them to 'think twice before making up their mind to face the Court again'.[32] In addition to blocking permits for IPC and other Middle East pipelines, the American domestic producers were also using their influence to hound their American multinational rivals on anti-trust grounds. When reports of Jersey and Socony joining Socal and Texaco in Aramco appeared, the domestic producers' Senate representatives cried foul. In 1949 a Federal Trade Commission investigation of the oil industry was launched, striking terror into the American majors.[33]

As it turned out, the FTC's report did not appear (in abridged form) until 1952. Antitrust was trumped by Truman's recognition of the oil cartel's importance in the Cold War effort. Gulbenkian nonetheless benefited from American concern that oil secrets might leak out and harm the status quo. A 1949 State Department memo indicates that it believed Gulbenkian's claim that he had leaked information to Tehran revealing Anglo-Iranian's manipulation of the numbers used to calculate the royalty paid to the Iranian state. Gulbenkian had supposedly done so 'in anger over [Anglo-Iranian] opposition to his suit against Standard of Jers[e]y and Socony for breaking the Red Line Agreement'.[34]

Though evidence to support this claim has yet to be found, in a sense it was beside the point. With Gulbenkian's reputation, recently burnished by his 'Memoirs' (cited in the same State Department memo) and photographs of him hobnobbing with Saudi princelings on the tarmac at Lisbon, was Jersey, Socony or Anglo-Iranian prepared to run the risk of finding out if such claims were true? As Gulbenkian might have put it, 'I hae me doots about it.'

'Grand Old Man' or 'Shrewd Trader'?

Thanks to Gulbenkian and CFP, the second, more formal phase of negotiations for a new working agreement (1947–8) took place under a hail of writs and counter-claims. Everyone involved in IPC was now being sued by at least two of their partners. Gulbenkian's Pandi issued writs on 7 January 1947. CFP had issued its writs a week before. Jersey–Socony followed in April and May. Much to the irritation of the judges, however, all parties sought to spin out proceedings as much as possible. Sir Cyril Radcliffe, Gulbenkian's main legal adviser, recognised litigation's value 'as a menace', but it was important 'not to bring it to a hearing before we must, since, as you know, I expect to lose rather than to win'.[35] A date for the hearings was finally set in July 1948, for 1 November 1948. On 1 November the judge agreed to a three-day adjournment. The 1948 Working Agreement was signed in the early hours of trial day, 4 November 1948.

In the twenty-odd years since the original 1924–8 negotiations the old guard had passed: Henri Deterding and John Cadman were dead, Walter Teagle and Ernest Mercier had retired. One of the few remaining veterans of the 'first "World War"' was Anglo-Iranian's Louis Lefroy, who briefed

the next generation. After rehearsing his account of the 1924–8 negotiations ('a story I have told you many times'), Lefroy concluded 'that G. will
be as tough in 1946 as 1924/8 over "rights" as a minority shareholder unless
he is ageing'.[36] The fact that his partners repeated the mistake of assuming that 'the grand old man' could be left until last suggests that many
of them did indeed see Gulbenkian as an ageing throwback, as 'history'.
Gulbenkian, however, recognised that 'history' could be a weapon. 'We
must exhume all the past history,' he instructed Nubar, 'which, I am sure,
contains very valuable stuff.'[37]

Whishaw and Gulbenkian's other representatives in London played
little part in thrashing out the new set of 'Heads of Agreement' finalised
in late May 1947. Much of the detail (on 'Flexibility Clauses') did not seem
likely to be of any importance to Pandi. As well as five weeks of drafting committee meetings, this involved considerable bilateral negotiation
between CFP and Near East Development. CFP agreed to drop its suit as
well as its prior claim for Vichy-era losses in return for the right to 'overlift'
and a promise that IPC would get its Big Inch built by 1952. To tide it over
while it waited, CFP would be allowed to move into a Venezuelan concession controlled by Pantepec.[38]

This went against Gulbenkian's strategy, which was to focus on securing a royalty on the Saudi oil lifted by Jersey–Socony – Gulbenkian's price
for allowing them to enter Aramco. Gulbenkian's 5 per cent of Jersey–
Socony's 40 per cent of Aramco worked out at two cents per barrel of
Saudi crude. For Gulbenkian everything else, including offers of bigger
pipelines or access to concessions outside the red line, was at best a distraction and at worse represented deliberate stalling on the part of the
Americans. The deteriorating political situation in Palestine also made
Gulbenkian less keen than CFP to push for rapid construction of a new
pipeline, whatever its diameter.

Gulbenkian's refusal to sign the 'Heads of Agreement' caused a crisis
in the summer of 1947. CFP faced the 'most serious decisions' about
whether to abandon their former ally and proceed to implement the new
agreement without Pandi. The latter seemed possible, at least in the short
term, as the new working agreement did not refer to the 1928 Red Line
Agreement at all. If Gulbenkian won his case and the Red Line Agreement
was declared valid, then the Red Line and the new agreement could run
side by side.[39] All agreed to send Jersey's vice-president, Orville Harden, to
Lisbon to negotiate directly with Gulbenkian. In the run-up to Harden's

visit, Gulbenkian put in long nights at the Aviz, regularly poring over documents until 1 a.m. Far from sounding exhausted, his letters to Nubar suggest that he relished the coming duel. 'We shall have momentous times,' Calouste wrote, 'we must give the problem our concentrated attention from all corners, and be ready in every respect.'[40]

Harden spent the first week of September 1947 closeted with Gulbenkian at the Aviz, the former assisted by David Shepard (another Jersey man), the latter by Nubar and Whishaw. On the 8th negotiations stopped without a settlement having been reached. For Harden the demand for two cents a barrel was ludicrous: assuming production at half a million barrels per day, this would work out at $30 million a year. Gulbenkian said that he would take his chances in the court. Harden reported to his IPC partners that 'the conversations had taken place in the most friendly atmosphere and that [even] if they had got nowhere the door was still open but unfortunately there did not seem to be any path leading to it'.[41] The US ambassador also reported an 'atmosphere of great cordiality'. Given the lack of progress, he presumed that the dispute 'will follow legal course and end up in [the] House of Lords'. Harden did not share this view. Gulbenkian had not said his final word, Harden told Baruch, being a 'shrewd and patient trader'.[42]

CFP was now strongly urging the others to sign the 'Heads of Agreement' and proceed, leaving room for Pandi to join if Gulbenkian subsequently changed his mind.[43] In the absence of any consensus, however, CFP's Cayrol began negotiating a compromise with Nubar in London, under which Pandi would also benefit from the 'Flexibility Clauses'. Reusing a gambit from his father's playbook, Nubar reassured Calouste that he was handling his talks with Cayrol as

> a strictly private arrangement Cayrol-Nubar which does not commit Mr C.S.G. in any way, or the other Groups. That being the case, it is perhaps as well that I should take full responsibility so that you in due course will be able to turn the proposal down or squeeze a little more from it when (a) the Americans and (b) the other Groups, are definitely committed and commission Cayrol to come out to Lisbon to try and convince you to accept it. If I refer to you in my negotiations then you will be committed and it will be more difficult for you to stand firm.[44]

Cayrol duly went out to Lisbon in March 1948 for his own round of direct talks, which focused on arrangements to protect Gulbenkian from a devaluation of sterling as well as Gulbenkian's demand for 300,000 extra tons of oil per annum.

To his partners it seemed as if Gulbenkian was raising new objections every time compromise was reached on the old. CFP blamed Gulbenkian's delays for the failure to enter the (lucrative, as it turned out) Kuwaiti Neutral Zone concession, which Royal Dutch-Shell had offered to share with them if they only backed down.[45] Gulbenkian felt that more credit was due to him for having renounced a royalty on Aramco production. He could certainly not be blamed for the delays caused by currency restrictions. For the British, Iraq was an important source of 'sterling oil', invaluable in addressing the 'dollar drain'; for the French, it was the only source of 'franc oil'.[46]

By September 1948 it was becoming difficult to keep the various court cases in suspense. After further consultation, it was agreed that Cayrol should return to Lisbon and offer Gulbenkian an extra 225,000 tons a year. Twelve days of negotiations on increasingly technical matters ensued. Finally agreement was reached. Gulbenkian got his 'Special Allocation' of 250,000 extra tons a year, and received reassurances that a thirty- to thirty-two-inch Kirkuk–Banias pipeline would be completed in 1952.[47] The self-denying clause was dropped. Gulbenkian's holding company Pandi retained its 5 per cent in IPC and all IPC's subsidiaries. The latter covered most of the former red-line area and ranged from companies with working concessions to ones that had yet to apply for a concession, but did so later: Basrah Petroleum, Mosul Petroleum, Petroleum Developments (Syria), Petroleum Developments (Lebanon) and similarly named companies for Cyprus, Palestine, Transjordan, Hadramaut (today's Yemen and Oman) and the Trucial Coast (Abu Dhabi, Dubai, Sharjah and other emirates). The agreements were signed in London between 1.30 and 2 a.m. on 4 November, hours before the 10.30 a.m. deadline at which hearings would have begun.

Cayrol wrote to Anglo-Iranian chairman William Fraser that he took two lessons from the three-year slog. The first was that it had been 'most unfortunate' to exclude Pandi from the early negotiations. The second was that 'Mr Calouste Gulbenkian in spite of his defects and keen bargaining power can give us wise advice and considerable help in all negotiations that we will have to carry on with the several Governments in the Middle

East.' Cayrol pointedly referred to Gulbenkian's 'considerable influence with the Government of Iran'.[48] As with the Americans, so the French may have overrated Gulbenkian's pull in Tehran.

Around the same time Gulbenkian had also managed to draw a line under the even more interminable dispute with Royal Dutch-Shell over Venezuelan Oil Concessions, which had been quietly festering since the dramatic proxy fight of 1926. December 1948 found Gulbenkian feeling understandably pleased with himself. As he noted to his old friend Herman Baruch (now retired):

> My oil associates are now very happy, and I think they are all praising me. I told them that the American Groups can go around in the Saudi Arabia Desert without being haunted by Gulbenkian, and the Shell Group will be going about the Pampas of Venezuela, without the spectre of your friend, checkmating them!![49]

Mr Walker of Washington

Sir Kenneth Clark's decision to resign as director of the National Gallery at the end of the war led Gulbenkian to send a telegram accusing him of 'upsetting my plans which were so much initiated and furthered by your sympathetic collaboration both personally and as Director National Gallery'.[50] Credit for 'upsetting' Gulbenkian's plans belongs, in fact, not to Clark but to his successor, Philip Hendy, and to the opportunism of John Walker, chief curator of the National Gallery in Washington. Regular visits to Lisbon by Clark and lobbying by various members of the British Establishment struggled to regain Gulbenkian's confidence. By 1949 it was not yet clear that Gulbenkian had definitively settled on Washington as the final destination of his art and fortune, but it was clear that London had missed the bus. 'After playing for it desperately,' Walker noted, Clark had lost.[51]

A charmless man of left-leaning views, Hendy was incapable of pandering to Gulbenkian or other would-be benefactors. Neither was Hendy particularly taken with Gulbenkian's paintings, which had returned to a heavily bomb-damaged Trafalgar Square at the war's end. Reconstruction of the destroyed galleries took years, and to that extent it was not Hendy's fault if there was not room to hang all Gulbenkian's loans. Given the vast endowment on offer, however, Hendy was remarkably loath to provide Gulbenkian with the required updates on the 'health' of his beloved 'children', let alone explain his reasons for not hanging particular works from the Gulbenkian collection. By May 1946, therefore, Gulbenkian was writing to Clark that he would have to look elsewhere for a home, as 'my dear "children" should in no way remain in [*sic*] sufferance'.[52]

Gulbenkian's Egyptian collection had been on loan to the British Museum since 1936, but had not been unpacked since being evacuated in 1939.[53] The museum had no space to show it, facing similar pressures to the National Gallery: heavy bomb damage and a Ministry of Works insistent 'that little or no labour would be available for Museums until demands for housing had been met'. This would, incidentally, also prevent any Gulbenkian annexe from being built at Trafalgar Square for at least a decade.[54] During a transatlantic crossing on the *Queen Elizabeth* Walker met the British Museum's director, Sir John Forsdyke, and asked about Gulbenkian's loan. Forsdyke replied that, if Walker were interested, the British Museum would be happy for the Gulbenkian collection to travel to the US. With the assistance of the US Embassy in Portugal, Walker duly paid court, travelling to Lisbon in July 1947 and organising a viewing at the embassy of a promotional colour film. Walker and Gulbenkian had several long conversations which lasted until the early hours.[55]

Gulbenkian knew that when business associates came to praise, they came to bury as well. *Chan-chan* was cheap, flattery especially so. With regard to his collections, however, Gulbenkian was a different man. Walker recognised this and, over his six-year courtship of Gulbenkian, he laid it on thick: it would be hard to imagine Clark penning *billets doux* confiding that 'I think of you constantly.' 'Museum directors are predators by nature,' Walker later recalled; 'no prey seemed as tempting as the Gulbenkian Collection, no prize as desirable as some future Gulbenkian Foundation.'[56] Whether by accident or design, Walker used Forsdyke's off-the-cuff remark to create an impression in Gulbenkian's mind that Forsdyke was another Hendy, reluctantly providing Gulbenkian's 'children' with room and board.

Gulbenkian agreed to lend his Egyptian collection to Washington, along with eleven paintings from 51 Avenue d'Iéna. Walker roped the US ambassador, Jefferson Caffery, into a complex 'insurance policy' he and Gulbenkian had cooked up to pre-empt any attempt by France to prevent the paintings from leaving French soil. The paintings would be driven from Avenue d'Iéna in vans under US Embassy seal, without the need for the usual export permits. If challenged, the French authorities were to be told that the paintings were the property of the National Gallery in Washington, and Gulbenkian would call on the State Department to defend gallery property 'which he will then deliver to us to become a part of our collection without restrictions'.[57]

Fortunately for a nervous Caffery, the plan was dropped after the British Museum successfully lobbied Gulbenkian to reconsider the withdrawal of his Egyptian collection. The museum's defence was led by Kenneth Clark's friend David Lindsay (28th Earl of Crawford), who happened to be a trustee of both the British Museum and the National Gallery. Lindsay encouraged fellow trustees to write fulsome letters of regret, in which they distanced themselves from Forsdyke and sought to assuage Gulbenkian's concerns about the Labour government's taxation policies. Lindsay reported that the Victoria and Albert Museum's director, Sir Leigh Ashton, would be very interested in Gulbenkian's collection: an annexe could be built opposite the main entrance. Ashton, too, paid court at the Aviz.[58]

The Archbishop of Canterbury was probably not the most qualified adviser on tax, admittedly, but as chairman of the trustees of the British Museum it fell to him to write to Gulbenkian praising his generosity and assuring him that, even if a capital levy were to be introduced, it would not apply to chattels such as works of art.[59] Gulbenkian relented. Whether or not he found it embarrassing having to turn Walker down, the pair continued to develop plans to bring Gulbenkian's dispersed collections and fortune together in Washington. As Gulbenkian's new confidant at the US Embassy in Lisbon, Ted Xanthaky, noted, 'in his opinion the British Museum was not being very "chic" about the whole matter but in view of the important people involved he did not feel that he could over-ride their request at this juncture and suggested that the matter be allowed to simmer down'.[60] It did not simmer down for long. Within months Walker's director and trustees were beginning to wonder: was their chief curator about to land the gallery's biggest benefaction, firmly establishing Walker's claim to the top job, or were they all being played by Gulbenkian, who simply wanted to find a temporary safe haven for his 'children'? Walker had even proposed sending a US Navy warship to carry Gulbenkian's paintings across the Atlantic.[61] Was Walker a 'predator', as he liked to think, or prey?

EIGHTEEN

THE CARAVAN PASSES, 1949–55

In August 1949 Gulbenkian returned to Paris. He had intended to do so earlier, but had been prevented by his inability to secure a visa for his valet, a Russian. The curator of his collection, Marcelle Chanet, took care to ensure that his art treasures were ready to receive him. Gulbenkian's reunion with his 'children' at 51 Avenue d'Iéna was not a happy one, however:

> He did not evince the slightest satisfaction at seeing his wondrous possessions again ... he even asserted that some of them were not his! He seemed not to recognize the paintings which had resumed their wonted places. Instead he searched for *The Sleeping Village* by Corot: an imaginary work which he could nonetheless describe in great detail.

Suspicious as always, Gulbenkian seems to have come to the unsettling conclusion that cherished elements of his collection had been disposed of, only to be replaced with lesser works. Fortunately for Chanet, a *catalogue raisonné* listing all Corot's works had been published. There was no mention of *The Sleeping Village* in any of the five volumes. Despite this evidence, Gulbenkian continued to doubt its non-existence. Three years later he was still telling the staff at 51 Avenue d'Iéna that he expected to find the imaginary painting in place on his next trip to Paris.[1]

After seven years during which he had rarely left Lisbon, Gulbenkian was on the move again. Each year he escaped the heat of the Lisbon summer, spending July in Deauville overseeing improvements at Les Enclos, such as the 'chicken garden city' (as Rita described it) intended to house more exotic birds.[2] August was spent in Paris. Thanks to the de Havilland Comet, the world's first commercial jet airliner, it was now possible to make the journey from Lisbon to Paris in just two hours and thirty-five minutes – although Gulbenkian was concerned about the effects the Comet's novel pressurised cabin might have on his health.[3] After her years at Estoril, Nevarte was now living in Paris, where she once again found herself struggling to keep Rita and twenty-three domestic staff in line.

There was little love lost between mother and daughter. When events in Korea led many to make contingency plans for a third world war, Nevarte secured three stand-by tickets on Pan-American Airways. She informed her daughter that the extra seats were for her maid and doctor, not for Rita.[4] It was in Paris that Nevarte and Calouste celebrated their sixtieth wedding anniversary in June 1952, posing for a family photograph on the terrace. Two weeks later, to everyone's surprise, Nevarte was dead.

Nevarte's death does not seem to have upset Calouste terribly much. After the heady days of courtship the pair had enjoyed a decade of happiness together. Mutual jealousies and suspicions, however, had then brought the relationship to breaking point in 1914. Though the marriage held, thereafter the pair pursued separate lives, rarely passing a night under the same roof. In the few letters between them which survive Calouste comes across as preoccupied and cross, repeatedly asking his wife to keep her letters short. It is important to remember that this was a union of two Ottoman Armenian *amira* clans: neither side expected the husband to remain faithful, for example.

In the 1920s the Gulbenkians still kept up the fiction of a joint *ménage* in Paris, at their apartment on the Quai d'Orsay, perhaps because Calouste still felt the need of Nevarte's considerable talents as a hostess. From the move to 51 Avenue d'Iéna (1927) onwards, however, even this pretence was dropped: the house was a fortress rarely used for entertaining, a gilded cage in which Calouste sought to pen his family alongside his other 'children' (the art collection). The 1930s saw Nevarte pass some of the unhappiest moments of her life there, among her husband's treasures, left to deal with the crises surrounding Rita, Nubar and Mikhael almost single-handed – continually spied on by her husband's staff. The outbreak of the Second World War, therefore, must have felt like something of a liberation. As her brother recognised, Nevarte enjoyed the attention which came with being 'Mrs Five Per Cent', even if she now spent only a few weeks a year in the same hotel as 'Mr Five Per Cent'. Her final years were a happy round of luncheon and dinner parties.

Nevarte's unexpected death did not lead Gulbenkian to question his own life expectancy. He was fond of informing people that his grandfather had died at the age of 105, adding that he intended to live even longer.[5] His address book listed forty-four doctors based in Paris and Lisbon, including a Professor Fonseca, who became his chief physician.[6] Fonseca was much in demand as Gulbenkian passed through a series of increasingly serious health crises, which began in January 1951 and continued on an almost annual basis until February 1955, when a cerebral thrombosis struck, heralding a final decline. Alongside his heart trouble and lumbago, Gulbenkian suffered from neuritis in his legs, which at one point in 1953 became sufficiently gangrenous for Fonseca to conclude that his patient would not live a fortnight. Yet Gulbenkian survived. As a thanks offering he paid for two rams to be ritually slaughtered by his baptismal church in Istanbul, Surp Takavor, and the meat to be given to the poor of the parish.[7]

La Theis

Back in 1930 a twenty-five-year-old accountant named Isabelle Theis had joined the staff at 51 Avenue d'Iéna, where she worked alongside Madame Soulas. While Soulas remained in Paris in 1940, Theis (whose husband had since died) accompanied Gulbenkian to Vichy, and later to Lisbon. By 1942, even British Intelligence had worked out that she was Gulbenkian's 'girl friend'. In 1951 Nevarte and Nubar agreed to keep a 'watching brief' on Theis, concerned at her influence over Calouste.[8] Within a few days of his wife's death Calouste repeatedly informed Nubar that he had no intention of marrying Theis, and denied paternity of Theis's child. 'This assurance was quite spontaneous,' Nubar reported, 'as Mme. Theis's name had not even been mentioned.'[9]

Apart from this curious statement, Gulbenkian never commented on his relationship with Isabelle Theis. Theis was equally discreet. Had it not been for the survival of a letter written several years after Gulbenkian's death, we would know next to nothing about the nature of the relationship. In this letter Theis recorded at some length how

I loved, I served, in total devotion, sacrificing, freely and spontane-
ously, every aspect of my life ... What did I care?! Years and years of
incessant work, great responsibility, increasingly exciting, enormous
and varied – I devoted myself to him, as I dedicated myself to the well
being of the private life of a Great and kindly Friend and Master ...
I speak with the calm certainty of someone who lived His life, was
with Him constantly, because that's what he wished – rather, what
He demanded. I saw, heard, observed, discovered, always by His side,
discreet, reserved, proud and touched by the absolute trust he placed
in me. I swore, for my part, that I would never let him down.

Though remarkably revealing in one sense, Theis's letter does not indicate
whether she had hopes of marrying Gulbenkian. There were precedents
from the Gulbenkians' social circle, such as the Aga Khan, who had
married his social secretary (also French) in 1944. In the same letter Theis
recalled how, growing tired of 'the tedium of living in hotels, here, there
and everywhere', she had dreamed of having a house and garden 'all mine'.
'We made so many plans, so many ... for years we looked without ever
finding anything that we liked, until it was too late for Him to fulfil his
now old promise.'[10]

Nubar and Theis did not believe each other to have Gulbenkian's
best interests at heart. Although Nubar's relationship with his father had
steadily improved in the decade after their dramatic court case in 1939,
fear of being sidelined by him and denied a role in shaping his legacy led
Nubar to resume attempts to bully Gulbenkian.[11] In particular he used
Nevarte's death to manufacture a crisis which poisoned relations for the
rest of Gulbenkian's life. Ostensibly this crisis centred on Nevarte's testamentary wishes, recorded in a 1942 letter instructing her brother Yervant
to sell her jewels on her death and use the proceeds to establish an orphan-
age for Armenians. This was hardly a formal testament, however, merely
a one-sentence aside in a personal letter. Nubar nonetheless inflated the
document's significance even as he refused to show it to his father. In
claiming that this letter gave him the power to foil Gulbenkian's own testamentary plans, Nubar knowingly caused his father significant distress.[12]

If family disputes wearied Gulbenkian, oil ones revived him. The last
oil crisis of Gulbenkian's career was triggered by the nationalisation of
Anglo-Iranian's facilities by Iranian prime minister Mohammad Mosaddegh in May 1951. These facilities included the refinery on the Persian

Gulf at Abadan, then the world's largest. Calouste and Nubar were both stripped of their Iranian diplomatic appointments in June. There was talk of a British invasion; instead the refinery's non-Iranian staff were evacuated. This Iranian crisis took several years to resolve itself.

Mosaddegh's demand for a greater share of Anglo-Iranian's profits was triggered by Aramco's shock announcement in January 1950 that it had agreed to share profits 50:50 with the Saudi Arabian government. This was roughly equivalent to a royalty of thirty shillings per ton, when Iraq was receiving twelve shillings from IPC.[13] Spotting a Jersey Standard executive in a corridor at the Aviz, Gulbenkian pounced. The American companies behind Aramco, 'only mindful of their own interests, and without in any way consulting their associates, had thrown the news of their arrangement with Saudi Arabia like a bomb-shell,' he thundered.[14]

Gulbenkian was soon advising Tehran on how best to respond. He noted that Aramco would be able to offset increased payments to the Saudis against the tax they paid to the United States. Under this so-called 'Golden Gimmick' the US Treasury was paying, not Aramco. The Iranians should not nationalise Anglo-Iranian, Gulbenkian counselled, as they would find themselves unable to run Abadan. Gulbenkian's old friend Hassan Taqizadeh was now president of the Iranian Senate and he blamed the crisis on Anglo-Iranian's failure to 'make a good and appeasing "gest[e]" until it was too late'. Gulbenkian agreed that Anglo-Iranian had been foolish, but certain 'high personalities' (Mosaddegh, presumably) were also guilty of having 'allowed public opinion and passions to get beyond control'. Nationalisation and 'other high-sounding slogans will have fatal results'.[15]

Having failed to avert a crisis in Iran, Gulbenkian and his IPC partners were now faced with finding some kind of formula to appease the Iraqis' demand for their own 50:50 arrangement. In London the Iraqi prime minister, Nuri al-Said, used Nubar and Kevork as back-channels to send messages to IPC, just as Anglo-Iranian used Nubar to send messages to the Iranians.[16] Under the settlement reached in February 1952, IPC committed itself to a rapid increase in production and to pay the Iraqi government a sum equivalent to 50 per cent of profits – Iraq ended up with better terms than Iran, Kuwait or even Saudi Arabia itself.[17]

London

In 1945 Gulbenkian's kitchen cabinet of advisers consisted of Whishaw, Nubar, Kevork and Hacobian, in descending order of influence and out-spokenness. Two of these four attended important meetings, each as a check upon the other. Gulbenkian expected to hear everyone's account and analysis.[18] Josef Henggeler (who ran Gulbenkian's Liechtenstein holding companies) and Sir Cyril Radcliffe continued to function as honorary cabinet members on taxation and legal questions, while being accorded a greater degree of respect. Unlike the rest of his London cabinet, Gulbenkian addressed them as near-equals. Over the following decade, as Gulbenkian's health and concentration declined, this cabinet began to take a more active role in setting policy. In November 1951 Gulbenkian gave the London office full discretion to act in his name, a step interpreted as 'virtual abdication to a regency council'.[19]

When it came to hiring new staff Nubar was persuaded that the English had lost any appetite for hard work, another casualty of those worrying socialist tendencies he and his father saw all around them. This influenced the choice of understudy for Hacobian, who would clearly need to be replaced sooner or later. In July 1949, therefore, Nubar Ekserdjian joined the London office. Born in Istanbul in 1912, 'Bill' Ekserdjian's main qualification as far as the Gulbenkians were concerned was his Armenian origin, taken as evidence of both complete discretion and readiness to give his life in the clan's service.

Far from aspiring to become the new Hacobian, Ekserdjian's plan was to work for the Gulbenkians just long enough to save up some money before entering politics. Whenever the antics of the London office became too much, he found relief in imagining how the Gulbenkians would react when they discovered that, far from being an Armenian drone without a mind of his own, their new employee was a keen Labour supporter, who spent evenings after work distributing copies of the *Clarion* and lobbying for selection as a parliamentary candidate.[20]

As Ekserdjian observed, he proved a success precisely 'because every-one except the Gs regards me as British and talking their language while the Gs look upon me as Armenian and attach great importance to that'. His diary provides a day-by-day account of the London office and the workings of Gulbenkian's cabinet, viewed with a fresh pair of eyes and a somewhat self-conscious detachment. Ekserdjian's first impression of Whishaw was of 'a keen and shrewd looking man [who] has a large hand in running the place'. Kevork seemed nervous, prone to pace the office carpet when alone. Nubar was 'fascinating, fascinating like a toad or something crawly. He even has a certain charm, if that is the word; he seems to realise his own horribleness and to revel in it.' When Nubar secured a doctor's certificate in order to claim twenty-six shillings National Insurance sickness benefit, Ekserdjian was disgusted rather than impressed.

Ekserdjian saw Nubar's 'oriental' costume for the fancy dress it was, openly challenging Nubar over the Gulbenkians' claim to have a special rapport with the Iraqis and Iranians, as fellow 'orientals'. Ekserdjian had served in the British Army during the war, rising to the rank of brigadier. He was not willing to have the family pull strings to get him exempted from military service so that he could remain in their service if and when world war three broke out. He would not be joining the others on the Mexican ranch Nubar had lined up as a bolt-hole.[21] If the balloon went up he would stay in the United Kingdom and take his chances with everyone else. The Gulbenkians were surprised to find that 'we cannot make our pilaff on [that is, cannot rely on] keeping Ekserdjian during the next war'. They were also impressed. Unable to grasp the real reasons behind it, they concluded that Ekserdjian was playing tough in order to get a pay rise.[22]

The workings of the Gulbenkian court were anything but efficient, Ekserdjian noted. Colleagues were still addressed with pre-war formality, as 'Mister Nubar' and 'Mister Charles'. When National Gallery director Philip Hendy referred to 'your son Nubar' in a letter, Gulbenkian noted the familiarity (Hendy should have written 'your son, *Mister* Nubar'): 'This must be Labour style!'[23] Gulbenkian continued to subject the accounts of 51 Avenue d'Iéna and his London staff to close scrutiny, leading to long discussions over trivial sums. Gulbenkian wondered, for example, if he could afford a Westclox 'Big Ben' alarm clock from W. H. Smith that he had set his heart on. At times Gulbenkian's health or impatience led him to demand shorter memos, only for the London staff to struggle to express complex agreements in 'so-called "baby talk"'.[24]

David Drysdale had joined the Gulbenkians as an accountant in 1928. During the war he and his wife had been evacuated with the London office to Dorking. Now Drysdale gave Ekserdjian his own explanation of the tensions which made the office such a challenging environment in which to work. Drysdale blamed them all on Gulbenkian's possessiveness, on his attempts to use money to control his family. These attempts had signally failed, in Drysdale's eyes at least:

> But all he has done is to alienate them all and yet, in his own muddled way, CSG was trying to help them and therefore feels hurt and frustrated at not getting affection and gratitude from his family. They, on the other hand, are miserable and bullied and sore and frustrated too because they have sold their souls to CSG – willy-nilly – and have not even had payment, since CSG by living so long has made them wait longer than they ever bargained for.[25]

During visits to Paris each summer Ekserdjian could reach his own conclusions. He found Gulbenkian 'a remarkable old man with a natural charm as well as simple dignity'. He was less impressed by the 'mutual sniping and general unpleasantness of the G. children' over lunch at 51 Avenue d'Iéna. Ekserdjian was right: the Gulbenkians felt little need to hold back in his company (even on his very first visit to their home), as they considered him a fellow Armenian.[26]

Ekserdjian succeeded in improving the atmosphere in the London office by regularly talking Nubar back from his latest 'clever' wheeze in a fashion which prevented him from losing face in front of Whishaw and Kevork.[27] When it came to Gulbenkian's plans for his art collection and foundation, however, Ekserdjian was not among the inner circle. He certainly noted the Gulbenkians' strong sense of entitlement, that sense that (in Rita's words) 'laws are made for everyone but us, the exalted US'.[28] Nubar encouraged this sense of entitlement in his father by regularly identifying instances in which the British authorities had supposedly shown themselves ungrateful. In March 1950 the chairman of the National Gallery trustees, Sir Alan Barlow, thanked Gulbenkian for the loan of his paintings collection and expressed hopes of their 'speedy return' to Trafalgar Square after their exhibition on loan in Washington. This was interpreted as further evidence of the British 'trespassing on my rights', by presuming to dictate what Gulbenkian did with his own property.[29]

That October Nubar and Whishaw met with senior Treasury official Sir Wilfred Eady to rehearse their grievances, many of which dated back to the war. These included Gulbenkian's enemy status, difficulties over the sale of his Reichsbank shares, the Brigade of Guards' refusal to take his grandson, Mikhael, as well as the 'curt' tone in which the Chancellor of the

Exchequer, Sir Stafford Cripps, had written to him. As Nubar reported, he and Whishaw took some pains 'drawing attention to your world-wide position and the fact that the British position in the Middle East and Venezuela oil was really due to you'. Eady acknowledged 'a considerable number of slights', recalling that upon leaving office John Maynard Keynes had warned Treasury mandarins 'not to fall out with Mr CSG'. Unfortunately, 'it was very difficult in (Socialist) England after the war, to obtain facilities for a rich man'. 'What can we do to put this right?'

Although Nubar replied that ten years' better treatment would help, Whishaw was probably being more realistic when he told Eady that nothing could erase these slights 'so that they would never be referred to again'.[30] A knighthood was offered, which Gulbenkian modestly refused, as he had the Légion d'honneur thirty years before.[31] Just because Whishaw felt these slights unforgivable by Gulbenkian did not mean, however, that Whishaw himself considered them unforgivable. Quite the contrary. When Nubar read him a letter from Gulbenkian rehearsing his own services to the United Kingdom,

> the first reaction of Whishaw, but in a very nice way as always, was the usual one that you as a British subject had done nothing!!! for this country; you had not bought them a squadron of bombers during the war and not even one Spitfire. When Mr. Hacobian pointed out that you had given them over a million dollars when dollars were so valuable to this country's economies, Whishaw's reaction was that these dollars were brought over for your personal purpose and the fact that this country benefitted was merely secondary. When your pictures were mentioned, his reaction was that they had originally been sent here for safety and that the fact that tens of thousands if not hundreds of thousands of people were enjoying them, was also secondary. When we mentioned the courtesy which was being displayed to you by the American Authorities, he countered by saying that it was not an English habit to 'fawn' on people.

As for the paintings, while Gulbenkian might get 'kudos' for a limited period after 'you had given them irrevocably, the possibility of getting kudos and appreciation for what you might do in the future, was about exhausted'.[32]

Washington

In December 1948 Gulbenkian re-established contact with the poet Alexis Léger, whom he had first encountered in the 1920s. Léger was a shining example of that French tradition of combining the vocation of poet with the *métier* of diplomacy. When the Banque Industrielle de Chine scandal erupted in 1921 Léger decided to remain at the Quai d'Orsay rather than follow his patron, Philippe Berthelot, into the wilderness. He became *chef de cabinet* (chief of staff) to Foreign Minister Briand. At quiet moments Léger would walk down the street to snatch a few hours of 'free and confiding talk' with Gulbenkian at 27 Quai d'Orsay.[33]

Léger subsequently rose to become secretary-general of the Quai d'Orsay, only to become disenchanted with France's policy of appeasement towards Hitler. He left France in June 1940, vowing never to return. He settled in Washington, but refused to serve as Vichy's ambassador. A highly respected poet whose works were translated by T. S. Eliot and who would win the Nobel Prize in 1960, Saint-John Perse (Léger's nom de plume) lived off a stipend from the Bollingen Foundation. When his stipend ran out Gulbenkian sprang into the breach with a significantly higher pension, which he gracefully referred to as a retainer, ostensibly payment for the odd report on 'the general situation' in Washington. This saved Léger from having to cast about for a university teaching post, 'the worst fate that destiny could subject me to'.[34]

Although Léger knew nothing about oil or business, he was popular on the Georgetown social circuit and enjoyed considerable influence among the Washington elite, gently urging America to fight for France, albeit without committing themselves to de Gaulle.[35] In the words of his biographer, Léger served as 'a clandestine, self-appointed advisor, ambassador of a phantom state, a France directed neither from London or Algiers or Vichy'.[36] Léger and Gulbenkian never met again, but their epistolary relationship came to mean a great deal to both men. Each consoled the other on his elective exile, while offering reassurance that this was the wisest course of action for 'the two loneliest men on the planet', the only men who remained faithful to true moral standards.[37]

Gulbenkian was not a literary man; as his curator recalled, 'He did not read novels.'[38] Léger recognised that he was uninterested in literary gossip. In Léger's letters, however, Gulbenkian found his isolation transformed into something noble and sublime – so appealing a pose, perhaps, that one might wish it not to end. Léger never visited Les Enclos, yet he constantly returned to Gulbenkian's Deauville estate in his imagination, gently flattering 'the sage of Les Enclos' for his achievements as a landscape designer, as well as a collector of art. Nature and art were two of the 'secret keys' Gulbenkian held, keys which allowed him to defy that 'Promethean ransom' which otherwise kept him chained to his business empire. On a more mundane level, Léger also recalled Gulbenkian's 'humour' (he employed the English word, which has no equivalent in French), Mehmed the Turkish chef and the roof terrace at 51 Avenue d'Iéna, 'where the pheasants soar over Paris'.[39]

'The future of my paintings, to which I have given the best of myself, torments me constantly,' Gulbenkian confided in Léger, inviting his friend's counsel. 'Where? To which institution should I finally entrust them? So many questions.' No longer his 'children', with time these paintings had matured into 'dear friends'. Gulbenkian did not want any 'kudos', he insisted, 'only that they should be happy, that they should remain together and their needs be catered to in the future'. Even if plans to lend his collections to Washington had come to nothing in 1947, John Walker had persuaded Gulbenkian that they 'would receive a warmer welcome there than elsewhere'.[40] In 1949 Walker tried again, securing the passage through Congress of a special Joint Resolution protecting Gulbenkian's estate from any tax claims in the event of Gulbenkian dying while his property was on loan in Washington.[41] By that point Gulbenkian's Egyptian collection had already left the British Museum for Washington. On 23 June 1950 the forty-one paintings on loan to the National Gallery followed, sailing on the *Queen Elizabeth*. After four years of negotiations, Walker had apparently secured his 'prey'.

One of the other conditions of the loan was that they be exhibited glazed, for their protection. Unfortunately, this made them difficult to view properly, contributing to a lukewarm reception by the American media. Although the repetition of such comments in the British press could be blamed by Nubar on 'an ulterior motive', otherwise the coverage worried Gulbenkian, who began wondering if his 'friends' were being given as warm a welcome as they had been promised.[42] Even worse, his loans led to the Aviz being besieged by reporters eager to interview the rich recluse, whom *Time* found as 'impassive and aloof as the [Egyptian] statuettes he collects'.[43] When their interview requests were refused, journalists bribed the staff for gossip about his eating habits.

'Next to Living Alone and Making Money,' *Life* revealed, 'the Most Important Interest in the Life of the Richest Man in the World Is Food.'[44] Even the tame Portuguese papers were not above serialising 'the astonishing life' of 'the boy from Baku' who became 'the king of petroleum'.[45] Gulbenkian's reply was to cite his favourite proverb, writing to Nubar, '"the dog barks but the caravan passes"; this is very appropriate ... The upshot is why leave the pictures in America if they do not appreciate them.'[46]

Before entrusting his paintings to Washington Gulbenkian had signed a will under which all his art would be held by a 'Gulbenkian Foundation' intended to further 'educational, artistic and benevolent ends'.[47] This foundation would house, care for and augment Gulbenkian's art collection. Smaller trusts would provide income for his family. If none of the latter wished to make 51 Avenue d'Iéna home, it was to be given to the United States for use as the ambassador's residence.[48] Meanwhile plans for a Gulbenkian annexe to be built on tennis courts between the National Gallery of Art and the Capitol were developed, but dropped in 1952 when Gulbenkian found the $5–8 million estimate 'rather astronomical'. It certainly was; unbeknownst to him the actual quotation was $3.5 million.[49]

Walker's apparent decision to inflate the estimate suggests that he may have lost perspective. After securing the loan of Gulbenkian's collection he was persuaded that 'if [Gulbenkian] does not decide on another solution I think there is a will leaving the pictures and Egyptian pieces to us!' Having already had to wait for 'this damnable oil deal' (that is, the 1948 Working Agreement) to go through and having secured the loans over the heads of the British Museum and National Gallery in London, Walker was fully committed. He even tried to persuade Gulbenkian to drop his insistence on keeping his collections together.[50]

When Gulbenkian mooted the possibility of the Chief Justice of the Supreme Court serving as a trustee of his foundation ex officio, Walker made arrangements. He inspected and bid on paintings Gulbenkian was interested in buying, liaised with American recipients of Gulbenkian's private charity and even sought to improve Gulbenkian's press.[51] The gallery's director and others began wondering if their chief curator might not be being strung along. Challenged by Walker for supposedly reconsidering their agreed policy of endeavouring to 'get them [Gulbenkian's collections] in any way we could within reason', gallery director David Finley replied, 'It simply seems as if Mr Gulbenkian wants to send them abroad just for security.'[52] The American ambassador in Paris, David Bruce, seemed far from enthused at the prospect of moving from 2 Avenue d'Iéna (the ambassadorial residence at the time) to the more opulent 51. Even worse, he told a Senate committee investigating oil cartels that Gulbenkian was 'poised for flight to any place in the world'.[53]

Both Gulbenkian and Walker were essentially playing for time, each waiting for the other to back down over the question of whether Gulbenkian's 'friends' would be displayed together or arranged chronologically among the gallery's other works. Walker seemed more aware than Gulbenkian that time was something Gulbenkian might not have much of. 'I have never known anyone so oblivious of "Time's winged chariot hurrying near"!' Walker wrote to Bruce.[54] Meanwhile Gulbenkian had, it seems, not given up entirely on the other National Gallery, in London, where trustee David Lindsay, Earl of Crawford, had replaced Kenneth Clark as Gulbenkian's liaison. In May 1951 Crawford was helping him negotiate to buy Hans Memling's *Donne Triptych* from the Duke of Devonshire. Were this a success, Gulbenkian informed Radcliffe, he planned to give it to the National Gallery in London '(if I can avail myself of the exemption of Death Duties)'.[55]

Gulbenkian's May 1950 will had been drawn up 'hurriedly, in anticipation of a definitive version', to quote the document itself.[56] It attempted to buy time Gulbenkian did not have: its first clause stipulated that Gulbenkian's fortune, including his business interests and all his private philanthropy, were to be maintained as a discrete entity for a period of at least five years. This fortune was to be administered by Nevarte, Nubar, Rita, Kevork, Mikhael and Chase Bank. It was left to them to establish the foundation, whose aims were vague. There was no indication as to where this foundation would display the art collections. Chase executives were supposed to meet with Gulbenkian and Henggeler in Paris over the summer and frame the foundation's statutes, taking those of the Rockefeller Foundation as a model. Instead Gulbenkian held off, perhaps because of the Iranian crisis, perhaps because he could not face the decision Henggeler presented him with, the choice of where (the United States, Panama or Canada) to base his foundation.[57]

A third factor was Gulbenkian's desire to ensure the involvement of his 'excellent friend' Cyril Radcliffe, who had recently been granted a life peerage as Baron Radcliffe of Werneth.[58] Their relationship went back to 1935, when Gulbenkian's lead counsel, Wilfred Greene, left the Bar. Radcliffe was then working in Greene's chambers, and the latter proposed him as a worthy replacement. Unfortunately for Gulbenkian, Radcliffe's legal career proved to be even more stellar than Greene's. While Greene had been appointed a Lord Justice of Appeal straight from the Bar, without any judicial experience (a remarkable achievement in itself), in 1949 Radcliffe was appointed a law lord straight from the Bar, an unprecedented promotion.

In October 1951 Gulbenkian invited Radcliffe to serve as 'lead Trustee' of his planned foundation. Radcliffe was in the midst of giving the prestigious BBC Reith Lectures and chairing a royal commission on taxation. But he flew down to Lisbon for Christmas.[59] The pair had not seen each other in almost two years, largely thanks to Radcliffe's work in India on the boundary commissions. The first of a series of intense face-to-face discussions over the Gulbenkian Foundation was held. Radcliffe tried to bring Gulbenkian's charitable vision into focus. Gulbenkian tried to prise Radcliffe away from Her Majesty's Service.[60]

Lisbon

In January 1952 Gulbenkian introduced Radcliffe to 'my Portuguese solicitor', José de Azeredo Perdigão. Gulbenkian had been introduced to Perdigão by a former Portuguese ambassador to Britain, Ruy Ennes Ulrich, probably in late 1942.[61] Perdigão seemed the natural choice for wealthy wartime refugees, counting Henri de Rothschild among his clients. By 1952 Perdigão's standing within the Portuguese legal profession was analogous to Radcliffe's in Britain. They were roughly the same age, around thirty years younger than Gulbenkian. Perdigão advised on the establishment of the Villa Flor Foundation and served as president of the Ordem dos Advogados, the Portuguese equivalent of the Bar Association. In his twenties Perdigão had helped found a liberal review, *Seara Nova*, which became a focus for intellectuals opposed to Salazar's dictatorship. He remained politically to the left of Salazar. In Salazar's own words, their relations were 'rather ceremonial'.[62]

Like Whishaw before him, Perdigão's progress to Gulbenkian's inner circle was marked by appointments to the boards of various holding companies. This process began in 1945, and by early 1951 Perdigão was serving as director of eleven companies registered in Canada, Venezuela, Hong Kong, Panama and Liechtenstein.[63] As none of Gulbenkian's interests were based in Portugal, however, Perdigão's role was small compared with that of Gulbenkian's other leading legal advisers, including Whishaw, Radcliffe and Henggeler. He knew nothing of the international oil industry.[64] Perdigão's role was limited to handling Gulbenkian's rare interactions with the Portuguese state. In 1951, for example, Perdigão met with PIDE (formerly PVDE, which handled immigration matters as well as internal security) to resolve the question of Gulbenkian's resident status.[65]

Although Henggeler took the lead, the drafting of Gulbenkian's 1950 will had drawn Perdigão further into the inner circle. Whereas Henggeler, Whishaw and Gulbenkian's other senior advisers weighed the pros and cons of various different fiscal regimes, from the beginning Perdigão pushed Portugal as the best place to establish the foundation. It would pay little or no tax if established in Portugal, he promised. Perdigão had a mutual friend 'on the most intimate terms' with Salazar through whom he proposed to get Gulbenkian all the reassurances he could want.[66]

One question on which Gulbenkian sought reassurance was whether the principle of *renvoi* would apply in his case. Under *renvoi* an estate was subject to restrictions imposed by the law of a country other than that in which the testator died: the will was 'sent back' to another state with some claim on the testator, be it of domicile, residency or nationality. Although Gulbenkian's nationality was simple (he was British), his domicile and residency were not. This was important because both French and Portuguese law protected the rights of a testator's children, while under English law the testator was free to leave them nothing. Under Portuguese law the children were entitled to half their parent's estate.

On this crucial question Perdigão failed to provide a clear answer. In late 1951 he advised Gulbenkian that the principle of *renvoi* would not apply in his case. A month later he advised that 'a British subject, domiciled and dying in Portugal, could dispose only of half his fortune, the other half being reserved by law to his direct descendants'. *Renvoi* did apply, therefore. The man 'considered to be the best jurist in Portugal' had reversed himself '(though he does not admit it)'.[67] Gulbenkian suspected that since his first statement Perdigão had gone away to study *renvoi*, and had adopted a new stance. As he wrote to Radcliffe,

> For your confidential information, I was much surprised to hear from Doctor Azeredo Perdigão this morning (Doctor Perdigão is my Portuguese Solicitor, and a very distinguished one, according to local

standards) that he always had maintained that a British subject, domiciled and dying in Portugal, could only dispose of half his fortune, the other half being reserved by law to his direct descendants. This came to me as a great surprise because, as far as I could remember, he had always said that, in Portugal a British subject could dispose of the totality of his fortune, as he wished. Entre nous, I believe that Doctor Perdigão has studied the 'procedure de renvoi' and he is interpreting same in accordance with the Portuguese law.[68]

In a further memorandum Perdigão reported that a Portuguese court would be free to invoke *renvoi* or not, 'as they saw fit'. Gulbenkian was further unsettled by the question of whether the Portuguese authorities would subject property held abroad to succession duty. When asked to clarify the legal position, Perdigão simply pointed out that the Portuguese state did not have the staff or expertise to investigate whether a testator had any property abroad. This did not reassure Gulbenkian at all. 'My mind is precise and meticulous,' he noted. He simply wanted to know what the law said. Gulbenkian acknowledged that Perdigão had intended his comments to reassure. 'And yet – and I am sorry to have to say it – your memorandum throws my mind into great confusion.'[69]

A week or so later Gulbenkian's health went into sudden decline, a crisis which lasted until early March. According to a letter written by Isabelle Theis in 1966, it was during this period of illness that she narrowly prevented Gulbenkian from being cajoled into signing certain documents by Nubar. Theis had taken to sleeping on a camp bed in Gulbenkian's room, and hence was able to work out what Nubar was trying to do and stymie him by summoning the doctors, under the pretence that Gulbenkian's health had suddenly deteriorated. Although she was not specific, the implication was that these documents would have given Nubar greater control over Gulbenkian assets. Gulbenkian himself may not have been fully conscious at the time. Theis may have shared her suspicions with him later.[70]

By the time Gulbenkian recovered in late April 1952 he was persuaded that Nubar, Whishaw and the London office had attempted to use the crisis to wrest control of his holding companies away from him. Contingency plans intended to protect Gulbenkian's interests in the event of his no longer being able to sign documents were misinterpreted as an attempted coup, in which Whishaw as well as Nubar were supposedly involved. Gulbenkian now asked Henggeler to scrutinise all the papers Gulbenkian himself had been sent to sign during his illness. He thanked Henggeler for not going along with London's contingency plans. The same day he thanked Theis for her loyalty by signing a statement confirming his previous gifts to her and promising her a pension of 40,000 francs a year after his death. He told Radcliffe that, once he recovered fully, he wanted to make a new will, and stated once again that he wanted Radcliffe to serve as 'the Leader of my Trustees'.[71]

In Paris Radcliffe and Gulbenkian began working on a new will. Henggeler having died in August 1952, Gulbenkian now looked to Perdigão to collaborate with Radcliffe, whom he introduced as 'an old friend ... a very eminent and important person who soars high above the English legal profession', adding, 'I am sure you will be delighted and interested to work with him.'[72] These discussions resulted in the will of 18 June 1953, which replaced the complex structure of the 1950 will with a simpler architecture, centred on a foundation to be established in Lisbon. The stipulated 'objects' of this foundation remained vague, however: ' charitable, artistic, educational and scientific'.[73] Radcliffe was named lead trustee on a generous salary of £20,000 (£500,000). Perdigão and Kevork were to assist him as trustees on just £4,000 (£100,000). Allowances were made for Nubar to join the board under certain terms.

As ever, time was of the essence. Though not involved in drawing up the will, Ekserdjian attended meetings in Paris with Gulbenkian on business matters a few days after the will was signed. He felt it was almost cruel 'to press him for rulings and directives when it is quite obvious that he is incapable and sees the problems vaguely through a haze'.[74] Gulbenkian's chief physician, Professor Fonseca, reported that Gulbenkian's heart could fail at any time. Gulbenkian's 'essentially suspicious' nature was getting worse, the doctor noted: 'He never relied on any one other person and always liked to check and countercheck, he always kept at least two doctors who advised him independently.'[75]

In September 1953 the Paris doctors were unsure whether Gulbenkian's heart was strong enough to allow him to return to Lisbon. Theis, Kevork and other family members sought to protect Gulbenkian, by keeping such potentially upsetting reports from him. Nubar did not, cruelly playing on his father's hypochondria. To Hacobian and Ekserdjian, it seemed as if Nubar hoped to trigger a fatal crisis by informing his father of his condition, in the expectation of the larger inheritance which would come to him should his father die on French soil.[76] 'In the course of time, I have acquired the painful conviction that [Nubar] will not shrink from any obstacle, lie, or blackmail, to reach his aim,' Gulbenkian observed to Radcliffe. 'Nor will he hesitate to calumniate such persons as are genuinely devoted to me, and whose assistance to me, he is resenting, and afraid of.'[77]

Kevork's years of uncomplaining devotion to Calouste's business had not passed unnoticed by Nubar, to whom they were a standing reproach. Kevork had also provided a grandchild, something Nubar was unable to do (owing to his infertility). In the 1930s and 1940s Nubar grew to resent as well as fear Calouste's reliance on Kevork. His resentment and fear expressed themselves in attempts to bully and intimidate Kevork. Their hatred of each other had become so strong by 1955 that Radcliffe drew a kind of comfort from it. By this point Gulbenkian was unable to sign his name independently: if a signature was required on a document someone had to hold the pen between two of Gulbenkian's fingers. The mutual suspicion of Kevork and Nubar was Gulbenkian's 'best safeguard' against either taking advantage of this.[78] While this might serve to protect Gulbenkian's philanthropic plans, it presumably did little to protect Gulbenkian from the constant anxiety, upset and confusion caused by such fierce brawling among his family. What anecdotes remain suggest Gulbenkian did spend some of his final three years in considerable distress, wondering whom he could trust and what he might have been cajoled into signing while semi-conscious.[79]

Distant Horizons

Writing to Léger in late March 1953, Gulbenkian noted:

> For many months now I have been suffering from a rather curious psychological state, one almost of apathy, because I do not really have the desire to do anything ... Medically I am told I have nothing to worry about; though I certainly bear the scars of my last two periods of illness as well as of the unfortunate events which subsequently weakened me there is nothing really alarming. What troubles me is my inability to shake off this apathy, which leads me to live on the margin of life and other living things, to neglect all outside contact.[80]

Back in the midst of the Iran crisis, Ekserdjian had noted how

Gulbenkian's health seemed to flourish in adversity. Gulbenkian had always liked a fight.[81] In early 1953, however, his oil interests were in rude health. Nubar calculated that 'we have now received back all the money we have put into the IPC venture, including any adjustment due to the depreciation of the £ sterling'.[82] The Big Inch pipeline from Kirkuk to Banias had been formally opened the previous November. As British Pathé noted in its newsreel coverage, the country's future was assured:

> From Kirkuk to Banias the oil now flows. 165,000 tons of steel pipe carry the precious fluid that means prosperity to the country from which it springs. Yet only the scarred earth tells where those riches now flow. Beneath the desert lies the fulfilment of men's dreams. Men of foresight and imagination, who thought, not of themselves, but of the people their enterprise could serve, from Kirkuk to Banias ... to the ends of the earth.[83]

A special feast had been laid on for the locals, it noted. 'But that's only the first of the good things that will come to Iraq – thanks to oil.'[84]

The development of Les Enclos proceeded apace, with plans for a new rustic chateau for the turkeys and pheasants.[85] Gulbenkian's grandson had begun working for Partex. But Gulbenkian showed less interest in acquiring new works of art, in the hunting of masterpieces which had provided a constant source of excitement for decades. Gulbenkian's refrain of 'Leave it to Radcliffe!' whenever his family or others sought clarity regarding his foundation's aims and purposes reflected this apathy as much as it did Gulbenkian's faith in an old friend.[86]

After signing the new will in June 1953, Gulbenkian continued to pester Radcliffe to drop his other activities, leave London and fly down to Lisbon, whereupon (Gulbenkian claimed) they would get the foundation up and running together. Radcliffe had urged Gulbenkian to do precisely this in order to ensure that the foundation was set on its course before the latter died. Now that Gulbenkian was ready, where was Radcliffe? 'As I wrote you before, it is altogether impossible for me to carry on and take decisions, single-handed as I am, even with the collaboration of Doctor Perdigão; the architecture of my contemplated Trust is still very sketchy.' In the case of the Gulbenkian Foundation, therefore, Gulbenkian also seemed to be immobilised, waiting peevishly 'until the blessed day when you will be free to take an active part in our plans'.[87]

Oil, art and the fate of his fortune no longer seemed to hold Gulbenkian's attention. But nature did. Gulbenkian delighted in paying visits to
the zoo in Lisbon, just as he had in London and Paris years before. He sent
the director a cheque. 'It gives me pleasure to show my lively sympathy in
this way,' he noted, 'for the animals which inhabit your beautiful garden
are my hosts too, in a way.'[88] Each morning when his physicians allowed he
had a car drive him two miles west to Montes Claros in Monsanto, which
Salazar had had transformed into a park. Here Gulbenkian took his solitary walk, after which he sat under 'my tree', having first removed his shoes
and socks so that he could feel the grass under his feet.[89]

'I am somewhat of a dreamer,' Gulbenkian had once told Deterding,
'and in my early youth was destined to follow the study of astronomy, but
my father put me into business ... However, I still like to look for distant
horizons and conceptions.'[90] On warm evenings he would return to
Montes Claros, accompanied by Isabelle Theis, two chairs and a telescope.
While the driver waited patiently in the car, Gulbenkian and Theis would
sit quietly together, looking up at the stars.[91]

At 9.40 a.m. on 20 July 1955 Gulbenkian died, peacefully, in his bed
at the Aviz. He was eighty-six.

CONCLUSION

Though one struggles to imagine Gulbenkian as much of a 'dreamer', his skill in carving out a place for himself among the emerging giants of the cut-throat world of big oil was clearly founded on a vision: the orderly development and consolidation of a fragmented oil industry through vertical integration and international cartels. The spectacular waste of oil he witnessed during his short expedition to Baku in 1888 clearly left a deep impression. So did the price wars fought among Standard, Royal Dutch, Shell and other companies before 1900, and the logjam produced by rival powers' attempts to secure the Mesopotamian oil concession before 1914.

Building on Frederick Lane's experience of forming large oil marketing syndicates, Gulbenkian saw the potential for cartels to take the politics out of upstream activities (that is, production), by ensuring that no single power predominated. Empires and states, diplomats and statesmen, spheres of influence and national champions, all were distractions to Gulbenkian: to be ignored if possible, or else coached and coopted – as he did so successfully with France. Talk about British, French or American 'control' was 'very largely nonsense', nothing but 'a matter of sentiment'. 'If by transferring control to the Hottentots we could increase our security and our dividends, I don't believe any of us would hesitate for long.'[1] The words are Waley Cohen's, but they could just as well be Gulbenkian's.

Gulbenkian thrived in the pre-1914 world of free trade, the gold standard and minimal state regulation. This was the age of the robber barons, but also the first age of globalisation.[2] Like another of his mentors, the Anglo-German banker Ernest Cassel, Gulbenkian's internationalism was 'a symptom of a new epoch ... part of a new kind of supranational socio-economic structure' that 'threatened to transcend and make obsolete the nineteenth-century boundaries of the nation and the state'.[3] This supranational structure was more global in 1914 than in any decade before the 1990s.[4] Faster flows of goods and information were rendering the partnership-based 'general merchant' model followed by S. & S. Gulbenkian outmoded.[5] Calouste could have taken his brothers with him as he specialised in mining and oil finance: M. Samuel and Co. (of Shell fame) made this transition. Instead, he turned his back on Karnig and Vahan, exhibiting an indifference to the clan's reputation that shocked many fellow Ottoman Armenians. Behind the story of the would-be astronomer stymied by his father may lie a deeper resentment, such as might explain his shocking decision not to attend his beloved mother's funeral.

What is clear is that Gulbenkian adopted a sometimes stark individualism, which seems more American than Armenian. As his daughter recognised, Gulbenkian was 'a Genius, a Special Number' who permitted 'himself to do everything in his own way', one to whom the rules (on taxation, for example) did not apply.[6] But there may be an Ottoman Armenian aspect to this attitude. Within the Ottoman Empire the Armenians were exempt from many of the usual requirements of modern citizenship, such as military service. Different sets of rules and taxes applied to different ethnic groups. The *amiras'* ability to navigate these rules, their mobility and their polyglot households surely prepared Gulbenkian well, even if he showed little interest in the Armenian Republic or Armenian patriotism. Meanwhile for non-Armenians the label 'Armenian' was immediately recognisable, yet carried reassuringly little baggage. Armenians were everywhere and nowhere; nobody had to worry that Gulbenkian might be following orders from Yerevan.

Gulbenkian's vision of international cooperation could not have been realised without sacrifice, without allowing his share of the Turkish Petroleum Company to be repeatedly reduced, for example, in order to admit new partners. To his brother-in-law, this demonstrated that Gulbenkian was not only a bad Armenian 'from the point of view of charity', but had 'a racial inferiority complex' to boot.[7] Yet Gulbenkian was evidently a gifted negotiator. Unfortunately, Gulbenkian's network of contacts, relentless focus and softly spoken persuasiveness have left few traces, apart from the odd aside in memoirs written by associates and snide comments by jealous relations, including his only son.

Yet it was these attributes, rather than any 'nose for oil' or 'oriental' expertise, which laid the foundations of the Gulbenkians' fabulous wealth. Had he not made a small fortune on 1 per cent and 2 per cent commissions he earned on a galaxy of bond and share issues and sales contracts for Royal Dutch-Shell, Gulbenkian would not have been able to afford to pay the calls on his 5 per cent of IPC – that is, to pay his share of the considerable upfront costs associated with exploration, drilling and building pipelines and other facilities. When IPC's Big Inch pipeline came onstream in the early 1950s, Gulbenkian's small fortune became a very large one very quickly.[8] At his death he was the world's richest man, rivalled only by Getty.

Founded in 1912, TPC had been a long shot. It took considerable courage as well as capital to stay the course in the face of political risks and repeated urging by Gulbenkian's closest advisers to sell out while the going was good. This is not, however, how it has been remembered. The biggest irony of Gulbenkian's career is that, having spent thirty years consolidating the international oil industry into one ruled by a few 'sisters', he spent the last twenty-five desperately fighting not to be squashed by them, and even came to be remembered as an ornery obstacle to further consolidation.

Gulbenkian's relationship with that other, more volatile genius Henri Deterding encapsulates this irony. For Gulbenkian it was the most rewarding relationship of his life, personally as well as financially. Gulbenkian knew that his talents and Deterding's complemented each other, and took great pleasure and pride from the success of their joint effort to turn Royal Dutch-Shell from an upstart into the world's largest international company. Encouraged by his second wife's jealousy and his own paranoia, after their 1925 falling-out Deterding tried his best to evict the Gulbenkians not only from IPC, but from the whole industry. Though he failed to achieve either goal, he did ensure that his former friend's contribution to Royal Dutch-Shell's development would be forgotten.

Instead Gulbenkian's reputation has been yoked to the Iraq Petroleum Company. He certainly played an important role in the company he had established as Turkish Petroleum, if not quite as significant a one as he liked to claim. It would be foolish to think that Gulbenkian was the first to draw attention to Mesopotamia's oil riches. The fact that powerful European financiers like Cassel and Deutsche Bank's Arthur von

Gwinner sought his advice on the development of the Ottoman Empire's oil reflected Gulbenkian's ability to persuade others that he possessed privileged access to mysteriously 'oriental' regimes.

Like his Ottoman and Persian/Iranian diplomatic status, this access was more apparent than real. Gulbenkian's role in securing TPC's Mosul concession and, later, in negotiating IPC's royalties with the Iraqis was almost non-existent. Though happy to circulate among French resorts, Gulbenkian had no desire to travel to Istanbul or Baghdad. Nor (in the 1940s) did he want to travel to Tehran to run a new national oil company. The 1888 expedition to Baku remained his sole experience of an oilfield, and he never set foot in Iran, Iraq or any other Arab country. Nor did he ever visit the United States.

Gulbenkian's contribution to IPC was not in its operations, but in the principle of international cooperation and the self-denying clause which underpinned it. This was the architecture in which Gulbenkian took such pride: the details of construction were left to others, and regularly adapted to fit changing circumstances. The result was what an American oil executive described as 'one of the outstanding instances of international sharing and cooperation'.[9]

As 'an archetypical example of cosmopolitan business interests', however, after 1914 the company represented 'a cross-current to the rise in the international tensions'. Having matured in a world of free trade, currency convertibility and capital mobility, Gulbenkian found the tide running against him, particularly after 1929, as globalisation went into reverse.[10] In the deteriorating international climate of the 1930s a willingness to cut deals across borders (notably across that border dividing the Soviet Union from the West) came to be viewed with suspicion. Gulbenkian's love of privacy only served to encourage conspiracy theorists who viewed his wealth and influence as illegitimate.[11] By the 1940s it had become easier to see Gulbenkian as a nefarious spider in an oily web than as the David struggling against the Goliath of big oil.

Gulbenkian was, admittedly, used to being viewed unkindly. Years of experience of negotiating unlikely alliances only to be calumniated afterwards by both sides allowed him to perfect his 'philosopher' pose. Yet it also seems to have caused him considerable personal disillusionment, to discover that 'healthy principles' played so little part in big business. At times, for example during his assignations with the *Morning Post* editor Howell Gwynne, he could even find himself espousing state intervention in the oil industry. He did not oppose the 1944 Anglo-American Petroleum Agreement in principle, but on account of its failure to create an international body which could force the majors to behave in a more principled manner. At the end of the day, however, one wonders if Gulbenkian felt that statesmen could be trusted any more than oilmen. The 'philosopher' pose allowed the elderly Gulbenkian to appear shrewd without having to come down on one side or the other.

Like other members of the pre-1914, London-based 'aristocratic bourgeoisie' described by historians Jose Harris and Pat Thane, so Gulbenkian 'combined grand dynastic aspiration with an unpretentious devotion to the ethic of work'.[12] Gulbenkian preached this work ethic to his son and grandson, and practised it to an almost Stakhanovite degree himself. Though his itinerant lifestyle orbited around grand hotels and resorts synonymous with opulence, his was not a life of ease. His dress was formal, yet modest: in middle age he sometimes evaded paparazzi simply by dint of not looking like a millionaire. Irritated to discover that his expensive Patek Philippe had broken yet again, Gulbenkian asked his valet where he had purchased his own more reliable watch. Upon hearing how cheaply such watches could be procured from Prisunic (a French chain of cheap department stores) he ordered the valet to go out and buy ten, which Gulbenkian successively wore until they broke.[13]

Just because Gulbenkian neglected much of his Ottoman Armenian birthright as a member of an *amira* dynasty did not mean that he was uninterested in starting a new dynasty of his own. This dynasty was to be built on his ineffable 'healthy principles'. His relationship with Nevarte began promisingly, with her submitting to her fiancé's somewhat priggish love letters. As husband and wife, however, Nevarte and Calouste struggled to live in close proximity. Though Nevarte had accepted her husband's regimen of regular sex with young women, the companionship offered by Isabelle Theis was something else entirely. Happily, in the circles in which they moved communicating bedrooms were not a requirement, and by the time they found themselves in Portugal (where they *were* required) their seniority shielded them from censure. In her final years Nevarte had a jolly good time being 'Mrs Five Per Cent'.

As head of the family, Gulbenkian took the same approach to major issues (the 'Rita Question', his grandson's education) as he did as head of Pandi: memos were solicited from all parties, then he reached a decision. Day-to-day expenses of the various households, too, were carefully monitored. Gulbenkian had no time or patience for everything else in between. His approach to parenting as well as marriage was that of an Ottoman Armenian *amira*. Educated in Britain, Rita and Nubar naturally chafed against this. Neither had the stamina to break free from the allowances (and promises of a legacy) which tied them to their father.

Gulbenkian's curator, Marcelle Chanet, could not help but spot an analogy between her employer's approach to Nubar and Rita and his approach to his other 'children', his art collection: 'A great solicitude ... but from a distance; correspondence by letter, cable and telephone over thousands of miles; specialist practitioners ordered hither and yon, but hardly ever a celebration spent with all the family together, and not a gallery without its deplorable gaps.'[14] Though possessive and controlling, Gulbenkian kept the objects of his solicitude at a distance. Whether out of a desire to protect his art from war or a more generous-minded wish to share it with the public, Gulbenkian's many loans to museums meant that he rarely had the opportunity to enjoy his own paintings and artefacts. He never slept at 51 Avenue d'Iéna and never constructed a house in his garden near Deauville (except for his beloved peacocks, pheasants and ducks). He was always a visitor, never at home.

The buccaneer element in Gulbenkian relished the pursuit of great masterpieces, a pursuit which took up a significant part of his time. Researching provenance, evaluating condition and attribution, gathering intelligence from multiple sources and studying market fluctations drew on the same skills which had made Gulbenkian such a renowned and envied figure on the stock market and within the oil industry. In this 'leisure' pursuit, as in his business and family affairs, Gulbenkian gave full vent to his suspicious nature. Even trusted advisers like Kenneth Clark had to accept that their actions were closely monitored and their statements checked against those of other advisers. They were not, in fact, 'trusted' very far.

Gulbenkian also drew on his own taste, of course, which he constantly sought to educate, and which became more catholic over time. He brought to this study an eye for colour and respect for craft that were partly an inheritance from his *amira* ancestors. The contemplation of his treasures and of his garden at Les Enclos enabled an otherwise restless business titan to snatch moments of restorative calm. Art provided 'consolation and relief' whenever one found oneself facing disappointments in life.[15] The quote is from a 1926 letter to Nubar – in the vast traffic of correspondence noted by Chanet, this is the only instance of Gulbenkian explaining why he collected. Whether the children in question were human beings, birds, cats, paintings or sculpture, Gulbenkian kept his feelings for them private.

Rita and Nubar were well aware of their father's plans to leave his art collection, investments and Pandi (that is, the famous 5 per cent) to a charitable foundation. Indeed, they had probably been aware of this since the late 1930s. There is no evidence that either resented it, or took much of an interest in the form this element of Gulbenkian's dynastic vision would take. Gulbenkian wished his foundation to be international in scope. This was unusual, if characteristic. Charity began at home. Gulbenkian having no home, his largesse would benefit humanity at large. Other than caring for his art, however, the Calouste Gulbenkian Foundation's aims were vague. Nor did Gulbenkian's lifetime giving offer much by way of guidance: although he gave to a wide variety of charities throughout his life, gifts were frequent – and small.

Andrew Carnegie, author of the famous *Gospel of Wealth* (1889), had begun giving on a large scale in his thirties (in the 1870s), developing his own signature schemes (donating church organs, for example, as well as public libraries) and taking full advantage of the press and politicians to explain how his philanthropy related to his views on the questions of the day, from labour relations to international peace. He was the first of a new breed of entrepreneurial philanthropists 'who use their power to accumulate more power, extend their social and political influence, and increase their capacity to shape society according to their will'.[16]

Gulbenkian shared many of the values of Carnegie, as well as John D. Rockefeller and Henry Ford, who established foundations in 1909 and 1936: self-help, a strong work ethic and a visceral hatred of 'socialism', above all. Even before 1914 Gulbenkian claimed that 'the trend of the taxation plainly points to vicious attacks by political parties upon one section of the community, in order to catch the votes of the other and larger section'.[17] By the 1950s Gulbenkian had become so fixated on protecting his fortune, however, that he seemed uninterested in the purposes for which it was being preserved.

'You are my son,' he told Nubar (in Armenian) in a moment of lucidity in February 1955, 'don't forget what I'm telling you. You are strong, you must defend our fortune, it will be a shame if it all goes.'[18] The fortune had become an end in itself. A few months later Gulbenkian's executors faced the unenviable task of establishing a new kind of international philanthropic foundation, in a country where only a handful of foundations existed, where the laws relating to foundations were ill-defined, and where the head of state was a dictator hostile to international organisations, Boy Scouts included. For one whose mantra had been 'check, check, check', this was something of an oversight.

THE SPOILS OF
GULBENKIAN, 1956

*'He was terrified that his family and entourage would lose
their heads, overwhelmed by the colossal fortune which he had
amassed, and which he alone was capable of managing.'*
Marcelle Chanet

*'The modern substitution of Combination for Competition as
the principle of capitalism is producing a new crop of individual
fortunes so monstrous as to make their possessors publicly ridiculous.
Unloading is, for the moment, the order of the day.'*
Bernard Shaw

Gulbenkian had few illusions about how his family would react to his death. Within minutes of his passing, he predicted, Nubar and Rita would be found 'wedged in the door of Jack Barclays', the renowned Bentley dealership in London's Berkeley Square.[1] Under the will, each received $1 million ($8.8 million/£6.8 million) in cash, as well as income from trusts. The £196,508 (£4.6 million) assessment of Gulbenkian's estate for British probate was, of course, only the tip of the iceberg. For 1955 his profits on his 5 per cent of IPC were £3.9 million (£92 million). These profits were more than ten times greater than in 1947, when Jersey had valued the stake at around £500 million (in today's values); so perhaps £5 billion (again, at today's values) would be a very rough estimate. Had he lived, this would have placed Gulbenkian at the top of the first 'Rich List', compiled by *Forbes* two years later. He died the world's richest man.

Gulbenkian had appointed his son-in-law, Kevork, an executor alongside Perdigão and Whishaw. The 1953 will also stipulated that Kevork serve alongside Perdigão as a trustee of his foundation, under the leadership of Radcliffe. Nubar was not a trustee, but Radcliffe had ensured that the will explicitly empowered the trustees to coopt him if they wished. The will also named Mikhael Essayan as a possible future trustee. The foundation itself had yet to be established, however. Its statutes remained to be written. To enjoy exemptions from estate duty and other taxes it would need to have statutes approved by the Portuguese government and enshrined in a decree law.

Gulbenkian's body lay in state in the chapel of the British Embassy in Lisbon. There being no facilities in Portugal, his body was flown to Geneva for cremation. The ashes were then taken to London. Barely eight days after his father's death Nubar began issuing threats to use possession of the ashes to establish his father's residency in the United Kingdom. If successful this would have radically altered the tax burden imposed on the estate. Though Ekserdjian recognised this for yet another of Nubar's 'clever' if impracticable schemes, Kevork took the threat seriously. While Gulbenkian's death energised Nubar, it seemed to rob Kevork of any initiative. Kevork was concerned that Nubar and the Portuguese government were seeking to make trouble for the future foundation, yet seemed incapable of organising any countermeasures.[2]

The memorial service at St Sarkis Church in London was thinly attended, so much so that the London office decided not to have the names of those present published in the papers. Newspaper obituarists repeated all the old stories about Gulbenkian's supposed idiosyncrasies. Armenian and Turkish coverage combined pride in Gulbenkian's origins with complaints that he had never paid sufficient tribute to the region to which he owed his birth and fortune – in life or in death.[3] Ekserdjian sought to provide the British press with material for a more rounded portrait, but struggled: Gulbenkian was 'a legend rather than a person'.[4] Gulbenkian's former secretary D. H. Young felt less constrained. In exchange for 'a sum of money which would see him through until the end of his life', he sold his memoirs to the *People*, which serialised them. 'They Called Him Gulbenkian the Gentle', ran their headline, 'But He Held All of You to Ransom.' Despite giving lurid accounts of Gulbenkian taking 'girls from the gutter' as mistresses, Young could not help but admit to an abiding affection for his former master. Young might have been 'Gulbenkian's slave for 26 years', 'yet I almost loved him!'[5]

Radcliffe offered a more measured assessment of 'The Gulbenkian I Knew' in the *Sunday Times*. Gulbenkian 'had a native intellectual force, unharnessed by logic and unabated by conventional reading,' Radcliffe noted. 'He had an enormous vitality, a nervous intensity, which charged his body and mind with electricity and set him to work upon anything he turned to with a concentration that was frightening.' Far from being the vain despot depicted by Young, Gulbenkian only took pride in the 'intricate and complicated structure ... which he had built up as the fortress and temple of his wealth'.

It was through this structure that Gulbenkian sought immortality:

> In his later years it became his obsession. I wish that it had not, because in the end it isolated him for good from the two countries which in all the world had done most to form him and to give him his opportunities, England and France; and Portugal, a pleasant and kindly refuge, could never take their place. But death duties and income taxes and exchange controls, which seemed to be all that post-war England and France had to offer their former lover, were to him nothing but the moth and rust that were to corrupt his finely wrought treasure. He did not want to understand the reasons that made them necessary. He wanted instead to sulk and be unreasonable and, secretly, to hope that by some sweeping personal concession these erring countries would absolve him from all the burdens but restore to him all the graces of their connection. This is not what happened.[6]

During their long discussions in London, Paris and Lisbon regarding the foundation, Radcliffe had repeatedly urged Gulbenkian to increase the number of trustees, by adding high-ranking representatives of the British and Portuguese governments. On their own, Radcliffe, Kevork and Perdigão would struggle to administer an international philanthropic organisation, he argued, not least because none of them had any relevant experience. It was foolish of Gulbenkian to presume that such a wealthy foundation could be kept 'private'. 'It will be too large, too wealthy, and the interests that will belong to it are too important, economically and politically, to allow of that.'

'I have seen too much of Governments to trust any of them to leave such sources untapped,' Radcliffe continued, 'unless it clearly suits them to do so, or it would be too obviously embarrassing to do otherwise.' By giving equal weight to British and Portuguese representatives on his foundation's board, Gulbenkian could ensure that it would not be captured by either side. Right up until his death, however, Gulbenkian had resisted this logic. Although an undated memo in his hand sketches out a proposal for an expanded board of seven trustees (two family representatives, two British, two Portuguese, under Radcliffe's chairmanship), this plan was never put in place during Gulbenkian's lifetime.[7]

Perdigão kept Salazar informed of Gulbenkian's testamentary plans. He informed Salazar when the 1953 will was signed, at the same time placing himself at Salazar's disposal, 'with formal discretion and in professional secrecy'. Perdigão later requested a meeting to discuss the will and even promised Salazar that it would never be changed.[8] At one of these meetings Salazar instructed Perdigão to ensure that the foundation's board had a Portuguese majority, only to find that Perdigão had already had the same idea. As Salazar noted to the Portuguese ambassador in London, Pedro Teotónio Pereira, 'we must not forget that the Foundation is Portuguese by the express wish of the founder, that the act of creating the foundation and its nationality represent a gift to Portugal'.[9]

In September 1955 the three trustees (Radcliffe, Kevork and Perdigão) met to discuss the general principles to be embodied in the statutes of the new foundation. In keeping with his desire for rapprochement, Radcliffe invited Nubar to take part in this and other discussions regarding his father's foundation. Radcliffe suggested the Dutchman Eelco Van Kleffens as an appropriately international addition to their number.[10] A distinguished international jurist, Van Kleffens had worked in the Secretariat of the League of Nations before the war, then became Dutch Foreign Minister. After the war he served as ambassador to Portugal and in 1954 had been appointed president of the UN General Assembly. Van Kleffens was, in short, a highly qualified candidate. Perdigão rejected Radcliffe's proposal to increase and internationalise the board. Enlarging the board would have the unintended consequence, Perdigão claimed, of leading the Portuguese government to demand a Portuguese majority.

Radcliffe made it clear that if a Portuguese majority was written into the statutes he would not serve as chairman. Agreement was, however, reached that Portugal and the United Kingdom each had 'first claim' on the foundation, with Armenia, France and the Middle East deserving 'special consideration'. Kevork and Nubar agreed with Radcliffe's proposal that they should seek guidance from established American and British foundations. At David Rockefeller's suggestion, all four met with the leaders of the Rockefeller Foundation, which had been established in 1913 with the goal of 'promoting the well-being of humanity throughout the world'. A series of meetings were held with foundation president Dean Rusk (who would later serve Kennedy as Secretary of State) and Arthur Dean, a leading corporate lawyer who had helped negotiate the armistice ending the Korean War. As far as Perdigão was concerned, these consultations were a waste of time; he decided to draft the foundation's statutes on his own.[11]

Radcliffe asked Arthur Dean to come up with a list of questions regarding Portuguese testamentary and foundation law, an exercise intended to clarify the parameters within which the foundation would operate. These questions were put to two leading jurists from the University of Coimbra, António de Arruda Ferrer Correia and Afonso Rodrigues Queiró, who delivered a joint response in December 1955. Radcliffe continued to insist that the statutes respect certain basic conditions: no Portuguese majority (indeed, no majority for any nationality), no set minimum for grants to Portugal and no other restrictions on where and how the foundation distributed its largesse. Perdigão relayed these demands to Salazar, who became increasingly concerned at what the former referred to as 'Radcliffe's persistence, born more of stubbornness than intelligence'.[12]

To Radcliffe's surprise, Perdigão began awarding scholarships in the foundation's name, even though the statutes had yet to be drafted, let alone formally adopted.[13] Perdigão continued to extend such private patronage in the years that followed, much to the consternation of Radcliffe and Whishaw. For Radcliffe and Whishaw, such philanthropy was scattergun, and both argued that it did not represent a responsible use of Gulbenkian's wealth. As Whishaw noted a few months later in a letter to Perdigão:

> My own Church needs money; the Church School in my neighbour-
> hood, of which my wife is Chairman of the Governors, badly needs
> money to keep abreast of the standard of the Government schools in
> equipment, but I wouldn't dream of making any proposal for them,
> for their need is no greater than the needs of hundreds of Churches
> and Church Schools throughout the country. Picking out individual

institutions almost at random is not, I submit, the way to carry out Mr. Gulbenkian's trust.[14]

Despite complaints from fellow trustees about Perdigão's fondness for giving grants without consultation, such grants only became more frequent.[15] By directing Gulbenkian's inheritance to individuals and institutions he knew personally, Perdigão may have appeared to be acting irresponsibly to Whishaw and Radcliffe. Yet clientism governed all aspects of public life in Portugal. Rather than being seen as random or corrupt, personal knowledge was held to be the best means of establishing this or that individual or institution's claim on the foundation's largesse.

As the French ambassador to Portugal noted, there was a 'shocking contrast between the concentration of wealth in the hands of a few families and the misery which persists as much in the country as among the proletariat, and which is even found among the *petit bourgeoisie* of the towns'. Though Salazar had brought order where there had been 'anarchy', the ambassador noted, prosperity gains had again been enjoyed by 'a narrow oligarchy'. During the Second World War the masses had nonetheless acknowledged that, for all their deprivation, they were better off than those in countries caught up in the conflict. Now peace had broken out, now Portugal was a member of NATO and the OECD, however, those same masses were (according to the ambassador) beginning to see their position rather differently.[16] As Salazar noted, Gulbenkian's 'gift' provided the means to address these problems: 'The Gulbenkian Foundation has unexpectedly created a public resource that could radically modify the conditions under which we seek to resolve certain fundamental problems facing Portugal.'[17] It was therefore vital that the 'gift' was delivered to Portugal.

In their reply to Arthur Dean's questions, Queiró and Correia did their bit. They noted that under Portuguese law the Gulbenkian Foundation would not be subject to any restrictions on the nationality of board members or the destination of its grants. A founder's wishes would always be respected. The wording of Gulbenkian's will, however, made it equally evident to them that the founder's wish had been that Portugal benefit more than any other country. Queiró and Correia drew attention to the stipulation that the foundation's activities 'shall be exercised not only in Portugal, but also in any other country where its directors may see fit'.

Those four words ('not only in Portugal'), the pair argued,

demonstrated a 'special appreciation for Portugal, so warmly expressed by the Testator' that it 'must be one of the essential guideposts in interpreting the will and filling in its lacunae':

> In virtue of an express provision of the will Portugal is the only country where the Foundation cannot fail to exercise its activity. All this expresses over-abundantly a preference for Portugal, preference to which the executors and trustees – who must first and foremost comply with the testator's purposes and respect his intentions – have to remain faithful under all circumstances whatever.

Correia and Queiró further remarked that the Portuguese government would be well within its rights to insist on a Portuguese majority on the board, thanks to a 1944 law on 'public utility undertakings and companies administering public property or engaged in activities of essential interest to the national economy'.[18] The law in question applied to gas companies and other utilities. It was something of a stretch to apply its provisions to a charitable foundation.[19]

But then again, as the pair noted, 'There are many gaps in Portuguese legislation on foundations in general.'[20] The 1867 Civil Code then in force did not mention foundations at all. The 1940 Administrative Code did, but understood them as 'institutions of local utility' whose foundation required the approval of the local intendant. The handful of foundations in Portugal in 1955 had indeed been established to benefit specific regions. While a new Civil Code was introduced in 1966, in the late 1950s the law governing foundations in Portugal was in flux.[21]

In January 1956 Radcliffe returned to Lisbon, and met with Salazar at the Palace of São Bento. Radcliffe told Salazar of how he was torn between his career in Britain and the foundation chairmanship. He feared that it would be difficult for him, as a non-Portuguese, to lead the foundation. Salazar urged Radcliffe to take the chairmanship, but stated that the majority of the board had to be Portuguese citizens. The will had established the foundation in Portugal, and it stood to reason that it was Portuguese and hence should be controlled by Portuguese nationals. When challenged, Radcliffe conceded that he could not think of any other foundations where one nation did not have a de facto majority.[22]

Minister of the Presidency Marcello Caetano also emphasised this point in his informal meetings with Van Kleffens, who was trying to broker a settlement. Van Kleffens argued that the Rockefeller Foundation (whose trustees were all American) was not a helpful analogy: whereas the Rockefellers and their oil companies were American, neither Gulbenkian nor Pandi was Portuguese, nor had Gulbenkian made his money in Portugal. The foundation's Portuguese nationality was 'a matter of form', a flag of convenience, similar to shipping companies nominally registered in Liberia or Panama. Caetano found these arguments insulting. The refusal to accept a Portuguese majority implied that the Portuguese could not be trusted to run a large philanthropic organisation. 'It all is a matter of prestige,' Van Kleffens observed, 'arising out of that unfortunate feeling of inferiority which plagues this country.'[23]

At meetings with Perdigão, Radcliffe continued to insist that no one nation should have a majority on the board, and that grants to Portuguese institutions should not exceed 20 per cent. Perdigão explained that the tax relief which the foundation would receive from the Portuguese Ministry of Finance was a quid pro quo for grants: 'It would be truly incomprehensible were the Portuguese legislature to allow a nominally Portuguese foundation to enjoy total exemption from taxes.' The government would insist that at least a third of grants were distributed within Portugal. This direct relationship between tax relief and philanthropy was nowhere laid down in Portuguese law, but formed part of the Portuguese legal mind-set.[24]

Radcliffe's demands were now an ultimatum: he would not take the chairman's role unless the above conditions were met. Perdigão asked Kevork and Nubar to give their views on the board question. In his memo Nubar acknowledged that his father had failed to 'crystallise' his wishes before his death. It was nonetheless clear that Gulbenkian had wished 'humanity to profit rather than any limited circle of persons'. Given his visceral dislike of 'publicity and ostentation', Gulbenkian would probably not have relished the idea of large numbers of people 'of public standing or not' running what he saw as 'a purely personal family concern'.

> That was, in my opinion, why he specified that his great friend, in whom he had such confidence – Lord Radcliffe – be the Chief Trustee, to whom he added the illustrious Portuguese lawyer whom he thought he knew so well ... The possibility of an outside majority being imposed had never been envisaged by my Father, and I do feel that if it had been brought to his attention during his lifetime he would have taken other steps than he did about his Foundation. Being an Armenian with an

international outlook, and having made his fortune internationally, he did not feel it fair for any one community, except perhaps the Armenians, to be the sole or even the chief direct beneficiary of his fortune.

It was important to think practically, however. The key point as far as Nubar was concerned was to ensure that Radcliffe accepted the chairmanship. If the Portuguese government insisted on a minimum share, then Nubar advocated the creation of a separate Portuguese foundation to which that share could be ceded by a parent foundation to be established elsewhere.[25]

Kevork's statement was characteristically modest in noting that he had not been party to his father-in-law's estate planning. It was nonetheless clear to him that Gulbenkian had put his trust in Radcliffe, and that Gulbenkian expected 'members of his family to take great heed of [Radcliffe's] guidance and advice in the solution of our problems'. Kevork therefore supported Radcliffe's position.[26] This may have disappointed Perdigão, who had previously written appreciatively to Salazar of how Kevork was 'the loyal collaborator of the Portuguese trustee [that is, Perdigão himself]'.[27]

Perdigão did not shift his position, writing to Radcliffe that the government insisted on a Portuguese majority and a minimum 33 per cent of grants as their quid pro quo for registering the foundation as a tax-exempt philanthropic organisation. Radcliffe's reply was equally firm: 'In all the years during which [Gulbenkian] confided in me his ideas as to the eventual creation of a great public Trust – and they go back to 1937 – I never heard him express an intention to favour specially any particular country. He spoke always of "humanity" as his beneficiary.' Were the Portuguese Ministry of Finance to impose the 33 per cent requirement as a prerequisite for the decree law establishing the foundation 'it would not be realising the founder's intentions: it would be flouting them. It would not be carrying out the terms of the Will: it would be defeating them.' Gulbenkian had chosen Portugal because its tax regime exempted charitable foundations from estate duty (unlike, say, the French tax regime). 'I must say with all respect that I consider it quite inadmissable that after his death the Minister of Finance should seek to introduce by administrative decision a substantive alteration of the purposes of the Foundation.'[28]

It had become unclear to Radcliffe whether Perdigão's demands were his own or those of the Portuguese government. Was Perdigão speaking as

Gulbenkian's executor or was he a spokesman for Salazar? In March 1956 Perdigão insisted that his letters to Radcliffe had been 'my own exclusive aut[h]orship and responsibility', and denied that he had been showing Radcliffe's letters to Portuguese ministers. These statements were incorrect: Perdigão had shown Radcliffe's letters to both Salazar and Caetano, and asked Salazar for instructions on how to reply. That same letter in which Perdigão issued his denial had itself been sent by Perdigão in draft to Salazar, with a request that Salazar check it. Perdigão later wrote thanking Salazar for his suggestions.[29]

By this point Radcliffe recognised what was going on. When Van Kleffens suggested he and Perdigão put matters before mediators at the International Court of Justice, Radcliffe replied that it was pointless. To do so would be to 'avoid the plain fact that the other party is the Portuguese gov[ernmen]t and <u>their</u> claims, not his. [Perdigão] merely shelters behind them and says "They want this and have the power to get it – I agree."'[30] Radcliffe was nonetheless shocked to discover that Perdigão had also been cooperating with the Portuguese government in negotiations for the export of Gulbenkian's art from France to Portugal.

Starting in January 1956 the Portuguese ambassador to France, Marcello Mathias, had been negotiating with the French arts minister, under instructions from Salazar, Caetano and Perdigão (without the knowledge of Radcliffe or Nubar). As Perdigão noted in a letter to Mathias, the three were in 'full agreement' as to how the 'Portuguese interests of the Gulbenkian Foundation' were to be defended.[31] The French Ministry of National Education (which handled such questions) initially identified sixty objects among the collections at 51 Avenue d'Iéna which they considered *patrimoine* – that is, items of national heritage subject to an export ban. As a ministry official noted, the Gulbenkian collection had been 'both famous and at the same time unknown'. That was no reason, however, to let it escape.[32] Mathias made good use of the carrot and the stick: offering to give the French Les Enclos (and even 51 Avenue d'Iéna itself), while threatening to prevent any foundation grants going to France if the French government did not prove more amenable to the collection's export to Lisbon.[33] A final settlement of these questions would eventually be reached in 1959.

In 1956, however, Mathias was taking decisions regarding property which did not belong to the Portuguese government, and making policy commitments on behalf of a foundation which did not (yet) exist. For

Radcliffe it was premature to allow decisions regarding 'basic questions of Foundation policy' to be made 'before the Foundation itself has Articles legally approved by the Government, a legal existence and a Board of Governors who can duly take decisions on its behalf'.[34] He told Nubar that he considered Perdigão's actions 'a breach of faith'.[35]

Perdigão deeply resented this language. He confessed to Mathias in Paris that he sometimes toyed with the idea of pushing matters to a complete break with Radcliffe. Perdigão and Mathias, as well as Salazar, were all keen to avoid such a break, fearing a public outcry and 'international repercussions' if Radcliffe were to resign and publicly declare himself unable to realise Gulbenkian's wishes. The Portuguese ambassador in London, Pedro Teotónio Pereira, was charged with meeting Radcliffe and defending the Portuguese position.[36] Meanwhile Perdigão seems to have won Kevork over to his side. In March 1956 he wrote to Kevork, citing Radcliffe's 'breach of faith' comment as 'yet another example of his hostility to Portugal'. Radcliffe having yet to accept his trusteeship, it was time for Perdigão and Kevork to act.[37]

Kevork's reply made it clear how far his position had shifted in just six weeks, from deference to Radcliffe to veiled disdain. 'I don't think it is necessary to attach much importance to London's reaction,' he reassured Perdigão. 'It's an open secret that a game of chess is going on. In the near future the general position regarding Nubar and Radcliffe is bound to clarify itself one way or another, and that is when we will take final steps ... if the opposition becomes too overt then we will just have to ignore it.'[38] Kevork approved of the negotiations for the export of the art.[39] Considering that he had been the first to suspect that Perdigão intended 'to swallow the Foundation (with the help of and at the instigation of Salazar) for Portugal', Kevork's shift of position is difficult to explain.[40] Described by his son as 'a born second in command', Kevork may simply have left Gulbenkian's orbit to join Perdigão's. Standing over six feet tall, Perdigão was a confident and highly charismatic individual. After thirty-five years of being Gulbenkian's loyal understudy and enduring Nubar's bullying, it may have been rather inspiring to be told by Perdigão that 'you, my dear friend, and I, we are the only persons fully competent and fully authorised to carry out the provisions of the late Mr. C. S. Gulbenkian'.[41]

With Kevork and the Portuguese government behind him, Perdigão wrote to Radcliffe in a much firmer tone: 'My relationship of so many years with Mr Gulbenkian gave me the exact notion of the interest he had

for his Foundation.' It was a truly remarkable claim to make to the man
Gulbenkian himself had repeatedly identified as the person who knew his
intentions best. Radcliffe's response was to walk away. In May 1956 he notified Perdigão of his intention to resign. A press release was issued. On 18
July 1956 the Calouste Gulbenkian Foundation was duly established by
decree law, which stipulated a Portuguese majority.[42] Perdigão appointed
three fellow Portuguese to the board, as well as Whishaw. As Perdigão's
secretary remarked to the American ambassador, it had been 'a personal
victory of Perdigão, all the more remarkable ... in that it was effected
without scandal'.[43]

For Ekserdjian, Radcliffe had been 'the biggest disappointment of all'.
In contrast to Nubar and Kevork, Ekserdjian had expected more of Radcliffe, 'and I think the old man did too'. Radcliffe had missed his chance to
'come down off his pedestal and get into the fight, using the press, public
opinion and so on'. He had ceded the high ground to Perdigão by 'talking
of his own emoluments'.[44] As Radcliffe put it to Nubar in May 1956, 'on
top of other things' new tax rules had 'put the lid on it for me, because
[they] so much disimprove my personal position'.[45] Portuguese ministerial
correspondence suggests that Ekserdjian was correct: Radcliffe had more
leverage than he knew, given Salazar's fears of 'international repercussions'.
The Portuguese had not expected him to go quietly.

After all, 'national prestige' cut both ways: while it supported the
Portuguese government's case for a Portuguese majority on the board, it
also suggested that the foundation's leadership would be scrutinised by
outside observers. Months after Radcliffe's resignation, Pereira reminded
Salazar of one of Radcliffe's parting remarks: Radcliffe stated that those
who ended up administering the foundation 'would be tested'.[46] Pereira
himself would be among those 'tested'. Like Mathias and Correia, Perdigão
would later appoint Pereira a trustee of the foundation.

Perdigão, Nubar and Kevork had each been something of a 'disappointment', too. But Gulbenkian had demanded less of them than he had
of his 'great friend' Radcliffe. It is Gulbenkian himself, however, whose
actions and inaction ultimately brought this remarkable situation about.
As early as August 1955 Ekserdjian had, with his usual insight and detachment, detected a certain irony in the general predicament:

> [Gulbenkian] so distrusted all those around him that he did not consult
> any of them about his will and turned to a comparatively strange – and

as it seems none too honest – Port[uguese] Lawyer. Obsessed with protecting his fortune from the feared depredations of his family and friends (if he can be said to have had any), of his partners and of the gov[ernmen]ts to whose benevolence he owes it, he failed to take the most elementary measures to protect it against the greed and corruption of the dictatorial régime which he disregarded and forgot to fear. There will be a certain divine justice in it if the whole lot is pinched by the Portuguese – but what a tragedy from the point of view of what good might have been done.[47]

Gulbenkian had certainly not observed his own mantra of 'check, check, check' when it came to Portuguese law. When Perdigão gave his interpretations regarding the question of *renvoi*, Gulbenkian had noted the inconsistency. Rather than consulting another lawyer or insisting that Perdigão 'check, check, check', he let the matter drop. Gulbenkian also failed to recognise that there was very little by way of a precedent for the international foundation he intended to establish. Radcliffe and Van Kleffens had no precedents to refer to when Salazar and Caetano asked them to give an example of a foundation with an international board. By failing to take steps to elaborate his vision, Gulbenkian left his legacy exposed.

In the preamble Salazar wrote to the 1956 decree law and in Perdigão's speeches as president of the Gulbenkian Foundation there are repeated references to the trust that Gulbenkian had placed in Portugal.[48] In a sense they were right. Whether this can be taken as a compliment, however, is far from clear. As Van Kleffens noted, Portugal was another Panama or Liechtenstein as far as Gulbenkian was concerned. 'He thought he could use them for tax-dodging purposes,' Ekserdjian remarked, 'and that they w[oul]d be content with a few crumbs. Instead they have grabbed the lot and have thus managed to levy a 100% Death Duty.'[49]

Ekserdjian was, of course, exaggerating. In the first three years of its existence, Portugal secured 45 per cent of the foundation's grants, not 100 per cent (this percentage rose dramatically in later years, admittedly). Writing to Radcliffe just a few months before, Van Kleffens recognised that the Gulbenkian legacy was too large and extensive to be 'pinched' or 'grabbed' as easily or as definitively as Ekserdjian's caricature suggested. The foundation, Van Kleffens observed, 'is going to operate with the eyes of the world on it':

What it does or omits will also reflect on Portugal, for better or for worse, most especially if the Portuguese Government intervenes directly or more discreetly, through its nationals in the affairs of the Foundation, or subjects it to unreasonable contributions or limitations. Such things can always be ferreted out by a clever reporter. Portugal has a great opportunity here, but also a terrible choice: according to what it cho[o]ses its prestige in the world will go up or down. The story does not end with it having been chosen as the seat of the Foundation. That was only the beginning; whether the honour will finally give Portugal credit depends entirely on the way it uses the honour. All friends of Portugal will hope and expect that it will choose wisely.[50]

* * *

Nubar continued to defend his father's original vision. He accepted an invitation to become a trustee in May 1956, only to back out – wisely, as it turned out, as Perdigão saw the offer as 'virtually a trap'. Once brought inside, Perdigão argued, Nubar could be 'strangled and suffocated'.[51] The next year Nubar sued the foundation trustees, noting that the increased salaries they had awarded themselves were excessive relative to those paid by other charities. Two years later he made his case on John Freeman's well-known BBC television programme *Face to Face*.[52] As always, Nubar's motivations were not entirely disinterested. Like Kevork, he was looking to the foundation to allow him to commute the trust established by the will into a lump-sum payment. A settlement between Nubar and the foundation was achieved in 1958, and Nubar dropped his case against the trustees the following year.[53]

Nubar did not let his dispute with the foundation stop him from enjoying the rest of his life to the full. He continued to cultivate a somewhat shallow celebrity as a fabulously wealthy bon viveur, chauffeured around London in a converted London taxi, riding to hounds from his Buckinghamshire estate and estivating at Eden Roc. For British Pathé News, his monocle, beard, bushy eyebrows and orchid buttonhole were gifts which kept on giving, adding an exotic note to car and agricultural shows, state visits, Ascot and international cooking competitions.[54] In 1967 society photographer Patrick, 5th Earl of Lichfield, assembled a group of celebrities for a portrait of 'Swinging London': Nubar was front and centre, surrounded by Susannah York, David Hockney and Roman

Polanski.[55] If Calouste had thought Nubar's fondness for monogrammed Russian cigarettes *rastaquouère*, it is perhaps just as well that he was spared the spectacle of conspicuous consumption which only ended with Nubar's death in 1972.

Rita settled in Paris and kept a lower profile, refusing to get drawn into her brother's disputes with the foundation and continuing to enjoy a lively social life. In 1958 she was elected president of the Gourmettes de France. She published two slim volumes of poetry in French before her death in 1977.[56] Her husband, Kevork, remained in Portugal and helped administer the small share of foundation money allotted to Armenian causes. After military service in the British Army their son, Mikhael, had spent several years working for IPC, at his grandfather's insistence. With Gulbenkian's death he was free to blaze his own trail, training as a barrister, marrying and starting a family of his own. None of the Essayans settled in Portugal. Robert Gulbenkian, Calouste's nephew, did, and several of his children went on to work for the Gulbenkian Foundation.

The early years of the foundation had been challenging. Under Perdigão's close supervision, the foundation built a massive modernist complex on a former fairground in the north of Lisbon. This complex included a museum to house the founder's collection, a concert hall, art library, conference centre and spacious offices. It opened in 1969 and remains Lisbon's pre-eminent cultural centre. A scientific institute opened in Oeiras in 1961. Under the dictatorship, the foundation provided the Portuguese people with a window on the outside world, through concerts, travel scholarships and its fleet of mobile libraries. In those troubled early years, Salazar had thought of replacing Perdigão with Pereira. In time, however, he came to appreciate Perdigão's achievement. 'We must do justice to Azeredo Perdigão,' he wrote in his diary. 'The foundation directed by him constitutes an admirable Ministry of Culture.'[57]

And what of Gulbenkian's other legacy, his 'house'? IPC's response to the death of its founder was muted, almost offensively so. At the board meeting held on 2 September 1955 it was noted 'with regret' that Gulbenkian had died, but there were no condolences extended, no moment's silence and nobody stood as a mark of respect. Though Gulbenkian had rarely attended meetings himself (preferring to send alternates), he had been a board member for forty-three years. Perhaps the 'philosopher' would have appreciated the fact that poor old Hacobian received far more by way of a send-off when he died in 1962, after seven years of service.[58]

Along with Gulbenkian's collections and the majority of his investment portfolio, the foundation also received Pandi, the holding company through which Gulbenkian held his famous 5 per cent. Thanks to the opening of the Kirkuk–Banias pipeline (1952) and another line from Basra to Fao (on the Persian Gulf), Pandi's Iraq-based revenues increased dramatically in the 1950s. In 1958 a military coup saw the end of the Iraqi monarchy, and the violent murder of Nuri al-Said and King Faisal II. The first prime minister of the Republic of Iraq, Abd al-Karim Qasim, put pressure on IPC to relinquish some of its territory (which covered the whole of Iraq). In 1960 he invited leaders of other oil-producing nations to a conference in Baghdad, where they formed OPEC.

Although the Iraqis stripped it of all its undeveloped lands, IPC continued operations until 1972, when it was nationalised. Its subsidiary, Basrah Petroleum, was nationalised a year later. While the Yom Kippur War and other external events played their part, IPC was as much a victim of its own internal dissensions as anything else.[59] Pandi's Portuguese identity afforded little protection. In stripping it of its 5 per cent in Basrah Petroleum, Iraq Law 101 of 20 December 1973 characterised Portugal as 'a racist state which perpetrates violent acts of terrorism and annihilation against the peoples of Africa fighting for their liberty and independence'.[60]

There were other IPC subsidiaries, however, operating in other parts of the red-line area. While some were liquidated within a few years of Gulbenkian's death, others remained active.[61] IPC had secured the concessions to Oman and Abu Dhabi in 1937 and 1939 respectively. Exploratory drilling only began in the 1950s. Oil was struck in the Abu Dhabi concession in 1960, but Oman proved so challenging that several of Pandi's IPC partners pulled out. In the 1970s 60 per cent of Pandi's 5 per cent holdings in Oman were nationalised, leaving it with 2 per cent. Persistence, however, paid off. That 2 per cent of what became Petroleum Development Oman has proved extremely profitable.

In January 2014 the onshore Abu Dhabi concession, the last of the Gulbenkian-era concessions, expired. Pandi has been transformed into Partex Oil and Gas, a small upstream oil company which survives to this day, and which has invested some of the proceeds from earlier concessions in joint ventures in former Portuguese colonies. Partex is fully owned by the Calouste Gulbenkian Foundation. Valued at just over €500 million, its interests represent around a sixth of the foundation's €3 billion asset portfolio. This endowment places the foundation thirty-sixth in the list of the world's wealthiest foundations, a few places below the Rockefeller Foundation. While similar foundations in the United States are required to draw down 5 per cent of their capital each year, it faces no such obligation. It intends to be a perpetual foundation, a permanent legacy to its founder, Calouste Sarkis Gulbenkian.

GULBENKIAN'S WEALTH

Calculating Gulbenkian's wealth is fiendishly difficult. Throughout his adult life he was trading oil and mining shares as well as other equities, securities, gold and currencies. From the 1920s onwards this activity was moved offshore, and by Gulbenkian's death he controlled a network of interlocking holding companies based predominantly in Liechtenstein. The shares of TPC/IPC were never traded, so the value of his 5 per cent is difficult to ascertain. The figures below should be considered rough estimates.

Year	Raw (£m)	2015 RPI (£m)	2015 Economic Power/ Share of GDP UK (£m)
1894	0.25	26	321
1898	0.12	12	132
1932	2.7	169	1,223
1951	13	368	1,678
1955	201	4,756	19,410

Notes

1. All historical conversions are made using Lawrence Officer and Samuel H. Williamson's Purchasing Power Calculator, acccessible online at www.measuringworth.com.
2. Estimates for 1894 and 1898 do not include the value of S. & S. Gulbenkian Frères, Sarkis Gulbenkian Fils, C. & G. Gulbenkian or other Gulbenkian family firms.
3. 1898 estimate does not include balances or liabilities in Gulbenkian's joint accounts with Horatio Bottomley, Whitaker Wright and brokers.
4. 1932 estimate does not include Gulbenkian's 5 per cent share in IPC, which had yet to show a profit.
5. 1951 and 1955 estimates include a valuation for Gulbenkian's share in IPC, calculated using a profits/earning ratio based on Jersey Standard's valuation of Gulbenkian's 5 per cent made in 1947, in a private communication to Anglo-Persian, as well as profit figures from CFP's annual reports given in Zuhayr Mikdashi, *A Financial Analysis of Middle Eastern Oil Concessions: 1901–1965* (New York: Frederick A. Praeger, 1966).

— APPENDIX 2 —

GULBENKIAN'S FAMILY TREE

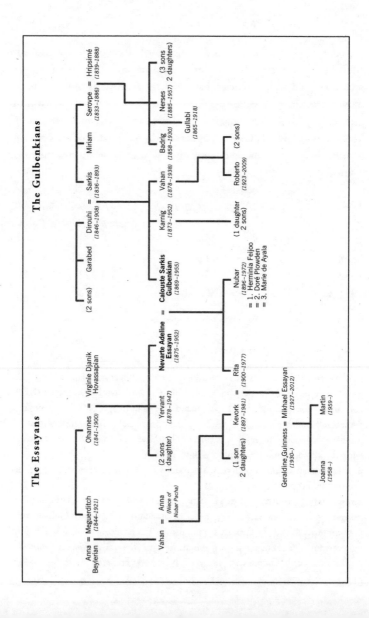

NOTES

LIS   Gulbenkian Foundation, Lisbon Office Files
MBZ   Foreign Ministry, Brussels
MCG   Calouste Gulbenkian Foundation, Museum Files
memcon Memorandum of Conversation
NARA   National Archives and Records Administration II, College Park, MD
NGA   National Gallery of Art, Washington, DC
OBA   Ottoman Bank Archive, Istanbul
PIO   Nubar Gulbenkian, *Portrait in Oil: The Autobiography of Nubar*
        Gulbenkian (New York: Simon & Schuster, 1965)
PRES   Gulbenkian Foundation, Presidencia Files
PRS   Gulbenkian Foundation, Paris Office Files
RGAE   Russian State Archive of Economy, Moscow
SHA   Shell Historical Archive, The Hague
SJP   Vasco Graça Moura (ed.), *Saint-John Perse Calouste Gulbenkian*
        Correspondance 1946–54 (Paris: Gallimard, 2013)
SLA   Shell London Archive, The Hague
SM   Science Museum Archives, Swindon
TA   Tate Archive, London
TBA   The Baring Archive, London
TNA   The National Archives, Kew
TT   Torre do Tombo National Archive, Lisbon

Introduction: Drawing the Line

1. Ralph Hewins, *Mr Five Per Cent: The Biography of Calouste Gulbenkian* (London: Hutchinson, 1957), p. 141.

2. William Stivers, *Supremacy and Oil: Iraq, Turkey, and the Anglo-American World Order, 1918–1930* (Ithaca, NY: Cornell University Press, 1982), p. 128. Stivers even claims in the same passage that Gulbenkian had no 'capital resources'.

3. Daniel Yergin, *The Prize: The Epic Quest for Oil, Money, and Power* (New York: Free Press, 1991), pp. 557–8. See also Geoffrey Jones, *The State and the Emergence of the British Oil Industry* (London: Macmillan, 1981), p. 20. For a similar assessment, see Gregory P. Nowell, *Mercantile States and the World Oil Cartel, 1900–1939* (Ithaca, NY: Cornell University Press, 1994), p. 66.

4. http://www.aljazeera.com/indepth/opinion/2016/05/iraq-sykes-picot-percent-oil-160515065650996.html.

5. CSG, 'Memorandum to be read to Mr Nichols', 20 June 1925. LDN00866. For context, see Peter J. Beck, '"A Tedious and Perilous Controversy": Britain and the Settlement of the Mosul Dispute, 1918–26', *Middle Eastern Studies*, 17:2 (April 1981), 256–76.

Chapter 1: Istanbul, 1896

1. In 1869 the Gulbenkians were living in Üsküdar, also on the Asian side, moving to Kadıköy by 1873. Calouste was reportedly baptised in Surp Haç, in Üsküdar. Fire later destroyed the church's registers, however, and the only scholar to record a date of birth or baptism does not give his sources. Kevork Pamukçiyan, *Zamanlar, Mekanlar ve İnsanlar* (Istanbul: Aras Yayıncılık, 2003), pp. 37–8. For claims that Calouste had a sister, Haiganush (of whom no other trace remains), see ibid., p. 40. See also Pamukçiyan's edition of Drtad Kahana Oughourlian, *Badmoutiun Gulbenkian Kertastani* (Antilias: Gatoghigosoutiun Medzi Dann Giligio, 2006).

2. Razmik Panossian, *The Armenians: From Kings and Priests to Merchants and Commissars* (New York: Columbia University Press, 2006), pp. 84–5; Philip Mansel, *Constantinople: City of the World's Desire* (London: John Murray 1995), App. 1.

3. Sarkis's father, Gullabi, was cousin to Dirouhi's father, Krikor. Gullabi and Krikor were sons of brothers Gulbenk and Garabed Gulbenkian.

4. Fatma Müge Göçek, *Rise of the Bourgeoisie, Demise of Empire: Ottoman Westernization and Social Change* (Oxford: Oxford University Press, 1996), p. 96.

5. *Jehri* (*Reseda luteola*) is known in English as dyer's weed. Richard G. Hovannisian (ed.), *Armenian Kesaria/Kayseri and Cappadocia* (Costa Mesa, CA: Mazda, 2013), pp. 237 (population), 238 note 19 (Gulbenkians and *jehri*); Sarkis Teke, personal communication, 21 November 2013.

6. Gertrude Bell, *Amurath to Amurath* (London: William Heinemann, 1911), p. 354.

7. Sokratis Mouratoglou (b. Talas 1895), cited in Hovannisian (ed.), *Armenian Kesaria*, p. 249 note 60.

8. Mansel, *Constantinople*, App. 1.

9. CSG to Cavid, 1 December 1923. LDN00519.

10. For an American perspective on Talas, see the reports of missionaries the Reverend James and Carrie Fowle (1894–1900) and Stella Loughridge (1901–17), who ran the American school. Houghton Library, Cambridge, Mass. American Board of Commissioners for Foreign Missions Archive, 16.9.4 (Fowles); 9.5.1, files 14–15 (Fowles) and 77.1, Box 45 (Loughridge).

11. Alan Duben and Cem Behar, *Istanbul Households: Marriage, Family and Fertility, 1880–1940* (Cambridge: Cambridge University Press, 1991), pp. 206, 209.

12. James Forsyth, *The Caucasus: A History* (Cambridge: Cambridge University Press, 2013), pp. 277–9.

13. For one example, see 'The Armenian Atrocities', *Northern Echo*, 31 December 1894.

14. Henry C. Barkley, *A Ride through Asia Minor and Armenia* (London: John Murray, 1891), pp. 137, 145, 154 (quote).

15. Ralph Hewins, *Mr Five Per Cent: The Biography of Calouste Gulbenkian* (London: Hutchinson, 1957), p. 20.

16. Archag Alboyadjian, *Les Dadian*, translated by Anna Naguib Boutros-Ghali (Cairo: Dar Al Maaref, 1965), pp. 112, 124; Dorothy George, *Merchants in Exile: The Armenians in Manchester, England, 1835–1935* (Princeton, NJ: Gomidas Institute, 2002), pp. 104, 105, 108.

Chapter 2: Marseille, London and Baku, 1883–8

1. SG to Hagop Selian, 17 January 1885. LIS00416, f. 149. Confirmed by Chanet, p. 20, presumably on the basis of CSG's own account.

2. SG to CSG, 15 December 1883. LIS00416, f. 4.

3. SG to Alfred Clayton Cole, 19 August 1884, SG to CSG, 27 September 1884. LIS00416, ff. 14, 24. A William Cole (b. 1857), son of Samuel Cole of Haverhill, Essex, attended the school in 1873–4.

4. King's College School Archive, Wimbledon. The register incorrectly gives 'American College, Constantinople' as Gulbenkian's previous school.

5. SG to CSG, 8 November 1884. LIS00416, f. 59.

6. CSG, cited in SG to CSG, 25 April 1885. LIS00416, f. 202.

7. Frank Miles and Graeme Cranch, *King's College School: The First 150 Years* (London: KCS, 1979), p. 133.

8. For the Bourdas case, see KCL Archives, KA/IC/B79; for building plans, see K/PHI/2/4.

9. Miles and Cranch, *King's College School*, pp. 134–7.

10. Thomas Hinde, *A Great Day School in London: A History of King's College School* (London: KCS, 1995), p. 35.

11. Belcher to J. W. Cunningham, n.d. [before September 1884] and 24 September 1884, KCL Archives, KA/IC/B77. See also Agnes Quidd, 'Katakaua's Hawaiian Studies Abroad Programme', *Hawaiian Journal of History*, 22 (1988), 170–207.

12. According to CSG's account to NME many years later. ED, 19 June 1951.

13. SG to Miriam and Khosrov Balian, 30 September 1884; SG to CSG, 7 October 1884. LIS00416, ff. 33, 40.

14. SG to CSG, 20 January 1885. LIS00416, f. 104.

15. SG to CSG, 14 October 1884. LIS00416, f. 43.

16. SG to CSG, 2 December 1884. LIS00416, f. 86.

17. SG to Baxter (W. H. Cole & Co.), 12 December 1884. LIS00416, f. 104.

18. SG and Dirouhi Gulbenkian to Hagop Selian, 30 December 1884; SG to CSG, 27 December 1884, 6, 10, 13 and 17 January 1885. LIS00416, ff. 120, 132, 136, 140, 145, 157.

19. Belcher to Cunningham, 10 January 1885. KCL Archives, KA/IC/B80. KA-E-E5, f. 230.

20. SG to CSG, 18 and 21 October, n.d. [early November] and 15 November 1884. LIS00416, ff. 45, 48, 52, 64.

21. CSG to [A. C.] Cole, 27 July 1885. LIS00416, ff. 212, 213v.

22. *Calendar of King's College, London, for 1885–6* (London: KCL, 1885), p. 182.

23. *Calendar ... for 1886–7* (London: KCL, 1886), pp. 239–40; *Calendar ... for 1887–8*, p. 222. He first appears among the associates in *Calendar ... for 1888–9* (London: KCL, 1888), p. 620.

24. Advanced certificates were administered by the Department of Science and Art, based in London's South Kensington. Of the 14,001 candidates, Gulbenkian came eighteenth. CGF, GuiaD2/003.

25. Ralph Hewins, *Mr Five Per Cent: The Biography of Calouste Gulbenkian* (London: Hutchinson, 1957), p. 14. As Ekserdjian noted, 'He is proud – and rightly – of having studied under Kelvin and Rutherford and having been made an AKC of King's, London "with distinction".' ED, 10 June 1950.

26. 'John Millar Thomson', *Obituary Notices of Fellows of the Royal Society*, 1:2 (1933), 91–4.

27. 'Herbert Tomlinson', *Obituary Notices of Fellows of the Royal Society*, 1:2 (1933), 89.

28. Herbert Tomlinson, 'The Scientific Papers of Herbert Tomlinson', KCL Archives, C/PP4.

29. The claim that Gulbenkian made the journey in 1889 is incorrect, as he describes himself rushing to Tbilisi in order to be there for the visit of Tsar Alexander III, who arrived on 29 September 1888, and did not return in 1889 or 1890.

30. Calouste S. Gulbenkian, *Transcaucasia and the Apcheron Peninsula: Travel Memories*, translated by Caroline Beamish (Lisbon: Calouste Gulbenkian Foundation, 2011), p. 33.

31. Alexandre Dumas, *Le Caucase: impressions du voyage* (Montreal: Le Joyeux Roger, 2006); Théophile Gautier, *Constantinople* (Paris: Michel Levy Frères, 1853).

32. G. Perrot to CSG, 25 July, 20 October 1890 and 8 June 1891 (quote). EP.

33. Gautier, *Constantinople*, p. 6.

34. In 1912 one of the founders of the Merchant Bank of Tiflis [Tbilisi] was a certain 'S. Giulbenkyan'. Khachatur Dadayan, 'Armenian Commercial Presence in Tiflis', *21st Century*, 2:4 (2008), 69–89 (78).

35. For Mantashev, see ibid., 85–6.

36. Gulbenkian, *Transcaucasia and the Apcheron Peninsula*, p. 185.

37. V. S. Ziv, *Inostrannye kapitaly v russkoj neftjanoj promyshlennosti* (St Petersburg: Tip. Red. perīodicheskikh izd. Ministerstva finansov, 1916), p. 1.

38. For Branobel, see Budar N. Seidov, *Arkhivy Bakinsski Neftyanykh Firm: XIX–Nachalo XX veka* (Moscow: Modest Kolerov, 2009), pp. 38–44; Robert W. Tolf, *The Russian Rockefellers. The Saga of the Nobel Family and the Russian Oil Industry* (Stanford, CA: Hoover Institution Press, 1976).

39. See Bertrand Gilles, 'Capitaux français et pétroles russes (1884–1914)', *Histoire des entreprises*, 12 (1963), 9–95. In anglo- and francophone literature (Daniel Yergin's *The Prize*, for example) scholars frequently refer to 'BNITO' when they mean to refer to the Société Caspienne de la Mer Noire. 'Bnito' is not, in fact, the acronym of the latter Rothschild-controlled firm, but of the Batumi firm they originally acquired: Batumskoye Neftepromyshlennoye i Torgovoye Obschestvo.

40. Rothschilds charged 6 per cent interest when Russian banks charged 10 per cent. Seidov, *Arkhivy Bakinsski Neftyankykh Firm*, p. 104.

41. Daniel Yergin, *The Prize: The Epic Quest for Oil, Money, and Power* (New York: Free Press, 1991), pp. 23, 26 (quote), 35.

42. Ibid., p. 45.

43. Whether it was invented by Mendeleyev, Shukhov, Gavrolov or Burton is disputed. See Miryusif Babayev, *Concise History of Azerbaijani Oil* (3rd edn, Baku: privately printed, 2010), p. 84; Geoffrey Jones, *The State and the Emergence of the British Oil Industry* (London: Macmillan, 1981), p. 3.

44. Jones, ibid.

45. Ibid., p. 51.

46. Gulbenkian, *Transcaucasia and the Apcheron Peninsula*, p. 189.

47. Ibid., pp. 191 ('shower'), 178 ('dazzling').

Chapter 3: Young Man in a Hurry, 1889–96

1. CSG to NAE, n.d. [summer 1889]. EP.

2. Istanbul Branch to Cellurier, 12 April 1893. Crédit Agricole, Paris. Fonds Crédit Lyonnais, DAE2288.

3. Arsen Yarman, *Osmanlı sağlık hizmetlerinde Ermeniler ve Surp Pırgiç Ermeni Hastanesi tarihi* (Istanbul: Ermeni Hastanesi Vakfi, 2001), p. 506.

4. Quoted in NAE to CSG, n.d. [September 1891]. EP.

5. Among the personal effects of CSG preserved in the Gulbenkian Foundation in Lisbon is a silver platter engraved with NAE's and CSG's monograms beneath the dates 'June 5th 1889–Nov' 18th 1891'. It seems reasonable to assume that this commemorates the gap separating the first and second proposals of marriage.

6. NAE to CSG, n.d. [summer 1890]. EP.

7. Essai Essayan took British citizenship in 1871. Working on the assumption that he applied as soon as the required five years' residence was complete (as Gulbenkian and many other Armenians did), we can presume he arrived in 1866.

8. *Slater's Royal National Commercial Directory of Manchester and Salford* (Manchester: Slater, 1867), p. 178. Joan George claims that the Essayans arrived in Manchester in the late 1840s from Izmir. There are no Essayans listed in *Slater's* directory for 1863, nor do any Essayans appear in the 1861 census. Joan

George, *Merchants in Exile: The Armenians in Manchester, England, 1835–1935* (Princeton, NJ: Gomidas Institute, 2002), p. 9.

9. A. Mantashev is first listed in *Slater's* directory in 1869, Pervanoglou and Karayoussoufoglu in 1874, Manoukian, Elizarian, G. Essayan and P. & E. Mosditchian in 1876. 'Shaum' also appears as 'Shahum' and 'Shamum'.

10. Nevarte's grandfather Kevork Essayan (not to be confused with her son-in-law of the same name) married an Anna Mosditchian.

11. George, *Merchants in Exile*, pp. 24–5.

12. The 1871 census found him boarding with Henry Pendleton, a joiner in Huyton-cum-Roby, Merseyside. He appears as a married merchant born in Istanbul.

13. Ohannes Essayan to Virginie Essayan, 24 July, 4, 11 and 20 August (weather) 1874. PRS00897.

14. The description of Ohannes Essayan is from notes taken during an interview with Aram Frenkian, son of Nevarte's sister Anna. I am grateful to Melinée Frenkian for sharing these with me. For Virginie Essayan, see NAE to CSG, n.d. [Monday]. EP.

15. Family album. EP.

16. E. Sweeney to CSG, 26 and 31 March and 4 November 1891. EP.

17. C. S. Gulbenkian, 'Voyages dans les pays des tapis d'Orient', *Levant Herald and Eastern Express*, 25 May 1889.

18. CSG to P. Würzburger, 21 January 1889. EP.

19. For an example of a more successful Caucasus travelogue, see Charles Marvin, *The Region of the Eternal Fire* (London: W. H. Allen, 1884).

20. CSG to NAE, n.d. [after 3 March 1891]. EP.

21. NAE to CSG, n.d. and n.d. ('Jeudi'). EP.

22. NAE to CSG, n.d. ('Lundi'). 'Z.' may have been the Zareh referred to in NAE to CSG, n.d. ('Friday morning'). EP.

23. NAE to CSG, 19 August 1891. EP.

24. NAE to CSG, 3 September 1891 (Ohannes), n.d. [1891] (blackmail), n.d. [August 1891] (stalking). EP.

25. NAE to CSG, n.d. [August 1891]. EP.

26. CSG to NAE, 23 August [1891?]. EP.

27. NAE to CSG, n.d., and 'H. Leonardi' [CSG] to 'Mrs C. James' [NAE], n.d. EP.

28. NAE to CSG, n.d. [November?] 1891. EP.

29. NAE to CSG, 31 August 1891. EP.

30. CSG to NAE, 8 February and 19 April 1892. EP.

31. CSG to NAE, 16 February 1892. EP.

32. CSG to NAE, 14 February ('aristocratic'), 12 March (hospital) and 23 April (flat) 1892. EP. For 'flats' in London, see Jonathan Conlin, *Tales of Two Cities* (London: Atlantic, 2013), Ch. 1.

33. When Nubar began making problems over Nevarte's will shortly after her death, Gulbenkian was considering countering, somewhat legalistically, that owing to

this lack of civil registration 'from a European point of view, we were not legally married'. CSG to JAP, 7 August 1952. CGF, CSCSA00234.

34. CSG's uncle Hagop Selian officiated as best man. CSG's parents were back in Istanbul by July. SG to Miriam Selian, 4 July 1892. LIS00416, f. 393.

35. Chanet, p. 17.

36. *Post Office Directory* (1892), pp. 310–11, 1009. Gulbenkian may have moved in in January 1891, as a letter from Chabert congratulates him on finding new London office accommodation. Chabert to CSG, 24 January 1891. EP.

37. Like his elder brother, Karnig stayed with the Selians in Marseille. SG to Garabed Gulbenkian, 4 October 1888; SG to Dirouhi Gulbenkian, 12 September 1889. LIS00416, ff. 278v, 326.

38. SG to CSG, 23 December 1892. LIS00416, loose letter.

39. For CSG's *Guadalquivir* travel diary, see LIS00367. For Adana, see J. S. Warburton to CSG, 27 April 1893; SG to Harutyun Gulbenkian, 6 March 1886. LIS00416, loose letter and f. 214.

40. The ledgers of IOB in Istanbul show Sarkis Gulbenkian Fils making large withdrawals in 1895 (totalling more than £T 700,000) and no deposits. There was no further activity in 1896 and only one small payment in 1897. OBA, Caisse Ledgers, Mouvement des Fonds 1893–1897. See also LDN00922.

41. The list of shareholders prepared when the firm was wound up (shareholders receiving just 8s 4d per share) includes O. Essayan (450 shares) and O. & M. Essayan (960). Some of the former must have been held for relations, however, as Gulbenkian Frères and Vahan Essayan each received 100 shares in the new firm established from the ruins of the old. TNA, BT34/968/40698.

42. In the aftermath O. & M. Essayan appeared on a table of 'Principaux Comptes courants débiteurs', with £T 21,049 secured by 2,000 New Rietfontein shares, albeit with ample means to pay any debt. Archives nationales du monde du travail, 207AQ189. Though New Rietfontein declined from $6^{3/16}$ to $3^{15/16}$ between 2 and 29 October 1895, it was associated with Barnato, and acted as a 'bear' for the South African market. My thanks to Funda Soycal for this information.

43. The Gulbenkians sought to disavow Turabian's losses, and the resulting case between them and IOB went before the High Court in London in 1897. See OBA, XKLI-100/1005.

44. Vincent's associates at IOB took a more philosophical view, on the assumption that Vincent himself had (contrary to rumours which circulated subsequently) lost money in the crisis. Although they conceded that they should have monitored him more closely, they concluded that nobody could have predicted the crisis and that it would be foolish to risk alienating Vincent when he was the best man to wind down the positions the bank had adopted. Lander to Berger, 3 January 1896. Archives nationales du monde du travail, 207AQ151.

45. Richard Davenport-Hines and Jean-Jacques van Helten, 'Edgar Vincent, Viscount d'Abernon and the Eastern Investment Company in London, Constantinople and Johannesburg', *Business History*, 28:1 (1986), 35–61. For 'Armenian intrigue' see 'The Money Market', *The Times*, 2 November 1895.

46. For an eyewitness account, see Auboyneau to IOB London, 27 August 1896. OBA, CD-CLCA-001.

47. These included the *Adana*, *Tarsus* and *Hadide*, coal-powered vessels the Ottoman Navy admired and was trying to buy at the time. Navy Construction Commission Report, 6 January 1896, and Navy Council memo, 7 January 1896. BOA, Y.MTV 134/79.

48. His wife, Virginie, and his children Anna and Atvart are listed on the same passport. PRS00909.

49. The claim is made in a letter of 18 September 1896 from 'Une Groupe de Musulmans' to the MAE. AMAE, 75ADP/40.

50. For dragomans' reports on Commission hearings, see TNA, FO195/1928. One dragoman drew up figures (see Devey's report of 10 October 1896, in the above file) proving that far more Armenians than Muslims were being brought before the Commission. Those Muslims who did appear were rarely charged with anything worse than looting.

51. Adam Block to Herbert, 10 August 1896. TNA, FO195/1927.

52. Devey to Block, 1 October 1896. TNA, FO195/1928.

53. In 1896 the Ottoman security service believed Mantashev's tankers were being used to run guns to Armenian revolutionary groups. See BOA, HR.SYS 2770/29, DH.TMIK.M 27/35, A.}MKT.MHM 631/18 and Y.PRK.ESA 29/32.

54. Ralph Hewins, *Mr Five Per Cent: The Biography of Calouste Gulbenkian* (London: Hutchinson, 1957), p. 47.

55. Mantashev thanked Gulbenkian for sending a copy of *La Transcaucasie* in 1899. If the pair had met in 1896 and had Gulbenkian been seeking to establish a connection he would surely have presented him with a copy much earlier. Mantashev to CSG, 3 June 1899. LDN00023, f. 80.

56. NAE to CSG, n.d. [October 1891?]. EP.

57. NAE to CSG, n.d. ('Friday morning'). EP.

Chapter 4: Nothing More Than a Sport, 1897–1901

1. David Kynaston, *The City of London*, Vol. 2 *Golden Years, 1890–1914* (London: Chatto & Windus, 1995), p. 174.

2. See James G. D. Nye, 'The Company Promoter in London, 1877–1914', unpublished PhD dissertation, King's College London, 2011, pp. 207–39.

3. Geoffrey Jones, *Merchants to Multinationals: British Trading Companies in the Nineteenth and Twentieth Centuries* (Oxford: Oxford University Press, 2000), pp. 161–2.

4. Joint Stock Institute to CSG, 21 August 1897. LDN00034, f. 113. Bottomley to CSG, 19 November 1897. LDN00895, f. 96.

5. Bottomley to CSG, n.d. [February 1898]. LDN00895, f. 72.

6. Gulbenkian, 'Position Loans a/c to January 1901'. LDN00923.

7. The word 'holiday' is written in English. CSG to H. Malcolm, 13 February 1901. LDN00923, loose letter.

8. Bottomley to CSG, n. d. [February 1898]. LDN00895, f. 93.

9. 'R. D. T.' to CSG, 10 November 1897. LDN00895, f. 82.

10. NAE to CSG, 10 January (Nubar) and n.d. [early 1898] (bicycling). LDN00895.

11. NAE to CSG, n. d. [February 1899]. LDN00026, f. 48.

12. Seymour Hicks to CSG, 13 July 1898. LDN00895, f. 35.

13. Escoffier to CSG, 22 June 1898; César Ritz to CSG, 22 June 1898. LDN00895. Richard D'Oyly Carte to CSG, 31 May 1899. LDN00025, f. 101. CSG to 'John' [chef hired by Escoffier for CSG], 28 January 1902. LDN01480. Hilda Moody to CSG, 2 March 1899. LDN00025, f. 70. NAE to CSG, n.d. LDN00895. CSG to Virginie Essayan, 22 August 1905 (quote). LDN01500, ff. 33, 35.

14. CSG to Hall, 1 January 1900. LDN00019, f. 9.

15. Pride of Gwalia (Liquidator) to CSG, 19 February 1901. LDN00019. See also LDN00005.

16. Bottomley to CSG, 22 September 1903; CSG to Bottomley, 22 September 1903. LDN00974.

17. CSG to Case, 18 January 1902. LDN01480.

18. Georg Spies, *Erinnerungen eines Ausland-Deutschen* (1926; St Petersburg: Olearius, 2002), p. 228.

19. Geoffrey Jones, 'Frederick Lane', in David J. Jeremy (ed.), *Dictionary of Business Biography* (5 vols., London: Butterworth, 1984), Vol. 3, pp. 652–4.

20. Spies, *Erinnerungen eines Ausland-Deutschen*, p. 228.

21. Gulbenkian, 'Memoirs of Calouste Sarkis Gulbenkian', unpublished typescript (1945), pp. 5, 6. The earliest contact between Gulbenkian and Lane is a letter of 21 March 1898. LDN00012.

22. Indeed, Bottomley was an investor in the firm. Bottomley to C. G. Penney (Russian Industrial), 10 April 1899. LDN00021, f. 5.

23. Lane to CSG, 22 December 1899 and 9 January 1900. LDN00020, ff. 16, 18.

24. M. Ja. Gefter et al., 'O proniknovenii anglijskogo kapitala v neftjanuju promyshlennost' Rossii (1898–1902)', *Istoricheskij arkhiv*, 6 (1960); Xavchatur Dadayan, *Armiiani v Baku* (Erevan: Novabank, 2007), pp. 25, 28 (original figures in *pudi*).

25. Budar N. Seidov, *Arkhivy Bakinsski Neftyanykh Firm: XIX–Nachalo XX veka* (Moscow: Modest Kolerov, 2009), p. 118.

26. Presumably this was Beilby Lawley, 3rd Baron Wenlock (1849–1912), former Governor of Madras. Lane and Macandrew to CSG, 15 April 1898. LDN00895, f. 118.

27. Spies Stücken to Brunner & Co., 2 December 1898. LDN00027, f. 35.

28. The new company also took over the properties of Terek Syndicate. Lane to CSG, 10 and 25 October 1900. LDN00019, ff. 11, 3.

29. These fields were owned through the Byrd Syndicate, who later sold the Texas properties in order to focus on the Indiana ones. Grady to CSG, 23 February and 3 March 1899. LDN00023, ff. 14, 19. Grady to CSG, 14 May 1901. LDN00033, f. 22. Lane and Macandrew to CSG, 7 January 1898. LDN00034, f. 13.

30. Grady to CSG, 8 and 9 December 1898. LDN00023, ff. 21, 20.

31. Lane to CSG, 10 November 1900. LDN00035, f. 26.

32. For the agreement between Terek Syndicate, Gulbenkian, Georg Spies, Wilhelm von Ofenheim and Spies Stücken of 19 December 1900, see LDN00009. For Paris introduction, see Wilhelm von Ofenheim to CSG, 8 March 1901. LDN00006.

33. CSG was allotted 5,800 shares in Bibi-Eybat, whose shares proved difficult to place, and by 1901 Lane was advising him to sell. Lane and Macandrew to CSG, 5 November 1900 and 7 March 1901. LDN00033, ff. 59, 1. Boverton Redwood to CSG, 3 October 1900. LDN00009.

34. KSG to CSG, 18 May 1904. LDN00003. KSG to CSG, 4 August 1898. LDN00031. Serovpe Turabian to CSG, 29 November 1899. LDN00028, f. 18. Report on Tien-Sing [Tianjin], 16 April 1898. LDN00018, f. 3.

35. Harutyun Gulbenkian to Hovhannes C. Gulbenkian, 25 December 1897. LDN00034, f. 71.

36. Karnig wanted to shut Varna and move the staff to Bradford, where their mohair business needed sorting out. KSG to CSG, 8 March 1900. LDN00024, f. 105.

37. Ohannes Essayan to CSG, 21 April 1900. LDN00035, f. 10. KSG to CSG, 6 November 1899, 20 and 28 April 1900. LDN00028, ff. 79, 91, 92. For the Gulbenkians' commercial property in Varna and Devnya, see Hovassapian to CSG, 30 October 1898. LDN00007.

38. W. H. Cole & Co. to Sarkis Gulbenkian Fils (Istanbul), 5 January 1899. LDN00027, f. 62. W. H. Cole & Sons to CSG, 20 March 1899. LDN00023, f. 25. Dikran Turabian to CSG, 30 March 1899. For a full list, see LDN00023, f. 31.

39. KSG to CSG, 14 June and 23 July 1898. LDN00031. In 1914 Hagopian established that there was indeed some sort of warrant out for CSG (presumably on account of his being a 'fugitive' since 1896) but that, provided CSG paid a fine, the matter could be taken care of. Hagopian to CSG, 3 October 1914. LDN00072.

40. NAE to CSG, n.d. [March 1898?]. LDN00895.

41. Miriam Selian to CSG, 10 October 1899. LDN00028, f. 59.

42. KSG to CSG, 23 February 1899. KSG to CSG, 17 and 21 February 1900. LDN00028, ff. 92, 91. In Britain Vahan sought to register copyright for several photographs of famous actresses. TNA, H0405/17191.

43. Karnig Turabian to CSG, 7 February 1899. LDN00023. Sadly no packing list survives.

44. J. Mordaunt Crook, *The Rise of the Nouveaux Riches: Style and Status in Victorian and Edwardian Architecture* (London: John Murray, 1999), p. 62. For the distribution of bankers' residences in London, see Youssef Cassis, *City Bankers, 1890–1914*, translated by Margaret Rocques (Cambridge: Cambridge University Press, 1994), p. 245.

45. LDN02491.

46. LDN00975.

47. The changes were backdated to 1 January 1901. *London Gazette*, 31 May 1901. For copies of this and related papers, see LDN00922.

48. Garabed Gulbenkian to CSG, 12 April 1901. LDN00033, f. 31. Hagop Meldjian to CSG, 29 May 1900 (doubting CSG's ill-health). LDN00036, f. 45.

49. CSG to Hovhannes Gulbenkian, 7 June 1901. LDN00029, f. 57.

50. Garabed Gulbenkian to CSG, 24 September 1902. LDN00003. Meguerditch Essayan to CSG, 24 December 1903. LDN00002.

51. Cited in Kynaston, *Golden Years*, p. 339.

52. TNA, H0334/34/13044.

Chapter 5: Asiatic and European, 1902–8

1. The relevant chapter of Hewins's biography is entitled 'Factotum'. Ralph Hewins, *Mr Five Per Cent: The Biography of Calouste Gulbenkian* (London: Hutchinson, 1957), pp. 47–50.

2. George Philip, *The Political Economy of International Oil* (Edinburgh: Edinburgh University Press, 1994), p. 27.

3. Deutsche owned 50.4 per cent of EPU, the French Rothschilds 24 per cent, Nobel Brothers 20 per cent and the rest was held by the Belgian Waterkeyn group.

4. It is unclear why this attempt failed. See J. D. Archbold to John D. Rockefeller, 15 October 1901. Rockefeller Archive Center, Sleepy Hollow, NY. RG2C/115/864. Jonker and van Zanden suggest that Marcus Samuel feared bad publicity immediately before assuming the London mayoralty. HRDS, Vol. 1, pp. 68–72.

5. Lane had been chartering for Royal Dutch since at least 1898. The earliest letter between CSG and Deterding known to the present author dates from 1902. Sent to Deterding's home address, it seems to refer to personal investments CSG is managing on the latter's behalf. Lane to August Kessler, 11 May 1898; CSG to Deterding, 17 June 1902. SHA 3/208 and 3/160.

6. Daniel Yergin, *The Prize: The Epic Quest for Oil, Money, and Power* (New York: Free Press, 1991), p. 47.

7. HRDS, Vol. 1, pp. 65, 116; Geoffrey Jones, *The State and the Emergence of the British Oil Industry* (London: Macmillan, 1981), p. 209; [Stanley Naylor], *An International Oil Man* (London: Ivor Nicholson and Watson, 1934), p. 17.

8. HRDS, Vol. 1, p. 75.

9. Lane recognised Deterding's ambitious plans to use Asiatic and EPU to make Royal Dutch into the chief rival to Standard, but did not see them as feasible. Lane to Baer, 11 January 1906. ANMT, 132AQ155, 'Asiatic Correspondence 1906'.

10. CSG to Mantashev, 4 March 1903. LDN01616, ff. 23–8.

11. CSG to Goukasoff, 25 December 1901. LDN01479, tipped-in letter.

12. Unfortunately, the sources rarely specify which Goukasoff (Boghos, Abraham or Paul) they are referring to and it is unclear which attended this meeting. Lane to CSG, 27 December 1901. Abraham seems to have been envious of Gulbenkian's relationship with Mantashev. See CSG to Mantashev, 20 February 1903. LDN01614, ff. 480–87.

13. Lane to CSG, 25 and 29 August 1902. LDN00037.

14. Goukasoff to CSG, 29 November 1902. LDN00011.

15. Founded in November 1902 with £1 million capital, the Caucasian Petroleum Export Company was renamed Home Light in 1904. Jones, *The State and the Emergence of the British Oil Industry*, p. 36.

16. [Paul?] Goukasoff to CSG, 30 October 1901. LDN00001.

17. Christopher Rice, 'Party Rivalry in the Caucasus: Socialist Revolutionaries, Armenians and the Baku Union of Oil Workers, 1907–8', *Slavonic and East European Review*, 67:2 (April 1989), 228–43; Yergin, *The Prize*, p. 114.

18. Figures from Ronald W. Ferrier, *The History of the British Petroleum Company*, Vol. 1 *The Developing Years, 1901–1932* (Cambridge: Cambridge University Press, 1982), App. 0.1.

19. CSG to Lane, 5 April 1903. ANMT, 132AQ152, Folder 1. CSG to Lane, 3 April 1905 (quote). LDN01498. Lane to CSG, 19 December 1908. LDN00038.

20. Lane to Baer, 6 April 1903. ANMT, 132AQ152, Folder 1.

21. Lane to Baer, 20 October 1905. LDN00037.

22. ANMT, 132AQ216. In 1903 its capital was increased to 6.5 million Reichsmarks.

23. Baer to CSG, 1 December 1902. LDN00002.

24. HIDB, S1612.

25. Baer to CSG, 19 February 1903; CSG to Abraham Goukasoff, 21 February 1903. LDN00007. CSG to Mantashev, 20 February 1903. LDN01614, ff. 480–87. Wisely holding himself back, Mantashev told Gulbenkian and Tchigianoff to divide up the 10 per cent among themselves. Mantashev to CSG, 21 February 1903. Agreement was reached on 19 May 1903.

26. Deutsch-Rüssische to CSG, 16 February 1903. LDN00002.

27. Richard M. Francis, 'The British Withdrawal from the Bagdad Railway Project in April 1903', *Historical Journal*, 16:1 (March 1973), 168–78; Roger Adelson,

London and the Invention of the Middle East: Money, Power, and War, 1902–22 (New Haven: Yale University Press, 1995), pp. 40–41, 44–5.

28. Under the so-called Zander Concession. Dietrich Eichholtz, *Die Bagdadbahn, Mesopotamien und die deutsche Ölpolitik bis 1918* (Leipzig: Leipziger Universitätsverlag, 2007), pp. 22–5. For the Ottoman perspective, see BOA, Y.PRK.HH 35/44 and Y.MTV 260/15.

29. For an 1884 report of oil being found on properties recently acquired by the Sultan in Mosul *vilayet*, see BOA, Y.MTV 16/71. By an *irade* of 5 Chaban 1306 (8 April 1889) exclusive oil rights to the Sultan's lands in the *vilayet* of Mosul were granted to the Civil List. That of 5 Djamajul-Ewell 1316 (24 September 1898) did the same for the *vilayet* of Baghdad. See BP, 163011. For Agop's role, see Edgar Vincent to Philip Currie, 11 November 1889. BL, Add MS 48938, f. 61. The need for improved technology is highlighted in Es-Seyyid Hüseyin Galib to Sultan's Properties Commission, 2 June 1889. BOA, HH.THR 233/54. See also Albertine Jwaideh, 'The *Sanniya* Lands of Sultan Abdul Hamid II in Iraq', in George Makdisi, *Arabic and Islamic Studies in Honor of Hamilton A. R. Gibb* (Leiden: Brill, 1965), pp. 326–36.

30. Cesare Porro to Gwinner, 28 March 1905; Quandt to Gwinner, 23 May 1905; Huguenin to Gwinner, 4 September 1905. HIDB, OR1058.

31. Georg Spies, 'Exposé über die rumänische Organisation der "Steaua Romana"', 10 August 1904. HIDB, S1633.

32. The Deutsche Petroleum Aktiengesellschaft (DPAG), which in 1906 became Deutsche Petroleum Verkaufs-Gesellschaft (DPVG). Hans Pohl, 'Die Steuea Romana und die Deutsche Bank (1903–20)', in Hans Pohl (ed.), *Wirtschaft, Unternehmen, Kreditwesen, soziale Probleme* (2 vols., Stuttgart: Franz Steiner, 2005), Vol. 2, pp. 946–65.

33. Gwinner to Spies, 13 April 1904. HIDB, S1633.

34. 'F. Lane General Understanding Europe and England', n.d. [December 1904]. LDN00009.

35. Jones, *The State and the Emergence of the British Oil Industry*, p. 37. Lane and Gulbenkian struggled, however, to get Home Light to follow EPU's instructions. See Lane to CSG, 21 and 29 July 1908. LDN00012.

36. Spies to Gwinner, 29 May 1906. HIDB, S1633.

37. KSG to CSG, 1 May, 12 and 22 July 1904. LDN01492, f. 32.

38. Cited in Hovhannes C. Gulbenkian to CSG, 1 September 1908. LDN00016. See also CSG to Garabed Gulbenkian, 15 August 1904. LDN01494, f. 53.

39. Badrig Gulbenkian, 8 July ('fire') and 22 April (commercial prospects) 1904. LDN00003.

40. 'Avis officiel', *Moniteur oriental*, 30 April 1907: £19,900 of these debts were owed to branches in Beirut (Hovhannes C. Gulbenkian) and Mosul. Garabed Gulbenkian to CSG, 5 April 1907. LDN00016.

41. Bischoff & Co. to CSG, 24 May 1907. LDN00012.

42. See *İkdam*, 9 April 1907; 'Faillite des Sieurs Gulbenkian et Fils', *Moniteur oriental*, 17–30 April 1907. For Armenian coverage, see undated clippings from *Arevelk* and *Manzumei Kefikar*, OBA, XKLI-010/4215, and from *Byzantion* (10, 12 and 13 April 1907), LDN00043.

43. A collection from 1877 was sent by the French consul to Paris with a note explaining the risks they posed to the market. AN F^{12} 7189.

44. This had been remarked on by Karnig Gulbenkian. KSG to CSG, 8 February 1907. LDN00003.

45. Picu to Ministère du Commerce, 13 November 1907. AN, F^{12} 7279. In the case of C. & G. Gulbenkian, IOB certainly adopted a firm stance, refusing their request to appoint a voluntary liquidator and so avoid formal bankruptcy proceedings. Deffès and Nias to IOB London, 16 and 27 April 1907. OBA, CD-DPLCA-2, ff. 199, 222.

46. VSG to CSG, 2 September 1908. LDN00016.

47. VSG to CSG, 20 October 1905. LDN00003.

48. For the divorce, see TNA, J77/915/773 and 95 (consolidated). For VSG's other struggles, see Garabed Gulbenkian to CSG, 2, 17 January and 7 May 1908. LDN00016; Andreassian to CSG, 23 August, 12 and 15 September 1907. LDN00012.

49. KSG to CSG, 12 August 1904. LDN00003.

50. Garabed Gulbenkian to CSG, 12 August 1908. Badrig Gulbenkian to CSG, 19 and 22 August 1907. LDN00016. Garabed Garabedian to CSG, 8 July 1908, and CSG to Garabedian, 15 August 1908. LDN00015.

51. KSG to CSG, 22 December 1914. LDN00084.

52. CSG to Lane, 2 January 1902. LDN01479. For the Delaunay, see LDN00012.

53. This phrase is one Gulbenkian uses repeatedly in his letters to Karnig, without ever specifying what he understood by it. CSG to KSG, 3 and 28 September 1907. LDN01511, ff. 30–32, 77–8. CSG to KSG, 11 October 1907. LDN01512, f. 6.

54. CSG to Hagopoff, 18 April 1907. Gulbenkian blamed Badrig for the article in *Byzantion* of 12–13 April 1907. CSG to Vahan Essayan, 18 April 1907. LDN01509, ff. 11–12 (quote), 15–18. See also CSG to Hagopoff, 30 April 1907. Ibid., ff. 53–5.

55. Garabed Gulbenkian to CSG, 24 December 1903. LDN00003.

56. CSG to Fox, 21 January 1902. LDN01480, f. 36.

57. Camille Benoît to CSG, 18 December 1903. LDN00002.

58. D. C. Thomson (Agnews) to CSG, 17 December 1903. LDN00001. There is no evidence that CSG ever met BB, although he had bought a copy of the latter's *Duty and Criticism of Italian Art* in 1901. Henry Glaiser to CSG, 26 November 1901. LDN00003.

59. Stephen Duffy, 'French Eighteenth-Century Painting in England and the Opening of the Wallace Collection', in Christoph Vogtherr, Monica Preti

and Guillaume Faroult (eds), *Delicious Decadence: The Rediscovery of French Eighteenth-Century Painting in the Nineteenth Century* (Farnham: Ashgate, 2014), pp. 141–57 (153). When some of the Wallace's French furniture was regilded in 1933, CSG complained, to the fury of its curators. See TNA, AR1/340.

60. For 1901–3 correspondence with Lalique, see LDN00005. See also Maria Fernanda Passos Leite, *René Lalique at the Calouste Gulbenkian Museum* (Milan: Skira, 2008).

61. CSG to Charles Romer Williams, 1 June 1914. LDN00066.

62. For the earliest correspondence with Kevorkian (1897–8), see LDN00017. For his Persian dealings, see the correspondence with Bedros Mikaelian (1906) and B. Aghayantz (1907–8), both of Tehran. LDN00006 and LDN00012.

63. Maria D'Orey Capucho Queiroz Ribeiro, *Iznik Pottery and Tiles in the Calouste Gulbenkian Museum* (Lisbon: CGF, 2009), pp. 9–13.

64. *Byzantion*, 12 April 1907. LDN00043.

65. Gulbenkian's previous personal telegraphic addresses had been 'Aiglon', then 'Mimula'. CSG to Dawkins, 8 May 1907. LDN01509.

Chapter 6: Young Turks, 1908–14

1. For purchases around Adana, see Kerovpe Gulbenkian to CSG, 9 December 1908. LDN00016. For a 21,000 *dunum* farm at Mutevelli (near Manisa), bought from Serko Baliozian for £T 10,000, see A. Apikian to CSG, 1 December 1908. LDN00012; CSG to M. Essayan, 29 April 1909. LDN02052. A *dunum* is forty-four square *arsheens*, an *arsheen* approximately thirty-three inches.

2. Among the companies brought under Royal Dutch-Shell's control in 1910–13 were Standard Russe (also known as 'Russostand'), North Caucasian Oil Fields, Grozny-Sundja, New Schibaieff and Ural Caspian. J. B. Aug. Kessler, 'Overzicht van de Russische Belangen der Koningklijke-Shell-Groep' (1916). SLA, SC70/35. For letterbooks of these companies in these years, see SLA, SC70/20 and /25, SC70/17/5/8/1.

3. Enclosed in Lane to Loudon, 7 December 1908. SHA, 195/208. Contrary to the consensus view that NBT was a 'British' bank established by Cassel to further a Foreign Office agenda, as Hardinge noted to Bertie, Cassel got involved 'not at our initiative' but at the request of 'the Turks'. 'We have done nothing for him.' Hardinge to Bertie, 4 February 1909. TNA, FO800/80.

4. For examples, see Gwinner to Cassel, 21 February 1913. TBA, 200197, f. 290. Belgian Embassy report of 1 July 1913. MBZ, CP Turquie 1913.

5. David Kynaston, *The City of London*, Vol. 2 *Golden Years, 1890–1914* (London: Chatto & Windus, 1995), p. 301.

6. Lothar Gall et al., *The Deutsche Bank, 1870–1995* (London: Weidenfeld & Nicolson, 1995), p. 77.

7. Lane's letters to Jules Aron of Rothschild Frères inviting them to join Gulbenkian's bank scheme repeatedly refer to Gulbenkian's personal connections (including his supposed friendship with Noradunkyan) and ethnicity as vouching for its potential. Lane also claims that Cassel had developed a similar idea independently. Lane to Aron, 12 (Noradunkyan), 16, 18 September and 11 November (Cassel) 1908. ANMT, 132AQ137, 'Affaire Ottomane'.

8. CSG to Essayan, 16 December 1908. LDN02052. Gall et al., *Deutsche Bank*, p. 74.

9. Cassel cited in Cambon to Pichon, 16 December 1908. AMAE, CP Turquie 361, f. 225.

10. Mohammed Şerif Paşa, an Ottoman Kurd and former ambassador to Stockholm, and Hasan Fehmi Paşa, President of the Council of State. Şerif resigned noisily from the Unionist Party on 23 March 1909 and left for Paris, where he became a focus of monarchist counter-revolutionary agitation. Fehmi Paşa resigned on 13 February; in April he served as Minister of Justice for a few days. Another attendee, Prince Said Halim Paşa, served as President of the Council of State and Foreign Minister in 1913. Aykut Kansu, *Politics in Post-Revolutionary Turkey, 1908–1913* (Leiden: Brill, 2000), pp. 50, 67, 87, 183–5, 439–40.

11. CSG to Essayan, 12 January 1909. LDN02052.

12. The minutes of the meeting of 29 January 1909 are given in the minutes for the NBT meeting of 5/18 September 1909. LDN02045.

13. Cassel arrived 9 March and was seen off by Cavid on 17 March.

14. Sorgoudje (O. & M. Essayan, London) to CSG, 18 February 1909. LDN00014.

15. Sorgoudje to CSG, 25 January 1909. LDN00014.

16. Sir Edward Hamilton, cited in Pat Thane, 'Finances and the British State: The Case of Sir Ernest Cassel', *Business History*, 28:1 (1986), 80–99 (80).

17. Einstein to State Department, 15 July 1909. NARA, RG59/20784/1095.

18. Report of 11 July 1909. MBZ, CP Turquie 1909–10, f. 2.

19. Ozan Ozavci, 'Diaries of a Young Turk: Cavid Bey's Notes on the Great Powers, the Unionists and the Armenians, 1908–14', conference paper presented at 'The Clash of Empires: WWI and the Middle East', CIRMENA, University of Cambridge, 13–14 June 2014.

20. Mehmed Cavid, 'Neşriyatımız ve Vaka-i İktisadiye', *Ulum-u İktisadiye ve İçtimaiyye*, V (1909), 123–35 (128).

21. Mehmed Cavid, 'Neşriyatımız ve Vaka-i İktisadiye', *Ulum-u İktisadiye ve İçtimaiyye*, IV (1909), 554–74 (562).

22. Tevfik Paşa to CSG, 4 and 28 December 1909. LDN00014. Foreign Secretary Edward Grey noted that the FO could not enter the name of 'a naturalised British subject', let alone 'any official engaged in the trade in this country', in the printed list of the Diplomatic Corps, but had notified other government

departments of the appointment. Edward Grey to Tevfik Paşa, 22 December 1910. LDN00046.

23. BOA, BEO 3783/28371. In January 1910 he was also promoted from the Third to the Second Class of the Order of Osmaniyeh. BOA, BEO 3805/285532.

24. Bompard to MAE, 17 September 1909. AMAE, CP Turquie 363, f. 123.

25. Bompard to MAE, 5 October 1909. AMAE, CP Turquie 363, f. 141.

26. Cassel to Babington Smith, 27 July 1910. Trinity College, Cambridge. Babington Smith Papers, HBS28, f. 108. The pair had, admittedly, already met in Istanbul in 1909. W. S. Churchill, *The World Crisis, 1911–18* (5 vols., London: Odhams, 1939), Vol. 2, p. 432. I am grateful to Ozan Ozavci for this reference.

27. George Frisby to CSG, 26 July 1910. LDN00014.

28. Cassel reports his undertaking in Cassel to CSG, 3 September 1910. LDN00039.

29. Bénard et Jarislowsky, Louis Dreyfus, Gulbenkian and the Syndicat des Banquiers de Province all had 15 per cent participations; Bemberg 10 per cent; Hirsch and Thalmann split the remaining 30 per cent between themselves. LDN00043.

30. 'Siyasiyat: İstikraz Etrafında', *Tanin*, 19 August 1910, p. 1.

31. Bompard to MAE, 17 October 1910. AMAE, CP Turquie 366, f. 90. For another perspective, see reports of 18 August and 17 September 1910. MBZ, CP Turquie 1909–10, ff. 69, 79.

32. 'İstikraz Hakkında: Cavit Bey'in Beyanatı', *Tanin*, 23 August 1910, p. 1.

33. For Laurent, see Ozan Ozavci, 'A Man in the Middle: The Mission of Charles Laurent and the Young Turks', in Gokhan Çetinsaya and Gül Tokay (eds.), *Festschrift to Feroze A. K. Yasamee* (Istanbul: ISIS Publications, forthcoming).

34. *Le Temps*, 20 September 1910. Hüseyin Cahit immediately picked up on this story, citing *Le Temps* as his source. 'Yeni İstikraz', *Tanin*, 20 September 1910, p. 1.

35. Cassel to CSG, 26 September 1910. LDN00039.

36. Cassel and Babington Smith, 'Memorandum on Recent Ottoman Loan Negotiations', 4 October 1910. TBA, 200196, f. 2.

37. Cassel to CSG, 1 October 1910. Ibid. See also Babington Smith to CSG, 1 October 1910. LDN00043.

38. CSG to Naoum Paşa, 22 October 1910. AMAE, CP Turquie 366, f. 130.

39. Noted in Naoum to Rifaat, 26 September 1910. BOA, HR.ID 209/37.

40. Pichon is reported as advocating this plan to Gulbenkian in Hugo Baring to Revelstoke, 14 October 1910. TBA, 200196, f. 84.

41. NSG to CSG, 23 October 1910. LDN00048.

42. Cavid to CSG, 10 October 1910. LDN00043.

43. CSG to Cavid, 8 October 1910. LDN00910.

44. Syndic since 1895, de Verneuil had been the Quai d'Orsay's choice to lead the Anglo-French 'Société d'Etudes' in 1906. Jacques Thobie, *Intérêts et impérialisme*

français dans l'empire ottomane, 1895–1914 (Paris: Imprimerie Nationale, 1977), p. 635.

45. Steeg to Gout, 26 November 1910. AMAE, CP Turquie 367, f. 126.

46. Helfferich to Weitz, 12 October 1910, cited in John G. Williamson, *Karl Helfferich, 1872–1924: Economist, Financier, Politician* (Princeton, NJ: Princeton University Press, 1971), p. 92. The Belgian Embassy in Istanbul also heard similar reports. Reports of 12 October and 4 November 1910. MBZ, CP Turquie 1909–10, ff. 81, 87.

47. CSG to Cavid (letter and telegram), both 24 October 1910. LDN00043 and LDN00931.

48. Kansu, *Politics in Post-Revolutionary Turkey*, pp. 175–6; Ozavci, 'Diaries of a Young Turk', p. 8.

49. Reports of 17 and 21 October 1910. MBZ, CP Turquie 1909–10, ff. 82 (quote), 83.

50. 'Propositions of Henry Babington Smith', 19 October 1910, and Bessborough to Barry, 14 December 1910. London Metropolitan Archive, CLC/B/172/MS24013. Daeschner to Pichon, 3 November 1910. AMAE, CP Turquie 384, f. 105.

51. Hardinge to Cassel, 19 September 1910. TNA, FO371/994/33592.

52. As a further sweetener, Crédit Mobilier were to give a £T 1.5 million participation in their loan to NBT. Babington Smith to Cassel, 11 November 1910. TBA, 200196, f. 34.

53. Babington Smith to Revelstoke, 12 July 1911. TBA, 200196, f. 312. Despite fears that the bills would not be placeable in London, almost a third were taken by the Rhodesian mining holding company Charter Trust and Agency; Cassel, Hamar Greenwood and the Swiss Bank Corporation took £150,000 each. A list is at LDN00055.

54. For Deutsche Bank, see Council of Ministers minutes, 7 July 1913. BOA, MV 179/5. For Périer, see Thobie, *Intérêts et impérialisme français dans l'empire ottomane*, pp. 283–7.

55. In the words of a new British ambassador, Louis du Pan Mallet, to Tyrrell, 26 April 1914. Balliol College, Oxford. Mallet IV.2. For earlier discussions, see Grey to Lowther, 18 February 1910. TNA, FO800/79.

56. Hugo Baring to Babington Smith, 19 February 1913. TBA, 200197, f. 271. Cavid, diary entry for 28 July 1913. *Tanin*, 3 June 1944.

57. Cavid diary, 11–22 December 1912. *Tanin*, 21 February 1944. Rifaat Paşa to CSG, 3 January 1913. LDN00079.

58. The most detailed account of these early attempts to secure the concessions is Stephen H. Longrigg, *The Origins and Early History of the Iraq Petroleum Company* (London: privately printed, 1969), Ch. 5. For the Civil List, see Arzu T. Terzi, *Hazine-i Hassa Nezareti* (Istanbul: Türk Tarih Kurumu Basımevi, 2000).

59. Kautz report, 3 August 1908. HIDB, OR1320.

60. Nichols, 'Report about the Moussoul Petroleum Mines' [August 1909?]. BP, 163011. Nichols to D'Arcy Exploration, 27 August 1908 (quote). BP, 072655. See also Williamson, *Karl Helfferich*, p. 80. For Deutsche Bank, Halliss Mustechar (Undersecretary at the Ottoman Civil List) was 'that bandit'. Huguenin to Anatolian Rwy (Berlin), 21 June 1909. HIDB, OR1059.

61. P. Weitz to Helfferich, 9 March 1909. HIDB, OR1320.

62. Arzu T. Terzi, *Bağdat-Musul'da Abdülhamid'in Mirasi: Petrol ve Arazi* (Istanbul: Timaş Yayınları, 2009), pp. 239–41.

63. Glasgow claimed to represent J. G. White & Co. Straus to State Department, 23 September 1909. NARA, RG59/5012/426.

64. LDN00943. See also Lane to Emanuel Nobel, 23 September 1909. LDN00038.

65. CSG to M. Essayan 27 March and 29 April 1909. LDN02052. Cassel to Babington Smith, 13 August 1910. Trinity College, Cambridge. HBS28/113.

66. Lane to CSG, 4 and 8 September 1909 and 2 February 1910. LDN00038.

67. CSG to M. Essayan, 18 June, 9 July ('<u>hook</u>'), 18 August ('backsheeshes'), 3, 17 and 25 September 1909. LDN02052. For Essayan's contract, dated 31 July 1909, see LDN00169. D'Arcy's agent, H. E. Nichols, was certainly aware of Essayan's activities. See Longrigg, *The Origins and Early History of the Iraq Petroleum Company*, p. 53.

68. CSG to M. Essayan, 13 May (quote) and 6 September 1909. LDN02052.

69. CSG to M. Essayan, 18 August 1909. LDN02052.

70. John Hands to CSG, 28 November 1910. LDN02052. Essayan appealed, but then agreed to settle out of court. See CSG to D. H. Young, 17 August 1910. LDN01528.

71. BOA, DH.MUi 58/31, DH.MUi 91–1/21 and DH.MTV 38/25. See also Wiet (French Consulate, Baghdad) to MAE, 25 May 1910. AMAE, CP Turquie 384.

72. The present author has struggled to track down this famous report, which Gulbenkian claimed to have submitted 'round about 1890/1892' to Minister of the Civil List Agop Paşa, who 'thanked me profusely' and stated that to serve the Sultan was 'to serve your conscience' ('Memoirs', pp. 3–4). Agop died in late September or early October 1891. The earliest Gulbenkian might have submitted any report is 1889, yet even at that early date the Civil List had reports from its own staff in Mesopotamia. It seems more likely that the report was submitted in 1899, and that Gulbenkian received the Osmaniyeh in 1900 as his reward. If so, then this may be the report (an incomplete copy) addressed to Minister of Public Works Selim Melhame, found at LDN00009 and datable by internal evidence to the mid- to late 1890s. This report is thin and less informative than the 1889, 1898, 1899 and 1901 Civil List surveys carried out by G. Alan, M. Weiss, Émile Jacquerez and Otto Groskopf, for which see BOA, HH.THR 233/49, HR.THR 239/55, HH.THR 248/10, Y.MTV 188/7 and Y.PRK.OMZ 2/22. See also Volkan Ediger, *Enerji Ekonomi-Politiği Perspektifinden Osmanlı'da*

Neft ve Petrol (Ankara: ODTU Yayıncılık, 2007), pp. 170–87; Hikmet Uluğbay, *İmparatorluk'tan Cumhuriyet'e Petropolitik* (Istanbul: De Ki Yayınları, 2008), pp. 42–3, 62; Terzi, *Bağdat-Musul'da Abdülhamid'in Mirası*.

73. Gwinner to Anatolian Rwy, 15 March 1910. HIDB, OR0932. Lane to CSG, 9 September 1910. LDN00169.

74. Gwinner to Auswärtiges Amt, 28 October (quote) and 5 December 1913. HIDB, OR1329.

75. Babington Smith to Cassel, 18 May 1911. LDN00055. For Deterding's reaction see Lane to CSG, 12 February 1912. LDN00064. Cassel may have also been bound to bring in Deutsche by a previous agreement with Gwinner. See 'Sir Henry Babington Smith', undated memo. ANMT, 132AQ198, 'Royal Dutch 1911'. The agreement between Deutsche and NBT was signed on 21 October 1912.

76. Gulbenkian had defeated Gwinner's alternative suggestion, by which NBT would go in with both Deutsche Bank and Ottoman Bank. Babington Smith to Cassel, 20 July 1910. Trinity College, Cambridge. HBS28 f. 107.

77. In July 1910 he proposed to Babington Smith a scheme which included Royal Dutch, Shell and Rothschild Frères, 'in connection with the Standard Oil Company'. The inclusion of the American firm is noteworthy, but no further evidence of Gulbenkian's contacts with Standard Oil has been found. Babington Smith to Cassel, 20 July 1910. Trinity College, Cambridge. HBS28/107.

78. Babington Smith to Cassel, 21 October and 1 November 1911. Trinity College, Cambridge. HBS31/61 and /69.

79. Babington Smith to CSG, 18 December 1911. LDN00861.

80. For the letters agreeing to this condition, see Deutsche Bank to TPC, 19 October 1912; Hecht (NBT) to TPC, 22 October 1912; Waley Cohen (Anglo-Saxon Petroleum) to TPC, 23 October 1912. LDN00861. For discussions of concession area, see Kliemke, memo, 26 October 1912. HIDB, OR1326.

81. Eyre Crowe to Babington Smith, 28 September 1912. TBA, 200187, f. 121. Babington Smith, 'Petroleum in Turkey. Memorandum of Interview', [September?] 1912; 'Turkish Petroleum Coy. Memorandum of Interview', 25 October 1912. TBA, 200187, ff. 123, 136.

82. Alwyn Parker memo, 28 November 1913. TNA, FO371/1761, E53892. CSG's shareholding was known to the Board of Trade. Percy Ashley to Stauss, 14 February 1914. HIDB, OR1330.

83. Alwyn Parker memos, 1, 9 and 11 December 1913. TNA, FO371/1761, E54440, E55551 and E55859. See also Cavid's diary entries for 3 and 9 December 1913. Servet Avşar and Hasan Babacan (eds.), *Meşrutiyet Ruznamesi II* (Ankara: Türk Tarih Kurumu, 2015), pp. 362, 387.

84. CSG reserved for himself 12,000 of the 40,000 TPC shares held by NBT. Hecht to CSG, 24 October 1912. LDN00055. As Hugo Baring noted, the sacrifice of 10 per cent was compensated for by the gain of diplomatic support

for TPC. Hugo Baring to CSG, 9 March 1914. LDN00068. See also Lane to CSG, 20 March 1914. LDN00081.

85. Eyre Crowe to Babington Smith, 4 December 1913. TNA, FO371/1761, E53892.

86. The information came from Stauss at Deutsche Bank. Ashley memo, 22 December 1913. TNA, FO371/1761, E57611.

87. Liquidation required a 75 per cent majority of shareholders, which Babington Smith argued made Gulbenkian's position unassailable. Babington Smith to Gwinner, 2 March 1914; Gwinner to Babington Smith, 4 March 1914 (quote). HIDB, OR1130. See also Stauss to Helfferich, 16 January 1914. HIDB, OR1329.

88. Gwinner to Guenther, 14 March 1913. HIDB, OR1330. Marian Kent, *Oil and Empire: British Policy and Mesopotamian Oil 1900–1920* (Basingstoke: Macmillan, 1976), p. 67.

89. For examples, see Gwinner to Helfferich, 18 November 1910; Gwinner to Guenther, 8 May 1913. HIDB, OR1060 and OR1328.

90. For their 'understanding' regarding TPC, see CSG to Deterding, 24 October 1913. LDN00861. Stauss to Kuhlmann, 11 January 1915; Stauss to Helfferich, 16 January 1914. HIDB, OR1329. Babington Smith to Gwinner, 12 March 1914 (Deterding offer). HIDB, OR1330.

91. Ronald W. Ferrier, *The History of the British Petroleum Company*, Vol. 1 *The Developing Years, 1901–1932* (Cambridge: Cambridge University Press, 1982), pp. 61–2.

92. Ibid., pp. 152, 166–9; Fiona Venn, *Oil Diplomacy in the Twentieth Century* (Basingstoke: Macmillan, 1986), pp. 28–9; T. A. B. Corley, *A History of the Burmah Oil Company, 1886–1924* (London: Heinemann, 1983), pp. 189, 191, 193 (quote), 201–2, 205.

93. Ottoman archives indicate that in 1914 Ottoman ministers were planning to auction leases to fields in the two *vilayets*, following the 1910 Concessions Law. See Council of State and Ministry of Public Works Minute of 17 March and 26 May 1914. BOA, BEO 4297/322227. Hakkı 'started' and 'required some smoothing down' when told by the German ambassador that TPC would not confine its activities to the two *vilayets*. Mallet to Grey, 23 March 1914. TNA, FO800/80, f. 270.

94. Lane to CSG, 23 July 1909. LDN00169.

95. NAE to Devgantz, n.d. LIS03059, H2a (quote). Moore received stock tips and chocolates from 'Carloust', but there is nothing to suggest anything more was going on. She met Nevarte as well as Calouste socially, and even suggested that Calouste buy his wife a theatre to give her a hobby. Mary Moore to CSG, 1 June and 3 November 1913. LDN00075. Mary Moore to CSG, 22 April 1914. LDN03059.

96. CSG to Devgantz, 19 June 1914 (Duz); CSG to NAE, n.d. [June 1914] ('pair'). LIS03059, ff. 5–10, 34.

97. Quoted in NAE to CSG, n.d. LDN03059, H2d.

98. Devgantz to CSG, 27 June 1914; Hagop Hagopian to CSG, 2 June 1914; CSG
    to Virginie Essayan, 30 June 1914; Virginie Essayan to NAE, 21 June 1914.
    LDN03059, H2e, ff. 41–2, 32–3, H2b.

99. Arthur Hort to CSG, 26 July (ill-health) and 4 October (football) 1910.
    LDN00041.

100.   Cited in Devgantz to CSG, 21 October 1912. LDN00051.

101.   NSG to CSG, 19 January 1913. LDN00084.

102.   Devgantz to CSG, 16 December 1912 ('bode well'). LDN00051. Harrow
        School Report, 26 June [1910?] ('uppish'). LDN00048. RSE to NAE, 13 August
        1913 ('blasé'). LDN00084.

103.   CSG to Hagopian, 27 June 1914. LDN03059, H25.

Chapter 7: Put Out More Flags, 1914–18

1. Soulas to Gulbenkian, 22 October 1914. LDN00079.

2. Chargé d'affaires to Gulbenkian, 31 July 1914. LDN00079. BOA, BEO
   4298/322303.

3. Soulas to Gulbenkian, 29 (Évian), 31 (Turkish flag) October and 1 November
   (death) 1914. LDN00079.

4. NAE to CSG, 31 July and 4 August 1914; NSG to CSG, 26 August 1914.
   LDN00084. For CSG's efforts to recover the vehicle, see CSG to Ritter's Park
   Hotel, 10 September 1914. LDN00078.

5. KSG to CSG, 5 (quote), 31 August (quoting CSG's telegram) and 31 October
   (Sarkis) 1914. LDN00084.

6. Gertrude Bell to Mallet, 26 March 1914. Balliol College, Oxford. Mallet IV/11.

7. Norman Scott to Mallet, 10 August 1914. TNA, FO195/2460/3494.

8. Norman Scott to FO, 8 September 1914. TNA, FO195/2460/3494.

9. H. W. Stock to Nichols, 25 August 1914. BP, 119156. For the draft concession, see
   H. E. Nichols to Stauss, 27 July 1914. HIDB, OR1332. For Ottoman views on
   royalties, see memcon Hakkı, Alwyn Parker and H. E. Nichols, 1 July 1914. BP,
   163011.

10. 'Sermon of Oubeid Ullah Effendi, St Sofiah', 20 August 1914. TNA,
    FO800/240, Pt 1, f. 626.

11. Kessler to Standard Russe, 7 December 1914; Brucken Fock to Braun, 6 January
    1915. SLA, SC70/17/1, ff. 168, 314.

12. For all these and more, see Annual Report, 22 June 1914. ANMT 132AQ232,
    EMBA Folder.

13. Deterding to Royal Dutch, 10 November 1914. LDN00070.

14. George Philip, *The Political Economy of International Oil* (Edinburgh:
    Edinburgh University Press, 1994), p. 31.

15. Daniel Yergin, *The Prize: The Epic Quest for Oil, Money, and Power* (New York:
    Free Press, 1991), p. 79.

16. George Sweet Gibb and Evelyn H. Knowlton, *History of Standard Oil Company (New Jersey)*, Vol. 2 *Resurgent Years, 1911–27* (New York: Harper & Brothers, 1956), p. 7, Table 1.

17. Geoffrey Jones, *The State and the Emergence of the British Oil Industry* (London: Macmillan, 1981), pp. 78, 151–5, 160, 171, 201.

18. HRDS, Vol. 1, p. 217.

19. Brian S. McBeth, *Dictatorship and Politics: Intrigue, Betrayal, and Survival in Venezuela, 1908–35* (Notre Dame, IN: University of Notre Dame Press, 2008), pp. 42–3.

20. Anglo-Saxon (that is, Shell) 63.75 per cent, Rothschild Frères 7.5 per cent, Rothschild and Sons, 3.75 per cent, General Asphalt 25 per cent. 'Capitalisation of Venezuelan Business with Regard to Taxation', 24 October 1921. SHA 195/177b.

21. SLA, VEN/B1/1. LDN00246.

22. Edwards to CSG, 16 March 1915. SHA, 195/177a.

23. CSG to Deterding, 20 and 21 April 1915. LDN02580.

24. Aranguren to CSG, 8 March 1918. LDN00127.

25. CSG to Deterding, 9 December 1915. LDN0090.

26. McBeth, *Dictatorship and Politics*, p. 145.

27. Brian S. McBeth, *Juan Vicente Gómez and the Oil Companies in Venezuela, 1908–35* (Cambridge: Cambridge University Press, 1983), p. 19.

28. SHA, 195/33c.

29. LDN02532.

30. HRDS, Vol. 1, p. 185.

31. For Hauser–CSG correspondence regarding the Royal Dutch introduction to New York in 1915–16, see LDN02043. CSG also worked closely with Kuhn Loeb in issuing Mexican Eagle in New York. See LDN02476, LDN00176. Mortimer Schiff to CSG, 27 March 1922. LDN00470.

32. Deterding to CSG, 25 July 1916. LDN0101.

33. Deterding to CSG, 7 August 1916. LDN0101.

34. CSG to Deterding, 4 April 1918 ('penetrated'). LDN01547. CSG to Deterding, 28 May 1918 ('inner life'). LDN01548.

35. Foreign Office to Anglo-Persian, 23 November 1915. BP, 67764.

36. Gunther to Wangenheim, 4 May 1915. HIDB, OR1063. See also Dietrich Eichholtz, *Die Bagdadbahn, Mesopotamien und die deutsche Ölpolitik bis 1918* (Leipzig: Leipziger Universitätsverlag, 2007), pp. 68–71.

37. Kriegsministerium to Stauss, 31 December 1927. HIDB, OR1067. The 1918 pipeline and refinery plans are in the same file.

38. Roberto Nayberg, 'Une stratégie pétrolière pour la France: la défense des intérêts nationaux dans les conférences interalliés du pétrole de 1918', *Revue Historique*, 2 (1994), 459–93 (461).

39. Quoted in J. Avenol to Ministère de Finance, 1 September 1917. AMAE, 370PO/CH/511. Unsurprisingly, this relatively minor official at the French Embassy in London was left with the feeling that this 'long chat' had 'not really been aimed specifically at me'.

40. Jean-Marie Bouguen, *Le Pétrole en France: genèse et stratégies d'influence (1917–24)* (Paris: L'Harmattan, 2013), p. 22.

41. 'Secret note of meeting at 88, Rue de la Grenelle', 17 December 1918. TNA, FO368/2095.

42. Georges Bénard acted for the Pearson group in their attempts to secure Algerian oil concessions, but first seems to have collaborated with CSG in 1912, developing abortive plans for an 'understanding' between Mexican Eagle and Royal Dutch-Shell (LDN00089). For lobbying of French officials in 1916, see LDN00099 and LDN00114 (including G. Bénard to CSG, 16 July 1916, in which Bénard describes himself as the latter's 'pupil'). For Bérenger's reliance on CSG for information about the oil industry and British oil policy, see Bérenger to CSG, 7, 17 November and 4 December 1917. LDN00956. For the flat, see D. H. Young, 'He Bribed a Minister with a Mansion', *The People*, 23 October 1955.

43. CSG to Deterding, 15 May 1917. SHA, 195/33c.

44. R. W. Ferrier, 'French Oil Policy, 1917–30: The Interaction between State and Private Interests', in D. C. Coleman and Peter Mathias (eds.), *Enterprise and History: Essays in Honour of Charles Wilson* (Cambridge: Cambridge University Press, 1987), pp. 237–62 (249).

45. Deterding to CSG, 5 April 1917. LDN00116. For 'les Boches', see the 1916 pamphlet *Le Trust des Carbures*. AN, F^{12} 7681.

46. Fitzgerald to CSG, 29 July 1916. LDN00514.

47. The French Ministry of Commerce appointed him to this position on 29 November 1917. Ministre de Commerce to Marquis de Chasseloup-Laubat, 27 May 1918. LDN00132. TNA, KV2/4426.

48. See, for example, LDN00956.

49. Gregory P. Nowell, *Mercantile States and the World Oil Cartel, 1900–1939* (Ithaca, NY: Cornell University Press, 1994), p. 140.

50. LDN00105.

51. Leathersellers Hall (St Helen's Place) to CSG, 24 January 1918. LDN00132.

52. NSG to CSG, 20 October 1914. LDN00084. For other Cambridge-related correspondence, see LDN00120.

53. The daughter of a certain Vohrab (Krikor Vohrab, perhaps?) and the son of a certain 'Mr. M.' were mooted. CSG to NAE, 1 July 1918, and CSG to Devgantz, 14 July 1918. LDN01549, ff. 40, 76. CSG to NAE, 28 July 1918. LDN01551, ff. 29–30. See also Elise Ananoff to CSG, 7 April 1921. LDN00404.

54. CSG to NSG, 6 August 1918. LDN00958.

55. CSG to Langton, 24 June 1918. LDN01550.

56. SLA, SC70/20.

57. Field Managers to UK Ambassador to Russia, 24 October 1917. SLA, ES/FNX1.

58. Diary for 28 April (quote) and 8 May 1913. *Tanin*, 15 and 27 April 1944. Ozan Ozavci, 'Diaries of a Young Turk: Cavid Bey's Notes on the Great Powers, the Unionists and the Armenians, 1908–14', pp. 21–2, conference paper presented at 'The Clash of Empires: WWI and the Middle East', CIRMENA, University of Cambridge, 13–14 June 2014. See also Robert Koptas, 'Zohrab, Papazyan ve Pastırmacıyan'in kalemlerinden 1914 Ermeni reformu ile Ittihatçi-Tasnak müzakereleri', *Toplumsal Tarih*, 5 (2007), 159–78; Feroz Ahmad, *The Young Turks and the Ottoman Nationalities* (Salt Lake City: University of Utah Press, 2014), pp. 38–9.

59. For 'unsere sogenannten Hammelwagen, in denen beispielsweise 880 Menschen in 10 Wagen befördert werden', see Eichholtz, *Die Bagdadbahn*, p. 74.

60. Boghos Nubar to Sir F. Bertie, 27 May 1915; Boghos Nubar, memorandum, 17 July 1915 (quote). TNA, FO371/2488, 96769. For post-war attempts to arrest Turkish ministers for war crimes, see FO371/4173.

61. Donald Bloxham, *The Great Game of Genocide: Imperialism, Nationalism, and the Destruction of the Ottoman Armenians* (Oxford: Oxford University Press, 2005), pp. 141, 144.

62. Hovhannes Massehian to CSG, 10 December 1918. LDN00135.

63. LIS00416.

64. Robert Henriques, *Sir Robert Waley Cohen, 1877–1952* (London: Secker and Warburg, 1966), pp. 147, 252. Henriques's claims for Waley Cohen's role within Royal Dutch-Shell are piously exaggerated. Although some personal papers survive (Southampton University Library Special Collections, MS363), they are not very numerous. Notes preserved at Southampton suggest that the rest of the papers were simply destroyed.

65. CSG to Deterding, 15 August 1918. LDN01551.

66. SHA, 195/176a; LDN02533; George Philip, *Oil and Politics in Latin America: Nationalist Movements and State Companies* (Cambridge: Cambridge University Press, 1982), p. 24.

67. CSG to Lane, 26 December 1907. LDN01512.

68. CSG to Deterding, 23 June 1914. SHA, 195/37. Deterding to CSG, 25 June 1914. LDN00070.

69. See his memo of 23 February 1914 sent to IOB, and presumably other French banks. Archives nationales du monde du travail, 207AQ399.

70. F. W. Brecher, 'French Policy towards the Levant 1914–18', *Middle Eastern Studies*, 29:4 (October 1993), 641–64; E. P. Fitzgerald, 'France's Middle Eastern Amibition, the Sykes-Picot Negotiations and the Oil Fields of Mosul', *Journal of Modern History*, 66:4 (1994), 697–725 (704).

71. 'C.T.', 26 October 1918. TNA, KV2/4426.

Chapter 8: Talleyrand, 1918–20

1. FO to D'Arcy Exploration, 23 November 1915. BP, 67764.

2. In December 1922 Deutsche Bank refused to hand over shares in Anatolian and Baghdad Railways (pledged in 1912 for its 25 per cent stake in TPC) to TPC's E. H. Keeling. Keeling, memo, 15 December 1922. LDN00863. The question was settled by the Anglo-German Mixed Arbitral Tribunal, which found on 29 June 1928 that the 1912 contract between the Anatolian Railway and TPC was void under Article 299 of the Treaty of Versailles. Deutsche Bank were then unsure, however, that they could capitalise on the railway's rights. Meissner to J. Jacoby, 12 March 1928, and Rechtsabteilung to Weigelt, 2 September 1930. HIDB, OR1068 and OR1069.

3. On 1 November 1920 the Nationalist parliament in Ankara retransferred them from the Civil List to the Treasury. As there were then two regimes claiming to govern Turkey, however, this did not clarify matters.

4. Helmut Mejcher, 'Oil and British Policy towards Mesopotamia, 1914–18', *Middle Eastern Studies*, 8:3 (October 1972), 377–91 (387–8).

5. Y. A. Dervichyan to MAE, 11 March 1915. MBZ, CP Turquie 1915.

6. FO memo, 19 May 1919. TNA, FO368/2095.

7. Oscar H. Heizer (US Consul, Baghdad) to State Department, 9 December 1919. NARA, RG59/800.6363/75. See also /58 and /134. John A. DeNovo, *American Interests and Policies in the Middle East, 1900–1939* (Minneapolis: University of Minnesota Press, 1963), pp. 169–77.

8. Andrews to Lane, 6 February 1919. LDN00140.

9. Cowans to CSG, n.d. ('Tuesday p.m.'). LDN00140.

10. CSG to Deterding, 12 July 1919. SHA, 195/175b.

11. Cowans to CSG, 27 December 1919. LDN00140.

12. Cowans makes this clear in Cowans to Noble, n.d. [summer 1919]. SLA, GHC/IRAQ/DI. See also Deterding to Cadman, 28 January 1919. SHA, 195/30a.

13. Cowans to CSG, 26 January 1921. LDN00412.

14. Cowans to CSG, 23 April 1919. LDN00140.

15. Actually, Rear-Admiral Henry Priaulx Cayley (for it was he) was an Australian admiral. Memo, 14 November 1919. TNA, FO371/4209.

16. Cowans to CSG, n.d. [1919]. LDN00140.

17. *The Nation and Athenaeum*, 13 May 1922, p. 4.

18. CSG to Lane, 24 July 1918. LDN01551.

19. Daniel Yergin, *The Prize: The Epic Quest for Oil, Money, and Power* (New York: Free Press, 1991), p. 167.

20. For Pearson, see Jonathan Brown, 'Domestic Politics and Foreign Investment: British Development of Mexican Petroleum 1889–1911', *Business History Review*, 61 (1987), 387–416.

21. Linda B. Hall, *Oil, Banks, and Politics: The United States and Postrevolutionary Mexico, 1917–24* (Austin: University of Texas Press, 1995), p. 61.

22. Cowdray, 'The British Imperial Oil Co.', 14 February 1916. SM, PEA C44/9.

23. Geoffrey Jones, *The State and the Emergence of the British Oil Industry* (London: Macmillan, 1981), pp. 152 (quote), 174. Ferrier notes the 'sobering and almost incredible fact' that Anglo-Persian's first shipment to the Admiralty was found to be unusable, owing to its viscosity. Ronald W. Ferrier, *The History of the British Petroleum Company*, Vol. 1 *The Developing Years, 1901–1932* (Cambridge: Cambridge University Press, 1982), p. 199.

24. This arrangement would have established a voting trust to ensure that British nationals controlled a list of Royal Dutch-Shell subsidiaries. 'Onderhandelingen Engelsche Regeerung 1917–20', SHA 102/1; TNA, FO608/75/12/1282; CAB24/132/37. Jones, *The State and the Emergence of the British Oil Industry*, pp. 209, 213; T. A. B. Corley, *A History of the Burmah Oil Company 1886–1924* (London: Heinemann, 1983), Ch. 19. For hints that the purchase of Burmah's shares by Royal Dutch-Shell might have been on the *tapis* in January 1922 but that Gulbenkian missed the opportunity, see Evelyn Fitzgerald to CSG, 12, 17, 19, 20 and 23 January 1922. LDN00456.

25. Cited in Tanner memo, 9 October 1918. SM, PEA C44/3, Folder 1.

26. Exactly what figure was to be taken as the basis for Gulbenkian's brokerage fee was unclear even to those immediately involved. One memo (by Cowdray?) among the Pearson archive notes: 'I never for a moment understood that this selling arrangement with Mr Gulbenkian – for shortness expressed in the draft R.D.-Shell agreement as the pooling arrangement – was ever intended to be a real pooling arrangement such as is understood in the City.' The memo goes on to say that 'I' never intended Gulbenkian to have 20 per cent of the dividends and bonus shares involved. [Cowdray?], 'Memo for Mr Tanner', 2 March 1919. SM, PEA C44/3, Folder 1. J. E. F. de Kok (BPM) to CSG, 6 August 1919, does indeed suggest that the 20 per cent excluded dividends and was calculated on the difference between £4 18s and the price at which Gulbenkian actually sold the said Águila shares. LDN00140.

27. With Georges Bénard of Bénard Frères. In 1919 CSG offered them a participation in his pool, but they declined. CSG to Georges Bénard, 10 February 1919. LDN00970.

28. CSG to Tanner, 18 May 1919. LDN00957.

29. Tanner to CSG, 15 May 1919. LDN00126.

30. Cowdray to CSG, 26 September 1921. SM, PEA C44/3, section 3.

31. Águila memo, 2 August 1935. SM, PEA C44/3, section 6. George Philip, *Oil and Politics in Latin America: Nationalist Movements and State Companies* (Cambridge: Cambridge University Press, 1982), p. 206.

32. CSG to Colijn, 5 March 1921. LDN00435.

33. CSG to Deterding, 29 July 1918 ('digestion'). SHA, 195/175a. See CSG to Colijn, 1 March 1921, in which he surveys the state of the markets in London, Paris, Amsterdam and New York. LDN00435.

34. Deterding to CSG, 12 January 1922. SHA, 195/29; CSG to Colijn, 1 March 1921. LDN00435. CSG to Deterding, 10 January 1922. SHA, 195/176f.

35. Deterding, marginalia added to CSG to Deterding, 23 June 1924. LDN00568.

36. Pierre Soulaine, 'Elles en ont toutes', undated clipping enclosed in Soulas to NSG, 20 April 1920. LDN00182.

37. Bérenger, 'Rapport Secret sur la Politique Française du Pétrole et de la Paix', 5 November 1918. CAEF, B0031973, 'Roumanie – Pétroles, 1918–23'.

38. CSG to Colijn, 18 December 1919. LDN00957.

39. Bérenger to Ministre des Finances, 3 January 1920. CAEF, B0064326, 'Règlement des fournitures de pétrole effectuées par la Royal Dutch (1919–21)'.

40. CSG to Deterding, 8 January 1920. LDN01451, f. 1.

41. For Articles of Association and board minutes, see LDN00149.

42. This participation rested on a letter from Deterding. Exactly what kind is unclear because the letter was lost or stolen from Gulbenkian's secretary, D. H. Young, in February 1920, resulting in an explosion of temper that left Gulbenkian with 'no heart for business'. CSG to NSG, 6 February 1920. LDN02574. An earlier letter refers to a 15 per cent carried interest in Royal Dutch-Shell's 60 per cent SEP shareholding; CSG refers to '5% which you had ceded and the 10% which I got from the French'. CSG to Deterding, 17 July 1919. SHA, 195/175b. Of course, CSG enjoyed carried shareholdings and overall sales commissions in tandem in many Royal Dutch-Shell subsidiaries, so perhaps he had both.

43. CSG to Kessler, 31 March 1920. LDN00175.

44. This was the Directeur du Mouvement des Fonds, and the meeting was held on 30 May 1919. Eric Bussière, 'La France et les affaires pétrolières au lendemain de la Première Guerre Mondiale – la politique des groupes financiers à travers celle de la Banque de l'Union Parisienne', *Histoire, économie et société*, 1 (1982), 313–28 (314).

45. As Jones notes, Greenway had tried to acquire full control of TPC in 1917, shortly after it acquired BP for £2 million (much of it borrowed from the trustee). Jones, *The State and the Emergence of the British Oil Industry*, pp. 180–81. Ferrier, *The Developing Years*, pp. 217–19, 223, 241.

46. The agreement did, however, protect 'existing British concessions' in the area assigned to France. Jones, *The State and the Emergence of the British Oil Industry*, p. 195.

47. Edward Peter Fitzgerald, 'France's Middle Eastern Ambition, the Sykes–Picot Negotiations, and the Oil Fields of Mosul', *Journal of Modern History*, 66:4 (1994), 697–725; Roberto Nayberg, 'La politique française du pétrole à l'issue de la première guerre mondiale: perspectives et solutions', *Guerres mondiales et conflits contemporains*, 4 (2006), 125–9. The link between Mosul and the 'buffer Republic including the coal mines on the Rhein [*sic*]' was more explicit when Syria was discussed in February 1919. Louis du Pan Mallet was the FO official

charged with briefing Balfour at the time, and this quote comes from his diary.
Balliol College Archives, Oxford. Mallet IV.7, entry for 2 February 1919.

48. Yergin, *The Prize*, p. 173.

49. Kidston, memo, 5 June 1919. TNA, FO368/2095. As in London, disagreement
reigned in Paris in 1919: had Lloyd George disavowed Bérenger–Long (French
ambassador De Fleuriau thought not), was it worth ratifying (Pichon at the
Quai d'Orsay hoped for 50 per cent of Mosul's oil, rather than the 25 per cent
on offer through TPC), and what compensation had Clemenceau secured in
exchange for giving Lloyd George Mosul back (here Berthelot's imagination
came into play)? De Fleuriau to Pichon, 23 June; Pichon to de Fleuriau, 23
June; Bérenger to Pichon, 25 June 1919; Paul Cambon to Pichon, 3 March 1920.
AMAE, 75CPCOM/194, ff. 20, 21, 22, 185. Bérenger memo, 24 December
1919. AMAE, 166PAAP/451. Millerand made a final push for 50 per cent at San
Remo in 1920, but was cut off by Lloyd George. See the transcript at AMAE,
75CPCOM/671.

50. Curzon, memo attached to Weakley, 'Memorandum on M. Beranger's [*sic*] Note
to M. Clemenceau relative to Petroleum', 13 December 1919. TNA, FO368/2095.
The cabinet nonetheless approved Lloyd George's policy on 23 January 1920.
Jones, *The State and the Emergence of the British Oil Industry*, p. 216.

51. CSG to Colijn, 14 January 1920. LDN00860.

52. CSG to Deterding, 28 April 1920. SHA, 195/175c.

53. CSG to Maurice Paléologue, 24 September 1920; memcon Paul Bargeton, 5
August 1921. PRS03446. The French ambassador in Tehran, Bonin (whose share
portfolio CSG was managing, see LDN00629, LDN00689), was so active in
pushing French interests that his British counterpart tried to have him recalled.
Cyrus Ghani, *Iran and the Rise of Reza Shah: From Qajar Collapse to Pahlavi
Rule* (London: I. B. Tauris, 1998), pp. 52–3.

54. CSG to Prince Firouz, 28 July 1919. LDN01448, f. 252. Ghani, *Iran and the Rise
of Reza Shah*, pp. 45–6.

55. SEP could not find the 500,000 tomans monthly dead rent that Prince Firouz
demanded in July 1921 in exchange for the concession. See the reports of Henri
Hoppenot (military attaché at the French Embassy in Tehran) in CAEF,
B0032866, Folder 6. For Khostaria, see J. Cornfeld to State Department, 18
November 1922. NARA, RG59 867.516/9887/17.

56. Michael A. Rubin, 'Stumbling through the "Open Door": The US in Persia
and the Standard-Sinclair Oil Dispute, 1920–25', *Iranian Studies*, 28:3–4 (1995),
203–29.

57. CAEF, B0031973, 'Steaua Romana'. As with Turkey, here again this proved
difficult, as Deutsche Bank had moved assets to Switzerland.

58. Gh. Buzatu, *A History of Romanian Oil*, translated by Laura Chistruga-
Schneider (Bucharest: Mica Valahie, 2011), pp. 162, 170–71.

59. French Embassy Bucharest to MAE, 18 June 1920 (quote). CAEF, B0031973, 'Roumanie – Pétroles, 1918–23'. Bratiano cited in MAE to Ministre de la Finance, 2 July 1923. CAEF, B0032313.

60. Deterding to CSG, 23 December 1919. LDN00434. For the ultimatum, see 'Note pour M. Celier', 8 July 1920. CAEF, B0064326.

61. Though Deterding was apparently unconvinced, Gulbenkian felt Payot's strong connections and 'ability in management and organisation' made him well worth his annual salary of 50,000 francs. CSG to Deterding, 4 September 1919. SHA, 195/175b.

62. Éric Bussière, *Paribas 1872–1992: l'Europe et le monde* (Antwerp: Mercator, 1992), pp. 106–8; Philippe Marguerat, *Banque et investissement industriel: Paribas, le pétrole roumain et la politique française* (Geneva: Droz, 1987), pp. 36–9; Éric Bussière, *Horace Finaly, banquier, 1871–1945* (Paris: Fayard, 1996), pp. 188–9.

63. CSG to Deterding, 20 September 1919. SHA, 195/175b. Bussière, *Horace Finaly*, pp. 190–93.

64. CSG to VSG, 24 March 1920. LDN01452, f. 272.

65. Matilda Miskdjian to CSG, 20 October 1920. LDN00159.

66. Roupen Selian to CSG, 2 and 3 July 1914. LDN00078. Selian to CSG, 6 April 1919 (quotes). LDN00148.

67. As Arnold Toynbee noted, Boghos's delegation was 'hardly more representative of the total population of Armenia than the Zionists are of the population of Palestine'. TNA, FO608/77/25, f. 229.

68. Evelyn Fitzgerald to CSG, 7 May 1920. LDN00170. André Autheman, *La Banque Impériale Ottomane* (Paris: Comité pour l'Histoire Economique et Financière de la France, 1996), p. 253.

69. CSG to Charles Serkis, 16 June 1918. LDN01549. CSG to Boghos Nubar, 9 May 1919. LDN00957. He also ignored an invitation to join a 'democratic committee' intended to foster moderate political parties in Armenia. Leon Gumushguerdan to CSG, 8 October 1920. LDN00171.

70. CSG to Boghos Nubar, 2 October 1920. LDN01454, f. 373. See also CSG to Their Beatitudes the Patriarch Presidents of the Conseil Mixte Arménien, n.d. [1921]. LDN00405.

71. His Beatitude Patriarch Zaven to CSG, 16 March 1922. LDN00449.

72. CSG to Abel Abrahamian, 1 January 1921. LDN00450. Abrahamian changed his surname to Nazarian later that same year. Nerses sued for divorce from his wife, Satenig, in 1925. TNA, J77/2162/7720. I am grateful to Felix Corley, Jakub Osiecki and Hratch Tchilingirian for sharing with me an advance copy of a forthcoming article devoted to Abrahamian/Nazarian, entitled 'London's "disgraceful vardapet": Armenian Priest, Adulterer, Soviet Secret Police Agent'.

73. There is no evidence to support D. H. Young's claim that the murder left Gulbenkian fearing for his own life, or led to his deciding never to sleep at the

Paris *hôtel* he later purchased, at 51 Avenue d'Iéna. John Lodwick, *Gulbenkian: An Interpretation of Calouste Sarkis Gulbenkian* (London: Heinemann, 1958), p. 191.

Chapter 9: Open Door, Close Ranks, 1921–3

1. D'Arcy Exploration to CSG, 1 July 1921; CSG memo, 5 July 1921; Anglo-Saxon Petroleum to CSG, 5 July 1921. LDN00860.

2. Cochrane to Agnew, 11 September 1924. SLA, RA262/1; 'L.M.L.', 'Gulbenkian Interest', 5 September 1924. BP, 67806.

3. The French feared being made to sacrifice part of their 25 per cent to let in 'native interests' under art. 8 of San Remo. Oliphant to Saint-Aulaire, 31 July 1922. AMAE, 19RC/B50, f. 9.

4. CSG, 'Memoirs', p. 22 (corridors). Briand to Deutsch de la Meurthe, 5 October 1921 (validity). A check of files had indeed been made. See 'Note au sujet de la lettre ... remis par M. Deutsch de la Meurthe', 28 September 1921. AMAE, B49, f. 52.

5. CSG's office ran Berthelot's financial portfolio up to his death and beyond. LDN02454. For Berthelot's role in supporting CSG and SEP, see Brylinski to CSG, 21 September 1921. LDN00860; CSG, 'Memoirs', p. 22. There is no mention of this relationship in Jean-Luc Barré, *Le Seigneur-Chat: Philippe Berthelot, 1866–1934* (Paris: Plon, 1988).

6. Briand to Doumer, 23 March 1922. AMAE, B49, f. 94. Poincaré, cited in Brylinski to CSG, 2 August 1922. LDN00860.

7. CSG to Brylinski, 26 July 1922. LDN00860.

8. CSG to Cowans, 14 November 1919. LDN01449.

9. Weakley and Tyrrell, 'Activities of Standard Oil', 30 November 1921. TNA, FO371/6362.

10. Hardinge to Poincaré, 12 July; 'Note pour le Président du Conseil', 17 July; Saint-Aulaire to MAE, 26 July; 'Note pour Monsieur de Peretti', 27 July; 'Note pour le Président du Conseil,' 29 July 1922 (quote). AMAE, 19RC/B49, ff. 118, 144, 167, 171, 207. Pineau, report on London mission, 18 September 1922. CAEF, B0032308.

11. Board of Trade minutes, 7 December 1922; FO to Curzon, 7 December 1922. TNA, FO371/7785/53 and POWE33/98.

12. *Daily News*, 2 December 1922, p. 17.

13. A. C. Millspaugh, 'The Chester Project in Turkey', 1 March 1921. NARA, RG59 867.6020T81/9890/180. CSG to Deterding, 11 December 1922 (quote). LDN00860.

14. CSG to Yervant Essayan, [?] February 1925; British Trust to Mohsin Bey Yaghin, 18 March 1925. PRS00879, ff. 70, 7. Stephen Longrigg, *The Origins and Early History of the Iraq Petroleum Company* (London: privately printed, 1969), p. 158.

15. Hikmet Uluğbay, *İmparatorluk'tan Cumhuriyet'e Petropolitik* (Istanbul: De Ki Yayınları, 2008), p. 329.

16. CSG to H. E. Nichols, 17 January 1923. LDN00532.

17. Joseph C. Grew, *Turbulent Era: A Diplomatic Record of Forty Years, 1904–45* (2 vols., London: Hammond, 1953), Vol. 1, p. 584 ('third degree'); Richard Washburn Child, *A Diplomat Looks at Europe* (New York: Duffield, 1925), pp. 18 (denial of oil as factor), 118 ('eggs'); Sevtap Demirci, *Strategies and Struggles: British Rethoric [sic] and Turkish Response: The Lausanne Conference, 1922–23* (Istanbul: Isis, 2005), pp. 177–9.

18. Henderson to Andrew Ryan, 17 July 1923. TNA, FO800/240, Pt 1, f. 1356. William Stivers, *Supremacy and Oil: Iraq, Turkey, and the Anglo-American World Order, 1918–30* (Ithaca, NY: Cornell, 1982), p. 156.

19. John A. DeNovo, 'The Movement for an Aggressive American Oil Policy Abroad', *American History Review*, 61:4 (1956), 854–76.

20. The French also received strong representations from President Wilson. Washington Embassy to Millerand, 31 July 1920. AMAE, 19RC/142. For more lurid British conspiracies, see Oil conference, 12 January 1921, and W. E. D. Stokes to Warren Harding, 24 October 1921. NARA, RG59, 800.6363/238 and 306.

21. FRUS, 1923, Vol. 2, pp. 80–84. See also A. C. Millspaugh, 'Memorandum on the Grand Vizier's Letter of June 28, 1914', 24 October 1921. NARA, RG59 890G.6363/49a.

22. A. C. Millspaugh, memo, 23 May 1921. NARA, RG59 841.6363/135/8766/200. See also A. C. Millspaugh, 'Informal and Provisional Memorandum on the General Petroleum Situation', 19 February 1921. RG59 800.6363/325. For the Chester Concession's potential to harm US prestige in the region, see Mark Bristol to State Department, 16 April 1923. FRUS, 1923, Vol. 2, pp. 1202–4. G. Howland Shaw to Allen Dulles, 11 June 1923; Thomas Owens to State Department, 10 May 1923;. NARA, RG59 867.6020T81/9891/378 and /333.

23. The adventurer Henry Woodhouse was the source of much Anglophobic copy, probably funded by the Hearst media group. See clippings in BP, 71220. Cadman could see value in having the Americans in north Persia, 'as a buffer to the general Bolshevik tendency which is naturally more active in that part than in the South'. Cadman memo, 26 November 1921. BP, 78128.

24. The quotations are from Walter Teagle and John Gregory respectively. Carole Fink, Axel Frohn and Jürgen Heidekry, *Genoa, Rapallo and European Reconstruction in 1922* (Cambridge: Cambridge University Press, 1991), pp. 43, 155. See also Child, *A Diplomat Looks at Europe*, p. 30.

25. See the correspondence between Charles E. Hughes, Richard Washburn Child and A. C. Bedford. NARA, RG59 861.6363/9569/52A, /54, /59 and /63. For Joe Boyle's negotiations with Krasin, see SLA, GHC/USSR/C15 USSR Vol 3a., 'Genoa Conference'.

26. V. Trifonoff to STO Commission, [?] September 1922. GARF, f. 1726, op. 1, d. 55, doc. 6.

27. Report, 16 October 1922. RGAE, f. 2309, op. 1, d. 88, doc. 34.

28. 'Note pour Monsieur le Ministre', 2 July 1921. MBZ, B36.

29. NSG to Kessler, 4 and 22 August 1921. SHA, 195/31. CSG to Deterding, 6 and 11 May 1920. SHA, 195/175c.

30. Daniel Yergin, *The Prize: The Epic Quest for Oil, Money, and Power* (New York: Free Press, 1991), pp. 220, 214. R. W. Tolf, *The Russian Rockefellers: The Saga of the Nobel Family and the Russian Oil Industry* (Stanford: Stanford University Press, 1976), p. 214.

31. Adjemoff to M. Vinaver, 25 February 1919. GARF, f. 5913, op. 1, d. 808, doc. 1.

32. PIO, pp. 68–72.

33. RSE to CSG, n.d. [1925]. LDN00599.

34. Although some sources give 1922, letters to CSG from KLE and his father, Vahan, refer to KLE moving to Paris for a 'happy event' in April 1920. Vahan Essayan to CSG, 5 April 1920; KLE to CSG 20 April 1921. LDN00164. CSG to NSG, 14 August 1920. LDN02574. When KLE was proposed for the Légion d'honneur in 1967 both he and RSE submitted statements giving 1920 as the date of their wedding. AGT, 90ZY935–4.

35. CSG to NSG, 14 Aug. 1920. LDN02574.

36. Like other London bankers of German origin, the Ansbachers had changed their name during the First World War, to Ansley. Yervant later stated that he had refused because there had been 'too much electricity in the air'. *Gulbenkian* v. *Gulbenkian*, witness statement, 19 February 1927. NSG00001.

37. George Ansley to CSG, n.d. [December 1920]; NSG to Herminia Feijóo, 23 December 1920; NSG to CSG, 23 May 1921. NSG00001.

38. PIO, pp. 56–59. CSG had asked Trinity College to prevent NSG from travelling down to London. CSG to E. Harrison, 7 July 1916. LDN01342.

39. NSG to Herminia Feijóo, 21 March 1921; George Ansley to NSG, 7 April 1921. NSG00001. PIO, p. 59.

40. PIO, p. 80. 'Victims of Auto Smash Are Known', unidentified clipping [1922]. LDN00474.

41. CSG to Devgantz, 3 April 1914 ('merits'); CSG to NSG, 2 April 1914 (North British, dissertation). LDN01342.

42. J.-M. Waterkeyn to MAE, 25 October 1923. MBZ, B36.

Chapter 10: The End of the Affair, 1924–6

1. Chanet, pp. 33 (quote), 36 (travelling pharmacy).

2. Deterding to CSG, n.d. ('Tuesday morning') ('rhino') and 28 April ('dividends') 1923. LDN00496.

3. HRDS, Vol. 1, p. 249.

4. CSG to August Philips, 18 February 1923. LDN00510. See also CSG to August Philips, 14 February 1923. LDN00513.

5. A secondary dispute arose between Gulbenkian and Deterding over whether the former was committed to purchase shares at par under the 1921 pool agreement, even though their price had dropped well below. CSG to Deterding, 24 August and 30 July 1921. SHA, 195/176c and 195/177b.

6. CSG to Deterding, 23 (two letters) and 24 June 1924. LDN00568.

7. Brian S. McBeth, *Juan Vincente Gómez and the Oil Companies in Venezuela, 1908–35* (Cambridge: Cambridge University Press, 1983), p. 31.

8. George Philip, *Oil and Politics in Latin America: Nationalist Movements and State Companies* (Cambridge: Cambridge University Press, 1982), p. 45.

9. Deterding to CSG, 6 July 1923. LDN00496. HRDS, Vol. 1, p. 298.

10. CSG to Deterding, 8 July 1923. LDN00049; CSG to Deterding, 4 January 1923 (quote). SHA 195/177b.

11. Deterding to CSG, 4 April 1923. LDN00496.

12. [Deterding], 'Draft,' n.d. [1925?]. SHA, 190C/113. Prepared in 1955, this collection of documents does not include the VOC/BPM agreement at the centre of the dispute.

13. CSG to Deterding, 13 April 1923 ('poet'). LDN00496. CSG to Deterding, 10 March 1918 (friend). LDN01547.

14. CSG to Philips, 9 January 1924; CSG to Beatty, 23 February 1924; CSG, memos, 5 March and 1 July 1924. LDN00399.

15. NSG to CSG, 30 December 1925. LDN00866.

16. D. H. Young to CSG, 10 February 1926. LDN00681.

17. CSG to KLE, 31 December 1923. LDN00399.

18. *Daily Express*, 15 ('mystery') and 28 (headline) January 1926; *The Times,* 17 Feb. 1926 (report of meeting).

19. Waley Cohen to Lionel de Rothschild, 17 February 1926. Southampton University Library, Special Collections, MS363/1/3/33.

20. *Financial Times*, 23 June 1926, p. 17 ('reports'); *The Economist*, 30 January 1926, p. 42 ('experts').

21. CSG to Clive Pearson, 9 July 1926. LDN02505.

22. HRDS, Vol. 1, pp. 298 ('enemy'), 321 ('opportunities').

23. 'She loved you so much,' wrote Deterding shortly after his first wife's death in 1916. Deterding to CSG, n.d. [1916]. LDN00101.

24. Geoffrey Jones, *The State and the Emergence of the British Oil Industry* (London: Macmillan, 1981), p. 236. Nubar, however, thought she was being scapegoated. See his memo, 20 June 1929, LDN02938; PIO, p. 102. For Deterding's view of CSG as a Bolshevik agitator, see Deterding to Rudeloff, 13 April and 1 May 1933. SHA, 195/22-G.

25. Although Deterding's dismissal of NSG was offensive, NSG's correspondence with his father suggests that NSG was aware of the impossible position in which

his refusal to take the post in Spain placed Deterding, and was thinking of resigning. NSG to CSG, 23 December 1925. LDN01344.

26. NSG to Deterding, 30 December 1925; Riedemann to NSG, 30 December 1925. LDN00602. See also PIO, p. 119.

27. The terms under which NSG replaced CSG on these boards were themselves contested by Gulbenkian and Deterding. See Deterding to CSG, 21 July and 29 September 1925; CSG to Deterding, n.d. [October 1925]. LDN02504.

28. Royal Dutch-Shell files suggest that directors were already trying to work out how to disconnect themselves from Gulbenkian the previous May. Waley Cohen to J. E. F. de Kok, 21 May 1925. SHA, 190/190D/696.

29. CSG to NSG, 25 April 1925. NSG00001.

30. Quoted in Deterding to CSG, 11 April 1924. LDN00535. See also HRDS, Vol. 1, pp. 291–5, 305–6.

31. Deterding to CSG, n.d. [between 15 March and 2 April 1924]. LDN00535. Given the raft of unsupported claims alleging that Deterding supported Hitler, it is salutary to consider Deterding's 1933 correspondence with Rudeloff. This makes clear that Deterding was not a fervent supporter of Nazism. His general view of Nazism was that 'the whole movement will do a lot of good, especially as it is directed against Communism'. Deterding to Rudeloff, 4 February 1933. Though deplorable, Deterding's anti-Semitic sentiments were not unusual for the time: examples of Cadman and others making similar remarks could be given. See also HRDS, Vol. 1, pp. 477, 481.

32. CSG to NSG, 4 November 1925. LDN00866.

33. NSG to J. E. F. de Kok, 30 December 1925. LDN00602.

34. CSG to Deterding, 10 March 1918. LDN01547.

35. PIO, pp. 72 ('apple'), 126 ('career').

36. CSG to Sir Charles Russell, 4 March 1926. LDN00675.

37. See the file 'Re: Herminia' in NSG00001.

38. Richard Washburn Child, *A Diplomat Looks at Europe* (New York: Duffield, 1925), pp. 16 ('average'), 17 ('appetite').

39. 'A. E. F.', 'At the Embassy Club', *Sunday Express*, 21 September 1924.

40. MCG00070 (MacGregor); MCG00015 (cat). The private commission agent Arthur Ruck was also active in assisting CSG with the MacGregor collection. See LDN00432. Luis Manuel de Araujo, *Egyptian Art: Calouste Gulbenkian Collection* (Lisbon: CGF, 2006), p. 50.

41. JAP, *Calouste Gulbenkian: Collector* (Lisbon: CGF, 1969), p. 11.

42. E. S. G. Robinson, *A Catalogue of the Calouste Gulbenkian Collection of Greek Coins* (Lisbon: CGF, 1971), Pt 1 *Italy, Sicily, Carthage*, pp. 13 ('step'), 14 ('austere').

43. CSG to Joseph Duveen, 8 January 1920 (quote). LDN01451, f. 13. See also Otto Gutekunst to CSG, 8 February 1921. LDN00412; CSG to Lockett Agnew, 19 January 1916. LDN00066. Arthur Ruck to CSG, 3 September 1923. LDN00513.

Edward Fowles, *Memories of Duveen Brothers* (London: Heinemann, 1976), p. 172.

44. Ibid., p. 174.

45. Kenneth Clark, speech at the opening of the Calouste Gulbenkian Museum in 1969. TA, 8812.2.2.371–2. For plans and photographs, see Centre Culturel Calouste Gulbenkian, *L'Hotel Gulbenkian 51 Avenue d'Iéna: Mémoires d'un lieu* (Paris: CCCG, 2011).

46. Herminia Feijóo's divorce petition carefully listed the many instances during which Nubar appeared naked in the presence of servants, which she presented as further evidence of Nubar's abuse of her. NSG00001, 'Re: Herminia'.

47. The peacock later moved to Les Enclos, CSG's estate in Normandy. Chanet, p. 126.

48. CSG to John Walker, 18 August 1947. NGA, RG28 Box 8–13.

49. Kenneth Clark, *Another Part of the Wood: A Self-Portrait* (London: John Murray, 1974), p. 229.

50. CSG to NSG, 12 June 1926. NSG00019.

51. CSG to NSG, 11 June 1926. NSG00019.

Chapter 11: Fighting or Making Love, 1926–8

1. Draft minutes, 5 August 1924. BP, 67764.

2. Anglo-Persian and Royal Dutch-Shell, for example, created Consolidated Petroleum (share capital £100), pooling their sale facilities in the Middle East and Africa, sharing profits 50:50. BP, 202439. Ronald W. Ferrier, *The History of the British Petroleum Company*, Vol. 1 *The Developing Years, 1901–1932* (Cambridge: Cambridge University Press, 1982), p. 509; HRDS, Vol. 1, pp. 439–44.

3. Heinrich Riedemann to Teagle, 2 September 1925. Cited in George Sweet Gibb and Evelyn H. Knowlton, *History of Standard Oil Company (New Jersey)*, Vol. 2 *Resurgent Years, 1911–27* (New York: Harper & Brothers, 1956), p. 349.

4. Cited in PIO, p. 96.

5. A. W. Dulles, memo, 10 May 1923. NARA, RG59 890G.6363/T84/92.

6. 'S.K.H.', memo, 11 May 1923. NARA, RG59 890G.6363/T84/92.

7. Allen Dulles, 'The Turkish Petroleum Company – Status of Negotiations', 19 September 1924. NARA, RG59 890G.6363/T84/167.

8. Teagle and Howard Cole to Nichols, 31 July 1924. BP, 67764.

9. Nichols to Louis Tronchère, 17 November 1925. BP, 123039.

10. Stephen Longrigg, *The Origins and Early History of the Iraq Petroleum Company* (London: privately printed, 1969), p. 155.

11. Richard F. Kuisel, *Capitalism and the State in Modern France: Renovation and Economic Management in the Twentieth Century* (Cambridge: Cambridge University Press, 1981), p. 68.

12. Horace Finaly of Paribas and Standard Franco-Américaine was Jersey Standard's chief adviser on French oil policy. He viewed Pineau as 'a diligent agent for Sir H[enry] D[eterding]', while Mercier was 'a friend of ours', albeit one whose 'high character' would keep him impartial. Finaly to Teagle, 1 August 1922 (Pineau) and 1 April 1924 (Mercier). Archives BNP Paribas, Combs La Ville-Quincy. 744/2.

13. Nichols to Agnew, 8 January 1925. BP, 067807.

14. Nichols to Mercier, 6 February 1924. AGT, 81ZX916–54 (81.1/54).

15. It had proved impossible, admittedly, to locate sufficient Iraqi capital for equity to be practicable. Peter Sluglett, *Britain in Iraq: Contriving King and Country* (London: I. B. Tauris, 2007).

16. Teagle to Mercier, 7 December 1924. AGT, 81ZX916–53 (81.1/53). For the negotiations over this royalty, see Nichols to Mercier, 19 February 1925. AGT, 81ZX916–54 (81.1/54).

17. For a discussion, see 'Memorandum by Messrs. Linklaters and Paines with regard to the revised Draft Agreement prepared by Mr Gulbenkian's Solicitors', 15 July 1925. BP, 067807.

18. A. W. Dulles, memo 11 November 1924. NARA, RG59 890G.6363/T84/176.

19. 'Turkish Petroleum Company', *The Economist*, 23 August 1924, p. 310. Greenway also refers to this as a 'commission' in his account of the Foreign Office Agreement negotiations. Greenway, 'Fusion of D'Arcy and Other Interests', 2 October 1934. BP, 070229.

20. CSG to Deterding, 23 June 1914. SHA, 195/37.

21. CSG to Lane, 8 May 1907 ('slice'). LDN01509. CSG to Ofenheim, 12 January 1914 ('solidarity'). LDN01538.

22. CSG to Louis S. Levy, 8 August 1924. LDN00864.

23. William Fraser, cited in NSG to CSG, 18 January 1945. PRS00669.

24. CSG to Riedemann, 19 October 1923. LDN00532. For similar claims, see CSG to Deterding, 22 December 1922. LDN00860. CSG did not send this letter, suggesting that he knew Deterding would be able to see through the claim.

25. See Lefroy to Greenway, 2 October 1934. BP, 070229.

26. Tyrrell to CSG, 10 October 1924. LDN00864. Though the first surviving letter between them dates to 1914 (LDN00070), the relationship does not appear to have been close before 1921. By 1922 CSG was close enough to be advising Tyrrell's wife on her plans for a children's history book and other projects. See LDN00473.

27. Cadman to Lancelot Oliphant, 11 December 1925; Cadman to CSG, 7 January 1926; Oliphant to Cadman, 5 July 1926. BP, 068820. CSG to Cadman, 9 September 1927. BP, 71534.

28. Pineau to Mercier, 6 October 1926; Berthelot to Mercier, 3 March 1927. AGT, 81ZX916–41. Pineau to Gulbenkian, 24 July 1926. PRS03438. As the FO noted,

'the French moves have merely consisted of endorsing everything that Mr Gulbenkian claimed'. Minute 31 March 1926. TNA, FO371/11455/E2207.

29. Leslie Burgin to Louis Tronchère, 11 and 19 April 1927. AGT, 81ZX916–45. Burgin to Tronchère, 12 February 1927; Burgin to Mercier, 7 February 1927. AGT, 81ZX916–41.

30. Keith M. Wilson, *A Study in the History and Politics of the 'Morning Post', 1905–1926* (Lewiston, NY: Edwin Mellen Press, 1990), Ch. 7.

31. [CSG] to Gwynne, 5 January 1926. LDN00600.

32. Gwynne to CSG, 24 September 1928. LDN00749.

33. Gwynne to CSG, 6 and 25 November 1925. LDN00600. Memcon Inverforth/A. Chamberlain, 3 December 1925; Gwynne to Amery, 22 December 1925. TNA FO371/10829.

34. CSG to Gwynne, 11 January 1927. LDN00693.

35. Gwynne to CSG, n.d. 1925. LDN00600. For the press coverage, see 'Mosul Oil Fields. The True Facts', *Morning Post*, 19 November 1925. Compare 'Armenian Blocks Oil Plan in Mosul', *New York Times*, 11 October 1926. By 1927 Gwynne was rather fed up with CSG pouring out 'his woes' to him. Gwynne to Tyrrell, 16 February 1927. TNA, FO371/12263/140. For another madcap scheme, see Gwynne to Kells, 21 September 1939, KV2/4426.

36. Entry for 6 November 1927. BP, 110741.

37. Chanet, pp. 18–19.

38. NSG, 'Piesse memo', 13 February 1928. LDN02938.

39. Piesse to Mercier, 9 April 1926. AGT, 81ZX916–54. (81.1/54).

40. Tronchère to Mercier, 31 March 1926. AGT, 81ZX916–54. (81.1/54).

41. Georg Spies, *Erinnerungen eines Ausland-Deutschen* (1926; St Petersburg: Olearius, 2002), p. 228.

42. Sir John Simon and C. J. Conway, joint opinion, 2 February 1927. AGT, 81ZX916–41 (81.1/41).

43. Memcon Wilfred Greene, n.d. [October 1924]. LDN00864.

44. Sir Douglas Hogg to CSG, 10 February 1926. LDN00640.

45. Malkin note, 29 January 1927. TNA, FO371/11456/E342/104/65

46. CSG to NSG, 17 July 1926. LDN01316.

47. CSG to NSG, 2 September 1926. LDN01316.

48. CSG to Nichols, 26 October 1923. LDN00510.

49. Note by Lancelot Oliphant, 28 February 1928; Tyrrell to Sir John Anderson, 19 March 1928. TNA, FO372/2436, T2163.

50. Hossein Khan Ghadimy to CSG, 7 October 1924. LDN00553. For 'Isa Khan, see CSG, confidential memo, 11 February 1929; NSG, 'Issa Khan memo', 13 February 1929. LDN00832.

51. H. E. Mirza Hussein Khan Ala (Iranian ambassador to France) and Ali Akbar Khan Davar acknowledged CSG's input at the abortive negotiations held in the Iranian Embassy in Paris, 8–10 February 1933. The pair were too fearful of

retribution in Tehran to negotiate, however. BP, 69363. The Gulbenkians did not welcome Ala's appointment to Paris, considering him overly hostile to both Armenians and the British. NSG, 'O.K. memo', 25 June 1929. LDN00832.

52. CSG, memo, 24 February (portraits) 1926; CSG to Massehian, 6 June and 17 August 1926. LDN00669. Samad was nonetheless described as 'in the hands of Gulbenkian, an Armenian', in Hardinge, 'Report on Heads of Foreign Missions in Paris', 16 August 1922. TNA, FO371/8274/184.

53. H. Massehian to CSG, 14 May 1926. LDN00669.

54. CSG to Deterding, 19 July 1921. PRS03446. NSG, 'O.K. memo', 1 July 1929. LDN00832.

55. 'List of cheques sent to H. E. Samad Khan', 31 January 1923. LDN00494. SEP to H. E. Samad Khan Mometazos Saltaneh, 26 January 1921. LDN00430. For embassy refurbishment, see memo, 22 September 1927. LDN00915. The same file contains letters referring to sums given as gifts to a number of Iranian ministers and officials.

56. When Massehian resigned as ambassador he vowed he 'would do nothing without consulting very closely with us', and praised NSG to his successor, Taqizadeh. NSG, 'O.K. memo', 1 July and 8 August 1929. LDN00832. Unfortunately for Gulbenkian, Massehian went to the Tokyo embassy and died shortly afterwards. Adjemoff to CSG, 24 September 1929. LDN00756.

57. CSG to Massehian, 14 May (quote) and 17 August 1926. LDN00669.

Chapter 12: The Big Scheme, 1928–30

1. CSG to NSG, 18 December 1926. LDN00702.

2. CSG to A. Chester Beatty, 11 June 1924. Selection Trust Papers, London School of Economics. ACB/216. For Beatty's dining habits, see David Kynaston, *The City of London*, Vol. 3 *Illusions of Gold, 1914–45* (London: Chatto & Windus, 1999), p. 339.

3. A third key figure in London was Hermann Marx, head of the brokers Cull & Co. CSG's relationship with Marx went back to at least 1912, when Marx worked at the brokers Nelke Philips. See CSG, 'Tetiuhe Mining Corporation Guarantee', 16 March 1931. LDN01094. For the origins of Tetiuhe, see V. V. Veeder, 'The Tetiuhe Mining Concession 1924–32', in *Liber Amicorum Claude Reymond: Autour de l'arbitrage* (Paris: Éditions de Juris-Classeur, 2004), pp. 325–42.

4. Chicherin memo, 3 November 1927. Foreign Policy Archives of the Russian Federation, Moscow. File 05, op. 79, folder 29, delo 5, doc. 7.

5. For an overview, see Geoffrey Jones and Clive Trebilcock, 'Russian Industry and British Business: Oil and Armaments', *Journal of European Economic History*, 11 (1982), 61–103.

6. Gustav Nobel and Moise Adjemoff, undated memo. LDN00675, filed under 'Timurtash'. The basic outlines of the scheme were not secret, being described in

articles in the *Berliner Tageblatt* and *Courrier des Pétroles*. See David Williamson to State Department, 16 August 1929; David H. Slawson to State Department, 30 July 1929. NARA, RG59 891.6363/645 and /646.

7. For their correspondence, see LDN00535, LDN00593.

8. CSG to Kuhn Loeb, 10 January 1927. LDN00702. CSG to unidentified correspondent, 12 April 1928. LDN00758.

9. CSG to Émile Francqui (Vice-Gouverneur, SocGen), 25 April and 12 October 1928. LDN00749.

10. A. Chester Beatty to Charles Hayden, 3 January 1927. Selection Trust Papers, London School of Economics. ACB/217.

11. CSG to Colijn, 7 March 1927. LDN00702.

12. Deterding to Teagle, 9 ('loyalty') and 27 ('sleeping') June 1927. SHA, 195/30g.

13. E. J. Sadler to 28 August 1923. Cited in George Sweet Gibb and Evelyn H. Knowlton, *History of Standard Oil Company (New Jersey)*, Vol. 2 *Resurgent Years, 1911–27* (New York: Harper & Brothers, 1956), p. 344.

14. Neftsyndikat to Pineau, 19 December 1924. RGAE, f. 2309, op. 4, d. 21.

15. Pétrofina's French sales were through a subsidiary, Pétrofina Française. It bought back Neftsyndikat's 45 per cent of Pétronaphte in 1937. See Total Chemie et Raffinage, Brussels. 'Compagnie Financière Belge des Pétroles – Procès-Verbale 1920–36', minutes for 31 March 1924, 30 January 1925, 10 November 1926 and 9 October 1929. RGAE, f. 2309, op. 4, d. 21; f. 2309, op. 4, d. 21; f.2309, op.4, d.81. Michael Dumoulin, *Pétrofina* (2 vols., Leuven: Peeters, 1997), Vol. 1, pp. 47–9.

16. CSG to Adjemoff, 25 July 1925. LDN00866. NSG to Deterding, 14 December 1925. SHA, 195/35.

17. Teagle to Riedemann, 21 August 1925. Cited in Gibb and Knowlton, *Resurgent Years*, p. 348.

18. CSG to NSG, 10 March 1924. LDN00563.

19. Waley Cohen to August Philips, 11 May 1922; CSG to Waley Cohen, 13 May 1922. SLA, GHC/USSR/C2 USSR Vol. 3b, 'Undertaking given to British government'.

20. It seems that in 1925 CSG used H. A. Gwynne and Deterding to lobby William Tyrrell (FO) and Home Secretary Sir William Joynson-Hicks to persuade Cadman to stop negotiating with the Russians (Anglo-Persian was planning to purchase Russian oil for Germany). See CSG to Tyrrell, 17 September 1925. LDN00593. Gwynne to CSG, 13, 20, 27 August and 25 November 1925. CSG to Gwynne, 31 October 1925. LDN00600. Joynson-Hicks to Cadman, 26 October 1925, and 'Note of agreement between Cadman and Deterding', 7 November 1925. BP, 68864. NSG to Deterding, 23 January 1925. SHA, 195/35. NSG to CSG, 9 November 1925. LDN00866.

21. Cited in W. Joynson-Hicks to A. B. Houghton, 18 February 1926. NARA, RG59 861.6363/262.

22. Teagle to Riedemann, 17 August 1926. Cited in Gibb and Knowlton, *Resurgent Years*, p. 352.

23. Robert F. Kelley, memcon, 8 February 1927. NARA, RG59 861.6363/222.

24. Sir John Broderick (commercial counsel, UK Embassy Washington), cited in W. R. Castle (Asst. SOS), memcon, 4 February 1928. NARA, RG59 861.6363/239.

25. CSG to Hans Meyer (Warburgs), 17 December 1928. LDN00758. See also CSG to Hans Meyer, 6 June 1927. LDN00702.

26. CSG memo, 20 March 1929. CGF, MCG02429.

27. CSG to NSG, 15 October 1926, LDN00675. CSG to Timurtash, 23 October 1926. LDN00669.

28. The treaties were signed on 3 July 1924 and 17 December 1925 respectively. For the purchase agreement between Baryshnikoff of Russo-Persian Bank and Khostaria (24 August 1924) and the agreement between Russo-Persian Bank and Kevir-Khurian (28 August 1924), see B. Z. Shumyatsky's report of 28 February 1925. GARF, f. 374, op. 28, d. 1269. For Khostaria and his firmans, see GARF f. 5446, op. 71, d. 125; George W. T. Barnett, 'An Account of the Kavir-i-Khourian Oil Concession in North Persia', 13 June 1945. TNA, FO371/45506. Barnett's report is reproduced word for word (without acknowledgement) in M. Abdullahzadeh, 'The Kavir-i Khurian Oil Concession', *British Institute of Persian Studies*, 33 (1995), 161–4.

29. Of Kevir-Khurian's capital of 5 million tomans, Russo-Persian Bank held 3.25 million, Khostaria 1 million, Reza Shah 250,000, Timurtash and Daver (another minister) 150,000 and 100,000. GARF f. 5446, op. 8a, d. 84.

30. B. Z. Shumyatsky to Chicherin, 5 February 1925, cited in B. Z. Shumyatsky report, 28 February 1925. GARF, f. 374, op. 28, d. 1269.

31. Shortly after leaving Moscow, Timurtash claimed that the USSR opposed Gulbenkian's scheme because they did not want a third party (the French element of the scheme) having a foothold in the Caspian. There is no evidence in the Russian archives to support this claim. Vanetzian to Adjemoff, 3 December 1926. LDN00675. Commission on Semnan Oil, Protocol 2, 5 October 1926. GARF f. 5446, op. 71, d. 125, doc. 1. Karahan to Rukhimovich (copied to Mikoyan), 28 November 1926. f. 5446, op. 8a, d. 84, doc. 3. Pineau to Berthelot, 25 January 1927; CSG, 'Semna' memo, 2 February 1927. LDN00725. Perlin to Rakovsky, 5 February 1927. RGAE, f. 5240, op. 18, d. 2631, doc. 94.

32. 'Pétrole du Semnan' memo, 1 October 1927. LDN00725. Russo-Persian Bank had transferred the Kevir-Khurian shares in question to Azneft. See also CSG to Timurtash, 9 October 1927; CSG to unidentified correspondent, 28 March 1928; CSG to Vossough Dowley, 1 March 1928. LDN00715. CSG to Timurtash, 6 August 1928. LDN00779.

33. Piatakoff to Mikoyan (quote), 23 March 1928; Piatakoff to Chicherin, 30 March 1928. GARF f. 8350, op. 1, d. 3138, docs. 72 and 76.

34. Chicherin to Politburo, 30 May 1928. RGAE f. 5240, op. 18, d. 903, doc. 214.

35. Politburo memo, undated; Goldin to Khinchuk, 11 June 1928. RGAE f. 5240, op. 18, d. 903, docs. 207 and 192.

36. Politburo memos, 14 and 22 June 1926. Russian State Archives of Socio-Political History, Moscow, f. 17, op. 162, d. 6, docs. 107 and 111.

37. Elena Solomacha, 'Verkäufe aus der Eremitage', in Waltraud Bayer (ed.), *Verkaufte Kultur* (Oxford: Lang, 2001), p. 56.

38. Robert C. Williams, *Russian Art and American Money, 1900–1940* (Cambridge, Mass.: Harvard University Press, 1980), pp. 157–8; Semoynova and Iljine, *Selling Russian Treasures*, p. 269.

39. Martin Conway to Katrina Conway, 4 ('empty world') and 16 ('suicide') June 1924. Cambridge University Library, Conway Papers. Add 7676/D217 and 223.

40. Conway urged the National Gallery in London to buy, and proposed a return visit to the USSR in 1931. See C. J. Holmes to Robert Witt, 3 October 1924. National Gallery (London) Archives, NG26/122; TNA, FO371/15621

41. Solomacha, 'Verkäufe aus der Eremitage', p. 45.

42. For CSG's annotated copy of Pierre P. Weiner, *Les Chefs-d'oeuvre de la Galerie de Tableaux de l'Ermitage à Petrograd* (Munich: Franz Hanfstaengl, 1923), see CGF Art Library MS6 Res.

43. CSG, 'Liste de 8 Tableaux Remise à M. Piatakoff,' 30 Sept. 1928, '2nd List. Given à Mr. P on the day of his departure,' n.d.; 'Memorandum pour M. Aucoc,' 20 Sept. 1928, 'Memorandum,' n.d. MCG01147. A. Aucoc to CSG, 30 Oct. 1928; CSG to A. Aucoc, 25 April 1929; CSG, 'Memorandum concernant l'historique et les détails de l'achat d'objets à l'URSS, en 1928–9,' n.d. MCG01134.

44. CSG to Piatakoff, 19 December 1928. MCG02429. Piatakoff to Mikoyan, 2 January 1929. RGAE, f. 5240, op. 18, d. 2738, doc. 68.

45. Nikolaeff to unidentified correspondent, 8 March 1929. RGAE, f. 5240, op. 18, d. 2739, doc. 148.

46. Birenczweig to Khinchuk 25 October 1929. RGAE, f. 5240, op. 18, d. 2740, doc. 40.

47. CSG, memo for Piatakoff, 10 November 1929. Ibid., doc. 63.

48. Unidentified correspondent to Piatakoff, 15 June 1929. RGAE, f. 5240, op. 18, d. 2739, doc. 35. Birenczweig and N. G. Tumanoff (both Paris-based Russian trade representatives) met Gulbenkian in the months before this letter and may have written it, but it could have been penned by someone else entirely.

49. Troïnitsky to Mikoyan, 11 October 1928. RGAE, f. 5240, op. 9, d. 243, doc. 10. See also the report by D. A. Schmidt, 1 April 1929. The Hermitage Archives, St Petersburg. f.1, opis 5, chast 2, 859/72, doc. 212.

50. Solomacha, 'Verkäufe aus der Eremitage', p. 51.

51. CSG to A. Chadanian, 26 June 1930. MCG01139.

52. Edouard Leblond to CSG, 29 July 1930. MCG01141. This confirms the unattributed rumour cited by Oskina, 'De l'or pour l'industrialisation', *Cahiers du Monde russe*, 41:1 (2000), 5–40 (33).

53. Tatyana V. Sapozhnikova, cited in Elena Solomacha, 'The Destruction of the Hermitage', in Natalya Semyonova and Nicolas V. Iljine (eds.), *Selling Russian Treasures: The Soviet Trade in Nationalized Art, 1917–38* (New York: Abbeville Press, 2013), p. 139.

54. Paul Hocquart carried out the repairs. MCG01140.

55. Ministère des Affaires Etrangères to Mirza Hussein Khan Ala, 5 June 1930. MCG01138.

56. CSG to Piatakoff, 17 July 1930. LDN01030.

57. In 1931–2 Gulbenkian contacted Zatzenstein of the Berlin gallery Matthiessen, enquiring about antique Greek coins and Manets held in Russian collections, but nothing seems to have come of this. LDN01095 and LDN01154.

58. CSG to Émile Francqui, 12 October and 7 December 1928. LDN00749 and LDN00758. CSG to Piatakoff, 19 December 1928 (quote). MCG02429.

59. Unidentified correspondent to Piatakoff, 15 June 1929. RGAE, f. 5240, op. 18, d. 2739, doc. 35.

60. Toumanoff and Birenczweig discussed oil matters a couple of times in 1930. The last memo CSG sent Piatakoff on financial questions is dated 6 December 1930. LDN00990. A year later he was complaining to Piatakoff 'that I have no longer a link on this side [i.e. Paris] through whom I can correspond regularly with yourself'. CSG to Piatakoff, 8 April 1931. LDN01094.

61. Soviet oil exports peaked a few years later, in 1933, then declined. Hans Heymann Jr, 'Oil in Soviet-Western Relations in the Interwar Years', *American Slavic and East European Review*, 7:4 (1948), 303–16 (315).

62. See LDN01094; Veeder, 'The Tetiuhe Mining Concession 1924–32', pp. 337–42; V. V. Veeder, 'International Arbitration: Anglo-US Mining Concessions in Soviet Russia (1920–1925)', in Elizabeth Bastida, Thomas Wälde and Janeth Warden-Fernández (eds.), *International and Comparative Mineral Law and Policy* (The Hague: Kluwer Law International, 2005), pp. 99–126. My thanks to Johnny Van Veeder for sharing copies of his work on Tetiuhe with me.

63. For Wenger's correspondence with Batigne, who led the 1929–30 survey, see AMAE, 19RC/48. For the annual reports of the Syndicat d'Études Franco-Persane and its successors, the Société Franco-Persane de Recherches (established 1930, with a capital of 10 million francs) and the Société Franco-Iranienne de Recherches (established 1936), see Total Chemie et Raffinage, Brussels, 3/2/2/794.

64. Miron Rezun, 'Reza Shah's Court Minister: Teymourtash', *International Journal of Middle Eastern Studies*, 12:2 (1980), 119–37 (132); Ervand Abrahamian, *A History of Modern Iran* (Cambridge: Cambridge University Press, 2008), p. 75.

65. In 1926 Gulbenkian had tried unsuccessfully to interest Anglo-Persian in joining him in this venture. R. W. Ferrier, *The Developing Years*, p. 554. BP, 78/70/161 and 3A3097.

66. Gil Fortoul to CSG, 11 September 1926. LDN01316. E. H. Keeling to NSG, 6 December 1926. LDN01317. See also Selection Trust Papers, London School of Economics, ACB/218.

67. LDN00368. For Société Pétrolière de Caracas's attempts to secure both the *côte* and French state subsidies, see AN, 19780642/10 IND 12894.

68. Henry Lockhart to CSG, 26 October 1926. LDN00634. Blair & Co. made its 1928 offer of a credit line to Romania conditional on reforms to its 1924 mining law, which may have been related to the Romanian part of Gulbenkian's scheme. Gh. Buzatu, *A History of Romanian Oil*, translated by Laura Chistruga-Schneider (Bucharest: Mica Valahie, 2011), p. 407.

69. Paul Atterbury and Julia MacKenzie, *A Golden Adventure: The First 50 Years of Ultramar* (London: Hurtwood Press, 1985), pp. 17–19.

70. Robert Lenzner, *The Great Getty* (New York: Crown, 1985), pp. 53–8.

71. P. G. Vanetzian's firm was named Grivan Products. Hermann Marx to CSG, 12 December 1923. LDN00502; Vanetzian correspondence in LDN00619; PIO, p. 132 (in which NSG claims twenty-five tons). Nubar's references in the same passage to Douglas Hogg's gratitude for such gifts is confirmed by the Hogg letters cited above. See also LDN01692.

Chapter 13: Mr President, 1930–34

1. The relationship was distant enough to make any reconstruction tentative, but it appears that Aram Turabian may have been the son of Kerope Turabian and Vartouhi Selian, whose brother Hagop Selian married Miriam Gulbenkian, sister of Sarkis, Calouste's father – a 'cousin-in-law', in effect.

2. Aram Turabian, *Calouste Gulbenkian: Le milliardaire arménien et sa vie* (Marseille: privately printed, 1930), pp. 6 (Sarkis), 7 (egoism), 27 (brothers), 38 (money-making).

3. Aram Turabian, *Les volontaires arméniens sous les drapeaux français* (2nd edn, Marseille: Association Ouvrière, 1917). See also Feroz Ahmad, *The Young Turks and the Ottoman Nationalities* (Salt Lake City, UT: University of Utah Press, 2014), p. 75.

4. Aram Turabian to Soulas, 28 August 1929 (business); Aram Turabian to CSG, 10 (quote) and 25 November 1929. PRS00318. The cycle of self-righteous entreaty, threat and apology continued until at least 1934, with Turabian publishing another anti-CSG broadside in May 1933, after CSG refused to pay Turabian's hotel bill, which the hotel manager sent to CSG direct. See A. Fivel-Demoret to CSG, 26 January 1932. PRS00318. Between 1927 and 1929 CSG and NAE gave Turabian more than 3,500 francs.

5. V. Inayétian to CSG, 5 June 1908, LDN00014; Turabian, *Calouste Gulbenkian*, pp. 16 (Sarkis deathbed), 18 ('Calouste!'), 19 (doctor). See also Aram Turabian to CSG, 10 June 1928. PRS00318.

6. Balances as at 31 December 1932. LDN02750.

7. Calculation based on Mikdashi's figures. Zuhayr Mikdashi, *A Financial Analysis of Middle Eastern Oil Concessions: 1901–1965* (New York: Frederick A. Praeger, 1966), App. 2, Table 34.

8. For rent-seeking by Nuri al-Said and 'Abd al-Muhsin al-Sa'dun, see Peter Sluglett, *Britain in Iraq: Contriving King and Country* (London: I. B. Tauris, 2007), p. 258, note 60.

9. Cited in NSG, TPC memo, 3 March 1928. LDN02938.

10. When the Iraqi prime minister 'Abd al-Muhsin al-Sa'dun visited London in 1923 he wrote to Gulbenkian, but this was probably just a courtesy call. 'Abd al-Muhsin al-Sa'dun to CSG, 19 May 1923. LDN00496.

11. CSG to NSG, 7 October 1929. LDN00812.

12. NSG to CSG, 7 October 1929; CSG to NSG, 9 October 1929. LDN00812.

13. CSG to NSG, 2 January 1930. LDN01099.

14. NSG to CSG, 8 October 1929. NSG00001. The suggestion of NSG serving as managing director apparently came (twice) from Montagu Piesse. NSG, TPC Memo 43, 25 July 1929.

15. CSG to NSG, 2 January 1930. LDN01099.

16. Arakel Bey Nubar cited in CSG to Devgantz, 20 October 1930. LDN00990.

17. Nevarte's cousin Vahan Essayan married the daughter of Abraham Paşa, Nubar Nubarian's brother-in-law, and the Nubarian connection played an important role in CSG's early career, according to Essayan family tradition. Evidence to support this has yet to be found.

18. Report, 10 December 1931. NEF Dockets 1931–2. Near East Foundation Archives, Rockefeller Archive Center, Sleepy Hollow, NY.

19. CSG to Yervant Aghaton, 6 January 1931. LDN01096.

20. CSG memo, 7 November 1930. LDN01037.

21. Trust Officer (City Bank, NY) to NSG, 2 December 1930; CSG to Arshag Karagheusian, 8 December 1930. 'Union Générale Arménienne de Bienfaisance Memo', 27 November 1930. LDN01037.

22. Parekordzagan memo, 9 December 1930; CSG memo, 10 December 1930. LDN01037.

23. Raymond H. Kevorkian and Vahé Tachjian (eds.), *The Armenian General Benevolent Union: One Hundred Years of History* (2 vols, New York: AGBU, 2006), Vol. 1, p. 195.

24. CSG to Arshag Karagheusian, 1, 17 and 25 (quote) July 1931. LDN01096. Kevorkian and Tachjian (eds.), *The Armenian General Benevolent Union*, Vol. 1, pp. 251, 253.

25. NARA, RG59 390D.1162-GUL. This file is missing, but it is clear from the microfilmed index to this file series that this dispatch reported the foundation of the hospital.

26. Kevorkian and Tachjian (eds.), *The Armenian General Benevolent Union*, Vol. 1, p. 259.

27. Ibid., p. 206.

28. CSG to Leon Gumushguerdan, 21 January 1932. LDN01153. See also CSG to Vahan Malezian, 6 July 1931. LDN01096.

29. Arshag Tchobanian to CSG, 12 November 1930; CSG to Arshag Tchobanian, 17 November 1930. LDN01037.

30. CSG to Setrak Devgantz, 27 November 1930. LDN0990. For thoughts of resignation, see CSG to Arshag Karagheusian, 1 December 1930. LDN01037. There are interesting parallels to Robert Waley Cohen's activities on behalf of fellow Jews. A liberal and a 'Palestine Zionist', Waley Cohen's generosity and leadership received as little thanks from his community as Gulbenkian's did. For a surprisingly candid assessment, see Robert Henriques, *Sir Robert Waley Cohen 1877–1952* (London: Secker & Warburg, 1966), pp. 263–71, 343–8.

31. CSG to Setrak Devgantz, 18 October 1930. LDN00990.

32. Kevorkian and Tachjian (eds.), *The Armenian General Benevolent Union*, Vol. 1, pp. 261, 214.

33. NSG Memo 134, 31 October 1928 (far-fetched); Memo 142, 4 December 1928 (list). LDN02938.

34. See Thomas Palmer to Wallace Murray, 25 August 1930. NARA, RG59 890G.6363T84/431. The figure is Jersey Standard's. Edward Peter Fitzgerald, 'Business Diplomacy: Walter Teagle, Jersey Standard, and the Anglo-French Pipeline Conflict in the Middle East, 1930–32', *Business History Review*, 67 (1993), 219 note 17.

35. NSG memcon 17 June and 3 July 1929. LDN02937. NSG memcon, 20 February 1929. LDN02938.

36. For Mercier's claim, which he made to the Quai d'Orsay, see Anon., 'Note pour M. Berthelot', 29 May 1928. AMAE 19RC/61/67; Fleuriau to Aristide Briand, 16 August 1928. AMAE 19RC/61, f. 273. John Randolph to State Department, 18 December 1928 (Pachachi) and 9 September 1929 (Shell); Alexander K. Sloan to State Department, 14 January 1931 (Sinclair). NARA, RG59 890G.6363WEMYSS/1, 12 and 67. For Getty's own interest in an Iraqi concession, see Joseph C. Grew to State Department, 19 February 1930; Sloan to State Department, 8 October 1930 and 5 January 1931. NARA, RG59 890G.6363T84/405, 440 and 453.

37. There is little to justify Mascia's claim that this episode 'represented a great success for Italy in general'. Giacinto Mascia, 'La Nascita et lo Sviluppo dell'Azienda Generale Italiana Petroli (AGIP) negli fra le due guerre (1926–40)', University of Cagliari doctoral dissertation, 2012, p. 147. For suspicions of speculation, see ibid., pp. 125–7, 130, 134–5. For French investors in BOD, see AN 9780642/16 IND 12899.

38. Lady Wemyss memo, n.d., and Dudley H. Dibdin to Lady Wemyss, 17 May 1934 and 11 December 1935 (quote). Churchill Archives Centre, Cambridge. WEMYS 13/2.

39. CSG to Sir Adam Ritchie, 12 February 1929. BP, 176961. CFP and the Americans supported his idea, but Deterding opposed. Louis Tronchère to Borduge, 6 March 1929. CAEF B0032310, Folder 3 'TPC and Iraq 1929'.

40. Fitzgerald, 'Business Diplomacy', 207–45.

41. NSG to NAE, 11 May 1932. LDN01349, f. 13.

42. Mikhael Essayan, personal communication, 2012.

43. NSG to CSG, 19 March 1931 ('soft voice'). LDN01348, f. 140. NSG to CSG 12 June 1931 ('Clear out!'); CSG to NSG, 6 June 1931 (allowance); NSG to CSG, 12 June 1931 (refusal). LDN01099.

44. NSG to CSG, 26 October 1931. PRS01062.

45. Cited in Doré Gulbenkian, 'I Married into the Richest Family', *News of the World,* 25 October 1959.

46. 'The Royal Dutch-Shell Position', *The Investor*, 30 April 1932.

47. NSG, Grunwald memos, 24 ('sham') and 25 ('hitting') October 1932. LDN02623.

48. 'Sinistre Trinité', undated clipping from *Forces*. NSG blamed the piece on William F. Buckley of Pantepec, whom he unkindly described as 'a noted title-jumper, now in Paris, [who] is trying to upset our Caracas business, as he has, himself, some Venezuelan business he would like to introduce here'. NSG to CSG, 29 October 1932. LDN02623.

49. 'Kontra Deterding', undated clipping from *Vossische Zeitung*. SHA 15/132.

50. Gerhardt to Deterding, 20 April 1932; Deterding to Marcel Kapferer, 22 April 1932. Gulbenkian is named in Comtesse de Pluival Salges to Deterding, 1 May 1932. SHA 15/132.

51. LIS00439.

52. Vienna diary, entry for 8 October 1933.

53. Spain diary, entry for 25 March 1928, f. 31.

54. Marcelle Chanet was on both cruises, probably as secretary, and her insights into CSG's character were probably based on conversations on board. Chanet, pp. 152–6.

55. LDN00808.

56. Cruise diary, entry for 16 May 1932, f. 18.

57. For the painting, see Aram Hashadour to CSG, 8 June and 6 August 1934. Badrig Gulbenkian to Aram Hashadour, 11 November 1927. PRS00149.

58. Sylva Natalie Manoogian, 'Libraries of Armenian Jerusalemn', in Michael E. Stone, Roberta R. Ervin and Nira Stone (eds.), *The Armenians in Jerusalem and the Holy Land*, Hebrew University Armenian Studies, 4 (Leuven: Peeters, 2002), pp. 143–56. For Badrig's death, see *Pelham Sun* [Pelham, NY], 11 December 1931.

59. Astrig Tchamkerten's hagiographic account struggles to incorporate CSG in his family's pilgrimage tradition. Astrig Tchamkerten, *The Gulbenkians in Jerusalem* (Lisbon: Calouste Gulbenkian Foundation, 2006).

60. CSG to Dikran Turabian, 17 February 1930. LDN2449. CSG to Setrak Devgantz, 6 November 1932. LDN01113.

Chapter 14: Poor Pop Pays, 1935–8

1. P. Knabenshue to State Department, 1 November 1934. NARA, RG59 890G.6363T84/574.
2. Memcon CSG and Cadman, 5 November 1933. LDN01173.
3. P. Knabenshue to State Department, 24 January 1935. NARA, RG59 890G.6363T84/578.
4. NAE to NSG, 29 November 1934. LDN01274.
5. NAE to NSG, 11 October 1937. NSG00020.
6. PIO, pp. 38–9; Ralph Hewins, *Mr Five Per Cent: The Biography of Calouste Gulbenkian* (London: Hutchinson, 1957), pp. 180 (quote), 183–4. For the relevant extract from Young's serialised memoirs, see the *People*, 16 October 1955.
7. Malcolm Burr to YSE, 17 January 1928. PRS00902.
8. Rita Essayan, 'Pour Nubar', in *Les Papillons Repus* (n.p.: privately printed, 1973).
9. RSE to NSG, 19 [December 1935?], in which she describes the incident as occurring fifteen years before. Though a later hand has inserted the date 1938, 1935 fits the context better. NSG00021.
10. CSG revoked the gift to NSG of 30 Rue Émile Menier after their confrontation. NSG to CSG, 12 June 1931. LDN01099. The house may have been purchased from Adjemoff. Charles Letrosne to Adjemoff, 13 April 1929. PRS02004.
11. NSG to NAE, 2 November 1938. NSG00021.
12. NAE to NSG, n.d. [early February 1937]. NSG00020.
13. NAE to NSG, 6 January 1937. NSG00020.
14. NAE to NSG, 9 July 1937; RSE to NSG, 2 [January 1936?]. NSG00020.
15. A piece entitled *Une rue de Teheran*, for which Gulbenkian paid 2,000 francs. Receipt, 30 November 1932. MCG02511.
16. I am grateful to Mak's son, Dimitri Dourdine-Mak, for sharing this photo, the exhibition catalogue and other materials with me.
17. RSE to Dimitri Dourdine-Mak, 16 January 1977. Collection Dourdine-Mak, Brussels.
18. RSE to NSG, n.d. [1938]. NSG00021. RSE to CSG, 8 [Febuary 1934?]. PRS00184. For Mak's finances, see Directeur des RG to Cheberry (Directeur du Cabinet du Préfet de Police), 21 January 1938. My thanks to Dimitri Dourdine-Mak for sharing this information with me.
19. Martin Essayan, personal communication, 2014; NAE to NSG, n.d. [January 1938?]. NSG00021.
20. RSE to YSE, 17 August 1938. PRS00895.
21. RSE to NSG, 21 December 1937. NSG00020. NAE to NSG, 28 [December 1937?]. NSG00021. Charles Marcepoil to Bergery, 2 March 1938 (alien);

Marcepoil to de Hérédia, 24 March 1938 (Massot). Collection Dourdine-Mak, Brussels.

22. NAE to NSG, 23 [January 1938?]. NSG00021.

23. He had been attending Château de Bures's school in Orgeval. NSG to NAE, 18 June 1937. NSG00020.

24. RSE to NSG, 2 [January 1936?]. NSG00021. The letter and memo are written from Madrid. Other, dated, letters establish that Rita and Yervant Essayan were in Spain in January 1936.

25. NAE to NSG, n.d. [early April 1937]. NSG00020. RSE to NSG, 2 [January 1936?]. NSG00021.

26. RSE to NSG, 14 January 1938. NSG00021.

27. Martin Essayan, personal communication, 2015.

28. Mikhael Essayan to CSG, 29 December 1935. M. A. Rae to CSG, 29 December 1935. PRS00184.

29. NAE to NSG, 14 September 1937 [with marginalia by NAE in reply, n.d.]. NSG00020.

30. NSG to NAE [with marginalia by NAE in reply, 2 October], 1 October 1937. NSG00020.

31. NSG to NAE [with marginalia by NAE in reply, 20 November], 19 November 1937. NSG00020.

32. NSG memo, 12 April 1938. NSG00021.

33. 17 July 1935. LDN01625.

34. NAE to NSG, n.d. [January 1938?]. NSG00021.

35. *Gulbenkian* v. *Gulbenkian*, TNA J77/3470/5879J77/3581/1030.

36. 'Son's Trip in Portmanteau – Made Home in England', *Daily Mail*, 7 December 1937; 'Il n'est pas toujours drôle d'être le fils d'un milliardaire', *Paris-Soir*, 13 December 1937.

37. NSG to NAE, 18 May 1937 [with undated marginalia by NAE]. NSG00020.

38. More specifically, Nubar objected to the trusts on the ground that their asset portfolios were dominated by poorly performing US securities. The trusts' sole assets were shares in Gulbenkian Ltd, a holding company Calouste had used to park the 'safer' American railway bonds. Gulbenkian Ltd represented a small corner of Calouste's vast portfolio and hence, Nubar argued, it was unfair to have it serve as a vehicle intended to provide one individual with a steady income. See Gerald Russell to NSG, 27 July 1938, and other documents in 'Pleadings re. 1929 and 1938 Settlement'. NSG00021.

39. Cadman, 'Minute of Meeting at Shenley Park', 20 September 1938; NSG to Cadman, 24 September 1938. NSG00021. At the meeting Cadman recorded that NSG agreed to terms of a memo drawn up by CSG on 14 September, but in his subsequent letter NSG denies having done so.

40. NSG to Thomas Bischoff, 30 August 1938. LDN03082, f. 256. NSG to NAE, 18 November 1938. NSG00021. NSG to Wooster, 7 December 1938. LDN03082, f. 572.

41. NSG memo, 5 April 1938. NSG00021.

42. NAE to NSG, 26 February and 5 July 1938. NSG00021. Mary Cadman married a Major-General Bradshaw in 1939.

43. NAE to NSG, 1 April 1937. NSG00020.

44. NAE to NSG, 18 June 1937. NSG00020.

45. CSG to Turabian, 22 July 1922; CSG to Yervant Essayan, 27 June 1922. LDN00519.

46. Beatty to CSG, 20 February 1937. PRS04037.

47. CSG, 'Feuille d'instructions no. 1', 12 September 1937. PRS03407.

48. CSG to Achille Duchêne, 20 April 1938; Achille Duchêne to CSG, 18 September 1937. PRS00593.

49. CSG to Achille Duchêne 2 ('alone'), 4 ('book') and 9 ('office') February 1938. PRS00593.

50. Kenneth Clark, *Another Part of the Wood: A Self-Portrait* (London: John Murray, 1974), p. 230.

51. CSG, 'Résumé des Instructions Données par Mr C. S. G. à Monsieur Duprat, le 5 Mai 1938', PRS00588.

52. Duchêne, 'Abri pour Paons 2me Projet'. CGF 86.1.9.GVA3 116.

53. CSG coined this term to describe his plans for Les Enclos. Achille Duchêne to CSG, 11 February 1938. PRS00593.

54. NSG to NAE, 26 January, 6 and 27 February 1939. LDN03082, ff. 684, 711, 768.

55. 'Fight Over Rich Man's "Dangerous' Documents"', *Daily Herald*, 28 June 1939.

56. J. Mann to NSG, 3 March 1941. NSG00021.

57. NAE to NSG, 27 [October 1938]. NSG00021.

58. 'Saudi Arabia Western Area Concession', 25 May 1936. LDN02892. For analysis, see Walter Adams, James W. Brock and John M. Blair, 'Retarding the Development of Iraq's Oil Resources: An Episode in Oleaginous Diplomacy, 1927–39', *Journal of Economic Issues*, 27:1 (March 1993), 69–94.

59. Henrietta M. Larson, Evelyn H. Knowlton and Charles S. Popple, *History of Standard Oil Company (New Jersey): New Horizons, 1927–1950* (New York: Harper & Row, 1971), pp. 54–8.

60. Edward Peter Fitzgerald, 'The Iraq Petroleum Company, Standard Oil of California, and the Contest for Eastern Arabia, 1930–33', *International History Review*, 13:3 (August 1991), 441–65.

61. Federal Trade Commission, *The International Petroleum Cartel* (Washington: Government Printing Office, 1952), p. 75.

62. H. G. Seidel to Guy Wellman, 25 February 1938. Cited in ibid., p. 80.

63. Frank Holmes's famed Eastern and General Syndicate (EGS) was the first to secure oil rights in Arabia, then (1923) known as the Kingdom of the Hejaz.

Gulbenkian took a small stake in Holmes's syndicate, then asked Royal Dutch-Shell's view of its potential. Their geologist shared the consensus view, but also reminded CSG that in taking a share of EGS he was contravening the self-denying principle of the Red Line Agreement. See H. Marx to CSG, 9 January, 9, 30 November and 3 December 1923. LDN00502. CSG to Josef T. Erb, 3 December 1923, Erb to CSG, 7 January 1924. LDN00515.

64. Andrew Agnew cited in Mény, notes on Outside Concessions Committee, 6 April 1933. AGT, 81ZX916–110 (81.1/110).

65. For a full set of concession agreements (including with smaller Gulf emirates not named), see AGT, 82ZW519–4(82.5/4).

66. See Simon Davis, 'Keeping the Americans in Line? Britain, the United States and Saudi Arabia, 1939–45: Inter-allied Rivalry in the Middle East Revisited', *Diplomacy & Statecraft*, 8:1 (1997), 96–136 (102); Fiona Venn, 'A Struggle for Supremacy? Great Britain, the United States and Kuwaiti Oil in the 1930s', University of Essex Department of History Working Papers 2 (2000).

Chapter 15: For the Duration, 1939–42

1. Nubar incorrectly states that their case came to court in June 1939. PIO, p. 180.

2. YSE to NAE, 10 February 1940. PRS00905, f. 219.

3. NAE to NSG, 20 February 1940; NSG to NAE, 23 February 1940. NSG00021.

4. J. H. Macdonald to NSG, 20 September 1939. NSG's claim to have been on the point of winning is found in NSG to Macdonald, 9 April 1940. NSG00021. When NME later read a similar claim in PIO (p. 180), however, he denounced it as 'a travesty'. ED, 7 July 1957.

5. J. H. Macdonald memo, 26 March 1940. NSG00021.

6. For CSG's annotated copy of Charles Locke Eastlake, *Pictures in the National Gallery London* (Munich: Franz Hanfstaengl, [1899]), see CGF, E-P, 163.

7. Kenneth Clark, *Another Part of the Wood: A Self-Portrait* (London: John Murray, 1974), p. 229; CSG to Clark, 10 August 1937. TA, 8812.1.4.165a. For the loans, see MCG02905.

8. Clark, *Another Part of the Wood*, p. 230.

9. The Egyptian artefacts were lent 10 October 1936. See British Museum Archive, London. Standing Committee minutes, 13 December 1947.

10. CSG to Monteil, 27 February 1940. MCG02622.

11. Trustee minutes, 6 July 1937. National Gallery Archive, London.

12. Trustee minutes, 11 January and 8 February (Samuel) 1938. National Gallery Archive, London.

13. Jonathan Conlin, *The Nation's Mantelpiece: A History of the National Gallery* (London: Pallas Athene, 2006), p. 277. By CSG's day, however, Mond's paintings were no longer being kept together, something CSG found 'not very encouraging'. CSG to Radcliffe, 2 April 1951. CGF, Caixa CSG3, RAD199.

14. Trustee minutes, 11 January 1938. National Gallery Archive, London.

15. CSG to Clark, 10 January ('best example') and 17 February ('our building', 'new ideas') 1939. TA, 8812.1.4.165a.

16. Delano to Clark, 22 November 1939. TA, 8812.1.4.165a.

17. Clark to Delano, 1 September 1942. TA, 8812.1.4.165b.

18. Clark to Delano, 27 June 1939; CSG to Clark 9 August 1939; Clark to CSG, 4 August 1939. TA, 8812.1.4.165a.

19. Harold Brown to CSG, 14 February ('subjects') and 12 April 1939. CGF, CSCA00227. For heirs' rights, see the opinion of Patrick Devlin and Cyril Radcliffe, 11 April 1938, in the same file.

20. Charles Delautre to NSG, 19 December 1932. LDN01113. See also Mayor, Sworder & Co. receipt, 12 December 1936. LDN01696.

21. CSG to Dr Lenglet, 11 July 1940. LIS00154.

22. CSG to YSE, 19 July 1940. PRS00873. See also LDN02029.

23. Jean Lescuyer to MAE, 19 July 1940. AMAE, 4GMII/158.

24. Les Enclos reports, 28 April and 5 May 1941, December 1944. PRS02163. Philippe Normand, personal communication, 30 August 2016 (Christmas trees).

25. For APH (1876–1962), see *London Gazette*, 26 April 1921, p. 3324. APH to NSG, 6 December 1921. LDN00420. APH to KLE, 25 November 1929. LDN00803. NSG to CSG, 17 August 1942. LDN03085, f. 136.

26. NSG to APH, 15 July 1940. NSG00002. APH to KLE, 2 September 1939. LDN01826.

27. NSG to CSG, 1 March 1945. NSG00021.

28. Wilfred Greene to Rab Butler, 29 July 1940. TNA, FO371/24561.

29. Rab Butler minute. Ibid.

30. Petroleum Department meeting minutes, 29 July 1940. TNA FO371/24561. Near East Development to Montagu Piesse, 18 February 1941, enclosed in C. S. Morgan to Wallace Murray, 3 March 1941. NARA, RG59 890G.6363T84/653.

31. Anand Toprani, 'Germany's Answer to Standard Oil: The Continental Oil Company and Nazi Grand Strategy, 1940–42', *Journal of Strategic Studies*, 37:6–7 (2014), 949–73.

32. Dr Otto Wittrock to Obersturmführer Dr Maulatz, 18 February 1941. Bundesarchiv Berlin-Lichterfelde. HaPolXI 1694/41.

33. Minutes of meeting, 10 July 1940. AMAE, 17GMII/303, Subfile 1. Mercier to Charles-Albert de Boissieu, 21 September 1940. AGT, 90ZY935–4, 'Documents anciens CFP'.

34. Lagarde, 'Note sur les Pétroles du Proche-Orient', 10 July 1940. AMAE, 4GMII/55.

35. 'Protection des intérêts pétroliers français en Proche-Orient', 12 May 1941. AMAE, 17GMII/303, Subfile 1. Pascale Gemignani-Saxtad, 'La France, le Pétrole et le Proche Orient de 1939 à 1958', doctoral thesis, Université de Paris IV-Sorbonne, 1997, pp. 188–95.

36. NSG to Macdonald, 24 November 1940. LDN03083, f. 410a.

37. CSG to NSG, 4 December 1920. NSG00002. CSG to NSG, 23 December 1940 (quote). CGF, CSCA0228.

38. CSG to APH, 11 May 1941. PRS00711. For the proposed itinerary, see CGF, CSCA0228. For CSG's visa, see LDN02029.

39. CSG to NSG, 20 February and 28 March 1942. LDN01921. NSG to CSG, 21 April 1942. LDN03085, f. 36.

40. NAE arrived 28 May 1942. CSG to Ghadimy, 22 July 1942. PRS00697.

41. Admiral William Leahy to US Embassy Lisbon, 8 April 1942. NARA, RG59, 811.11 C. S. GULBENKIAN. CSG to NSG, 8 June 1942. LDN01921.

42. Cecil Farrer to Jeffes, 29 October 1942 ('hint'), A. Coombe Tennant, 23 October 1942 ('eaten'). TNA, FO837/282.

43. James E. Wood to George Kennan, 25 October ('disturbed') and 15 August ('ramified') 1943. NARA, RG84 Box File: Lisbon: Financial Attaché James E. Wood Commercial/Industrial Files, ARC1802194 (box 1) [350/67/13/6].

Chapter 16: Pays de Cocagne, 1942–4

1. NAE to NSG, 10 January 1944 ('no milk'). NSG00020. NSG to CSG, 1 December 1940 (food). NSG00002. NSG to RSE, 17 April 1945 ('Cocagne'). NSG00021. Pamela Robinson to CSG, 18 January 1949 (plums). PRS03980.

2. RSE to NAE, 12 November [1944?]. PRS04059. RSE to Marie Gulbenkian, 13 February 1957 ('mausoleum'). NSG00013. After the war KLE had to give up painting again. Chanet, pp. 55, 61.

3. NSG to CSG, 21 April 1942 ('frugal'); NSG to NAE, 24 May (typing). LDN03085, ff. 35, 567.

4. NAE to NSG, 12 October 1944 ('give and take'). NSG00006. NAE to NSG, 3 March 1943 (haddock). NSG00003.

5. NAE to NSG, 12 October (slippers) and 25 July 1944. NSG00006.

6. She did not specify which Legation. NAE to NSG, 19 [June 1943]. NSG00003.

7. Robert Coughlan, 'Mystery Billionaire', Life, 27 November 1950.

8. CSG to Agostinho Lourenço, 13 April and 4 May 1951. LIS00354.

9. CSG to JAP, 30 August 1953. CGF, CSCA00235.

10. Delano to Clark, 21 July 1942. TA, 8812.1.4.165b.

11. Soulas report, 6 August 1942. PRS00697. CSG to Ghadimy, 22 July and 6 August 1942. PRS00697. For Sardari's activities, see United States Holocaust Museum, 'Abdol Hossein Sardari (1895–1981)'. Holocaust Encyclopedia. http://www.ushmm.org/wlc/en/article.php?ModuleId=10007452 (accessed on 28 January 2016).

12. James E. Wood to Edward S. Crocker, 31 December 1943. NARA, RG84 Box File: Lisbon: Financial Attaché James E. Wood Commercial/Industrial Files, ARC1802194 (box 1) [350/67/13/6].

13. For these 3,000 1,000-Reichsmark shares, see LDN00598 and LDN01191.

14. Quoted in A. W. Barnett to R. A. B. Mynors, 18 June 1945. This document is misfiled with unrelated documents in TNA, FO371/45473.

15. In 1919 Herman and his better-known brother, Bernard Baruch, were part of the American Commission to Negotiate Peace, liaising with Clémentel on behalf of American oil companies. See Baruch to Clémentel, 12 June 1919. André Tardieu Papers. AMAE, 166PAAP/451.

16. Herman Baruch to CSG, 31 December 1951. NSG00007.

17. Hayes to State Department, 3 June 1944. NARA, RG59, Bureau of Economic Affairs, Office of International Trade Policy. Petroleum Policy Staff, Subject File. Box 5. [250/63/7/7].

18. CSG to Clark, 27 August 1943. TA, 8812.1.4.165b.

19. Clark to Anthony Eden, undated note [before 13 February 1944]. TNA, FO371/40215, E1301.

20. R. A. B. Mynors to E. F. Q. Henriques, 8 May 1944 ('whitewashing'); Anthony Eden, comment dated 12 February 1944 ('generously'), referring to W. H. Young's minute, 'Mr. C. S. Gulbenkian', 8 February 1944 ('flea-bite', 'diplomatic status'). TNA, FO371/40215, E2875 and E1301.

21. K. M. Crump to R. A. B. Mynors, 28 February 1944. TNA, FO371/40215, E2043.

22. In the words of HM Treasury's attaché to the Lisbon embassy, Sir Stanley Wyatt, cited in James E. Wood, 'Memorandum for Files: Re C. S. Gulbenkian', 13 May 1944. NARA, RG84 Box File: Lisbon: Financial Attaché James E. Wood Commercial/Industrial Files, ARC1802194 (box 1) [350/67/13/6]. See also NSG to CSG, 15 September 1943. NSG00003.

23. CPLW to Crane, Crane & Hawkins, 6 December 1944. LDN02142.

24. To cite just one example, in 1945 Charles F. Darlington was Chief of the State Department's Petroleum Division. Two years later he was working for Socony, and by 1951 he was president of Near East Development, the vehicle through which Jersey and Socony participated in IPC. Come 1954, Darlington was asking Gulbenkian for a second mortgage on his house. ED, 25 April 1954.

25. NSG to CSG, 4 July (quote) and 19 September 1945. PRS00669.

26. NSG to CSG, 27 May ('war') and 23 June ('divide') 1943. LDN03085, ff. 574, 623.

27. Anand Toprani, 'An Anglo-American "Petroleum Entente"?: The First Attempt to Reach an Anglo-American Oil Agreement, 1921', *Historian*, 49:1 (2017), 56–79.

28. Quoted in Irvine H. Anderson, *Aramco, the United States and Saudi Arabia* (Princeton, NJ: Princeton University Press, 1981), p. 32. A US consulate was established at Aden in 1918, but there was no representative in the Kingdom of the Hejaz/Saudi Arabia until May 1942, and even then he was a lowly chargé d'affaires, without ambassadorial rank. There was not even a consulate in Kuwait until 1951. See John A. DeNovo, *American Interests and Policies in the Middle*

East 1900–1939 (Minneapolis: University of Minnesota Press, 1963), pp. 361–5, 393.

29. Cited in Fiona Venn, 'The Wartime "Special Relationship"? From Oil War to Anglo-American Oil Agreement, 1939–45', *Journal of Transatlantic Studies*, 10:2 (2012), 119–33 (123).

30. 'Wartime Evolution of Postwar Foreign Oil Policy', 29 May 1947. NARA, RG59 811.6363/5–2947.

31. Cited in David Painter, *Private Power and Public Policy: Multinational Oil Corporations and U.S. Foreign Policy, 1941–54* (London: I. B. Tauris, 1986), p. 53.

32. Aaron David Miller, *Search for Security: Arabian Oil and American Foreign Policy, 1939–49* (Chapel Hill, NC: University of North Carolina Press, 1980), p. 82.

33. Reported in Robertson to John A. Loftus, 11 February 1946. NARA, RG59 Office on International Trade Policy, Petroleum Division, 1943–49, Box 3 'Middle East (General)'.

34. Simon Davis, 'Keeping the Americans in Line? Britain, the United States and Saudi Arabia, 1939–45', *Diplomacy & Statecraft*, 8:1 (1997), 96–136 (129). See also TNA, FO371/50385/10686/12/76.

35. As late as 1952 Gulbenkian was still grateful to Baruch for having 'helped me a great deal at the time to knock the Anglo-American Oil Pact'. CSG to Herman Baruch, 9 January 1952. CGF, CaixaCSG9, B115. For the Ickes meeting, see John C. Wiley to Loy Henderson, 12 November 1947. NARA, RG59 890G.6363/11–1247. For a French view of the agreement, see Pierre Mendès-France to MAE, 10 August 1944. CAEF, B0033849, 'Affaires Interalliés, Pétroles, 1944–9', red folder.

36. These views are cited in Skliros to APH, 4 December 1947 and 17 March 1948. BP, 164055.

37. These are the rates agreed in 1933 and 1934 respectively. Deadrents and other minimum payments, as well as clauses providing royalty oil or the opportunity to acquire oil at below-market prices, complicate the picture. For an analysis, see Zuhayr Mikdashi, *A Financial Analysis of Middle Eastern Oil Concessions: 1901–1965* (New York: Frederick A. Praeger, 1966).

38. CSG to René de Montaigu, 4 December 1944; CSG memos, 17 December 1944 and 7 January 1945. AGT, 81ZX916–75.

39. NSG to CSG, 22 January 1945. PRS00669.

40. René de Montaigu, 'Entretien avec M. Gulb le 8 Janvier 1945'. AGT, 81ZX916–75. Walter Adams, James W. Brock and John M. Blair, 'Retarding the Development of Iraq's Oil Resources: An Episode in Oleaginous Diplomacy, 1927–39', *Journal of Economic Issues*, 27:1 (March 1993), 69–94 (83).

41. CFP to CSG, 25 January 1945. AGT, 81ZX916–78.

42. NSG to CSG, 7 ('advisers') and 17 ('snags') January 1945. PRS00669.

43. Copies at PRES02083 and PRES00023; BP, 070229; NARA, RG59, 890G.6363/7729/3–448; AGT, 89ZY521–21. For further lending or gifts of copies to others, see Sir Nigel Ronald (UK Ambassador to Portugal) to CSG, 28 February 1949. CGF, CaixaCSG13. E. B. Swanson (Assistant Director of Oil & Gas, US Department of the Interior) to CSG, 13 April 1953. LIS00354.

44. One exception being Stephen Longrigg's insider history of IPC (sadly very hard to find), which rightly notes that the 'Memoirs' 'illuminate [CSG's] own character and approach rather than the events he describes'. Stephen H. Longrigg, *The Origins and Early History of the Iraq Petroleum Company* (London: privately printed, 1969), p. 26 note 2.

45. Gulbenkian's views as relayed in Franz von Schilling Jr (US Petroleum attaché, Cairo) to Charles F. Darlington (Socony), 28 February 1945. NARA, RG59 883.6363/2–2845.

46. CSG, 'Memoirs', p. 28. CGF, PRES02083.

Chapter 17: The Dogs Bark, 1945–8

1. NSG to CSG, 27 September 1943 ('Oiley'). NSG00003. Mikhael Essayan to CSG, 2 September 1944. PRS00686.

2. Jean-Anthelme Brillat-Savarin, *La Physiologie du Goût* (4th edn, 2 vols., Paris: Just Tessier, 1843), Vol 1., p. 13.

3. NSG to CSG/NAE, 4 November 1942; NSG to KLE, 12 November 1942 ('freak'). LDN03085, ff. 228, 244. RSE to NAE, 9 December [1944] (Protestant). PRS04059.

4. Chanet, p. 21.

5. RSE to NAE, 9 December [1944]. PRS03059.

6. The decoration was won in action near Mulhouse in December 1944. CSG to Georges Gulbenkian, 27 July and 7 December 1945. For these and seven copies of the citation, see PRS00718.

7. CSG to NSG, 11 October 1947. NSG00005.

8. French translation of article in unidentified newspaper, 27 August 1946. AGT, 04AH026–89. Adeed Dawisha, *Iraq: A Political History from Independence to Occupation* (Princeton, NJ: Princeton University Press, 2009), p. 105.

9. HRDS, Vol. 1, p. 319. George Philip, *Oil and Politics in Latin America: Nationalist Movements and State Companies* (Cambridge: Cambridge University Press, 1982), pp. 41 (on nationalism as a 'tactical stance'), 207 (quote), 225.

10. CSG to NSG, 11 October 1947. NSG00005.

11. IPC minutes, 8 and 9 October 1946 (CSG proposal). BP, 126859. Armand de Grouchy to René de Montaigu, 5 September 1946 (quoting Skliros). For these letters and other correspondence on this question, see AGT, 04AH026–89.

12. Jules Rondot to René de Montaigu, 18 December 1948. AGT, 04AH026–90
    (92.36). Total's files indicate that, having made regular requests up to 1948, the
    Iraqi government then went quiet until January 1956.

13. CSG, quoted in Armand de Grouchy to Victor de Metz, 29 June 1949. AGT,
    04AH026–47.

14. CSG to A. W. Barnett (Commercial attaché, US Embassy Lisbon), 27 January
    1946. CGF, Caixa CSG9, B171.

15. Cited in Fiona Venn, 'The Wartime "Special Relationship"? From Oil War to
    Anglo-American Oil Agreement, 1939–45', *Journal of Transatlantic Studies*,
    10:2 (2012), 119–33 (122). For an example of Congressional pressure, see Henri
    Bonnet to Georges Bidault, 6 October 1947. AMAE, 91Q0228, f. 94.

16. Francis Lacoste to MAE, 6 August 1945. Ambassade de France aux États-Unis,
    Washington. 4045 DE.4.2.

17. James Bamberg, *The History of the British Petroleum Company*, Vol. 2 *The Anglo-
    Iranian Years, 1928–54* (Cambridge: Cambridge University Press, 1994), pp.
    301–7. MAE to Henri Bonnet, 9 May 1947. AMAE, 91Q0228, f. 94.

18. IPC minutes, 24 September 1946; Vladimir Idelson, David Maxwell Fyfe and
    H. G. Robertson, joint opinion ('avoided'), 26 November 1946; Anglo-Persian
    to Near East Development, 26 December 1946; Sir Walter Monckton and H. L.
    Parker, joint opinion ('evidence'), 13 January 1947. BP, 126859.

19. Armand de Grouchy memo, 1 January 1947. AGT, 04AH026–9. David Painter,
    *Private Power and Public Policy: Multinational Oil Corporations and U.S.
    Foreign Policy, 1941–54* (London: I. B. Tauris, 1986), p. 107.

20. Pascale Gemignani-Saxtad, 'La France, le pétrole et le Proche Orient de 1939 à
    1958', doctoral thesis, Université de Paris IV-Sorbonne, 1997, pp. 512–13.

21. Loy Henderson to Dean Acheson, 16 January 1947. NARA, RG59
    890F.6363/1–1647.

22. French Embassy Lisbon to MAE, 20 January 1947. AMAE, 91Q0228, f. 74.
    See also Anand Toprani, 'The French Connection: A New Perspective on the
    End of the Red Line Agreement, 1945–48', *Diplomatic History*, 36:2 (April
    2012), 261–99 (287); Edward Peter Fitzgerald, 'The Iraq Petroleum Company,
    Standard Oil of California, and the Contest for Eastern Arabia, 1930–33',
    International History Review, 13:3 (August 1991), 441–65 (461–3); CSG to CFP,
    10 January 1947, cited in Gemignani-Saxtad, 'La France, le pétrole et le Proche
    Orient de 1939 à 1958', p. 519; J. Rives Childs to State Department, 4 March
    1947. NARA, RG59 890F.6363/3–347.

23. For the French ambassador's account, see J. du Sault to MAE, 15 January 1947.
    AMAE, 91Q0155.

24. This point was also noted by CFP's René de Montaigu. Memo 14 August 1947.
    AGT, 90ZZ478–20.

25. Olaf Sundt to State Department, 27 September 1948. NARA, RG59
    851.6363/6273/9–2748.

26. Actual total expenditure by IPC between 1948 and 1952 inclusive was much higher (£122 million). CSG's share was £6.1 million (£188 million). Calculations based on Zuhayr Mikdashi, *A Financial Analysis of Middle Eastern Oil Concessions: 1901–1965* (New York: Frederick A. Praeger, 1966), App. 2, Table 34.

27. Jersey Vice-President John R. Suman cited in Morris Bridgeman memo, 29 July 1947. BP, 126859.

28. NSG to CSG, 12 November 1947 (*'train de vie'*). NSG00005. NSG to CSG, 1 January 1945 ('hurry'). PRS00669.

29. Henri Bonnet to MAE, 28 December 1946 ('lost'). AMAE, 91Q0228, f. 29. Memcon John A. Loftus, Orville Harden, Harold Sheets, 9 January 1947 ('reprisals'). NARA, RG59 Office on International Trade Policy, Petroleum Division, 1943–49, Box 3 'Red Line Agreement 1947'. For the Bonnet démarche, see also CAEF, B0033849, 'CFP: Négociations avec l'IPC pour le rétablissement de ses droits, 1944–49'.

30. Funkhouser, 'Monthly petroleum report for France', 14 March 1947. NARA, RG59 800.6363/3–1447.

31. Such threats were made by the head of the Direction des Carburants (DICA), the post-war equivalent of ONCL. Pierre Guillaumat, 'Note pour le Ministre de la Production Industrielle', 28 February 1947. AGT, 81ZX916–82 (81.1/82).

32. CSG to NSG, 5 and 15 (quote) November 1947. NSG00005.

33. Burton I. Kaufman, 'The Oil Cartel Case and the Cold War', *Business History Review*, 51:1 (1977), 35–56 (39).

34. Lincoln MacVeagh to State Department, 7 March 1949; Mattison to Funkhouser, 'Oil Topics for Chiefs of Mission Discussions', 8 November 1949 (quote). NARA, RG59 Bureau of Near Eastern Affairs, Subject Files, 1941–54, Lot File 57D298, Box 1 'AIOC 1949' [250/63/7/7].

35. Cyril Radcliffe to CSG, 1 November 1947. NSG00005.

36. L. Lefroy to Taylor, 6 November 1946. BP, 126859.

37. Godber quoted in NSG to CSG, 19 July 1945 ('old man'). NSG00006. CSG to NSG 5 November 1947 ('stuff'). NSG00005.

38. For the ill-fated contracts with Pantepec, see Antoine Brandalac, 'Le mythe revisité de l'Eldorado: Aventures et mésaventures de la Compagnie Française des Pétroles au Venezuela de 1945 à 1957', unpublished MA thesis, Université Paris IV-La Sorbonne, 2014, Ch. 6.

39. Armand de Grouchy to Fletcher, 3 July (quote) 1947; Aiken Watson opinion, 10 July 1947. AGT, 04AH026–11.

40. CSG to NSG, 2 (1 a.m.) and 6 ('momentous') August 1947. NSG00005.

41. Cited in Armand de Grouchy memo, 11 September 1947. AGT, 04AH026–11.

42. John C. Wiley to State Department, 8 September 1947. NARA, RG59 890F.6363/9–847.

43. Group Meeting minutes, 23 September 1947. BP, 126859.

44. Nubar also noted that Cayrol was hungry for 'the personal kudos' of brokering a settlement. NSG to CSG, 5 November 1947. NSG00005.

45. CSG to Victor de Metz, 30 April 1947. AGT, 04AH026–9.

46. Robert Cayrol memo, 18 April 1948; Cayrol to CSG, 29 May 1948; CSG to Cayrol, 10 June 1948. AGT, 04AH026–10.

47. This special allocation of oil totalled 3.75 million tons, delivered between 1952 and 1966.

48. Robert Cayrol to William Fraser, 18 November 1948. BP, 126861.

49. CSG to Herman Baruch, 13 December 1948. CGF, CaixaCSG9, B110.

50. CSG to Kenneth Clark, 31 July 1945. TA, 8812.1.4.165c.

51. John Walker to David Finley, 11 July 1947. NGA, RG28 Box 8–4.

52. Clark to CSG, 13 March 1946; CSG to Clark, 12 May 1946 (quote); Clark to 28th Earl of Crawford, 25 June 1946. TA, 8812.1.4.165c. Hendy also made the mistake of speaking slightingly about a portrait CSG gave to Lisbon's Museu de Arte Antiga, Sir Joshua Reynolds's *Admiral Keppel*.

53. John Walker to David Finley, 22 October 1947. NGA, RG28 Box 8–4.

54. David M. Wilson, *The British Museum: A History* (London: British Museum Press, 2002), p. 252.

55. John Walker to CSG, 3 November 1947. MCG02448. CSG to 28th Earl of Crawford, 30 December 1947. MCG02450. John Walker, *Self-Portrait with Donors: Confessions of an Art Collector* (Boston: Little, Brown, 1969), p. 237.

56. John Walker to CSG, 19 March 1952 ('constantly'). CGF, CSCA00234. Walker, *Self-Portrait with Donors*, pp. 235–7 ('predators').

57. John Walker to David Finley, 17 July 1947. NGA, RG28 Box 8–4.

58. On the other side of Exhibition Road, where the Ismaili Centre now stands, and where the National Theatre was to have been located. Leigh Ashton to CSG, 16 September 1947; CSG to Leigh Ashton, 4 October 1947; 28th Earl of Crawford to CSG, 13 December 1947. MCG02450.

59. Geoffrey Fisher to CSG, 16 March 1948 (capital levy); 28th Earl of Crawford to CSG, 1 June 1948; Geoffrey Fisher to 28th Earl of Crawford, 9 January 1948. MCG02473.

60. Memcon CSG and Theodore A. Xanthaky, in John A. Wiley to State Department, 26 December 1947. NARA, RG59 883.4031/12–2647. Xanthaky later told NSG of his plans (never realised) to write a biography of CSG. NSG to JAP, 5 September 1958. NSG00013.

61. CSG liked this idea. CSG to John Walker, 1 April 1948. NGA, RG28 Box 8–14.

Chapter 18: The Caravan Passes, 1949–55

1. Chanet, pp. 135–6.

2. RSE to CSG, 19 November 1951. LIS00305.

3. CSG to Alexis Léger, 30 July 1953. SJP, pp. 297–8.

4. RSE to CSG 19 January 1950. LIS00305. See also NSG to CSG, 12 May 1949. PRS04057.

5. NSG to CSG 18 February 1952. NSG00007.

6. LIS00438.

7. ED, 16 December 1953 (doctors). KLE to Pestemalcian, 17 January 1954 (sheep). LIS00096. For earlier thank offerings, see His Beatitude Patriarch Maghakia Ormanian to CSG, 23 June 1907. LDN00012.

8. Gladstone to Kellar, 22 April 1942. TNA, KV2/4426. NAE to NSG, 7 July 1951 ('watching'). LDN03069.

9. NSG Memo, 15 July 1952. LDN03072.

10. Isabelle Theis to JAP, 12 December 1968. CGF, CSCA00238.

11. CPLW to NSG, 10 October 1951. LDN03069.

12. CPLW to NSG, 27 August and 21 November 1952. NSG00008. RSE to NSG, 10 December 1952. LDN03063. See also PRS00640.

13. The IPC royalty was four 'gold' shillings, but after the devaluation of 1949 it was worth twelve shillings sterling. Daniel Silverfarb, 'The Revision of Iraq's Oil Concession, 1949–52', *Middle Eastern Studies*, 32:1 (1996), 69–95 (74).

14. The executive was M. A. Wright, who later became chairman. Cited in CSG to NSG, 26 January 1951. NSG00007.

15. Taqizadeh to CSG, 29 March 1951; CSG to Taqizadeh, 16 April 1951. PRS03967.

16. NSG, Iraq memo, 5 October 1951. PRS04057. ED, 26 September 1949. Armand de Grouchy to René de Montaigu, 11 August 1949. AGT, 04AH026–47 (92.36/47).

17. Silverfarb, 'The Revision of Iraq's Oil Concession, 1949–52', 88; Zuhayr Mikdashi, *A Financial Analysis of Middle Eastern Oil Concessions: 1901–1965* (New York: Frederick Praeger, 1966), p. 249.

18. NSG to CSG, 21 September 1945. PRS00669.

19. ED, 12 November 1951.

20. ED, 5 October 1949 (*Clarion*), 5 February 1950, 17 July 1952 and 7 August 1953 (candidature).

21. ED, 18 July (CPLW), 8 August (KLE) and 16 September ('toad') 1949; 30 January (exemption), 20 February (ranch) and 15 March (CPLW quote) 1950.

22. NSG to CSG, 15 January 1951. NSG00007.

23. CSG to NSG, 8 January1950. NSG00007.

24. ED, 30 September 1949 (alarm clock); 9 October ('baby-talk') 1950.

25. Drysdale cited in ED, 7 August 1952.

26. ED, 7 ('dignity') and 10 ('sniping') June 1950.

27. ED, 8 June 1950.

28. RSE to YSE, 21 September 1945. PRS00888.

29. Alan Barlow to CSG, 14 March 1950. MCG02451. CSG to NSG, 18 March 1950. NSG00007.

30. Cited in APH to CSG, 5 October 1950. CGF, CSCA00231. NME thought that NSG did not himself believe these grievances to be serious, but only played them up to impress his father. ED, 7 December 1950.

31. D. H. F. Rickett to CSG, 1 December 1950. NSG00007.

32. Cited in NSG to CSG, 4 March 1948. PRS04057.

33. In the original French 'libre et confiante causerie'. It is difficult to know how best to translate *confiante* in this context. Alexis Léger to CSG, n.d. [1926]. LDN00665. Léger's appointment as *chef de cabinet* is also difficult to interpret. Renaud Meltz, *Alexis Léger dit Saint-John Perse* (Paris: Flammarion, 2008), pp. 257–8, 274.

34. CSG to Léger, 20 January 1949, Léger to CSG, 10 May 1949, in SJP, pp. 45, 54.

35. For a Gaullist view of Léger's status in Washington, see Maurice Dejean to Charles de Gaulle, 17 and 22 August 1942. AMAE, 288PAAP/24.

36. Meltz, *Alexis Léger dit Saint-John Perse*, pp. 621, 627 (quote).

37. Léger to CSG, 5 January 1950. SJP, p. 102.

38. Chanet, p. 29.

39. Léger to CSG, 10 May 1949 ('keys', pheasants and chef), 12 May ('sage') and 5 October ('Promethean') 1950. SJP, pp. 60, 129, 144.

40. CSG to Léger, 24 March 1953. SJP, p. 282.

41. House of Representatives Joint Resolution 497 of 29 June 1950 amended Section 863 of the Internal Revenue Code, exempting works of art on loan to the Trustees of the National Gallery of Art from the estate of a non-resident alien.

42. NSG to CSG, 10 October 1950 ('motive'). NSG00007. 'The Gulbenkian Collection. US Critics Lukewarm', *The Times*, 9 October 1950. CSG was insulted when the scholar hired to write the catalogue of his Egyptian collection, William Smith, declared two of his statuettes (ex-Rothermere Collection) to be fakes. CSG to Walker, 29 November 1948. NGA, RG28 Box 9–1. See Luis Manuel de Araujo, *Egyptian Art. Calouste Gulbenkian Collection* (Lisbon: CGF, 2006), p. 166.

43. *Time,* 14 February 1949.

44. Irving Johnson, 'Mr. Five Per Cent', *Life*, 14 November 1948 (quote); Robert Coughlan, 'Mystery Billionaire', *Life*, 27 November 1950.

45. 'A vida Fantástica do rei do petróleo', *Diário Popular*, 24, 25 and 26 June 1951. See also 'L'homme le plus secret et le plus riche du monde mène à 86 ans une vie de reclus dans une cage dorée', *Samedi-Soir*, 13 January 1951.

46. CSG to NSG, 17 October 1950. NSG00007.

47. CGF, CSCA00231.

48. Esmond B. Gardner to Sir William Wiseman, 18 March 1949; Wiseman to CSG, 21 March 1949; CSG memos, 3 May 1950. CGF, CSCA00231.

49. CSG to Walker, 28 November 1952; Vermilya-Brown to NGA, 28 October 1952. NGA, RG28 Box 7–12 and Box 8–6.

50. Walker to Finley, 25 August 1951 (quote); Walker to CSG, 18 February 1952. NGA, RG28 Box 8–6 and Box 7–13.

51. Walker wrote to *Life* attempting to correct their coverage, and tried to secure more balanced coverage from the *New Yorker*. Walker to CSG, 23 October 1950; Walker to Margit [surname absent], 11 November 1950; Janet F. Lanner to Walker, 2 December 1950. NGA, RG28 Box 9–6.

52. Memcon Walker, David Finley and Chester Dale, 28 June 1949. NGA, RG28 Box 8–6.

53. Walker, confidential memo, 5 July 1952; CSG to Walker, 9 June 1948 (quoting Bruce's statement). NGA RG28 Boxes 7–14 and 9–1.

54. Walker to David Bruce, 27 October 1949. NGA, RG28 Box 9–3.

55. CSG to Radcliffe, 13 May 1951. CGF, CaixaCSG3, RAD214. The *Donne Triptych* did enter the National Gallery's collection, but via Acceptance-in-Lieu, not purchase.

56. CGF, CSCA00231.

57. Dr J. Henggeler, 'Projet de Testament pour Monsieur C. S. Gulbenkian et Commentaire', n.d. [May 1951?]; Winthrop W. Aldrich to CSG, 18 May 1951; Anthony A. Bill to Josef Henggeler, 22 May 1951. CGF, CSCA00233.

58. CSG to NSG, 4 June 1949. NSG00019.

59. Radcliffe to CSG, 26 October 1951. CGF, Caixa CSG3, RAD228.

60. CSG to Radcliffe, 1 April 1952. CGF, Caixa CSG4, RAD298.

61. As recorded in CSG's address book. LIS00438. See also JAP, *Calouste Gulbenkian. Collector* (Lisbon: CGF, 1969), p. 21.

62. Salazar cited in J. M. Ferreira, 'A instituição', in Antonio Barreto (ed.), *Fundação Calouste Gulbenkian: Cinquenta Anos, 1956–2006* (2 vols., Lisbon, Calouste Gulbenkian Foundation, 2006), Vol. 1, pp. 69–163 (84). For biographical information on JAP, see PRES01933.

63. CSG to JAP, 15 February 1951. CGF, CaixaCSG8, JAP584.

64. CSG to JAP, 26 September 1945. CGF, CaixaCSG7, JAP235. A decade later, NME found JAP 'woefully ignorant of even the most elementary things' regarding IPC. ED, 31 January 1956.

65. See JAP invoice, 31 December 1951. CGF, Caixa CSG8, JAP602.

66. JAP to CSG, 9 August 1951. CGF, CSCA00233.

67. CSG to Radcliffe, 26 January 1952 (quote). CGF, Caixa CSG4 RAD263; CSG to Henggeler, 16 January 1952. CGF, CSCA00234.

68. CSG to Radcliffe, 26 January 1952. CGF, CaixaCSG4, RAD263.

69. JAP, 'Le Problème du renvoi', 19 January 1952 ('saw fit'); CSG to JAP, 20 February 1952 ('confusion'). CGF, CSCA00234.

70. Isabelle Theis to JAP, 12 December 1968. CGF, CSCA00238.

71. CSG to Henggeler, 21 April 1952. CGF, CSCA00234. CSG memo, 21 April 1952 (Theis). CGF, Caixa CSG2, CSG383. CSG to Radcliffe, 1 April 1952 ('Leader'). CGF, Caixa CSG4, RAD 298.

72. CSG to JAP, 7 September 1952. CGF, CSCA00234.

73. CGF, SF00121.

74. ED, 23 June 1953.

75. Cited in NSG, 'Professor Fonseca', 17 September 1952. NSG00008.

76. ED, 19 September 1953.

77. CSG to Radcliffe, 14 August 1952. CGF, Caixa CSG4, RAD367.

78. Cited in ED, 18 May 1955. NSG to APH, 23 February 1955 (signature), NSG00014.

79. An example is his anxiety over the whereabouts of a bag he attempted to keep by his bed, containing unidentified important documents. NSG, 'Mr CSG's Private Papers', 24 February 1955; NSG memo, 26 February 1955; KLE to APH, 7 March 1955. NSG00014.

80. CSG to Léger, 24 March 1951. SJP, pp. 279–80.

81. ED, 20 April 1951.

82. NSG memo, 10 February 1953. NSG00007.

83. British Pathé, 'News from Home & Abroad. King Feisal opens giant new pipeline', 24 November 1952.

84. British Pathé, 'New Oil Wealth for Iraq', 21 January 1952.

85. A. Agopian, 'Abri pour canards coureurs, oies, dindes, pintades, et paons', October 1953. LIS00096.

86. PIO, p. 247.

87. CSG to Radcliffe, 5 August 1953. CGF, Caixa CSG4, RAD500.

88. CSG to Dr Fernando Emilio da Silva, 23 April 1952. LIS00354.

89. CSG to NSG, 8 December 1951. NSG00007. After *Life* reported Gulbenkian's removal of his shoes, John Walker wrote refuting this claim. Walker had never seen him remove his shoes. But then Walker also denied that Gulbenkian had ever spent a night in jail. Walker to Margit [surname missing], 11 November 1950. NGA, RG28 Box 9–6.

90. CSG to Deterding, 6 February 1922. SHA 195/176k.

91. Mikael Gulbenkian, personal communication, 20 May 2013.

Conclusion

1. Waley Cohen to August Philips, 27 December 1923. Cited in Geoffrey Jones, *The State and the Emergence of the British Oil Industry* (London: Macmillan, 1981), p. 223.

2. Niall Ferguson, 'Sinking Globalization', *Foreign Affairs*, April 2005.

3. Jose Harris and Pat Thane, 'British and European Bankers, 1880–1914: An "aristocratic bourgeoisie"', in Geoffrey Crossick, Roderick Floud and Pat Thane (eds.), *The Power of the Past: Essays for Eric Hobsbawm* (Cambridge: Cambridge University Press, 1984), pp. 215–34 (228).

4. Robert Fitzgerald, *The Rise of the Global Company: Multinationals and the Making of the Modern World* (Cambridge: Cambridge University Press, 2015), p. 151.

5. Geoffrey Jones, *Merchants to Multinationals: British Trading Companies in the Nineteenth and Twentieth Centuries* (Oxford: Oxford University Press, 2000), p. 343.

6. RSE to NAE, 9 December [1944]. PRS03059.

7. Atvart Essayan, cited in Ralph Hewins, *Mr Five Per Cent: The Biography of Calouste Gulbenkian* (London: Hutchinson, 1957), pp. 20 (charity), 88 (complex).

8. See Appendix.

9. C. S. Morgan, cited in Federal Trade Commission, *The International Petroleum Cartel* (Washington: Government Printing Office, 1952), p. 67.

10. Fitzgerald, *The Rise of the Global Company*, pp. 174 ('archetypical'), 160 (reverse).

11. Anton Zishka and Frank C. Hanighen, *The Secret War: The War for Oil* (3rd edn, London: George Routledge, 1935), p. 61.

12. Harris and Thane, 'British and European Bankers', p. 228.

13. Chanet, p. 36.

14. Ibid., p. 140.

15. CSG to NSG, 12 June 1926. NSG00019.

16. Charles Harvey, Mairi Maclean, Jillian Gordon and Eleonor Shaw, 'Andrew Carnegie and the Foundation of Contemporary Entrepreneurial Philanthropy', *Business History*, 53:3 (2011), 425–50 (431).

17. CSG to NSG, 7 May 1914. LDN01342. For rates, see Martin Daunton, *Just Taxes: The Politics of Taxation in Britain, 1914–79* (Cambridge: Cambridge University Press, 2002), Ch. 2. Gulbenkian totted up the number of days spent each year between 1921 and 1928 (counting from April, for tax purposes) in London in his pocketbook. In 1921 it was seventy-two days, in 1928 just seven, but with a spike (to 109 and 101) in 1924–5. LIS00439.

18. NSG Memo, 26 February 1955. NSG00014.

Epilogue: The Spoils of Gulbenkian, 1956

1. Mikhael Essayan, personal communication, 10 May 2012.

2. ED, 28 July (urn) and 2 August 1955.

3. *Jamanag*, 21 and 29 July 1955. See also Mithat Cemal Kuntay's piece in *Son Posta*, reproduced in *Jamanag*, 7 August 1955. Vahan Malezian's articles are summarised by APH in an undated memo in NSG00012.

4. ED, 21 July (obituaries), 4 (service) and 7 ('legend') August 1955.

5. D. H. Young to KLE, 21 August 1955, London Office to Lisbon Office, 24 August 1955 ('money'). *The People* 2 ('gentle', 'slave'), 9, 16 ('gutter'), 23 and 30 October 1955. LDN04746.

6. 'The Gulbenkian I Knew', in Cyril Radcliffe, *Not in Feather Beds: Some Collected Papers* (London: Hamish Hamilton, 1968), pp. 61–5 (64).

7. Radcliffe to CSG, 2 May 1953. CGF, Caixa CSG4, RAD466. CSG memo, n.d. CGF, Caixa CSG2, CSG414.

8. JAP to Salazar, 24 June ('discretion'), 8 August 1953 and 13 April 1954. TT, AOS/CO/PC-44C, cx. 574.

9. Salazar to Pedro Teotónio Pereira, 11 September 1955. For similar comments, see Salazar to Armindo Monteiro, 25 August 1955. TT, AOS/CO/PC-44C, cx. 574.

10. Pedro Teotónio Pereira to Salazar, 7 September 1955. TT, AOS/CO/PC-44C, cx. 574.

11. Radcliffe, 'Draft memorandum of discussions on 20, 21, 22 Sep. 1955'; Radcliffe to JAP, 14 October 1955; JAP to Radcliffe, 20 October 1955. CGF, Caixa1, RAD77, RAD94 and RAD102.

12. JAP to Salazar, 21 December 1955. TT, AOS/CO/PC-44C, cx. 574.

13. Radcliffe to JAP, 11 December 1955. CGF, Caixa1, RAD134.

14. CPLW to JAP, 31 July 1956. PRES00096.

15. CPLW to JAP, 15 July 1958. KLE00014.

16. J. de Hauteclocque to MAE, 8 February 1956. AMAE, 200QO/62.

17. Salazar to Pedro Teotónio Pereira, 11 September 1955. TT, AOS/CO/PC-44C, cx. 574.

18. A. Ferrer Correia and A. Rodrigues Queiró opinion, translated by F. Vaz Pinto, January 1956, pp. 40 ('appreciation'), 49 ('companies'), 70 ('preference'). CGF, CSCA00003.

19. Lei 1:994. See https://dre.pt/application/file/596446 (accessed 27 October 2016).

20. Correia and Queiró opinion, p. 56. CGF, CSCA00003.

21. Marcello Caetano, *Das Fundações: Subsídios para a interpretação e reforma da legislação portugesa* (Lisbon, 1961), p. 11. I am grateful to Rui Hermenegildo Gonçalves for sharing with me material from his unpublished doctoral thesis on the history of Portuguese foundation law.

22. Memcon Salazar and Radcliffe, 11 and 30 January 1956. TT, AOS/CO/PC-44C, cx. 574 and AOS/CO/PC-8E1, cx. 562.

23. Eelco Van Kleffens to Marcello Caetano, 23 February 1956 ('form'); Van Kleffens to Radcliffe, 23 February 1956 ('inferiority'). NSG00015.

24. JAP to Radcliffe, 11 February 1956. TT, AOS/CO/PC-44C, cx. 574.

25. NSG, 'Calouste Gulbenkian Foundation. Views of Nubar Gulbenkian', 14 January 1956. NSG00015.

26. KLE, 'Caloust [*sic*] Gulbenkian Foundation, Views of Kevork Loris Essayan, Paris', 21 January 1956. PRES00107.

27. JAP to Salazar, 3 January 1956. TT, AOS/CO/PC-44C, cx. 574.

28. Radcliffe to JAP, 27 February 1956. CGF, Caixa 2, RAD262. Reproduced in PIO, p. 333.

29. JAP to Radcliffe, 22 March 1956 ('aut[h]orship'). NSG00015. JAP to Salazar, 21 and 23 March 1956. TT, AOS/CO/PC-44C, cx. 574.

30. Van Kleffens to Radcliffe, 2 March 1956. Radcliffe to NSG, 10 March 1956 (quote). NSG00015.

31. JAP to Marcello Mathias, 20 January 1956. AHD, Maço 344, 1958.

32. Indeed, the same official noted, to let the Gulbenkian collection depart would be tantamount to repeating the mistakes which had allowed a similar 'foreign' collection in Paris, that of Richard Wallace, to be exported to London. Anon., 'Note sur l'affaire Gulbenkian', n.d. [after February 1956]. AN, F^{12} 8603, Dossier Ministre.

33. JAP to Marcello Mathias, 23 August 1955; Marcello Mathias to Ministério dos Negócios Estrangeiros, 26 December 1955 and 5 January 1956. Ministério dos Negócios Estrangeiros to Marcello Mathias, 2 March 1956. AHD, Maço 344, 1958. See also Maço 561-A, n° 380, 1955–1960.

34. Radcliffe to JAP, 22 March 1956. Caixa2 RAD305. Reproduced in PIO, p. 345.

35. Radcliffe cited in NSG to KLE, 2 March 1956. KLE00046.

36. JAP to Marcello Mathias, 22 March 1956 ('repercussions'), AHD, Maço 344, 1958. Marcello Mathias to JAP, 10 April 1956. CGF, Caixa 2, RAD332. Pedro Teotónio Pereira to Salazar, 11 April 1956. TT, AOS/CO/PC-44C, cx. 574.

37. JAP to KLE, 7 March 1956. PRES00107.

38. KLE to JAP, 9 March 1956. PRES00107.

39. JAP to Marcello Mathias, 2 April 1956. AHD, Maço 344, 1958.

40. KLE cited in ED, 9 September 1955.

41. Mikhael Essayan, personal communication, 10 May 2012 ('second in command'); Maria Teresa Gomes Ferreira, personal communication, 6 June 2016 (charismatic). JAP to KLE, 14 March 1956 ('competent'). PRES00107. Reproduced in PIO, p. 341.

42. For the legal status of the foundation, see Emílio Rui Vilar and Rui Hermenegildo Gonçalves, 'Fundação Calouste Gulbenkian', in Jorge Bacelar Gouveia (ed.), *Dicionário Jurídico da Administração Pública* (3rd edn, Lisbon: Coimbra Editora, 2007), pp. 419–26.

43. Dr José Raposo de Magalhães, cited in Ellis M. Goodwin to State Department, 25 July 1956. NARA, RG59 853.57/7–2556.

44. ED, 10 ('pedestal') and 11 ('disappointment', emoluments) May 1956.

45. Radcliffe to NSG, 3 May 1956. NSG00015.

46. Pedro Teotónio Pereira to Salazar, 14 November 1956. TT, AOS/CD-18.

47. ED, 20 August 1955.

48. Decree Law 40/690, 18 July 1956, cited in CGF, *Chairman's Report, 20th July 1955–31st December 1959* (Lisbon: CGF, 1960), pp. 185–6.

49. ED, 12 May 1956.

50. Van Kleffens to Radcliffe, 13 January 1956. NSG00015.

51. NSG to JAP/KLE, 23 May 1956 (accepting trusteeship). NSG00009. JAP, cited in ED, 28 November 1956. NSG's trusteeship was firmly opposed by NME, CPLW and KLE.

52. Broadcast 15 July 1959. For a transcript, see PRES02053. When the BBC refused to honour their promise to provide NSG with a copy of the broadcast he sued them, winning minimal damages, but attracting further publicity in the process.

53. 'Son Drops Suit Against Gulbenkian Trustees', *Daily Telegraph*, 4 February 1959.

54. To view newsreels featuring NSG, see http://www.britishpathe.com/.

55. Patrick Lichfield, '"Swinging London" Group', February 1967. National Portrait Gallery, London. NPG x128489.

56. RSE to NSG, 19 December 1958 (presidency). NSG00017. Rita Essayan, *La Rue Barrée* (Lisbon: privately printed, 1967) and *Les Papillons Repus* (privately printed, 1970).

57. For JAP's fears of Pereira, see 'Extract from letter from Lisbon dated beginning of April 1957' and 'From Lisbon', 23 May 1957. NSG00015. Though the source of these letters is anonymous, the content is confirmed by ED, 14 November 1957 and 6 January 1958. Salazar cited in CGF, *Calouste Sarkis Gulbenkian: The Man and His Work* (new edn, Lisbon: Calouste Gulbenkian Foundation, 2012), p. 75.

58. IPC Minutes, 2 September 1955 and 21 March 1962. BP, 218096.

59. Samir Saul, 'Masterly Inactivity as Brinkmanship: The Iraq Petroleum Company's Route to Nationalization, 1958–1972', *International History Review*, 29:4 (2007), 746–92.

60. Cited in CGF, *Chairman's Report VI* (Lisbon: CGF, 1977), p. 47.

61. By the end of 1959 the following firms remained in existence: IPC, Basrah, Mosul, Petroleum Concessions, Petroleum Development (Trucial Coast), Petroleum Development (Oman), Petroleum Development (Cyprus), Qatar Petroleum Concessions and Syria Petroleum Concessions. CGF, *Chairman's Report, 20th July 1955–31st December 1959* (Lisbon: CGF, 1960), Ch. 5.

SOURCES AND SELECT BIBLIOGRAPHY

Public Archives

Belgium

Foreign Ministry Archive (Ministerie van Buitenlandse Zaken), Brussels

France

Archives du Ministère des Affaires Etrangères, Nantes
London Embassy Files
Archives du Ministère des Affaires Etrangères, Paris
Bellan Papers
C. P. Mexique (Roumanie, Turquie, Perse, etc.)
Relations Commerciales, Pétroles Perse (Mésopotamie, Russie, etc.)
Revoil Papers
Tardieu Papers
Y-Internationale (Pétroles)
Z-Europe (Pétroles)
Archives nationales, Peyrefitte
Comité Générale des Pétroles Files
Office Nationale des Carburants Liquides (ONCL) Files
Rapports Commerciaux (Constantinople, Baghdad, etc.)
Archives nationales du monde du travail, Roubaix
Banque Camondo Papers (1AQ)
Imperial Ottoman Bank Papers (207AQ)
Rothschild Papers (132AQ)
Centre des Archives d'Economie et des Finances (CAEF), Savigny Le Temple

Iran

Majlis Documentation Centre, Tehran
Ministry of Foreign Affairs Archive, Tehran
National Library and Archives Organization, Tehran

Portugal

Portuguese Foreign Ministry Archive (Arquivo Histórico-Diplomático), Lisbon
London Embassy Files
Marcello Mathias Archive
Paris Embassy Files
Portuguese National Archive (Torre do Tombo), Lisbon
Marcello Caetano Archive
Oliveira Salazar Archive
PIDE/DGS Files

Russia

Hermitage Archives, St Petersburg
Files on art exports (f1. opis 5. chast 2)
Russian State Archive of Economy (RGAE), Moscow
Concessions Committee Files
Neftsyndikat Files
VSNKh Presidium Files
Russian State Archives of Socio-Political History (RGASPI), Moscow
Neftsyndikat Files
Russian State Historical Archive (RGIA), St Petersburg
Mazout Archive (f.1450)

Nobel Archive (f.1458)
State Archive of the Russian Federation
(GARF), Moscow
Neftsyndikat, Kevir Khurian and
Piatakoff Files

Turkey
National Archives (Başbakanlık
Cumhuriyet Arşivi), Ankara
Ottoman Archives (Başbakanlık
Osmanlı Arşivleri), Istanbul
Civil List Files
Foreign Ministry Files
Interior Ministry Files
London Embassy Files

United Kingdom
British Library, London
Curzon Papers
D'Abernon (Sir Edgar Vincent)
Papers
British Museum Central Archive,
London
Standing Committee Minutes
London Metropolitan Archives,
London
Imperial Ottoman Bank Papers
Wallace Brothers Archive
National Archives, Kew
Board of Trade Papers

Cabinet Papers
Colonial Office Papers
Foreign Office Papers
Home Office (Naturalisation) Papers
Security Service Files, KV2/4426–7
Science Museum Archives, Swindon
Pearson Cowdray Archive
Tate Britain Archives, London
Kenneth Clark Papers

United States
French Embassy, Washington
Petroleum files (1946–52) not yet
transferred to Paris
National Archives and Records
Administration II, College Park
MD
Bureau of Commerce (RG151)
Bureau of Mines (RG70)
Federal Trade Commission (RG122)
Foreign Economic Administration
(RG169)
Foreign Service Posts (RG81)
International Conferences (RG43)
Petroleum Administration for War
(RG253)
State Department (RG59)
National Gallery of Art, Washington
Director's Files (RG2)
John Walker Papers (RG28)

Corporate Archives

BNP Paribas, Combs La Ville-Quincy
Finaly–Teagle Correspondence
Standard Franco-Américaine Files
Colnaghi, London (and Windmill
Hill, Waddesdon)
Letterbooks
Stockbooks
Crédit Agricole Archives, Paris
Crédit Lyonnais Archive
Deutsche Bank, Frankfurt
Orientbüro Files

Garanti Bank, Istanbul
Ottoman Bank Archive
ING, London (The Baring Archive)
Turkish Affairs Volumes
Rothschild Archive, London
Burlington Investment Files
Royal Dutch Shell Archives, The
Hague
Shell Historical Archive
Shell London Archive
Société Générale Archives, Paris

Banque de l'Union parisienne
    Archive
Banque Mirabaud Archive
Banque Salonique Archive
Crédit du Nord Archive
Société Générale Archive
Total Refining and Chemicals, Brussels
    Petrofina Board Minutes

Société Franco-Persane/Oléonaphte
    Reports
Total SA, Paris
    Compagnie Française des Pétroles
    Archive
University of Warwick, Coventry
    BP Archive
    Iraq Petroleum Company Archive

Other Collections

Balcarres, Fife
    Papers of the 28th Earl of Crawford
        and Balcarres
Balliol College, Oxford
    Louis Du Pan Mallet Papers
Bodleian Library, Oxford
    Cecil Rhodes Papers
Chanet Family, Paris
    Marcelle Chanet Papers
Churchill Archives Centre, Cambridge
    Mallet Papers
    O'Conor Papers
    Wester Wemyss Papers
Ekserdjian Family, Northamptonshire
    N. M. Ekserdjian Diaries
Essayan Family Archives, London
Gulbenkian Foundation, Lisbon
    Lisbon Files
    London Files
    Museum Files
    Nubar Gulbenkian Files
    Paris Files
    Presidencia Files
Harrow School Archives, Harrow
Houghton Library, Cambridge, Mass.
    American Board of Commissioners
        for Foreign Missions Archive

King's College Archive, London
    Secretary's In-Correspondence and
        Letterbooks
King's College School Archive,
    Wimbledon
    King's College Calendars
London School of Economics Archive,
    London
    Alwyn Parker Papers
National Library of Scotland
    Papers of the 28th Earl of Crawford
        and Balcarres
Nubarian Library, Paris
    AGBU Minute Books
    Nubar Nubarian Papers
Rockefeller Archive Center, Sleepy
    Hollow, NY
    Dean Rusk Papers (FA393)
    Near East Relief/Near East
        Foundation Archive
    Office of the Messrs. Rockefeller,
        Business Interests (FA312)
University of Southampton Special
    Collections, Southampton
    Cassel Papers
    Waley Cohen Papers

Select Bibliography

Adams, Walter, James W. Brock and John M. Blair, 'Retarding the Development of Iraq's Oil Resources: An Episode in Oleaginous Diplomacy, 1927–39', *Journal of Economic Issues*, 27:1 (1993)

Adelson, Roger, *London and the Invention of the Middle East: Money, Power and War, 1902–1922* (New Haven: Yale University Press, 1995)

Alboyadjian, Archag, *Badmoutioun Hay Guesario* (2 vols., Cairo: H. Papazian, 1937)

Anderson, Irvine H., *ARAMCO, the United States and Saudi Arabia: A Study of the Dynamics of Foreign Oil Policy, 1933–1950* (Princeton, NJ: Princeton University Press, 1981)

Autheman, André, *La Banque Impériale Ottomane* (Paris: Comité pour l'Histoire Économique de la France, 1996)

Bamberg, James, *The History of the British Petroleum Company*, Vol. 2 *The Anglo-Iranian Years, 1928–54* (Cambridge: Cambridge University Press, 1994)

Barreto, Antonio (ed.), *Fundação Calouste Gulbenkian: Cinquenta Anos, 1956–2006* (2 vols., Lisbon, CGF, 2006)

Beck, Peter J., 'The Anglo-Persian Oil Dispute of 1932–33', *Journal of Contemporary History*, 9 (1974), 123–51

Beck, Peter J., '"A Tedious and Perilous Controversy": Britain and the Settlement of the Mosul Dispute, 1918–26', *Middle Eastern Studies*, 17:2 (1981), 256–76

Bloxham, Donald, *The Great Game of Genocide: Imperialism, Nationalism, and the Destruction of the Ottoman Armenians* (Oxford: Oxford University Press, 2005)

Bonin, Hubert, *Les activités financières des banques françaises (1919–35)* (Paris: Plage, 2000)

Bonin, Hubert, *Les banques et les entreprises en France dans l'entre-deux guerres (1919–35)* (Paris: Plage, 2000)

Bonin, Hubert, *La Banque de l'Union parisienne (1874/1907–1974): De l'Europe aux outre-mers* (Paris: Société Française d'Histoire des Outre-Mers, 2011)

Bouguen, Jean-Marie, *Le pétrole en France: Genèse et stratégies d'influence (1917–24)* (Paris: L'Harmattan, 2013)

Brown, Jonathan C., *Oil and Revolution in Mexico* (Berkeley, CA: University of California Press, 1993)

Bussière, Eric, *Paribas, l'Europe et le monde, 1872–1992* (Anvers: Fonds Mercator, 1992)

Bussière, Eric, and Youssef Cassis (eds.), *London and Paris as International Financial Centres in the Twentieth Century* (Oxford: Oxford University Press, 2005)

Cassis, Youssef (ed.), *Finance and Financiers in European History 1880–1960* (Cambridge, Cambridge University Press, 1992)

Clark, Kenneth, *Another Part of the Wood: A Self-Portrait* (London: HarperCollins, 1975)

Conlin, Jonathan, *The Nation's Mantelpiece: A History of the National Gallery* (London: Pallas Athene, 2006)

Conlin, Jonathan, 'Philanthropy without Borders: Calouste Gulbenkian's Founding Vision for the Gulbenkian Foundation', *Análise Social*, 45:2 (2010), 277–306

Conlin, Jonathan, 'Debt, Diplomacy and Dreadnoughts: The National Bank of Turkey, 1909–1919', *Middle Eastern Studies*, 52:3 (2016), 1–21

Conlin, Jonathan, 'Drawing the Line: Calouste Gulbenkian and the 1928 Red Line Agreement', in T. G. Fraser (ed.), *The First World War and Its Aftermath* (London: Gingko Library, 2016), pp. 1–20

Conlin, Jonathan, 'The *Amiras* and the Ottoman Empire, 1880–1923: The Case of the Gulbenkians', *Turcica: Revue d'études Turques*, 48 (2017), 1–14

Conlin, Jonathan, 'Calouste Gulbenkian', in David Cesarani and Peter Mandler (eds.), *Great Philanthropists: Wealth and Charity in the Modern World, 1815–1945* (London: Vallentine Mitchell, 2017), pp. 167–94

Conlin, Jonathan, '"Renowned and Unknown": Calouste Gulbenkian as Collector of Paintings', *Journal of the History of Collections* (2017), https://doi.org/10.1093/jhc/fhx037

Dallakian, Karlen, *H.B.E. Miutian nakhagah K. Giulbenkiani hrazharakani hartsi shurj* [*On the Resignation of K. Gulbenkian*] (Yerevan, 1996)

DeNovo, John A., *American Interests and Policies in the Middle East, 1900–1939* (Minneapolis: University of Minnesota Press, 1963)

Deterding, Henri, with Stanley Naylor, *An International Oilman* (London: Ivor Nicholson and Watson, 1934)

Dumoulin, Michel, *Pétrofina: Un groupe pétrolier international et la gestion de l'incertitude*, Vol. 1 *1920–1979* (Louvain: Peeters, 1997)

Ediger, Volkan, *Enerji Ekonomi-Politiği Perspektifinden Osmanlı'da Neft ve Petrol* (Ankara: ODTU Yayıncılık, 2007)

Eichholtz, Dietrich, *Die Bagdadbahn, Mesopotamien und die deutsche Ölpolitik bis 1918* (Leipzig: Leipziger Universitätsverlag, 2007)

Eldem, Edhem, *A History of the Ottoman Bank* (Istanbul: Ottoman Bank Historical Research Centre, 1999)

Eldem, Edhem, *In Search of the Gulbenkians* (Istanbul: Sakip Sabanci Müzesi, 2006)

Ferrier, Ronald W., *The History of the British Petroleum Company*, Vol. 1 *The Developing Years, 1901–1932* (Cambridge: Cambridge University Press, 1982)

Fitzgerald, Edward Peter, 'The Iraq Petroleum Company, Standard Oil of California, and the Contest for Eastern Arabia, 1930–1933', *International History Review*, 13 (August 1991), 441–65

Fitzgerald, Edward Peter, 'France's Middle Eastern Ambition, the Sykes–Picot Negotiations, and the Oil Fields of Mosul', *Journal of Modern History*, 66:4 (1994), 697–725

Fursenko, A. A., *The Battle for Oil: The Economics and Politics of International Corporate Conflict over Petroleum 1860–1930*, translated by Gregory L Freece (Greenwich: Jai Press, 1990)

Galpern, Steven G., *Oil and Empire in the Middle East: Sterling and Postwar Imperialism, 1944–71* (Cambridge: Cambridge University Press, 2009)

Gemignani-Saxstad, Pascale, 'La France, le pétrole et le proche-orient de 1939 à 1958', doctoral dissertation, Université de Paris IV Sorbonne, 1997

Gerretson, F. C., *History of the Royal Dutch* (4 vols., Leiden: E. J. Brill, 1958)

Gharakhanyan, Vahram, *KhSHM petakan gortsich 'neri haraberut 'yunnerĕ Galust Kyulpenkyani het* [Calouste Gulbenkian's Relationship with the USSR] (Yerevan: Tir hratarakch'ut'yun, 2013)

Gibb, George Sweet, and Evelyn H. Knowlton, *History of Standard Oil Company (New Jersey)*, Vol. 2 *The Resurgent Years, 1911–27* (New York: Harper & Brothers, 1956)

Gulbenkian, Calouste S., *Transcaucasia and the Apcheron Peninsula: Travel Memories* (originally published as *La Transcaucasie et la Péninsule d'Apcheron: Souvenirs de voyage* (Paris: Hachette, 1891)), translated by Caroline Beamish (Lisbon: Calouste Gulbenkian Foundation, 2011)

Gulbenkian, Nubar, *Pantaraxia: The Autobiography of Nubar Gulbenkian* (London: Hutchinson, 1965)

Gwinner, Arthur, *Lebenserinnerungen*, edited by Manfred Pohl (Frankfurt: Knapp, 1975)

Hanioğlu, M. Şükrü, *A Brief History of the Late Ottoman Empire* (Princeton, NJ: Princeton University Press, 2008)

Heller, Joseph, *British Policy towards the Ottoman Empire, 1908–14* (London: Frank Cass, 1983)

Heward, E., *The Great and the Good: A Life of Lord Radcliffe* (Chichester, Barry Rose, 1994)

Hewins, Ralph, *Mr Five Per Cent: The Biography of Calouste Gulbenkian* (London: Hutchinson, 1957)

Heymann, Hans, Jr, 'Oil in Soviet–Western Relations in the Interwar Years', *American Slavic and East European Review*, 7:4 (1948), 303–16

Hotta, Takehashi, 'L'industrie du pétrole en France des origines à 1934', doctoral dissertation, Université de Paris X Nanterre, 1990

Hovannisian, Richard G. (ed.), *Armenian Kesaria/Kayseri and Cappadocia* (Costa Mesa, CA: Mazda, 2013)

Howarth, Stephen, Joost Jonker et al., *A History of Royal Dutch Shell* (3 vols., Oxford: Oxford University Press, 2007)

Ibragimov, M. Dzh., *Neftyanaya promyshlennost' Azerbaydzhana v period imperializma* (Baku, 1984)

Jones, Geoffrey, *The State and the Emergence of the British Oil Industry* (London: Macmillan, 1981)

Kent, Marian, *Oil and Empire: British Policy and Mesopotamian Oil 1900–1920* (Basingstoke: Macmillan, 1976)

Kevorkian, Raymond H., and Paul B. Paboudjian, *Les Arméniens dans l'Empire Ottoman à la veille du génocide* (Paris: Arhis, 1992)

Kevorkian, Raymond H., and Vahé Tachjian (eds.), *The Armenian General Benevolent Union: One Hundred Years of History* (2 vols., New York: AGBU, 2006)

Kubicek, Robert V., *Economic Imperialism in Theory and Practice: The Case of South African Gold Mining Finance, 1886–1914* (Durham, NC: Duke University Press, 1979)

Kuisel, Richard F., *Ernest Mercier, French Technocrat* (Berkeley: University of California Press, 1967)

Kuisel, Richard F., *Capitalism and the State in Modern France: Renovation and Economic Management in the Twentieth Century* (Cambridge: Cambridge University Press, 1981)

Kynaston, David, *The City of London*, Vol. 2 *Golden Years, 1890–1914* (London: Chatto & Windus, 1995)

Kynaston, David, *The City of London*, Vol. 3 *Illusions of Gold, 1914–45* (London: Chatto & Windus, 1999)

Lochery, Neil, *Lisbon: War in the Shadows of the City of Light, 1939–45* (New York: Public Affairs, 2011)

Lodwick, John, *Gulbenkian: An Interpretation of Calouste Sarkis Gulbenkian* (London: Heinemann, 1958)

Longrigg, Stephen H., *The Origins and Early History of the Iraq Petroleum Company* (London: privately printed, 1969)

Louis, William Roger, *The British Empire in the Middle East, 1945–51* (Oxford: Clarendon, 1984)

Mansel, Philip, *Constantinople: City of the World's Desire* (London: John Murray, 1995)

Marguerat, Philippe, with L. Jilek, *Banque et investissement industriel: Paribas, le pétrole roumain et la politique française, 1919–1939* (Neuchâtel: Université de Neuchâtel Press, 1987)

McBeth, Brian S., *Juan Vicente Gómez and the Oil Companies in Venezuela, 1908–35* (Cambridge: Cambridge University Press, 1983)

Mejcher, Helmut, *Imperial Quest for Oil: Iraq, 1910–28* (London: Ithaca Press, 1976)

Melkonyan, Ed. L. 'Calouste Gulbenkian-Khorhrtayin Mioutiun: Chkayatsats gortsunkeroutiun', *Lraber Hasarakakan Gitoutiunneri*, 3 (1998), 91–101

Mikdashi, Zuhayr, *A Financial Analysis of Middle Eastern Oil Concessions: 1901–1965* (New York: Frederick A. Praeger, 1966)

Miller, Aaron D., *Search for Security: Saudi Arabian Oil and American Foreign Policy 1939–1949* (Chapel Hill, NC: University of North Carolina Press, 1980)

Nayberg, Roberto, 'La question pétrolière en France, du point de vue de la défense nationale, de 1914 à 1928', unpublished doctoral thesis, Université de Paris I Panthéon-Sorbonne, 1983

Neilson, Keith, *Britain, Soviet Russia and the Collapse of the Versailles Order, 1919–39* (Cambridge: Cambridge University Press, 2006)

Nouschi, André, *La France et le pétrole de 1924 à nos jours* (Paris: Picard, 2001)

Nouschi, André, 'Pipe-lines et politique au Proche-Orient dans les années 1930', *Relations internationales*, 19 (1979), 279–94

Nouschi, André, 'Un tournant de la politique pétrolière française: les Heads of Agreement de novembre 1948', *Relations Internationales*, 44 (1985), 379–89

Nowell, Gregory P., *Mercantile States and the World Oil Cartel, 1900–1939* (Ithaca, NY: Cornell University Press, 1994)

Nye, James, 'The Company Promoter in London, 1877–1914', unpublished doctoral thesis, King's College London, 2011

Oughourlian, Drtad Kahana, *Badmoutiun Gulbenkian Kertastani* (Antilias, Gatoghigosoutiun Medzi Dann Giligio, 2006)

Painter, David S., *Private Power and Public Policy: Multinational Oil Corporations and U.S. Foreign Policy 1941–1954* (London: I. B. Tauris, 1986)

Pamukçiyan, Kevork, *Zamanlar, Mekanlar ve İnsanlar* [Times, Places and People] (Istanbul: Aras Yayıncılık, 2003)

Panossian, Razmik, *The Armenians: From Kings and Priests to Merchants and Commissars* (New York: Columbia University Press, 2006)

Pearton, Maurice, *Oil and the Romanian State* (Oxford: Clarendon, 1971)

Pelletier, François, 'Ernest Mercier, le pétrole et la France', unpublished doctoral dissertation, Université de Montréal, 2016

Philip, George, *Oil and Politics in Latin America: Nationalist Movements and State Companies* (Cambridge: Cambridge University Press, 1982)

Philip, George, *The Political Economy of International Oil* (Edinburgh: Edinburgh University Press, 1994)

Prewitt, Kenneth, et al., *The Legitimacy of Philanthropic Foundations: United States and European Perspectives* (New York: Russell Sage Foundation, 2006)

Rondot, Jean, *La Compagnie Française des Pétroles: du Franc-or au Pétrole-Franc* (Paris: Arno, 1977)

Rubin, Michael A., 'Stumbling through the "Open Door": The US in Persia and the Standard-Sinclair Oil Dispute, 1920–25', *Iranian Studies*, 28:3–4 (1995), 203–29

Sampson, Antony, *The Seven Sisters: The Great Oil Companies and the World They Made* (London: Coronet, 1975)

Samuel, Annie Tracy, 'The Open Door and U.S. Policy in Iraq between the World Wars', *Diplomatic History*, 38:1 (2014), 926–52

Sartor, Wolfgang, 'Die Europäische Petroleum Union G.m.b.H. 1906–1914', *Berliner Jahrbuch für Osteuropäische Geschichte* (1997), 147–73

Saul, Samir, 'Masterly Inactivity as Brinkmanship: The Iraq Petroleum Company's Route to Nationalization, 1958–1972', *International History Review*, 29:4 (2007), 746–92

Seidov, Vugar, *Arkivi Bakinsski Neftyanykh Firm: XIX–Nachalo XX veka* [The Archives of Baku Oil Companies] (Moscow: Modest Kolerov, 2009)

Semyonova, Natalya, and Nicolas V. Ilyine (eds.), *Selling Russian Treasures: The Soviet Trade in Nationalized Art, 1917–38* (New York: Abbeville, 2013)

Sluglett, Peter, *Britain in Iraq: Contriving King and Country* (London: I. B. Tauris, 2007)

Solomacha, E., *Gosudarstvennyj Jermitazh: Muzejnye rasprodazhi, 1928–1929* [The Hermitage Museum's Sale] (St Petersburg: Arhivnye dokumenty, 2006)

Spies, Georg, *Erinnerungen eines Ausland-Deutschen* (1926; reissued St Petersburg: Olearius, 2002)

Stivers, William, *Supremacy and Oil: Iraq, Turkey, and the Anglo-American World Order, 1918–1930* (Ithaca, NY: Cornell University Press, 1982)

Stivers, William, 'A Note on the Red Line Agreement', *Diplomatic History*, 7:1 (1983), 23–34

Terzi, Arzu T., *Bağdat-Musul'da Abdülhamid'in Mirası: Petrol ve Arazi* (Istanbul: Timaş Yayınları, 2009)

Thobie, Jacques, *Intérêts et impérialisme français dans l'empire ottomane, 1895–1914* (Paris: Imprimerie Nationale, 1977)

Tolf, R. W., *The Russian Rockefellers: The Saga of the Nobel Family and the Russian Oil Industry* (Stanford: Stanford University Press, 1976)

Toprani, Anand, 'The French Connection: A New Perspective on the End of the Red Line Agreement, 1945–8', *Diplomatic History*, 36:2 (April 2012), 261–99

Toprani, Anand, 'German's Answer to Standard Oil: The Continental Oil Company and Nazi Grand Strategy, 1940–1942', *Journal of Strategic Studies*, 37 (2014), 949–73

Uluğbay, Hikmet, *İmparatorluk'tan Cumhuriyet'e Petropolitik* (3rd edn, Istanbul: De Ki Yayınları, 2008)

Urselet, Laurent, 'L'Office National des Combustibles Liquides (1925–39)', unpublished *mémoire de maîtrise*, Université Paris IV Sorbonne, 1999

Venn, Fiona, *Oil Diplomacy in the Twentieth Century* (Basingstoke: Macmillan, 1986)

Venn, Fiona, 'Anglo-American Relations and Middle East Oil, 1918–34', *Diplomacy and Statecraft*, 1 (1990), 165–84

Walker, John, *Self-Portrait with Donors: Confessions of an Art Collector* (New York: Little, Brown, 1974)

Yergin, Daniel, *The Prize: The Epic Quest for Oil, Money, and Power* (New York: Free Press, 1991)

ACKNOWLEDGEMENTS

In November 1945 the Iranian ambassador to London thanked Gulbenkian for letting him read a short autobiographical memoir the latter had recently dictated. Gulbenkian's memoirs had been a fascinating read. Gulbenkian replied that 'the history I sent you covers only a fraction of my life. I have in my life seen so much, in various countries, with various men under various circumstances that it would be an offence to myself if I put everything down.' In sitting down to write my acknowledgements, I cannot help but share my subject's sentiments. In the five years it took to research and write this book I have seen so much in nine different countries, and have collaborated with or simply profited by the expertise and hospitality of so many men and women, that I have no choice but to cause offence – either by leaving someone out or, in the case of my editor, by trying to 'put everything down'.

My greatest debt is to the Calouste Gulbenkian Foundation, Lisbon. The grants they made to the University of Southampton freed me from my teaching and other responsibilities, providing the time and resources necessary to track down such a complex and evasive individual. Foundation presidents Emílio Rui Vilar, Artur Santos Silva and Isabel Mota, as well as Secretary-General Rui Esgaio, patiently supported the project and granted me privileged access to the Gulbenkian Papers held at the foundation. Crucially, they also granted me full editorial control. A supervisory panel of historians was appointed to monitor progress. Maria Fernanda Rollo, Richard Roberts and Joost Jonker brought considerable experience of similar research projects. I thank them for their wise counsel. Richard's untimely death in December 2017 robbed me of a friend as well as a mentor. My book cannot possibly relay more than a fraction of the expertise, wonder and good humour he brought to the project. It nonetheless seems fitting to dedicate it to his memory.

Ever since its establishment, the foundation has reserved one seat on its board for a member of Gulbenkian's family. Martin Essayan currently fills that position, having succeeded his father, Mikhael, Calouste

Gulbenkian's grandson. It was an honour to hear Mikhael's memories of his grandfather, and I am additionally grateful to him for allowing me to borrow Nubar Gulbenkian's personal archive. The more family correspondence I read, the more questions I wanted to ask Mikhael. I wish he had lived to read the final product. Mikhael and in particular Martin worked hard to make the triangular relationship between me, the family and the foundation work. Martin, his mother, Dina, and his wife, Tracy, were unstintingly kind and supportive.

I also thank other members of the family. Edward Jr and Carmen Gulbenkian, Melinée Frenkian, Mark Samuelson and Mikael Gulbenkian shared memories, papers and hospitality in the United States, France, Britain and Portugal respectively. Whether it was allowing me to rummage in their garage or stir up memories, they could not have been more open and helpful. Like the foundation itself, they recognised the value of having a thoroughly researched and objective biography of Calouste Gulbenkian, and left me free to draw my own conclusions from the vast amount of material they shared. The same was true of David Ekserdjian, who kindly granted me access to his father's extraordinarily detailed diaries of the Gulbenkians' London office.

Gulbenkian spent most of his life on the move. It was evident that if I wanted to track him down I would have to travel a great deal as well. Though I was not able to patronise quite the same class of hotel as Gulbenkian, I had excellent and exceptionally knowledgeable companions in Ozan Ozavci and Erman Ohanian. Resourceful, efficient and enviably polyglot, Ozan spent a year working on the project as Research Fellow, spending long periods in archives in Moscow, St Petersburg and Istanbul, locating, analysing and translating documents in Russian and Ottoman Turkish. He also kept me up to speed with Turkish-language scholarship. Erman did the same for Armenian-language sources and scholarship, as well as organising our whirlwind tour of Turkey in November 2014. Together with the director of the foundation's Armenian Communities Department, Razmik Panossian, Erman and Ozan helped me to understand the legacy of Gulbenkian's times for Armenian and Turkish politics today. They also helped me to interpret the raft of new information I received during our trip to Istanbul, Kayseri and Adana, gleaned from the late lamented Sarkis Seropyan, Archbishop Aram Ateshyan, Sarkis Teke and Leon Erarslan. An invitation from the Hrant Dink Foundation to speak at a conference allowed me to pay a second visit to Istanbul in October 2015. I must also thank Philippe Normand of the Mairie de Deauville for showing my wife Kate and me around Les Enclos, now the Parc Calouste Gulbenkian. It was a delight to be able to share this remarkable garden with Kate, who endured all my other oily absences so patiently.

Knowing little about the oil industry, I initially assumed that accessing the archives of Gulbenkian's partners and rivals would be a challenge. Thanks to archivists Peter Housego at BP, Cécile Benoit and Camille Pedenon at Total and Rosalie van Egmond at Royal Dutch-Shell, this was far from the case. I was permitted to view and quote almost anything I wanted. The BP archive also holds the archive of the Iraq Petroleum Company; I thank Andrew Whitehead of Abu Dhabi Petroleum (ADCO) for permission to consult it. ExxonMobil and Gulf, by contrast, refused even to acknowledge registered letters of enquiry about their archives. In the unlikely event that any of their employees read this page, may I observe that by denying scholars access to their records (or by claiming that they do not exist) such firms maintain a vacuum which conspiracy theorists are only too ready to fill.

Gulbenkian was as much financier as oilman and I spent many happy hours in the archives of banks in London, Paris, Roubaix, Frankfurt and Istanbul. Martin Müller of the Historisches Institut der Deutsche Bank was particularly helpful, inviting me to speak to a gathering of the Gesellschaft für Unternehmensgeschichte in Frankfurt. Lorans Tanatar Baruh of SALT in Istanbul was a mine of information on the Imperial Ottoman Bank. Inevitably there were some archives I could not visit myself for logistical or political reasons, or simply because I did not know the language. My thanks to Nareg Seferian, Khatchig Mouradian, Filipe Guimarães da Silva, Rosa Churcher Clarke, Vladimir Frilov, Rozina Sheikh, Hedayat Gravand, Azadeh Hassanin and Elena Stevens for research and translation help in Yerevan, Lisbon, London, Moscow, Tehran and Boston.

Sir David Cannadine was the first to suggest I tackle this subject, at a conference on twentieth-century philanthropy organised by the late Sir David Cesarani and Peter Mandler. I am grateful to all three for the inspiration and guidance. There is insufficient space for me to name all the other scholars who helped me, whether directly or indirectly, by assisting Ozan, Erman or Razmik to answer the many questions I peppered them with. Several individuals, however, went well beyond the call of collegial duty, sharing their unpublished research, reading my draft chapters and articles, or simply taking the time and effort to discuss this or that historical episode at length: Anny Bakalian, Alain Beltran, Christine Chanet, Richard Davenport-Hines, Dimitri Dourdine-Mak, Edhem Eldem, Peter Fuhring, Francesco Gerali, Keith Hamilton, Richard Hardman, James Nye, François Pelletier, Wolfgang Sartor, Funda Soysal, James Stourton, Ahsene Gül Tokay and Anand Toprani.

My colleagues at Southampton played a crucial role in handling the administrative, financial and legal aspects of the project, above all my dean, Anne Curry, but also Alison Leslie, Renée Lewin and Rita Oliver. My agent, Andrew Lownie, was indefatigable and adept in equal measure. At Profile I would like to thank Andrew Franklin for taking a second look, and Paul Forty for his shepherding of the manuscript through to print, a process which began with a reassuringly thorough copy-edit by Lesley Levene.

I shall end where I began, with the Gulbenkian Foundation. With over 600 metres of Gulbenkian papers to work with, I spent many happy weeks in an office kindly put at my disposal by the director of the Gulbenkian Art Library, Ana Paulo Gordo. Archivist Mafalda Melo de Aguiar explained to me the provenance of the archive and the principles by which this raft of material had been catalogued. Having been responsible for unpacking both the London and Paris office archives when they were moved to Lisbon, Mafalda's knowledge of the papers is unmatched. Without her suggestions, I quite literally would not have known where to start. Without her company at lunch in the foundation canteen, I could not have kept going. Every time I returned to Lisbon, it seemed, Mafalda had something new to show me, something exciting that had been discovered in a safe or a trunk somewhere in the foundation's vast basements. João Vieira joined the foundation as deputy-director in charge of archives halfway through my time on the project. Together with Mafalda he helped me to understand how Portugal and the foundation worked.

Among the past and present curators and directors of the Gulbenkian Museum I would like to thank Rita Albergaria, with whom I curated a small exhibition about Calouste Gulbenkian's early life, João Carvalho Dias, Maria Teresa Gomes Ferreira, João Castel-Branco and his successor as head of the Gulbenkian Museum, Penelope Curtis. Meanwhile, elsewhere in the foundation Isabel Moura, Ines Goncalves and Ana Barcelos Pereira helped with travel and accommodation. Rui Goncalves gave me a crash course in Portuguese law. Working in a basement office while the sun shone and the ducks quacked happily in the gardens outside, I must admit that there have been times when I flagged. But whenever I ran out of energy, Olga Gonçalves and Osvaldo Massapina were there with *uma bica* and a trolley full of files to get me started again. And after a long day, there was always Razmik's office at the end of the tunnel, where I could usually find good conversation and a glass of 7-star Ararat Armenian cognac waiting for me. To all my friends at 45A Avenida de Berna, I say *Genatset!*

Cholsey, 27 December 2017

INDEX

Illustrations are indexed as 'Pl (col)' for colour plates or 'Pl (b/w)' for black-and-white plates.

Calouste Gulbenkian is abbreviated throughout to 'CSG' except at the start of his own index entry.